EUROPEAN SOCIETY OF INTERNATIONAL LAW SERIES

International Law and Universality

EUROPEAN SOCIETY OF INTERNATIONAL LAW SERIES

The ESIL Book Series publishes high-quality volumes on the themes of ESIL Annual Conferences and ESIL joint events primarily. The volumes include chapters that are based on selected papers presented at ESIL events, revised to fit the theme and focus of the volume, and complemented by additional chapters that address topics that were not fully explored at the events, but that are essential for a full coverage of the theme.

International Law and Universality

Edited by
IŞIL ARAL AND JEAN D'ASPREMONT

Great Clarendon Street, Oxford, OX2 6DP,
United Kingdom

Oxford University Press is a department of the University of Oxford.
It furthers the University's objective of excellence in research, scholarship,
and education by publishing worldwide. Oxford is a registered trade mark of
Oxford University Press in the UK and in certain other countries

© The several contributors 2024

The moral rights of the authors have been asserted

All rights reserved. No part of this publication may be reproduced, stored in
a retrieval system, or transmitted, in any form or by any means, without the
prior permission in writing of Oxford University Press, or as expressly permitted
by law, by licence or under terms agreed with the appropriate reprographics
rights organization. Enquiries concerning reproduction outside the scope of the
above should be sent to the Rights Department, Oxford University Press, at the
address above

You must not circulate this work in any other form
and you must impose this same condition on any acquirer

Public sector information reproduced under Open Government Licence v3.0
(http://www.nationalarchives.gov.uk/doc/open-government-licence/open-government-licence.htm)

Published in the United States of America by Oxford University Press
198 Madison Avenue, New York, NY 10016, United States of America

British Library Cataloguing in Publication Data

Data available

Library of Congress Control Number: 2023948330

ISBN 978-0-19-889941-9

DOI: 10.1093/oso/9780198899419.001.0001

Printed and bound by
CPI Group (UK) Ltd, Croydon, CR0 4YY

Links to third party websites are provided by Oxford in good faith and
for information only. Oxford disclaims any responsibility for the materials
contained in any third party website referenced in this work.

Contents

List of Contributors vii

Introduction: The Universalizing Narratives of International
Law and their Binary Contestations 1
 Işıl Aral and Jean d'Aspremont

I THE IDEA OF UNIVERSALITY

1. The Spaces of the Universal and the Particular in International Law:
 Questioning Binaries and Uncovering Political Projects 23
 Gail Lythgoe

2. The Philosophical Problem of Universals and Universality Binaries
 in International Law: Hobbes and Leibniz Compared 43
 Ekaterina Yahyaoui Krivenko

3. Universalizing the Particular; or, Hotel and Carrier Bag 57
 Matthew Nicholson

4. International Legal Universalism: A Reactionary Ideology of
 Disciplinary Self-Aggrandizement 71
 Akbar Rasulov

II THE INVENTION OF UNIVERSALITY

5. The Assumption, Not Invention, of Universality Is the Problem 95
 Onuma Yasuaki

6. L'Invention de l'Universalité du Droit International 101
 Frédéric Mégret

III UNIVERSALITY AND RIGHTS

7. Universal Human Rights within Social Particulars 121
 Mark Retter

8. Human Rights Nationalism as Universality Challenge 135
 Tilmann Altwicker

IV UNIVERSALITY AND THE NON-HUMAN

9. Universalisms of Human Dominion   149
   Alejandro Lorite

10. The Universal Recognition of Animal Welfare and its Dark Sides   185
    Régis Bismuth

V UNIVERSALITY BEYOND EUROPE

11. Regionalism, Hegemony, and Universality in the International Order of the Far East   199
    Mohammad Shahabuddin

12. Universality in International Law Beyond the European: An Islamic Law Perspective   211
    Mashood Baderin

13. Beyond Co-option and Contestation: The Chinese Belt and Road Initiative and the Universality of International Law   239
    Kanad Bagchi and Milan Tahraoui

VI UNIVERSALITY AND THE LANGUAGES OF INTERNATIONAL LAW

14. The Power of Images: Questioning the Universality of International Human Rights Law   257
    Elisabeth Roy-Trudel

15. German 'Dogmatik'—An Untranslatable Concept if Ever There Was One?   279
    Markus Beham

VII CRITIQUE AND RESISTANCE TO UNIVERSALITY

16. The Retreat of the State in International Law? The Paris Agreement as a Case Study   295
    Maiko Meguro

17. Oscillating Justice: Between Universal and Particular   311
    Zinaida Miller

18. Conceptual Universality vs Pragmatic Particularity in International Adjudication   327
    Andreas Kulick

Index   339

List of Contributors

Tilmann Altwicker is an Associate Professor of Legal Data Science and Public Law and Head of the Center for Legal Data Science at the University of Zurich, Switzerland.

Işıl Aral is an Assistant Professor of International Law at Koç University, Turkey.

Jean d'Aspremont is a Professor of International Law at Sciences Po Law School, Paris, and at the University of Manchester, UK. He is the General Editor of the *Cambridge Studies in International and Comparative Law* and Director of Oxford International Organizations.

Mashood Baderin is a Professor of Laws at the School of Law, SOAS, University of London, UK. He specializes in Islamic law, international law, and human rights law. He was a onetime UN Independent Expert on the situation of human rights in the Sudan.

Kanad Bagchi is a postdoctoral researcher in international law at the University of Amsterdam, Netherlands.

Markus Beham is an Associate Professor at the University of Passau, Germany.

Régis Bismuth is a Professor at Sciences Po Law School, Paris.

Andreas Kulick is a Senior Research Fellow at Eberhard Karls University Tübingen, Germany, and a Visiting Professor at Albert Ludwigs University Freiburg, Germany, in the winter semester 2023–2024.

Alejandro Lorite is a Professor of Law at the University of Québec in Montréal, Canada.

Gail Lythgoe is a Lecturer in Global Law at the University of Edinburgh, UK.

Frédéric Mégret is a Full Professor and holds the Hans & Tamar Oppenheimer Chair in Public International Law at the Faculty of Law, McGill University, Québec, Montréal, Canada, where he also co-directs the Centre for Human Rights and Legal Pluralism.

Maiko Meguro is a Research Fellow of Public International Law at University of Amsterdam, Netherlands. She is also the Director for International Data Strategy at Government of Japan, where she leads the team of policymakers and lawyers. Previously, she served for the UN climate change negotiations and the regional economic partnership agreements.

Zinaida Miller is a Professor of Law and International Affairs at Northeastern University School of Law and the International Affairs Program of the College of Social Sciences and Humanities, Boston, Massachusetts.

Matthew Nicholson is an Associate Professor in International Law at Durham University in Durham Law School, UK.

Akbar Rasulov is a Professor of International Law at the University of Glasgow, UK.

Mark Retter is a Senior Research Fellow at the Cambridge Initiative on Peace Settlements and Associate Member of the Las Casas Institute, Blackfriars Hall, Oxford, UK.

Elisabeth Roy-Trudel holds a PhD in Humanities from Concordia University, Québec, Montréal, Canada, and is an independent researcher.

Mohammad Shahabuddin is a Professor of International Law and Human Rights at Birmingham Law School, University of Birmingham, UK.

Milan Tahraoui is a Researcher at the Berlin School of Economics and Law, Berlin, Germany.

Ekaterina Yahyaoui Krivenko is an Associate Professor of Human Rights at the Irish Centre for Human Rights, School of Law, University of Galway, Ireland.

Onuma Yasuaki was an Emeritus Professor at the Graduate Schools for Law and Politics, University of Tokyo, Japan.

Introduction
The Universalizing Narratives of International Law and their Binary Contestations

Işıl Aral and Jean d'Aspremont

The recurrence of debates about the idea of universality in the framework of annual conferences of the European Society of International Law (ESIL) is striking. At the 2004 inaugural conference of ESIL in Florence, Martti Koskenniemi delivered a keynote lecture on how the European international law tradition 'imagines itself as universal'.[1] At the 2008 Annual Conference in Heidelberg, Bruno Simma gave a keynote lecture where he addressed the theme of the Conference on 'International Law in a Heterogeneous World' by opposing the concept of heterogeneity to the universality of international law.[2] Yet again, a decade later 2018 Annual Conference in Manchester was entirely dedicated to the theme of international law and universality. It aimed to take a critical look at the mechanisms of inclusion and exclusion that come with the universalist discourses of international law and to disrupt preconceived ideas, ideologies, and mindsets about universality.[3] The omnipresence of the idea of universality in debates conducted under the aegis of the ESIL is not a coincidence. First, there has always been a specific European sensibility towards the idea of universality.[4] Secondly, the invocation of the idea of universality in international legal discourses is constant and the debates at annual conferences of the ESIL is only a tiny manifestation thereof. One could say that the question of universality may even be the starting point of any international legal discourse that seeks global outreach and global authority.

---

[1] Martti Koskenniemi, 'International Law in Europe: Between Tradition and Renewal' (2005) 16 European Journal of International Law 113.
[2] Bruno Simma, 'Universality of International Law from the Perspective of a Practitioner' (2009) 20 European Journal of International Law 265.
[3] Jean d'Aspremont, 'International Law, Universality, and the Dream of Disrupting from the Centre' (2018) 7(7) ESIL Reflections. Keynote lectures of the 2018 ESIL Annual Conference can be found at Manchester International Law Centre's YouTube Channel: <https://www.youtube.com/@manchesterinternationallaw2809/featured> accessed 20 December 2023.
[4] On the idea that concerns for Eurocentrism appear to arise from European preoccupations and political beliefs, see Martti Koskenniemi, 'Histories of International Law: Significance and Problems for a Critical View' (2013) 27 Temple International and Comparative Law Journal 215, 222.

The centrality of the idea of universality in international legal discourses is probably not difficult to fathom. Often, universality is invoked to refer to the *ratione loci* and *ratione personae* global bindingness of international law, that is its geographical outreach, its capacity to provide legal prescriptions that applies to every international law actor equally, its manifestation of the unity of the field and of its practices, etc. This spatial understanding of universality has useful explanatory virtues as it helps explain how international law creates and maintains a global legal order[5] both at a macro level and in everyday life.[6] The idea of universality is also used in international legal discourses in a more moral or substantive sense with a view to shedding a positive light on international law, endowing the latter with an image of agreement, harmony, inclusiveness, and integrity. Both in its spatial and its substantive dimensions, the idea of universality simultaneously plays a decisive role in the construction of a disciplinary history for the field.[7] By virtue of the idea of universality, the history of international law can be presented in a linear way whereby international law (and international lawyers) are seen moving from a world of coexisting legal systems towards a single legal system that speaks to everyone on an equal basis irrespective of power, size, religion, or culture. In that sense, universality is instrumental in consolidating the kinship between international law and progress.[8] It helps to tell a story where we have moved 'from a few original truths scattered in a void, through the rationalization of philosophy, to the development of modern institutional machinery'.[9] All in all, the idea of universality, in its spatial and non-spatial dimensions, has allowed international law to present itself and its advancement as a necessity.[10]

Unsurprisingly, all the achievements of the idea of universality and of its recurrent invocation in international legal discourses have been contested. And so has the very idea of the universality of international law. For instance, it has been shown that the process by which international law was made and conceptualized in Europe (the so-called *Ius Publicum Europaeum*) and then imposed on the rest

---

[5] Anne Orford, 'Constituting Order' in James Crawford and Martti Koskenniemi (eds), *The Cambridge Companion to International Law* (CUP 2012) 287.

[6] Luis Eslava, 'Istanbul Vignettes: Observing the Everyday Operation of International Law' (2014) 2 London Review of International Law 3.

[7] Thomas Kleinlein, 'International Legal Thought: Creation of a Tradition and the Potential of Disciplinary Self-Reflection' in Giuliana Ziccardi Capaldo (ed), *The Global Community: Yearbook of International Law and Jurisprudence 2016* (OUP 2016) 816. See also BS Chimni, 'The Past, Present, and Future of International Law: A Critical Third World Approach' (2007) 8 Melbourne Journal of International Law 502; Anne Orford, 'International Law and the Limits of History' in Wouter Werner and others (eds), *The Law of International Lawyers: Reading Martti Koskenniemi* (CUP 2015) 307.

[8] Thomas Skouteris, *The Notion of Progress in International Law Discourse* (Asser Press 2010).

[9] David Kennedy, 'A New Stream of International Law Scholarship' (1988) 7 Wisconsin International Law Journal 1, 15.

[10] It could also be added that the international lawyer often plays the role of the universal intellectual who counterposes power and injustice. On the extent to which the image of lawyers has shaped the image of the universal intellectual, see Noam Chomsky and Michel Foucault, *The Chomsky-Foucault Debate on Human Nature* (The New Press 2006) 165.

of the world can hardly be told as a story of progress, but rather deserves critical attention for the boundaries it drew, the exclusion it promotes, the cultural domination it serves, and the hegemony it strives to justify.[11] Among others, scholars associated with the critique of law and empire[12] or the Third World Approaches to International Law (TWAIL) levelled very compelling charges against narratives of universality of international law.[13] Similarly, feminist approaches to international law demonstrated how the claim of universality is indeed flawed by the gendered nature of the discipline.[14] It is noteworthy that the critique of universality has become so common that the lack of universality of international law and the comparison between the local particularities of international legal practices have

---

[11] On the universalization of a European tradition of international law, see Charles H Alexandrowicz, 'Doctrinal Aspects of the Universality of the Law of Nations' (1961) 37 British Yearbook of International Law 506; ONUMA Yasuaki, 'When Was the Law of International Society Born? An Inquiry of the History of International Law from an Intercivilizational Perspective' (2000) 2 Journal of the History of International Law 1; Brett Bowden, 'The Colonial Origins of International Law: European Expansion and the Classical Standard of Civilization' (2005) 7 Journal of the History of International Law 1. Alter argues that the problem of Western centrism is not about an unnecessary focus on that side of the world but rather the presentation of Western claims as universal: 'Historically European scholars wrote as if the authors were discovering fundamental truths that should apply everywhere' in Karen J Alter, 'Visions of International Law: An Interdisciplinary Retrospective' (2020) 33 Leiden Journal of International Law 849. On the dominance of English as a language in international law, see Justina Uriburu, 'Between Elitist Conversations and Local Clusters: How Should we Address English-centrism in International Law?' (*Opinio Juris*, 2 November 2020) < https://opiniojuris.org/2020/11/02/between-elitist-conversations-and-local-clusters-how-should-we-address-english-centrism-in-international-law/> accessed 20 December 2023.

[12] Among others, see Sundhya Pahuja, 'The Postcoloniality of International Law' (2005) 46 *Harvard International Law Journal* 459; China Miéville, *Between Equal Rights: A Marxist Theory of International Law* (Haymarket Books 2006); Martti Koskenniemi, 'Empire and International Law: The Real Spanish Contribution' (2011) 61 *University of Toronto Law Journal* 1. See also Emmanuelle Tourme-Jouannet, 'Universalism and Imperialism: The True-False Paradox of International Law?' (2007) 18 *European Journal of International Law* 379; Emmanuelle Tourme-Jouannet, 'Des origines coloniales du droit international: à propos du droit des gens modernes au 18ème siècle' in Pierre-Marie Dupuy and Vincent Chetail (eds), *The Roots of International Law/Les fondements du droit international: Liber Amicorum Peter Haggenmacher* (Brill-Nijhoff 2013) 648; Felix Lange, 'The Dream of a Völkish Colonial Empire: International Law and Colonial Law During the National Socialist Era' (2017) 4 *London Review of International Law* 343; Juan Pablo Scarfi, *The Hidden History of International Law in the Americas: Empire and Legal Networks* (OUP 2017); Liliana Obregon, 'Empire, Racial Capitalism and International Law: The Case of Manumitted Haiti and the Recognition Debt' (2018) 31 Leiden Journal of International Law 597.

[13] See eg Makau Mutua, 'What is TWAIL?' (2000) 94 American Society of International Law Proceedings 31; Makau Mutua, 'Savages, Victims and Saviors: The Metaphor of Human Rights' (2001) 42 Harvard International Law Journal 201; Anthony Anghie, 'The Evolution of International Law: Colonial and Postcolonial Realities' (2006) 27 Third World Quarterly 740; BS Chimni, 'Third World Approaches to International Law: A Manifesto' (2006) 8 International Community Law Review 18.

[14] See eg Hilary Charlesworth and Christine Chinkin, *The Boundaries of International Law: A Feminist Analysis* (Manchester University Press 2000); Doris Buss and Ambreena Manji (eds), *International Law: Modern Feminist Approaches* (OUP 2005); Anne Orford, 'Feminism, Imperialism and the Mission of International Law' (2002) 71 Nordic Journal of International Law 275; Dianne Otto, 'The Exile of Inclusion: Reflections on Gender Issues in International Law over the Last Decade' (2009) 10 Melbourne Journal of International Law 11; Gina Heathcote, *Feminist Dialogues on International Law: Successes, Tensions, Futures* (OUP 2019); Susan Harris Rimmer and Kate Ogg (eds), *Research Handbook on Feminist Engagement with International Law* (Edward Elgar 2019).

even been elevated into an object of study and a mode of engagement with international law.[15]

Charges against the universalizing narratives of international law thus abound. What is striking is that international lawyers, albeit with growing awareness of the limitations of the universalizing narratives, unflinchingly perpetuate them.[16] This perpetuation of the universalizing narratives of international law in spite of the growing consciousness of their limitations and contradictions can be understood in two different ways. First, it is as if there were hardly anyone seriously committed to the universality of international law and that universalizing narratives were perpetuated as a matter of routine.[17] This would mean that international lawyers have turned very cynical and very disloyal to their universal ideals.[18] Secondly, and alternatively, the perpetuation of universalizing discourses in spite of the critique of universality can be construed as the manifestation of the absorption of the latter by the former.[19] According to this reading, the critique of universality can be seen as having been absorbed in the very universalizing narratives of international law with which it takes issue and is now part thereof. In that sense, making oneself vulnerable to universality critique could be understood as another universalizing strategy.[20]

This chapter is not the place to determine what to make of international law's perpetuation of universality narratives in spite of an abounding critique of universality. For the sake of this volume, it matters more to emphasize that all those narratives critical of universality build on a wide range of distinct arguments on universality. In particular, many of them postulate that universality constitutes an efficiently void concept that allows one to construct both hegemonic and counterhegemonic narratives.[21] This is so because universality is defined through

---

[15] See Anthea Roberts and others, 'Conceptualizing Comparative International Law' in Anthea Roberts and others (eds), *Comparative International Law* (OUP 2018); see also Anthea Roberts, *Is International Law International?* (OUP 2017).

[16] For some general remarks, see Jean d'Aspremont, 'Martti Koskenniemi, the Mainstream, and Self-Reflectivity' (2016) 29 Leiden Journal of International Law 625–39.

[17] See Jean d'Aspremont, 'International Legal Methods: Working for a Tragic and Cynical Routine' in Rossana Deplano and Nicholas Tsagourias (eds), *Handbook on Research Methods in International Law* (Edward Elgar 2021) 42. On the idea of routine in legal scholarship, see Pierre Schlag, 'Normative and Nowhere to Go' (1990) 43 Stanford Law Review 167, 179 ('It is the highly repetitive, cognitively entrenched, institutionally sanctioned, and politically enforced routine of the legal academy—a routine that silently produces our thoughts and keeps our work channeled within the same old cognitive and rhetorical matrices'). See also Pierre Schlag, 'Spam Jurisprudence, Air Law, and the Rank of Anxiety of Nothing Happening (A Report on the State of the Art)' (2009) 97 Georgia Law Journal 803, 829 (where he writes that legal academics are destined 'to play out the myth of Sisyphus', the difference being however that Sisyphus had a real rock to push up the hill).

[18] Such a claim has been made as regards modernity as a whole. See Peter Sloterdijk, *Critique of Cynical Reason* (University of Minnesota 1987).

[19] See Pahuja, 'The Postcoloniality of International Law' (n 12).

[20] On the universalizing project of international comparative law, see Jean d'Aspremont, 'Comparativism and Colonizing Thinking in International Law' (2020) 57 Canadian Yearbook of International Law 89.

[21] Geoff Gordon, 'Universalism' in Jean d'Aspremont and Sahib Singh (eds), *Concepts for International Law: Contributions to Disciplinary Thought* (Edward Elgar 2019) 877.

what it is being opposed to.[22] To represent something that is shared by all or applied everywhere, it needs to define an 'other' or a 'particular' that is not shared. It is in that sense that Laclau famously argued that universality is not a standalone concept and that it can only be apprehended through its antagonism with particularity.[23] In his words, '[t]he universal emerges out of the particular not as some principle underlying and explaining the particular, but as an incomplete horizon suturing a dislocated particular identity.'[24] Said differently, universality is an empty frame that does not have an essence in itself and needs to draw from particularity in order to generate meaning. In that sense, what universality represents can hardly be apprehended without understanding the binary opposition that it creates within discourse.[25]

The creation of binaries whenever the idea of universality is invoked has a number of consequences. First, the idea of universality in international legal discourses, because it constitutes the binaries it needs to constitute itself, can be seen as supporting and perpetuating the binaries of modern legal thought.[26] Universality, just like dialectics,[27] reinforces the particulars it is meant to transcend and nourishes binary thinking about law. Secondly, and more importantly, universality in international legal discourses, when drawing the particularity it needs to define itself, turns itself into a colonizing concept[28] that absorbs all the particulars that it creates and supposedly transcends.[29] Indeed, universality and the particulars that constitute it are always determined from the start. If international lawyers are to find or establish universality, they must first presuppose it and define it according to their own descriptive categories, moral positioning, and political

---

[22] In legal argumentation, binary oppositions or 'philosophical pairs' can be used as an efficient tool of persuasion, see Chaïm Perelman and Lucie Olbrechts-Tyteca, *The New Rhetoric: A Treatise on Argumentation* (University of Notre Dame Press 1969) 420–36.
[23] Ernesto Laclau, *Emancipation(s)* (Verso 2007) 28–35.
[24] ibid 28.
[25] Pahuja calls the transformation of a concept into a universal and the stabilization of its meaning the 'operationalisation of universality', in Sundhya Pahuja, *Decolonising International Law: Development, Economic Growth and the Politics of Universality* (CUP 2011) 41.
[26] On the idea that modernity generalized modes of thinking articulated around identity and differences, see Michel de Certeau, *L'écriture de l'histoire* (Éditions Gallimard 1975) 59; Michel Foucault, *Les mots et les choses: une archéologie des sciences humaines* (Éditions Gallimard 1966) 68. See more generally Bruno Latour, *Nous n'avons jamais été modernes: essai d'anthropologie symétrique* (La Découverte 1997).
[27] On the idea that dialectical constructions reinforce dualism, see Latour (n 26) 77. See also Judith Butler, *Gender Trouble: Feminism and the Subversion of Identity* (Routledge 1999) 18–22.
[28] On the idea of a colonizing gesture, see generally Butler (n 27) 18.
[29] On the totalization of thought as a modern phenomenon, see Theodor Adorno and Max Horkheimer, *Dialectic of Enlightenment* (Verso 1997) 24. See more generally Theodor Adorno, *Negative Dialectics* (Routledge 1973). On the idea that culture is totalizing, see Edward Said, *The World, the Text, and The Critic* (Harvard University Press 1983) 14 ('in the transmission and persistence of a culture there is a continual process of reinforcement, by which the hegemonic culture will add to itself the prerogatives given it by its sense of national identity, its power as an implement, ally, or branch of the state, its rightness, its exterior forms and assertions of itself: and most important, by its vindicated power as a victor over everything not itself. There is no reason to doubt that all cultures operate in this way or to doubt that on the whole they tend to be successful in enforcing their hegemony').

preferences.[30] The particular is defined according to (and by) those that seek to invoke universality.

The foregoing does not however mean that the problematic idea of universality and its binaries, especially when applied to international law, can be jettisoned and abandoned. It has been shown that the total rejection of universality from international legal discourses is not an option.[31] Indeed, the very critique of universality and that of those that resort to universality need their own universality.[32] Said differently, it does not seem possible to articulate any legal discourse, let alone a critique of legal discourses, without a prior universalizing move. In that sense, the international lawyer aware of the emptiness of universality as well as its colonizing and hegemonic character, cannot simply take refuge in an utterly sceptical posture and must confront universality and the binaries it creates.

This book addresses the limits and inescapability of the idea of international law in the context of international legal discourses. It does so by engaging with the binaries accompanying the invocation of universality in international legal discourses. This introductory chapter maps some of binaries at work whenever the idea of universality is deployed by international lawyers and the criticisms that they have fueled . It then outlines the chapters of this volume which critically evaluate the binaries generated by the idea of universality and their inescapability .

1. Universality and its Binaries: A Few Examples

The invocation of universality and the creation of binary opposites can take diverse forms. This very brief summary sketches out some of the most common binaries that one can find in the international legal scholarship and which the authors of this book further engage with.

1.1 Particularity–Universality

Postulating that something is universal ultimately implies the existence of a particular. A universal concept transcends all cultural or historical belongings and

---

[30] See generally Foucault (n 26) 204.
[31] Laclau (n 23) 34, 59 ('The impossibility of a universal ground does not eliminate its need: it just transforms the ground into an empty place which can be partially filled in a variety of ways'; Pahuja, *Decolonising International Law* (n 25) 41 ('it is important to stress that I am not content only to reveal a "false" universality. Without more, such a revelation would simply lead us either to relativism or to an attempt to (re)found a "genuine" universality. Neither of these positions is theoretically tenable. Instead, I am trying to show that a universal orientation is unavoidable if there is to be law, but that even if the claim to universality is a familiar mode of power, it is nevertheless an unstable one, for it is always implanted with the seeds of its own excess').
[32] Said (n 29) 16, 25–26.

has to be freed from any aspect that might reflect a particularity. Butler defined this tension between universality and particularity as a hostility: 'The universal can be the universal only to the extent that it remains untainted by what is particular, concrete, and individual.'[33] The universal is in a constant struggle to detach itself from anything that might damage its distance from a particular. This, however, is a paradoxical task since whenever one makes the argument that something represents what is shared by all, that claim needs to draw from a particular. Universality has to be deduced from a particularity and it can never be authentic. Therefore, the claim to universality is always a hegemonic struggle that aspires to project what represents a particularity as what should belong to everyone. According to Martti Koskenniemi this is an antagonism that establishes the very premises of international law. As a hegemonic technique, international law is an exercise of presenting a particular political view as what should be accepted as universal.[34] In other words, universality can serve as a hegemonic tool that works in the service of those who want to impose their particular view through a legal vocabulary.

The idea that international law is universal and provides a legal system that can speak to all relies to a great extent on the objectivity of the discipline. The claim that international law consists of objective and neutral rules free from political interests, personal judgements, and particular concerns is central to the concept of universality. Several strands in international legal theory challenged this objectivity in relation to the universality of international law. Critical Legal Studies have long taken issue with the concept of universality when it is employed to describe a legal system that provides objective and neutral constraints against political power.[35] A classical argument of this strand has focused on the liberal project of separating law from politics through the rule of law. Critical legal scholars exposed the limits of liberal theory by demonstrating that this endeavour to provide a value-neutral legal system is doomed to fail since rules are indeterminate and do not lead to a single solution. Legal decisions will inevitably include particular political interests and it is therefore not possible to rely on the objectivity of international law, and hence claim it stems from universal values. International law cannot be conceived as 'the application of one unified method on the world' but rather it is 'a

---

[33] Judith Butler, 'Restating the Universal' in Judith Butler, Ernesto Laclau, and Slavoj Žižek (eds), *Contingency, Hegemony, Universality: Contemporary Dialogues on the Left* (Verso 2000) 23.
[34] Martti Koskenniemi, 'International Law and Hegemony: A Reconfiguration' (2004) 17 Cambridge Review of International Affairs 197, 198–99.
[35] Some seminal works include David Kennedy, *International Legal Structures* (Nomos 1987); David Kennedy, 'A New Stream of International Law Scholarship' (n 9); Nigel Purvis, 'Critical Legal Studies in Public International Law' (1991) 32 Harvard International Law Journal 81; Deborah Cass, 'Navigating the Newstream: Recent Critical Scholarship in International Law' (1996) 65 Nordic Journal of International Law 341; Martti Koskenniemi, *From Apology to Utopia: The Structure of International Legal Argument* (CUP 2006); Roberto Mangabeira Unger, *The Critical Legal Studies Movement: Another Time, a Greater Task* (Verso 2015).

conversation about the right thing to do in particular circumstances, constantly harking back to the political, the intimate and the subjective'.[36]

1.2 Hegemony–Universality

TWAIL's approach to universality has been about challenging the alleged unifying dimension of this concept. TWAIL has long been engaged in demonstrating how international law has served as a tool to legitimize power imbalances between states. Early TWAIL scholarship has been preoccupied with the decolonization process to demonstrate how international law has been complicit in the hegemonic policies of Western states.[37] While these writings discussed how international law could be improved by extending equal sovereignty to those who were marginalized by international law, a second wave of scholarship that started to take shape in the 1990s has concentrated on demonstrating how equal sovereignty is not the ultimate cure to remedy the power imbalances entrenched in the fundamental doctrines of the discipline. According to Antony Anghie, for instance, universality is used to mask how international law throughout history has been a tool in the service of an imperial project to advance European interests by relying on a 'dynamic of difference' between the so-called civilized and universal on the one hand, and particular and uncivilized on the other.[38] The main doctrines of international law are created to bridge the gap between these two fractions in order to extend the universality of the former to the latter. Sundhya Pahuja underlines how decolonization brought about formal sovereignty but did not establish a universality which would guarantee equality for all actors.[39] She claims that decolonization only replaced old forms of hegemony for new ones and a new form of universality.[40] Luis Eslava and Sundhya Pahuja highlight how, as a legal project, international law promotes a certain way of being as the universal and ask which universality can be accepted and which should be rejected.[41] Rather than a complete abandonment of the concept of universality, they propose to reform international law through a methodological turn in order to build a legal system that is also concerned with those that have so

---

[36] Martti Koskenniemi, 'International Law in a Post-Realist Era' (1995) 16 Australian Yearbook of International Law 1, 17.

[37] Georges Abi-Saab, 'The Newly Independent States and the Scope of Domestic Jurisdiction' (1960) 54 ASIL Proceedings 84; RP Anand, 'Attitude of the Asian-African States Toward Certain Problems of International Law' (1966) 15 International & Comparative Law Quarterly 55; Mohammed Bedjaoui, *Towards a New International Legal Order* (Holmes & Meier Publishers 1979); Frederick Snyder and Surakiart Sathirathai (eds), *Third World Attitudes toward International Law: An Introduction* (Brill 1987); Christopher Weeramantry, *Universalising International Law* (Brill 2004).

[38] Antony Anghie, *Imperialism, Sovereignty and the Making of International Law* (CUP 2007).

[39] Pahuja, *Decolonising International Law* (n 25).

[40] ibid 4.

[41] Luis Eslava and Sundhya Pahuja, 'Between Resistance and Reform: TWAIL and the Universality of International Law' (2011) 3 Trade, Law and Development 108.

far been at the periphery.[42] They argue that there cannot be one universality that can transcend all differences.[43] International law's universality should be understood as quasi-transcendent: not totally transcendent since there can never be an authentic universality. This understanding provides a space for plurality by recognizing that although law will necessarily have to emerge from a particular premise, that premise is ultimately contingent.[44]

The relationship between imperialism and international law can be told from various perspectives. According to Chimni, the proliferation of international organizations in the last few decades is a burden to reach universality. He states that most international organizations constitute a 'nascent global state' that functions in the service of powerful states and transnational capital to the detriment of Third World states.[45] In his opinion, this nascent global state can hardly be reformed to give way to a 'universal and homogenous state' due to the lack of social democracy within these institutions and also the way in which they treat Third World states. Jouannet's approach highlights the role that the concept of universality plays in legitimizing imperial policies through international law.[46] Classical international law emerged from a European legal tradition. This, however, did not prevent the founders of the discipline from arguing that international law enjoyed universal application. Jouannet claims that the projection of a legal system that originated in a specific region as a universal system was made possible on the basis of rationalism: 'It was Reason, common to all, that provided the foundation for the in-principle of the universality of the law of peoples, as it was from this basis that the rights and duties of individuals and states could be deduced.'[47] In that regard, in the classical period, rational universalism allowed the promotion of a regional legal system as a global one. The domination of a particular legal tradition could not be realized without erasing different juridical models. Universality of international law can therefore be said to have a dual life: on the one hand, in order to emancipate itself from its regional roots international law claimed to provide neutral norms of law that apply to all states; on the other, this universality, whose neutrality arguably stemmed from the abstract and formal nature of its rules, justified not only its global application but also European colonial imperialism.[48] In that sense, the universality of international law served as a tool to legitimize hegemonic policies.

---

[42] ibid 115–16.
[43] ibid 122.
[44] ibid.
[45] BS Chimni, 'International Institutions Today: An Imperial Global State in the Making' (2004) 15 European Journal of International Law 1.
[46] Emmanuelle Jouannet, 'Universalism and Imperialism: The True-False Paradox of International Law?' (2007) 18 European Journal of International Law 379.
[47] ibid 381.
[48] ibid 382.

1.3 Gendered Inequality–Universality

Feminist approaches to international law challenged the universality of international law by unravelling the gender bias inherent in the system. In a seminal work, Charlesworth, Chinkin, and Wright exposed this gender bias by demonstrating that international law was designed by men and marginalized women's voices and experiences.[49] From an organizational perspective, decision-making processes of international law hardly included female voices due to the low representation level of women within the primary subjects of the field, such as states and international organizations.[50] The invisibility of women can also be witnessed in the normative structure of international law, which divides between a male public sphere and a female private sphere.[51] *The Boundaries of International Law* expanded the depth and scope of studies from a feminist perspective by demonstrating how fundamental doctrines of international law, including statehood, use of force, law of treaties, and human rights, have either ignored or side-stepped concerns that are specific to women.[52] Universality has long been a great companion of human rights law. Otto questioned the process by which human dignity was constructed in international law discourse as a source of the universality of human rights.[53] She claimed that human dignity, rather than being a universal value, was a European and male discursive construct of dominant actors of international law that helped to transform differences in tradition, culture, and experience that did not conform with its way of being.[54] Other studies demonstrated the gendered nature of international law versus an alleged universality on various issues, including the use of force,[55] non-recognition of women's rights as human rights,[56] and humanitarian law.[57]

---

[49] Hilary Charlesworth, Christine Chinkin, and Shelley Wright, 'Feminist Approaches to International Law' (1991) 85 American Journal of International Law 613.

[50] ibid 621–25. See also Priya Pillai, 'Women in International Law: A Vanishing Act?' (*Opinio Juris*, 3 December 2018) <http://opiniojuris.org/2018/12/03/women-in-international-law-a-vanishing-act/> accessed 16 December 2021.

[51] ibid 625–34.

[52] Charlesworth and Chinkin, *The Boundaries of International Law* (n 14).

[53] Dianne Otto, 'Rethinking Universals: Opening Transformative Possibilities in International Human Rights Law' (1997) 18 Australian Yearbook of International Law 1.

[54] ibid.

[55] Gina Heathcote, *The Law on the Use of Force: A Feminist Analysis* (Routledge-Cavendish 2011).

[56] Karen Knop (ed), *Gender and Human Rights* (OUP 2004); J Oloka-Onyango and Sylvia Tamale, '"The Personal is Political" or Why Women's Rights are Indeed Human Rights: An African Perspective on International Feminism' (1995) 17 Human Rights Quarterly 691; Alice Edwards, *Violence Against Women under International Human Rights Law* (CUP 2013); Charlotte Bunch, 'Women's Rights as Human Rights: Toward a Re-Vision of Human Rights' (1990) 12 Human Rights Quarterly 486.

[57] Anne Orford, *Reading Humanitarian Intervention: Human Rights and the Use of Force in International Law* (CUP 2003).

1.4 Fragmentation–Universality

The proliferation of separate normative systems in international law and their independent development from each other has been a long-discussed phenomenon.[58] Fragmentation has been an efficient rhetorical tool in international legal scholarship. Anne-Charlotte Martineau traces different narratives of fragmentation and demonstrates that it can be used both in a positive sense to refer to the diversity of the discipline as a sign of progress and, equally, that it can be invoked to project a chaotic image of the field to demonstrate its underdevelopment.[59] When discussions on the fragmentation of international law centre around the growing number of different regimes with distinct problems, preferences, procedures, and institutions, the concept of universality can be used to refer to the unity of the discipline. Universality of international law can be opposed to the fragmentation of the field where the former implies the coherence of international legal rules as part of a legal unity.[60] In that sense, fragmentation poses a threat to the idea of universality by underlining the possibility of different normative systems coexisting at an equal level as part of international law.[61] The diversification of actors that generate international law norms, the differing nature of their application and scope, which at times conflict or overlap, can be interpreted as jeopardizing the ideal of preserving a coherent legal system. Mario Prost presents a different approach and argues that fragmentation should not be seen as the opposite of universality.[62] He differentiates between unity of the discipline and its universality and advocates for an attenuated version of the latter. According to his view, universality can only be realized if actors agree on the main principles and allow room for regional, substantive, or procedural deviation.[63] In that sense, the concept of universality refers to international law forming a system, rather than a coherent unity. The same interpretation is used by Jennings who argues that '[u]niversality does not mean uniformity. It does mean, however, that such a regional international law, however variant, is part of the system as a whole, and not a separate system.'[64]

---

[58] See 'Fragmentation of International Law: Difficulties Arising from the Diversification and Expansion of International', Report of the Study Group of the International Law Commission, Finalized by Martti Koskenniemi, UN Doc A/CN.4/L.682 (13 April 2006).

[59] Anne-Charlotte Martineau, 'The Rhetoric of Fragmentation: Fear and Faith in International Law' (2009) 22 Leiden Journal of International Law 1.

[60] Simma (n 2) 267.

[61] See generally Martti Koskenniemi and Päivi Leino, 'Fragmentation of International Law? Postmodern Anxieties' (2002) 15 Leiden Journal of International Law 553.

[62] Mario Prost, *The Concept of Unity in Public International Law* (Bloomsbury Publishing 2012) 34–37.

[63] ibid 37.

[64] Robert Jennings, 'Universal International Law in a Multicultural World' in *Collected Essays of Sir Robert Jennings* (Kluwer 1998) 342.

1.5 Regionalism–Universality

If fragmentation is used to refer to the diversification of not only local international law-making bodies but also to a greater extent, the growing number of actors, institutions, problems, and procedures to emphasize the coexistence of separate normative regimes in international law, regionalism has a particular focus on regional variations.[65] If international law is a system that has historically been intended to have global recognition, any local rule, process, or method that does not seek to have a global impact might be seen as diverting international law from its ultimate ideal of providing a universal system. Regionalism can be approached from different angles. It might refer to different approaches to international law that highlight the concerns of a particular region, such as African,[66] Asian,[67] European,[68] American,[69] or Latin American[70] approaches to international law, or it might also refer to regional law-making processes.[71] While in 1945 the international society was mainly organized around the United Nations as a global international organization and sovereign states as individual members of the international society, the proliferation of regional organizations in the following years challenged to a great extent the application of universal international norms. Regional organizations have been an effective mechanism for economic and political cooperation with their specialized focus and efficient decision-making processes.[72] If universality is perceived as inclusiveness and the ability of international law to reach all actors, regional variations stand in contrast with this understanding of universality with their limited area of validity.

---

[65] On the relationship between fragmentation and regionalism, see Report of the Study Group of the International Law Commission, Finalized by Martti Koskenniemi, (n 58) 102–14.

[66] Rowland JV Cole, 'Africa's Approach to International Law: Aspects of the Political and Economic Denominators' (2010) 18 African Yearbook of International Law Online 287; James Thuo Gathii, 'Africa and the History of International Law' in Bardo Fassbender and Anne Peters (eds), *The Oxford Handbook of the History of International Law* (OUP 2012).

[67] BS Chimni, 'Asian Civilizations and International Law: Some Reflections' (2011) 1 Asian Journal of International Law 39; ONUMA Yasuaki, 'The Asian Society of International Law: Its Birth and Significance' (2011) Asian Journal of International Law 71; Jin-Hyun Palk, Seok-Woo Lee, and Kevin Y L Tan (eds), *Asian Approaches to International Law and the Legacy of Colonialism: The Law of the Sea, Territorial Disputes and International Dispute Settlement* (Routledge 2012).

[68] Martti Koskenniemi, 'International Law in Europe' (n 1).

[69] Mark Weston Janis, *The American Tradition of International Law: Great Expectations 1789–1914* (OUP 2004); Emmanuelle Jouannet, 'French and American Perspectives on International Law: Legal Cultures and International Law' (2006) 58 Maine Law Review 292.

[70] Arnulf Becker Lorca, 'International Law in Latin America or Latin American International Law-Rise, Fall, and Retrieval of a Tradition of Legal Thinking and Political Imagination' (2006) 47 Harvard International Law Journal 283.

[71] For an account explaining how regionalism proliferated during the Cold War period, see Andrew Hurrell, 'One World? Many Worlds? The Place of Regions in the Study of International Society' (2007) 83 Foreign Affairs 127.

[72] Christoph Schreuer, 'Regionalism v. Universalism' (1995) 6 European Journal of International Law 477.

1.6 Heterogeneity–Universality

In his keynote speech delivered at the 2008 ESIL Annual Conference, Bruno Simma treated fragmentation as part of a broader concern. He posits universality as a concept that was created in international law as an antidote to the heterogeneity of the discipline where various treaties, customs, actors, judicial bodies, principles, binding and non-binding, instruments coexisted.[73] Universality serves as a concept that allows one to harbour in a legal system all these different elements which at times conflicted with each other. He argues that universality can be conceptualized at three different levels: it can, first, refer to the bindingness of international law as a legal system that applies to all states; secondly to the unity of the discipline as opposed to the fragmentation of international law due to the proliferation of international organizations, courts, and also different approaches to international law with the mushrooming of international law theories; and thirdly to a global system that provides a public order for all.[74] Simma's approach to universality is important for demonstrating how international law is in need of concepts that can conceal antagonisms within the discipline, whether about conflicting instruments and interests or various regulatory functions it is expected to perform. In other words, despite all the heterogeneity, disarray, and incoherencies that are part of the discipline, the concept of universality can restore our faith that the discipline still forms part of a single system after all. While Simma argues that there is no need for the constitutionalization of international law since the concept of universality ensures the unity of the discipline,[75] Allott's take on the heterogeneity of the discipline leads him to a different interpretation of universality. He claims that, in the twenty-first century, we are witnessing a sea change in the way we used to perceive what is international and what is national. In recent practice, due to the exponential growth of the international sphere, its frequent use in the national context, and the growing interaction between the international and national realms, the boundaries of these two legal systems are becoming increasingly blurred. Allott suggests that these developments give rise to the 'emergence of a universal legal system' that requires international lawyers to better understand the new international social reality.[76] He states that international lawyers need to restructure the way they conceive international society and find a way to establish 'the eventual structure of a universal legal system, the legal system of all legal systems'.[77]

---

[73] Simma (n 2) 265.
[74] ibid 266–67.
[75] ibid 297.
[76] Philip Allott, 'Emerging Universal Legal System' (2001) 3 International Law Forum du Droit International 12, 14.
[77] ibid 16.

1.7 Cultural Relativism–Universality

International lawyers have a paradoxical relationship with culture. While they might argue that international rules are neutral and transcend culture, they can hardly deny the specific cultural context from which these rules originated.[78] Despite the claim of universality, human rights law has been shaped by liberal Western thought and prioritizes certain values, stemming from a particular cultural legal tradition, over others.[79] While the universality of international law mainly refers to its bindingness in a formal sense, the universality of human rights describes a legal system that functions around certain common minimal standards.[80] The universality of human rights indicates that everyone shares fundamental rights just because they are a human being and postulates an idea of unity. On the other hand, cultural relativism highlights the diversity of what might constitute minimal standards in each and every culture.[81] Discussions on cultural relativism stem from this tension between unity and diversity. They centre around understanding whether human rights can transcend cultural differences to articulate some universal concerns or whether cultural particularities can provide a valid justification for not complying with universal human rights norms. Some international lawyers try to resolve the tension between cultural relativism and universality by stripping human rights from its cultural roots. They argue that although human rights are a product of a Western legal tradition, their emergence and consolidation did not rely on conditions that were specific to this culture.[82] In that sense, no cultural characteristic can be used to create a fundamental disagreement between different cultures when it comes to protecting human dignity. Others adopt a more nuanced approach and state that the universality of human rights should be seen as a process and cannot be imposed from outside upon regions which are resistant

---

[78] Annelis Riles, 'Aspiration and Control: International Legal Rhetoric and the Essentialization of Culture' (1993) 106 Harvard Law Review 723. On human universals from a cultural anthropology perspective, see Christoph Antweiler, *Our Common Denominator: Human Universals Revisited* (Berghahn Books 2018).

[79] Otto, 'Rethinking Universals' (n 46), David Kennedy, 'International Human Rights Movement: Part of the Problem?' (2002) 15 Harvard Human Rights Journal 101, 114–16. For a TWAIL perspective on human rights law, see generally Balakrishnan Rajagopal, 'Counter-Hegemonic International Law: Rethinking Human Rights and Development as a Third World Strategy' (2006) 27 Third World Quarterly 767; José-Manuel Barreto (ed), *Human Rights from a Third World Perspective: Critique, History and International Law* (Cambridge Scholars Publishing 2013).

[80] André Nollkaemper defines this universality as 'a pre-positive concept with aspirational value', see André Nollkaemper, 'Universality' in *Max Planck Encyclopedia of Public International Law* <http://opil.ouplaw.com/view/10.1093/law:epil/9780199231690/law-9780199231690-e1497> accessed 16 December 2021.

[81] Upendra Baxi, *The Future of Human Rights* (OUP 2008) 160–99; Marie-Bénédicte Dembour, 'Critiques' in Daniel Moeckli, Sangeeta Shah, and Sandesh Sivakuraman (eds), *International Human Rights Law* (OUP 2014) 52.

[82] Fernando Teson, 'International Human Rights and Cultural Relativism' (1984) 25 Virginia Journal of International Law 869; Rosalyn Higgins, *Problems and Process: International Law and How We Use it* (OUP 1994) 96; Jack Donnelly, *Universal Human Rights* (Cornell Universality Press 2013) 106–07.

to certain rights.[83] Some also argue that a balance should be struck between universality and cultural relativism since '[m]oral egoism easily leads to arrogance, and universalism to imperialism'.[84] A different perspective highlights how the emphasis on a dichotomy of cultural relativism and universality can serve as a hegemonic tool to differentiate between a public universal space which is impartial and a private cultural space which is particular.[85] This dichotomy presents liberal universalism as tolerant of particularities in a way 'to cabin difference within the terms of the public-private distinctions'.[86]

2. Contents of this Book: Binaries as Spaces of Contestation

Whilst the modern and cosmopolitan project driving international law since the eighteenth century has been the object of very extensive criticisms,[87] the idea of universality that supports it has rarely been systematically unpacked. With an emphasis on the binaries that accompany the invocation of the idea of universality in international legal discourses, this book sheds a new light on how the idea of universality plays out in international legal discourses and provides a site of contestation. Its chapters particularly examine how each of abovementioned binaries informing the idea of universality constitutes, enables, and delimits a new space for contestation of international law in international legal discourses.

It is important to note that, for the sake of this volume, universality is not reduced to the question of the geographical outreach of international law, but, drawing on the binaries sketched out in the previous section, is understood in the more general terms of boundaries. This also entails examining how the very idea of universality—which does not lend itself to a translation into all languages—was developed in some of the dominant vernaculars of international law—primarily English and French—before being universalized and imposed upon international lawyers from all traditions. This choice simultaneously offers an opportunity to revisit the ideologies that constitute the identity of international lawyers today, as well as the socialization, and legal educational processes which they undergo to

---

[83] Christina Cerna, 'Universality of Human Rights and Cultural Diversity: Implementation of Human Rights in Different Socio-Cultural Contexts' (1994) 16 Human Rights Quarterly 740, 752. In a similar vein, see Louis Henkin, 'The Universality of the Concept of Human Rights' (1989) 506 The Annals of the American Political Academy and Social Science 10.
[84] Costas Douzinas, ''The End(s) of Human Rights' (2002) 26 Melbourne University Law Review 445, 457.
[85] Vasuki Nesiah, 'The Ground Beneath her Feet: "Third World Feminisms"' (2003) 4 Journal of International Women's Studies 30, 35.
[86] ibid 37.
[87] See generally Martti Koskenniemi, *The Gentle Civilizer of Nations: The Rise and Fall of International Law 1870–1960* (CUP 2010).

become international lawyers. Special attention will be paid to the place which Europe has secured for itself by virtue of the progress and historical narratives built around the idea of universality.

2.1 The Idea of Universality

Part I of the book investigates the idea of universality in order to set the stage. Gail Lythgoe starts a discussion on what universality means in spatial terms. She looks at the spatial logics that function in legal regimes and how spatial characteristics inform international lawyers' political projects. She argues that the legal imaginary of international lawyers is dominated by two forms of particularity: geopolitical and networked particularity. Throughout her chapter, she analyses how international lawyers are inevitably concerned by one form of particularity or another, either consciously or unconsciously. The chapter brings to light our unquestioned assumptions about the spaces of universality and particularity that we generally take for granted.

Ekaterina Yahyaoui Krivenko questions the idea of universality through two philosophers: Hobbes and Leibniz. The comparison between the two philosophers' approach to universals brings a new perspective to the way we can apprehend binaries that the idea of universality is bound to generate. Krivenko demonstrates how examining the contrary views of Hobbes and Leibniz as to what constitutes a universal can be helpful in understanding the way these two philosophers conceptualized state and sovereignty and how in return this shaped their approach to international law.

Matthew Nicholson takes issue with the relationship between the universal and the particular and argues that formalist international legal thought is more concerned with the former rather than the latter. He associates formal universalism with the Bonaventure hotel analysis of Fredric Jameson. He further draws on Ursula K Le Guin's essay 'The Carrier Bag Theory of Fiction' and associates the universalization of the particular with the image of a carrier bag. He demonstrates how international law can be conceptualized as a carrier bag which conveys different particulars.

Akbar Rasulov is interested in an ideology critique of international legal universalism. He questions how international lawyers find in their profession a messianic endeavour to determine the true universals of the discipline. By examining the narratives of universality as reach, universality as representation, and universality as culture, Rasulov shows how this political project of international legal universalism is performed. By drawing insights from critical narratology and legal realist analysis, he lays bare the rhetorical manoeuvres used to put this universalism into practice.

2.2 The Invention of Universality

The idea of universality in international law is no doubt a legal construct, rather than a natural phenomenon that developed on its own. Part II discusses how this idea of universality was invented. It starts with a chapter introduced by Ishii Yurika which is based on the contribution that ONUMA Yasuaki was meant to deliver at the ESIL Annual Conference in Manchester in 2018, which he eventually—and sadly—could not attend. In his chapter, ONUMA Yasuaki criticizes the Western-centric premises of international law and inquires whether it would be possible to reach a universal that can be accepted by people from diverse cultures and backgrounds.

The second chapter in this Part makes a modest attempt at challenging the dominance of English as a language in international legal scholarship. Frédéric Mégret analyses in his chapter (in French) how the idea of universality is indeed a by-product of Western legal imagination. He advocates how universality was promoted to those who sought to escape the imperialist dispositions of American and European states based on the necessity of international law's universality.

2.3 Universality and Rights

Part III turns to the relationship between universality and rights. Mark Retter takes a natural law approach to justify the ethical foundation of universal human rights. By drawing insights from Alasdair MacIntyre's practice-based account of the political common good and natural justice, he addresses two issues: the consistency between its commitment to universal human rights and an understanding of moral knowledge formation, and the consistency of its commitment to universal human rights given certain facts of moral pluralism, and especially the presence of rival human rights theories about the foundations and content of such rights.

Tilmann Altwicker focuses on the European Court of Human Rights to explain how the Court developed an implicit universality jurisprudence while pretending not to intervene in theoretical discussions of human rights. He distinguishes three universality qualities of human rights, namely abstractness, inclusiveness, and rationality. He posits human rights nationalism against the universality of human rights, an idea that he argues is being advocated not only by political parties but also judges of domestic courts. He provides examples from the UK, Russia, and Switzerland to argue how there is a growing concern about the supremacy of international human rights adjudication. He analyses how this new binary, 'national relativism–universality', is challenging the idea of universality by prioritizing domestic interpretations of human rights over universalizing interpretations before international courts.

2.4 Universality and the Non-Human

The way we conceptualize, understand, practice, and interpret international law depends on several factors, including our political interests, personal biases, assumptions, predispositions, and cultural background. Nevertheless, it can be argued without much difficulty that anthropocentric thinking is predominant in the way we perform international law.[88] While anthropocentric thinking finds its rationale in placing the human at the centre of the legal imagination, it is crucial to acknowledge that there is a world beyond humans and that the world does not necessarily turn around us. It is to that end that Alejandro Lorite questions the relation between humans and animals in the first chapter in Part IV. He argues that the way legal regulations treat animals showcases how they are always positioned in a dualistic relationship with humans. Rather than being conceptualized as independent autonomous living beings, animals are seen as extensions of humans. To challenge this idea, Lorite posits what he calls Dominionism as opposed to the illiberal universal rule of Liberalism.

Régis Bismuth draws attention to the turn to animal welfare in recent years. While this concept has acquired some universality, it is used in several different meanings depending on the context. While animal welfare aims to protect the interests of animals, Bismuth demonstrates how it was instrumentalized to exploit animals. Through the example of the World Organisation for Animal Health, he explains how the concept is mostly used as an economic and efficiency-driven technical tool that can pave the way for the industrial exploitation of animals. While the *Seals* dispute before the WTO has become a precedent canonized in global animal law, Bismuth analyses it with a critical lens and demonstrates how the way the dispute has been handled showcases the anthropocentric thinking by discriminating between animal species.

2.5 Universality beyond Europe

The primary criticism that could be voiced against the universality of international law would be how this universality draws from the particularity of a European understanding of international law. Part V discusses how the idea of universality manifests itself beyond the European context. Mohammad Shahabuddin looks at the engagement of Japan with the idea of universality. After Japan opened up to the Western world in the nineteenth century, Japanese scholars had to engage with the European standard of civilization. Shahabuddin explains how they did

---

[88] See Jean d'Aspremont, 'The Foundations of the International Legal Order' (2007) 18 Finnish Yearbook of International Law 219.

so for instrumental purposes and used it to reclaim their supremacy in the region. He offers new analytical tools that allow us to go beyond mainstream narratives of European hegemony.

Mashood Baderin underlines how the universality of international law is perceived as a trojan horse of imperialist endeavours in the Global South and in particular in Muslim countries. From an Islamic law perspective, Baderin argues that a more inclusive universality is possible by taking into account the contributions made to the field by non-Western states. He investigates how the Eurocentric universality of international law is perpetuated through a historical narrative, norm formation, judicial interpretation, and political manipulations. He explains how a genuine universality can be reached by recognizing the contributions that an Islamic perspective can generate.

Kanad Bagchi and Milan Tahraoui inquire what might be the implications of the Chinese Belt and Road Initiative (BRI) regarding the universality of international law. They put into perspective common interpretations that are made about the BRI which suggest that it either strengthens or challenges the universality of international law. They go beyond this binary critique and explain how the BRI reinforces traditional doctrines of sovereignty and non-intervention, rather than dismantling the current international order. Through the lens of co-option and contestation, they analyse how BRI has been intentionally designed to oscillate between rhetoric and reality.

2.6 Universality and the Languages of International Law

Language, in Part VI, refers not only to particular languages, but also to methods of communication. It is in that sense that Elisabeth Roy-Trudel focuses in her chapter on visual methods of communication, and in particular the power of images. She inquires into the authority given to some images in human rights law to convey a certain message and underlines how visual discourse can be instrumental in reinforcing forms of domination and exclusion and prevent a genuine distribution of fundamental rights. She highlights some iconic images of human rights law to re-evaluate the meaning that they carry in mainstream discourses. She claims that drawing attention to the language of images is key in realizing human rights law's ultimate goal of reaching global justice.

Markus Beham focuses on the concept of 'Dogmatik', a German word that is hardly translatable into English. While the concept is widely used in the Germanophone legal traditions, in particular in Austria, Germany, and Switzerland, it does not lend itself to an easy counterpart in other languages. After mapping out the meaning of the concept within the Germanophone legal tradition, the chapter elucidates from a comparative perspective how this particular concept can support the universal aspirations of international law.

2.7 Critique and Resistance to Universality

The volume draws to a close with Part VII, which highlights how the idea of universality can be critiqued in different fields of international law.

Maiko Meguro takes a hard look at the impact of globalization on international law and investigates in particular the universality discourses regarding climate change. She analyses the scholarly discourses on the Paris Agreement that both have recourse to the concept of universality and particularity. She provides a new account by analysing the Paris Agreement under the United Nations Framework Convention on Climate Change and how there is a push and pull between universality and particularity, rather than an attempt to overcome the latter. She elucidates the underlying thinking patterns of scholars which affect both the empirical and epistemological claims on climate change.

Zinaida Miller argues how international justice acquires its legitimacy by a constant oscillation between universal and particular. While the universality discourse provides justification for the field's very existence, the particularity discourse protects it from criticisms of hegemony and neocolonialism. To demonstrate how this oscillation is performed, she examines in particular anti-impunity and truth-telling discourses. She shows how this tilt is consistently away from the racial and colonial dynamics that undergird the representation, reception, and practice of international justice. The chapter brings to light the constant struggle over universalist and particularist visions of international justice.

Andreas Kulick proposes a new binary in his examination of international adjudication discourses. Against the mainstream approach of conceptual universality, he posits what he calls pragmatic particularity. While international adjudication can be seen as a dominant narrative of dispute resolution since the end of the Cold War, he argues how this ideal is giving way to a pragmatic particularity due to the rise of China as a world power, the return of the nation state, and the diminishing interest and trust in international adjudication. Kulick examines how the idea that formalized mechanisms such as litigation or arbitration should be used to resolve disputes was advanced in particular by Western states. Against this conceptual universality of international adjudication, he investigates how the sinicization, re-etatization, and de-judicialization of international relations brought about the rise of pragmatic particularity.

I
THE IDEA OF UNIVERSALITY

1
The Spaces of the Universal and the Particular in International Law
Questioning Binaries and Uncovering Political Projects

Gail Lythgoe

In July 2018, New York became the first city to 'report directly to the international community on its efforts to reach global benchmarks in addressing poverty, inequality and climate change'.[1] Although voluntary, this event represents a wider shift in how the international community is being conceptualized. The term 'international community'[2] increasingly is used to describe more than the traditional society of states, referring also to non-state actors, such as international institutions, practitioners, non-governmental organizations, academics, and activists. The United Nations (UN) Forum where New York's proclamation was delivered saw not only states as delegates but also 'cities, businesses, and community organizations from around the world'.[3] Part of a wider initiative for achieving the Sustainable Development Goals (SDGs), it gave a platform to actors and entities long invisible to traditional accounts of international law.

---

[1] 'UN Forum Spotlights Cities, Where Struggle for Sustainability "Will Be Won or Lost"' (United Nations Sustainable Development, 12 July 2018) <https://www.un.org/sustainabledevelopment/blog/2018/07/un-forum-spotlights-cities-where-struggle-for-sustainability-will-be-won-or-lost-2/> accessed 16 January 2024.

[2] 'The concept is significant because it reflects a particular perspective on international relations: one that looks beyond States to include individuals, groups, companies', Christian Tams, 'International Community' in Jean d'Aspremont and Sahib Singh (eds), *Concepts for International Law: Contributions to Disciplinary Thought* (Edward Elgar 2019) 508.

[3] SDG Media Zone, 'SDG Media Zone: Sustainable Cities Update' (SDG Media Zone, 2018) at 00:11 minutes <www.un.org/sustainabledevelopment/blog/2018/07/sdg-media-zone-sustainable-cities-update/> accessed 20 July 2018. Of course, New York is not obligated, in law, to report on its SDG-promoting activities. It is difficult to see cities, no matter how big or how rich, as holding any real power, from an international law perspective, to effect or prevent (or be held responsible for) the kind of changes that the SDG programme envisages. However, when one considers that even for states SDGs are but political aspirations the pursuit of which entails no legal responsibility, the latter point seems somewhat moot. What is worth noting, in any event, is that the UN increasingly deals with an ever more diverse array of actors—not just at the level of informal political consultations, but as part of its official legal processes of norm creation, surveillance, and implementation of standards.

In the broader scholarly discourse there is also a 'turn' to non-state actors, including individuals, non-state armed groups, international institutions, and corporations. While the European Union (EU) and other international or regional organizations have prompted protracted debate as 'supra-statal' actors, a growing discourse seeks to better grasp the role in the international legal system of cities and local governments.[4] Yet the concepts of sub- or supra-statal entities are highly spatialized constructs evoking certain ideas of scale and scope, as well as hierarchy.

This New York proclamation episode is curious because of what it tells us about the various latent assumptions held about universality and particularity. There are many different angles from which one can dissect the tensions between 'the universal' and 'the particular'. One could argue, for example, that the involvement of cities and other actors in the SDG process ensures a more 'universal' participation rather than limiting the process to the 'particular' category of states. Moreover, the 2030 Agenda is universal in nature and ambition, given its goals of universal human rights; universal literacy; and universal access to education, affordable energy, and healthcare.[5]

Nevertheless, however laudable the concept of universality may be in the abstract, it is a deeply political project in practice. Designating anything—an idea, a value, a goal, an actor—as universalizable brings certain politics with it. The same holds true also for narratives of particularity and locality. Both the universal and the particular are categories used in international legal discourse to describe various processes, systems, structures, and organizational tactics; both are important tools of contestation and of argumentation, and I argue space plays an as yet unnoticed role in the construction of these ideas—indeed it is fundamental to their constitution and imaginary.

Universalities and particularities are understood in this chapter as mutually constituted. This does not mean that universality and particularity are indistinguishable concepts. They are most often oppositional to one another, but this opposition is analytically constitutive of each construct, its structure and content.

For both concepts evoke and are informed by sensibilities of space, scale, and scope. Yet, despite the attention paid by international lawyers to their use of these terms in their discourse, the spatial assumptions underpinning these concepts have remained largely unexplored. Thus, this contribution asks: what are the spaces that

---

[4] Helmut Aust and Janne E Nijman (eds), *Research Handbook on International Law and Cities* (Edward Elgar 2021); Janne E Nijman, 'Renaissance of the City as Global Actor' in Gunther Hellmann, Fahrmeir Andreas, and Milo Vec (eds), *The Role of Foreign Policy and International Law Practices in the Construction of Cities as Global Actors* (OUP 2016); Michele Acuto, 'City Leadership in Global Governance' (2013) 19 Global Governance 481; Helmut Aust and Anél du Plessis, *The Globalisation of Urban Governance* (Routledge 2020); Saskia Sassen, 'The Global City: Introducing a Concept' (2005) The Brown Journal of World Affairs 11(2) 27–43.

[5] 'Transforming Our World: The 2030 Agenda for Sustainable Development' (*Sustainable Development Knowledge Platform*) <https://sustainabledevelopment.un.org/post2015/transformingourworld/publication> accessed 14 January 2020.

international lawyers often attach to concepts like universality and particularity, how are they constituted, and how do they enable the imaginary of actors and legal regimes?

In the following I not only problematize the legal imaginaries of universality and particularity but suggest there are at least two forms of particularity: what might be called the *geopolitical particularity*, a concept that will be more intuitively familiar to many international lawyers, and what might be called *a networked or fluid particularity*, still emerging as a critical counterpoint. The spaces of cities and non-state actors are a good representation of this latter category.[6] This second particularity category is constituted by a different spatial ordering that confounds the spatial logic of traditional concepts of particularity and universality. In the following I explore the underlying spatial logics of these two particularities and the concept of universality to which they are dialectically related.

It is my hope the analysis offered here will prompt a critical awareness of the structuring role of implicit geographies and the latent spatial assumptions informing international law.[7] A spatially aware critique of international law not only gives clarity to legal analysis, but also allows for further contestation of often hidden agendas to take place. How we understand the relationship between these concepts has a direct impact on our understanding of law's relationship with society, culture, and epistemic frameworks. By exploring the usage of constructs like 'universal' and 'particular' in the contemporary international law discourses through a spatial lens, we can problematize the supposed binary between these constructs and understand what contributes to the creation of this binary in the first place.

This chapter explores these points in three stages. The first explores the spatial assumptions of international law and articulates why these are important to this inquiry. The second outlines the construction of the spatiality associated with the universal in contemporary legal discourse, highlighting its defining features and

---

[6] Another productive framework for understanding these phenomena might be transnational law. Yet, there is intellectual baggage with this framework that is avoided in this chapter. There is a similar thread running through transnational law literature which makes a fundamental connection between traditional international law's inveterate statocentricity and its preoccupation with territoriality. Notwithstanding the purported attempt to move away from the discipline's preoccupation with states, states continue to serve as a central anchor for most transnational law thinking and an integral structure to accounts of law. The concepts of state territory and state borders continue to operate as 'reference points' and 'crucial points of orientation' (Peer C Zumbansen, 'Defining the Space of Transnational Law: Legal Theory, Global Governance & Legal Pluralism' (2012) 21(2) Transnational Law and Contemporary Problems 305, 312, 324), a function they can only perform if they remain the stable background against which transnational (or indeed international) law exists. A certain degree of reliance seems inevitable: after all, without states, there would be nothing 'trans-' about transnational law. Yet, the extent of transnational law's dependence on statocentricity goes beyond that. This is a line of inquiry that is explored in Lythgoe *The Rebirth of Territory* (CUP forthcoming 2024) ch 2, but it would go beyond the scope of the chapter in this volume to examine.

[7] For similar analysis in practice, see Péter Szigeti, 'Territorial Bias in International Law: Attribution in State and Corporate Responsibility' (2009) 19 Journal of Transnational Law and Policy 311.

characteristics. The final section explores the spatial logic of the two identified forms of particularity: geopolitical and networked particularities. The proposed networked particularity offers a critical counterpoint to our understanding of how legal space is constructed, and this appreciation can offer further insights into the dialectical relationship between law and power. Taking each suggested concept of particularity in turn, I study its defining characteristics and discuss its actual and potential use for the purposes of legal discourse and analysis.

1. The Spatial Background of International Law: Interrogating the Modern Picture

Like any other discipline, international law incorporates a whole range of ideas, constructs, and preconceptions borrowed from other disciplinary traditions. Some of these borrowings and linkages most will usually be aware of, others less so. The linkage with geography often belongs in the latter category.

Geography is a body of knowledge that purports to give shape to the spaces which humans cannot otherwise know—either because they are 'far away' or because they are 'too big' and 'abstract' to experience physically. Every discipline, from economics[8] to public health,[9] has its own implicit geography: its own set of assumptions, in other words, about the various kinds of spaces, and the spatialities of the relevant actors, that exist in the world 'out there' and the various characteristics which these actors' spaces have.

As lawyers and scholars, we are all informed in our thinking by all manner of background assumptions that structure our understanding of concepts and narratives.[10] This inquiry shows that 'whenever and *wherever* law is at work, geographical knowledge already operates in the background'[11] and this knowledge shapes legal processes and arguments. There is an unconscious spatiality underlying most legal concepts and narratives: the idea of a legal system; the relevant actors to that legal system; the scope and application of a legal regime; the claim that a certain legal idea, value, or right has or does not have a universal validity, etc.

---

[8] Gordon L Clark and others, *The Oxford Handbook of Economic Geography* (OUP 2003).
[9] Trevor JB Dummer, 'Health Geography: Supporting Public Health Policy and Planning' (2008) 178 Canadian Medical Association Journal 1177.
[10] David Kennedy, *A World of Struggle: How Power, Law, and Expertise Shape Global Political Economy* (1st edn, Princeton University Press 2016); Andrea Bianchi 'Epistemic Communities' in Jean d'Aspremont and Sahib Singh (eds), *Concepts for International Law—Contributions to Disciplinary Thought* (Edward Elgar 2019) 251–66; Jan Engberg, Legal Meaning Assumptions—What are the Consequences for Legal Interpretation and Legal Translation? (2002) 15 International Journal for the Semiotics of Law 375–88; Rebecca Sutton 'How the Emotions and Perceptual Judgments of Frontline Actors Shape the Practice of International Humanitarian Law' in Susan A Bandes and others (eds), *Research Handbook on Law and Emotion* (Edward Elgar 2021).
[11] Philip Liste, 'Colliding Geographies: Space at Work in Global Governance' (2016) 19 Journal of International Relations and Development 199, 200.

A spatial lens is obviously not the only lens through which the concepts of universality and particularity could be studied. It is however a lens rarely utilized despite the fact our concepts of universalities and particularities are latently informed by our spatial assumptions about the basic qualities and characteristics constitutive of the spaces of actors and legal regimes—such as whether these have the qualities of being bounded, homogenous, or uniform. This spatial lens is thus significant in advancing the task of critical legal inquiry of these concepts.

1.1 The Modern Picture

Most contemporary legal regimes and associated political projects presume a space largely reminiscent of what one might call the spatiality of modernity:[12] abstract, homogenous, indivisible space with a static temporality.[13] State territory and geopolitical regions such as Europe or Asia (even 'Western Europe' and 'South-East Asia') offer classic examples of such construction. So too does the international human rights framework; treaty law; spaces governed by the law of the sea such as the territorial sea, EEZ, and continental shelf; and the assumption that states implement in their own territories legal norms emanating from international organizations. The examples—fitting universal impulses such as the international human rights project and more particular spaces, often regional organizations—are endless; what these all have in common is their background assumption that legal space is abstract and homogenous.[14]

Other spatial logics, however, depart from this mould. Legal spaces such as those that correspond to the 'offshore' in tax law today or the Hanseatic League in late-medieval Europe display constitutive characteristics more reminiscent of the ideas of flow, fluid temporality, and non-contiguity, often deliberately so in order to 'slip between the cracks' of bounded state space.[15] The Hanseatic League spatially expressed itself in only a handful of specific, circumscribed locations and yet, at the same time, was not limited to any single one of these locations but, rather, 'existed'

---

[12] By modernity I mean the broader project: 'modernism is the cultural, ideological, reflective, and, I will add, theory-forming response to modernization ... Modernism is, in essence, a "reaction formation", a conjunctural social movement mobilized to face the challenging question of what now is to be done given that the context of the contemporary has significantly changed. It is thus the culture-shaping, programmatic, and situated consciousness of modernity', Edward W Soja, *Postmodern Geographies: The Reassertion of Space in Critical Social Theory* (Verso Books 2011) 29.

[13] Robert Sack, *Human Territoriality: Its Theory and History* (CUP 2009); Soja (n 12).

[14] Francisco R Klauser, 'Rethinking the Relationships between Society and Space: A Review of Claude Raffestin's Conceptualisation of Human Territoriality' (2008) WP 37, Social Sciences Research Centre, National University of Galway, Galway <www.academia.edu/7934642/Rethinking_the_Relationships_between_Society_and_Space_A_Review_of_Claude_Raffestins_Conceptualisation_ of_Human_Territoriality> accessed 26 October 2023.

[15] Saskia Sassen, *Territory, Authority, Rights: From Medieval to Global Assemblages*, vol 4 (CUP 2006) ch 4.

simultaneously between them.[16] The spaces commonly identified as offshore can be found in the Cayman Islands and in the City of London.[17] Not every object, process, activity, or event taking place in tax havens is predetermined by the physical association of this location with a local or national authority.[18] Instead, activities occurring within the same physical space arise and might be said to be under the control of overlapping authorities. For example: buying a ticket for a bus passing through the City of London is not a transaction that will 'enter' the offshore legal space, and conversely certain transactions and activities will only arise within this offshore space.

Understanding the significance of the spatial logics informing the construction of these legal spaces is difficult to overstate. The legal spaces of global politics and global economy have always been diverse. Yet they have been dominated by one space in particular: the space of the state and spaces, like global space, that are made up of all state spaces.[19] But legal spaces are becoming especially diverse and numerous with the influx of new actors of law-making and governance. It is important that the theoretical sensibilities of international law—the 'professional world view' implicitly shared by international law academics and practitioners— can make sense of developments. Understanding the spatial logic of these legal spaces, including at the granular level of their basic characteristics, is important for maintaining analytical clarity and for our own political projects.

1.2 Interrogating the Modern Picture

Critical geography allows us to interrogate the background politics, history, and the general conditions of intelligibility behind implicit geographic assumptions.[20] The most common geographic assumptions made in contemporary social sciences are the product of specific historical 'events'. One of these was the emergence of

---

[16] Hendrik Spruyt, *The Sovereign State and Its Competitors: An Analysis of Systems Change* (Princeton University Press 1994) 12.

[17] For more, see especially William Vlcek, 'Behind an Offshore Mask: Sovereignty Games in the Global Political Economy' (2009) 30 Third World Quarterly 1465.

[18] For a more detailed exploration, see Gail Lythgoe, 'The Changing "Landscape" of Sovereignty Viewed Through the Lens of International Tax: Reterritorialising the Offshore' (2022) 59 Canadian Yearbook of International Law 171–99.

[19] See the article by John Agnew, 'The Territorial Trap: The Geographical Assumptions of International Relations Theory' (1994) 1 Review of International Political Economy 53. Yet, this analysis is not unproblematic. Shah highlighted that Agnew himself is stuck in a *territorial* trap, a trap that reproduces the same concept of territoriality. See Nisha Shah, 'The Territorial Trap of the Territorial Trap: Global Transformation and the Problem of the State's Two Territories' (2012) 6 International Political Sociology 57.

[20] Doreen Massey, *For Space* (SAGE Publications 2005); Derek Gregory, *The Colonial Present* (Blackwell Publishing 2004); Nicholas Blomley, 'The Spaces of Critical Geography' (2008) 32 Progress in Human Geography 285; David Harvey, 'Editorial: The Geographies of Critical Geography' (2006) 31 Transactions of the Institute of British Geographers 409.

the science of modern cartography with a claim both to practical accuracy and scientific precision. So popular proved the visual representations produced by cartography and so deeply engrained became the idea that these representations were scientific (and thus impartial and objective), that the cartographic picture of the world dominated.[21] The fact that most maps were drawn from 'the view from nowhere' further solidifies the assumption that the visuals these maps represent are 'scientific', and their objectivity is taken for granted. 'Cartography and the map' took up their positions 'at the heart of a scientific Enlightenment project'.[22]

Despite this, cartography's spatiality is deeply ideological. Not only does it privilege state space over all other types of political spaces, but it also projects its understanding of state spaces according to a very specific theory of power. The spaces controlled by states, from the perspective of international law's map, and thus the privileged model of spatial politics which cartography brings in its wake, are overwhelmingly understood to be:

- abstract—it is the French 'land, waters, and airspace' that constitute France, one does not need to know anything more concrete about the physical, cultural, or economic qualities of these spaces;
- internally homogenous—the cartographic perspective does not differentiate between the hinterland and the coastal area, between a multi-ethnic city and a natural reserve;
- indivisible—a French 'territory' can only be 'owned' by France, no one else at the same time;
- bounded and naturally objective—there is a certain self-evidence to the concept of French territory: it is all those physical lands, waters, and airspace that physically exist within these boundaries;
- temporally static—the French 'territory' is 24/7, its Frenchness neither grows, nor diminishes over time, there is no dialectics there, no evolution, only one single flat present; the moment it became French its status is fixed once and for all, until further notice.

The cartographic approach to configuring space is tied up with the project of modernity. As Bourdieu observed, 'map[s] replaced the discontinuous patchy space of practical paths by the homogeneous, continuous space of geometry'.[23] This representation of space chimes with the classical themes of the Enlightenment such as rationality, empiricism, progress, and the emergence and dominance of scientific

---

[21] Jordan Branch, *Cartographic State: Maps, Territory, and the Origins of Sovereignty* (CUP 2014) 40.
[22] John Pickles, *A History of Spaces: Cartographic Reason, Mapping, and the Geo-Coded World* (Routledge 2004) 14.
[23] Pierre Bourdieu, *Outline of a Theory of Practice or Esquisse d'une théorie de la pratique* (CUP 1977) 105.

'facts' such as geography. It also brought with it certain unexamined assumptions and consequences.

Contrast this with a critical geographical idea of space: space, this approach teaches us, is not an objective feature of the natural world, but a social construct. It is a 'product of interrelations' that is 'constituted through interactions'.[24] Our sense of space never remains the same across different contexts. It shifts constantly. Some interactions produce contestations, others alternative world pictures. What comes out of this is rarely homogenous or smooth either in terms of its form or content. Moreover, it is precisely because space is the product of, and constituted by, these interrelations and interactions that the ontology of space is neither static nor uniform: it is 'never finished, never closed ... [it] is a simultaneity of stories-so-far'.[25] Imagination is a key part of this process, and this applies to all forms and varieties of space: 'from the immensity of the global to the intimately tiny'.[26] It is from the immensity of the global space associated with universality to the tiny spaces associated with particularity that I now turn.

2. The Space of Universality

Like many disciplines with roots in the nineteenth century, international law absorbed the cartographic world view uncritically and enthusiastically. Its standard assumptions about geography and the organization of space to this day remain disciplined by the cartographic view. As a result, the spatiality of the concept of universality is also a product of the cartographic world view, and its theoretical construction is premised on the standard model of the state space described earlier.

Not only is the international law concept of universality spatially informed but it is a particular *actor's* space—state space—that, upon being put together, creates universal space.[27] Thus, the spatiality of universality is defined by the fact of its *difference from*, but also its *essential similarity to*, the concept of the state space. However, the 'wiping clean' of this relationality is part of the universalizing project and the political projects underpinning these. To put it differently: the spatiality of the universal shares *similar structural qualities*. While at first glance the spatial organization of universal jurisdiction, for example, differs from the spatial organization of national jurisdiction, there is actually a considerable degree of similarity between these concepts.

Examples of spatially informed understandings of universality can be seen everywhere in contemporary international law: from the idea of the universal

---

[24] Massey (n 20) 9.
[25] ibid.
[26] ibid.
[27] On this point more generally, see Jens Bartelson, 'The Social Construction of Globality' (2010) 4 International Political Sociology 219.

jurisdiction and the concept of 'universal human values [that are] applicable to daily lives—"everywhere in the world" '[28] to statements like the following from Schwarzenberger: '[o]n the level of unorganized international society, the geographical scope of international law is universal, in the sense that it extends to the whole world'[29] and '[i]nternational law is universal in the sense that its geographical scope is world-wide.'[30]

More often, however, there is an unwritten space into which claims of and for universality are projected into: ' "universalism" [is] the approach which considers a normative order of peace feasible even beyond the borders of a single state.'[31] The unspoken stage for this peace is the globe. This space is also unwritten in the following account of universal jurisdiction: 'jurisdiction is not truly "universal" until all states of the world have ratified the [respective] treaty.'[32] The focus here is on the primary subjects of international law which is 'sufficient' to represent the space because of an assumption that state space is natural geography, and all state space together constitutes universality for the purpose of jurisdiction. In other words, it is assumed because states are constituted by their territories[33]—their political space—in international legal theory. And it is states, assumed to be territorial actors, that together are supposed to represent the world and create universal space. The state and its territory are flattened analytically. Because cities, corporations, and other non-state actors are not usually understood to be relevant territorial actors for the purposes of international law, they do not often feature in accounts of universality. This reinforces the point that universality is a highly spatially informed concept and is a political project that prioritizes certain types of space.

The tendency to structure discussions of universal spaces around a statocentric perspective reveals itself in other contexts. 'If [rules and principles] become binding on all states,' writes Malanczuk, 'they are often referred to as "universal international law".'[34] Note again the suppression of the question of universality's spatial organization: the only spatiality to make an appearance in this narrative about 'universal international law' is the spatiality of the state. What this exposes is that the space that is valued is state space, which in turn shows the political project supported by international law.

---

[28] Dianne Otto, 'Rethinking Universals: Opening Transformative Possibilities in International Human Rights Law' (1997) 18 Australian Yearbook of International Law 3.
[29] Georg Schwarzenberger and ED Brown, *A Manual of International Law* (6th edn, Professional Books 1976) 7.
[30] ibid 96.
[31] Armin von Bogdandy and Sergio Dellavalle, 'Georg Wilhelm Friedrich Hegel (1770–1831)' in Bardo Fassbender and others, *The Oxford Handbook of the History of International Law* (OUP 2012).
[32] Luc Reydams, *Universal Jurisdiction: International and Municipal Legal Perspectives* (OUP 2003) 43.
[33] By this I mean that state territory is an essential ingredient of statehood, per art 1, Convention on the Rights and Duties of States (Montevideo Convention) 1933 (165 LNTS 19).
[34] Peter Malanczuk, *Akehurst's Modern Introduction to International Law* (Routledge 1997) 2.

Inevitably, this way of thinking about states and universal spaces tends to lead to all kinds of historical misrepresentations. As Bartelson remarks, for example, it is a common assumption among international lawyers that the global legal space has simply 'emerged out of intensified interaction and increased interdependence between states', a view which indicates that 'the global realm' is basically 'epiphenomenal in relation to the international system of states'.[35] A closer analysis of legal history, however, shows that 'the construction of such a single space on a planetary scale both antedated and conditioned the emergence of the modern international system, by providing the conceptual resources necessary for both territorial demarcation and national identity construction'.[36] Other scholars have noted the same theme: 'the globe was [first] rendered [into a] political space in the Iberian competition for trade routes to India during the second half of the fifteenth century'; only after that did 'Europeans create a unified cartographic representation to incorporate [this] spatial totality'.[37]

2.1 Universality's Spatial Characteristics and the Construction of Political Projects

In terms of the characteristics of this universal space, in international law it is usually constructed as homogenous, unified, uniform, and continuous space. It is a *smooth space* that has no internal gradations, no distinguishing local features, no uneven patches. It is flat and, being flat, it is inevitably devoid of all hierarchy and 'development'. It is a space that is assumed to be empty of any permanent structures and power balances—an arena that is not-yet-formalized and not-yet-ordered.[38] In such projections and representations of universality, the political project of state space is wiped from such recollections of universal space.

As critical geography literature highlights, always alongside smooth spaces there exists striated space. A *striated space* is one that has often been ordered and disciplined through the institutional division and delineation of the underlying expanse. The parcelling of physical geography into different administrative units,[39] for example, creates a space made up of heterogeneous particulars, patches, and discontinuities. The power of these insights allow us to better comprehend the dialectical and socially constructed relationship between the spaces of modern international law: the universal is comprised of multiple state spaces, the continuity between

---

[35] Bartelson (n 27).
[36] ibid 219–20.
[37] Jeppe Strandsbjerg, *Territory, Globalization and International Relations: The Cartographic Reality of Space* (Palgrave Macmillan 2010) 116.
[38] Gilles Deleuze and Félix Guattari, *A Thousand Plateaus: Capitalism and Schizophrenia* (University of Minnesota Press 1987) 474.
[39] Jeremy Larkins, *From Hierarchy to Anarchy: Territory and Politics before Westphalia* (Palgrave Macmillan 2010) 6.

THE UNIVERSAL AND THE PARTICULAR IN INTERNATIONAL LAW   33

which is interrupted by borders, even if each of these constituent spaces in turn is constructed as smooth, 'abstract, empty, and homogeneous' in form.[40] But the space international law associates with the idea of universality is directly premised on the idea of 'transcending'[41] and 'overcoming'[42] (note the political connotations) its apparent structural limitations, or its striatedness in other words. Compare this with the imperial or premodern understanding that conceived of political spaces 'as graduated, uneven, and discontinuous ... rather than abstract, empty, and homogeneous',[43] and we begin to see how political the international legal imaginary really is. To suggest that the defining feature of universality lies precisely in the transcendence of 'graduated, uneven, and discontinuous' space, in favour of a political arena that is 'abstract, empty, and homogeneous', signals a commitment to the politics of equality, sameness, a supposed absence of hierarchy.

The idea of a 'unified global space'—ie the characteristic of uniformity mentioned above—continues the 'political fabrication' that there can be found 'a level playing field for all actors'.[44] We know, of course, that a level playing field does not exist in international law. From the special position of the P5 in the UN Security Council to the unequal voting rights in the International Monetary Fund or the inability of postcolonial states to affect preexisting customary international law and distributions, the pretence of sovereign equality hides the unevenness of international law's political arena. Power is not equally distributed across the international legal order, yet the idea of the universal space of international law is built on precisely the opposite assumption, and the role which the cartographic view plays in enabling this misconception is central. It is the cartographic tradition of thinking of modern spaces as smooth and homogenous that, ultimately, enables the level-playing-field imaginary. It is this, too, which enables international law's project of universality and wipes out the politics that results from it.

To sum up, what characterizes the construction of the universal space in international law is, first, its statocentricity: the universal space is never conceived 'by itself', but only in reference to a prior conception of the state space (whereas Bartelsen and others suggest it was the other way around); secondly, universal

---

[40] Teemu Ruskola, 'China in the Age of the World Picture' in Anne Orford and Florian Hoffmann (eds), *The Oxford Handbook of the Theory of International Law* (OUP 2018) 25.

[41] Denis Badré, 'Reaffirming the Universal Nature of Human Rights' (Parliamentary Assembly, Council of Europe, 2011) 2, 5 <http://assembly.coe.int/CommitteeDocs/2011/ADOCUniversalHumanRights.pdf> accessed 28 May 2021; Anna Grear and Burns H Weston, 'The Betrayal of Human Rights and the Urgency of Universal Corporate Accountability: Reflections on a Post-Kiobel Lawscape' (2015) 15 Human Rights Law Review 21, 26; Otto (n 28) 5, 7.

[42] OHCHR, 'Vienna Declaration and Programme of Action, Adopted by the World Conference on Human Rights in Vienna on 25 June 1993' pt II, para 4 <www.ohchr.org/en/professionalinterest/pages/vienna.aspx> accessed 28 May 2021; Onuma Yasuaki, 'Towards an Intercivilizational Approach to Human Rights: For Universalization of Human Rights through Overcoming of a Westcentric Notion of Human Rights' (1997) 7 Asian Yearbook of International Law 21.

[43] Ruskola (n 40) 26.

[44] Strandsbjerg (n 37) 45.

space is thought to emerge out of interactions between states; thirdly, the embedded cartographic presumptions of flatness, internal homogeneity, and smoothness; and, fourthly, the spatial characteristics of universality help facilitate the legal fiction that all states are equal, even though in reality they are not.

3. Spatial Logics of Particularities

3.1 Geopolitical Particulars

The first type of particularity I explore is what I propose calling the geopolitical particularity. This term serves several purposes as it offers both a description and a critique. The geopolitical particularity is a product of a theoretical outlook associated with the discipline of political geography, which assumes many of the same spatial characteristics associated with the project of modernity outlined above.[45] At the same time, the concept of geopolitical particularity enables us to question the way legal and political systems can be flattened into distinct parcels of land, such that they are commonly understood to 'exist' across the globe, regardless of however different they may be otherwise.

A typical illustration of the concept of geopolitical particularity can be found in the discourse about regionalism. 'Regional arrangements,' writes Philip Jessup, 'are quantitatively non-universal.'[46] 'Regional institutional arrangements,' observes Laurence Boisson de Chazournes, 'surround the State, allowing it to act in a larger space ... regional initiatives can be more effective and easier to implement than actions carried out at the universal level. Regional organizations may therefore be better suited to protecting the values around which they were created.'[47] They are better suited, we understand, because there is a homogenizing of actors through the homogenizing of space—a deeply political act. Further, the structure of spatiality that is associated with regional space is given in international law discourse a distinctly cultural or quasi-cultural twist. A typical example can be found in scholarly exercises that propose, for example, to consider 'East Asian approaches' to human rights.[48]

---

[45] Gearóid Ó Tuathail, 'Localizing Geopolitics: Disaggregating Violence and Return in Conflict Regions' (2010) 29 Political Geography 256, 257. For more on critical geopolitics, see Klaus-John Dodds and James Sidaway, 'Locating Critical Geopolitics' [1994] Environment and Planning D: Society and Space 12.

[46] Philip Jessup, 'Non-Universal International Law' (1973) 12 Columbia Journal of Transnational Law 415, 420.

[47] Laurence Boisson de Chazournes, 'Relationships and Interfaces between Regional and Universal Organizations: Room for New Developments' (2012) 9 International Organizations Law Review 263, 265–66.

[48] Christina M Cerna, 'East Asian Approaches to Human Rights' (1995) 89 Proceedings of the Annual Meeting (American Society of International Law) 152.

3.1.1 Spatial characteristics

There are two insights to highlight in relation to the spatial characteristics of this particularity. First, that there is one characteristic of the geopolitical particular that almost by itself produces the binary between geopolitical particular and universal space; that is the quality of boundedness.[49] Secondly, that the geopolitical particularity exists because of a presumed equivalence between space and culture,[50] illuminating further the politics underlying this strand of contestation and discourse.

The dominant spatial paradigm of international law understands bounded parcels of space. Jurisdiction, territorial sovereignty, states, *and* regions are all bounded and presumptively contiguous spatial constructs. The politics this enables are the politics of order and containment (boundedness) and continuous homogeneity in terms of identity. This spatial paradigm can be seen in statements such as: '"particularism", claim[s] that order is possible exclusively within the individual polities, whereas between them only a limitation of disorder is achievable.'[51] Note the implicit homogenizing of the spaces of these individual polities: prepositions like 'within' and 'between' signal the interest in viewing each constituent polity as an imaginary container, of the kind associated also with the idea of state space. Also note the prioritized values: order and control. Note, finally, the allusion made to the phenomenon of borders and boundaries, which signposts the presumption that the space captured within these boundaries is both homogenous and smooth.

Boundedness is one of *the* fundamental spatial characteristics of this geopolitical particular. Indeed, it could be said that boundedness creates the core difference between the construction of universal spaces and geopolitically particular spaces: the universal space lacks boundedness; the geopolitically particular space is bounded. It is *in the characteristics of boundedness* that a binary is produced between the universality and geopolitical space.

Boundedness also creates the ability to project difference—different identities—into these spaces. The geopolitical particular makes certain assumptions about the 'isomorphism between space/place ... and society/culture'[52] where space and society are mapped onto each other and the relationship of cultures to geographical places is naturalized. The effect of this is to imagine cultures as having an 'integral relation to bounded space'[53] and as being internally coherent—an understanding of culture that is aided and reinforced by the ability to imagine space as

---

[49] For more on the way border making marks differences in space, see Gabriel Popescu, 'Borders and Boundaries' in *Encyclopedia of Geography* (SAGE Publications 2010) 293 <https://sk.sagepub.com/reference/geography/n115.xml> accessed 29 September 2019.
[50] For more on this relationship, see Benedict Anderson, *Imagined Communities: Reflections on the Origin and Spread of Nationalism* (Verso Books 2006) especially at 6.
[51] Armin von Bogdandy and Sergio Dellavalle, 'Georg Wilhelm Friedrich Hegel (1770–1831)' in Fassbender and others (n 31) 1127.
[52] Massey (n 20) 64.
[53] ibid 64–65.

homogenous—which enables, in turn, the tradition of separating cultures and societies into 'objectively' bounded spaces and naturalizing the effects of this separation. According to Gupta and Ferguson:

> [T]he premise of discontinuity forms the starting point from which to theorise contact, conflict and contradiction between cultures and societies. For example, the representation of the world as a collection of 'countries,' [or as regions] as in most world maps, sees it as an inherently fragmented space, divided by different colors into diverse national societies, each 'rooted' in its *proper* place.[54]

The politics legitimized by the discourse *enabled* by its spatial imaginary is thus an important issue in studying the use of concepts like universality and particularity in international law. It reinforces once again how crucial it is to understand the involvement of spatial assumptions in the contestations between universal and particular ideals.

3.2 Networked Particularity

This second category of *networked particularity* has a different spatial logic to the *geopolitical particularity*. In terms of its physical scope, the space in question is similar to universal space in that its potential 'reach' could cover the entire globe. Yet it differs from universal space as it is not internally homogenous. Neither is it (always) constructed as a flat space. Nor is it contiguous and continual. The patterns and spatial logics identifiable as belonging to a networked particularity could be said to belong to a different stage of modernity's understanding of space, compared to the stage that gave us state space and the rationalization of the universal. But neither is this space random. Trade, for example, does not happen at random across the globe; each step of a supply chain is driven by actors with their own spatial logics.

The binary between this particular and the universal is produced by different characteristics than those between geopolitical particular and the universal. It is a binary that is rarely noticed because of the dominance of the traditional conceptions of space. The fact the physical reach of networked spaces can potentially cover the entire globe often makes them equivalent in international legal imagination to universal spaces. But while the spatiality of universal spaces in international law, as noted earlier, derives from the traditional cartographic imaginary, which has disciplined us to think of spaces as overwhelmingly smooth, integrated, and internally homogenous, the spatiality of networks has a different logic. A networked

---

[54] Akhil Gupta and James Ferguson, 'Beyond "Culture": Space, Identity, and the Politics of Difference' (1992) 7 Cultural Anthropology 6, 6 (emphasis added).

space does not exist in the form of a bounded parcel or an integrated, continuous physical block of land, water, and airspace. Rather, it is often thought of as a non-physicalized space that jumps from one place (often referred to as a node) to another, leaving vast physical geography and spaces in between untouched.[55]

These patterns are not new, of course. One can think of some classic examples of premodern spatial networks.[56] The Hanseatic League was comprised of a multitude of trading cities, and it is in that space that its political and economic governance unfolded. The towns and countryside between these cities were not a part of its space and largely remained untouched by its political authority. Further examples of actors with non-contiguous physical expression include global cities and infrastructure space.[57] Having said that, these older political models and modern-day networked spaces are distinguishable: today's models subjugate space and time in a decidedly different manner from the Hanseatic League.

3.2.1 Spatial characteristics

The patterns identifiable in these networked spaces are entirely different to the homogenous, abstract, empty, bounded space of states and regions, or of the homogenous, abstract, emptiable, continuous space of the universal. Instead, the patterns are more reminiscent of webs, chains, and lines—depictable also using arrows that show directions of *flow*—rather than parcels, blocks, and borders.

The spatiality of this particularity speaks to us of a non-cartographic form (or not yet fully cartographically depictable) of spatial imagination. It is not necessarily new in terms of what sort of ontology ('real world patterns') it pays attention to, but new, rather, in terms of how it proposes to identify and understand these patterns that may have been there all along but have been invisibilized by the cartographic hegemony that has long dominated international law. Confronting and acknowledging this hegemony can not only allow us to see this category of 'fluid spaces', but also to understand better who uses them, how, and for what purposes. For example, space is instrumental to capitalist economics, and the ability of global economic processes to find new ways of order themselves far outstrips the ability of traditional legal and political theory to adapt their analytical lenses to follow them. While the international legal spatial imagination continues to be dominated by conceptions of space as flattened parcels of land—and the accompanying assumptions about how states exercise power in these spaces—many of the world's leading transnational corporations (TNCs) have long since respatialized their activities

---

[55] James Ferguson, 'Seeing Like an Oil Company: Space, Security, and Global Capital in Neoliberal Africa' (2005) 107 American Anthropologist 377, 377.

[56] Saskia Sassen, *Territory, Authority, Rights: From Medieval to Global Assemblages* (CUP 2006) compared these and found that global assemblages possess similar characteristics but other characteristics were dissimilar.

[57] To understand infrastructure space see Keller Easterling, *Extrastatecraft: The Power of Infrastructure Space* (Verso Books 2014) and Martín Arboleda, *Planetary Mine: Territories of Extraction under Late Capitalism* (Verso 2020).

and political presence precisely such that their spaces take advantage of that dominant concept of political space. This has allowed TNCs to 'open up new opportunities for super-profits, to find new ways to maintain social control, to stimulate increased production and consumption'.[58]

A spatial lens helps us understand why the existence of networked spaces to date has received so little recognition from the perspective of international law. There are two key reasons. The first is the dominance of the state-territorial system of international law, which can be understood both in terms of the actual political power of states as legal actors, but also in terms of the rather appealing sense of simplification and order statocentricity brings to international legal thought. The second is the general change in our common sensibilities: for one reason or another, it appears the dominant spatial paradigm is increasingly being replaced by networks and spaces of flow.

The hegemony of the state-based system, unchallenged in any serious way, has led the legal mind into a 'territorial trap'.[59] After all, it is a system designed for order: 'on political maps, different countries may be marked by different colours, but all states are coloured uniformly monochrome, never bleeding into one another'.[60] It is a system disciplined by a geographical imagination that persisted for much of the twentieth century. Real space—especially legal space—does not usually manifest itself so neatly. Nor indeed do states necessarily want this. Cartographic representations conceal a large part of what states have purposely chosen to do, often in the hope that no one outside the narrow circle of specialists and affected communities will notice or perhaps know what to do with. Take the example of borders.[61] In the real world, the location of a state's border for legal purposes will often have no immediate connection to its cartographic representation, as evidenced, for example, by the US-Canada Smart Border[62] and EU Carrier Sanctions.[63] Borders as offshored nodes are increasingly experienced by migrants and refugees detained on islands like Lesbos and Manus.[64] Borders between different national jurisdictions are becoming temporally separable for tax avoidance purposes.[65] These are only a handful of examples. The ideal whereby the spaces

---

[58] Soja (n 12) 34.
[59] Agnew (n 19). See also an illuminating response to this article by Shah (n 19).
[60] Ruskola (n 40) 25.
[61] Ayelet Shachar, *The Shifting Border: Legal Cartographies of Migration and Mobility* (Manchester University Press 2020).
[62] Efrat Arbel, 'Shifting Borders and the Boundaries of Rights: Examining the Safe Third Country Agreement between Canada and the United States' (2013) 25 International Journal of Refugee Law 65; Immigration, Refugees and Citizenship Canada (IRCC), 'Canada-U.S. Safe Third Country Agreement' (16 September 2003).
[63] Tilman Rodenhauser, 'Another Brick in the Wall: Carrier Sanctions and the Privatization of Immigration Control' (2014) 26 International Journal of Refugee Law 223.
[64] Reece Jones and others, 'Interventions on the State of Sovereignty at the Border' (2017) 59 Political Geography 1.
[65] Prem Sikka, 'The Role of Offshore Financial Centres in Globalization' <https://papers.ssrn.com/sol3/papers.cfm?abstract_id=467682> accessed 12 July 2017; see also Simon Hildrey, 'Jersey and

of governance, jurisdiction, and sovereignty are contiguous with the state's cartographic representation has an ever-growing list of exceptions.

Turning to the second, it is possible to claim that in recent decades there has been a shift in perspective. One can call this the postmodern turn,[66] or the arrival of late modernity.[67] I am not overly concerned with what labels we choose. What is important is the idea that something significant has changed. Modernity has tainted thought with ideas of rationality and geometry. Its effect on the discipline of international law and its discourses has been to programme assumptions about continuity of jurisdiction, state space, and sovereignty. Increasingly international lawyers are noticing new patterns to global governance, political authority, and trade emerging, making a late or postmodern turn. But noticing something is not the same thing as being able to engage well with it on an analytical level. Adopting a spatial lens makes it possible to problematize why the state-territorial regime dominated for so long and whose interest the old and new spatial logic suits. The lens offers insights into the assumptions held about international law, economics, and international relations, and the constitution of space and projection of values into concepts such as universality and particularity. And upon cracking the spatial code, it allows those wishing to, to challenge and contest.

4. Conclusion

New structures and actors are emerging and becoming entrenched in international law; therefore, a more nuanced and critically aware understanding of legal spaces—of the spatial logics and patterns of these either universal or particular regimes and actors—must also emerge. But while a new sensibility offers potential for contestation there are new problems and pitfalls. An increasingly growing part of the world's population today live in urban areas. Yet we should not overlook the lives and stories of the world's non-urban population. This makes the task of understanding the role of the 'networked particular' actor of cities an increasingly urgent one. Moreover, a challenge this presents, at least in part, is one of granularity: global cities are often viewed homogenously. This is erroneous when it is the financial districts and sites of law-making which form the actual nodes of the respective global networks and are thus the intended focus of such studies. I doubt

---

Guernsey Avoid OECD Blacklist' (*Citywire Money*, 27 February 2002) <http://citywire.co.uk/money/jersey-and-guernsey-avoid-oecd-blacklist/a235050> accessed 2 February 2018.

[66] According to Jennifer Wicke 'there are more than thirty-one flavors of postmodernism ... postmodernism was the term that marked the eighties on the critical map.' She suggests the term is 'stretched' from trying to cover too many things, 'a debate in theory, a set of discourses and disciplines, a criterion of style in aesthetics, a historical period, and a way of life', Jennifer Wicke, 'Postmodern Identity and the Legal Subject' (1991) 62 University of Colorado Law Review 455, 456.

[67] Zygmunt Bauman, *Liquid Modernity* (Polity Press 2000).

very much the Bronx feels as internationally connected and socially mobile as parts of Wall Street in New York, Hackney as connected as Canary Wharf in London,[68] or Transvaal-Noord as Statenkwartier in The Hague.[69] Even within each of these globalized nodes there is to be found a great deal of further social diversity: the experience of these cities as sites of global governance is hardly as relevant for food delivery couriers as for lawyers and financial advisers in the same locations. There is a risk of further entrenching upon failing to recognize these inequalities. However, a spatially aware critique can inoculate against that.

As has hopefully been demonstrated, the spatial lens and in particular comparisons with the concept of networked and fluid particularities present a useful alternative vantage point from which to tackle the questions of international law's politics. It can also be used to further a critical agenda that promotes solidarity, the 'transcendence' of xenophobia and racism, and other progressive political causes. At the same time, those using this category must also remain wary of inducing further disembodiment and alienation and ignoring important socio-economic differences present within the networked nodes.

The old understanding of the universal as homogenous empty space seems no longer fit for purpose, not least because of its unwarranted assumptions that every road to universality in international law leads to egalitarianism. International law does not apply everywhere equally. There are parts of the world untouched, and others unequally touched, by international law. There is no such thing as an inherently universal set of values that are held by every human being. Critical scholars have poked holes in this simplistic conception of universality. Rather, as Butler, Laclau, and Žižek have argued, what needs to be emphasized in our discussion of universality is its basic contingency.[70] What is universalized, or construed to be particular, is ultimately always contingent on space and time. This idea of contingent universality, contrary to the static and permanent connotations created by Enlightenment notions of space, may even help remove the heightened stakes in the use of these concepts in contemporary discourse.

Global space is not empty. It is filled with unevenness, discontinuities, particularities, and localities. Law is realized and implemented in concrete *places*. Values, such as human rights, are held and shared not in bounded containers but across networks. Being present *within* the space of one network does not preclude the possibility of being simultaneously present within the spaces of other networks or for that matter other non-networked spaces. New York, the site of the human rights

---

[68] 'Poverty across London', Trust for London <www.trustforlondon.org.uk/data/poverty-across-london/> accessed 23 June 2021.

[69] Spatial concentration of poverty in The Hague, Netherlands. Source: Regional Income Statistics (2000), Central Bureau of Statistics <www.researchgate.net/figure/Spatial-concentration-of-poverty-in-The-Hague-Netherlands-Source-Regional-Income_fig1_248974118> accessed 23 June 2021.

[70] Judith Butler, Ernesto Laclau, and Slavoj Zizek, *Contingency, Hegemony and Universality: Contemporary Dialogues on the Left* (2nd edn, Verso 2011).

proclamation, is both a US city and a global city; its priorities are different from other global cities, but its domestic interests are also different from other parts of the US, which is neither a monolithic idea nor a legal regime.

How we use and create different spaces and in what ways a certain spatiality structures our social, economic, and political life, and our thinking about these, is a critical question in an increasingly complex world. How international lawyers imagine the universal and the location of the particular is illuminating. It reveals much about the politics of international lawyers. The politics I speak of here is much more than just everyday apolitical debate; there is an innate politics to this: mastering the space of the 'global' is a fundamental element of the project of modernity.[71] The understanding of space outlined in this chapter can allow us to contest the standard hegemonic frameworks associated with this project, while providing insights for critical research.

---

[71] Peter Sloterdijk, 'Geometry in the Colossal: The Project of Metaphysical Globalization' (2009) 27 Environment and Planning D: Society and Space 29, 29 and 33; Martin Heidegger, 'Age of the World Picture', The Question Concerning Technology and Other Essays. Translated and with an Introduction by William Lovitt. (Garland Publishing, Inc 1977) 129–34; Lauren Benton, *A Search for Sovereignty: Law and Geography in European Empires, 1400–1900* (CUP 2010) 12–13; Wolfgang Natter, 'Is Universality the Object of Globalization? Political Geographies of Contingent Universality' [2008] Current Perspectives in Social Theory 138.

2
The Philosophical Problem of Universals and Universality Binaries in International Law

Hobbes and Leibniz Compared

Ekaterina Yahyaoui Krivenko

When we talk about universality in international law today, there is a shared assumption of the self-evident nature of the idea of universality. Whether we talk about universal values, universal validity of law, or other similar issues, we tend not to question what 'a universal' means, what can actually be 'a universal'. The question of the nature of 'a universal' is distinct from the simplicity with which we assume the self-explanatory though still often debated meaning of 'universal' as an adjective in the language of international law. This contribution argues that the philosophical debate on the nature and existence of universals can significantly contribute to international law discussions on universality binaries. To demonstrate this relevance, the contribution focuses on the problem of universals as discussed by two early modern authors: Leibniz and Hobbes. The early modern period is selected because during this time scholars often engaged in discussions of a wide variety of topics since the tradition of polymaths was still alive. Therefore, it is possible to identify scholars who discussed both the problem of universals and the concepts such as state, law, or international law. This in turn facilitates the demonstration of dependency of the conceptualization of international law by an author on his approach to the problem of universals. Moreover, since the concept of international law in the contemporary sense was still in the process of being formed, some scholars adopted divergent views on the regulation at the global level. Coupled with differences in views on the problem of universals, this divergency makes the claim about dependency between the two stronger. Leibniz and Hobbes debated to a comparable level of detail both the problem of universals and the nature of regulation at the global level. They held opposing views on key tenets of the problem of universals, which as this contribution demonstrates led them into divergent conceptualizations of international law. Finally, the demonstration of dependency between the views of each of the two authors on the problem of universals and their views on international law sheds light on some of the ways several

Ekaterina Yahyaoui Krivenko, *The Philosophical Problem of Universals and Universality Binaries in International Law*
In: *International Law and Universality*. Edited by: Işıl Aral and Jean d'Aspremont, Oxford University Press.
© Ekaterina Yahyaoui Krivenko 2024. DOI: 10.1093/oso/9780198899419.003.0003

of the binaries that inform the idea of universality in contemporary international law detailed in the introduction to this volume continue to operate as discussed in the penultimate section of this chapter.

Based on the comparison of Hobbes's and Leibniz's views this chapter suggests that international law does not have to choose between the particular and the universal or between hegemony and universality nor does it need to mediate between both. Instead, a deeper reflection on the meaning and structural requirements of its vision of the universal is needed. This will open new spaces for contestation and constructive development of international law. In addition, it can break some vicious circles of enduring debates in international law, opening up new directions for research. The chapter does not argue that Hobbes's and Leibniz's views of the universals or of international law are the only available or possible ones, but simply uses the contrast between the views of the two authors to achieve the objectives of the chapter. The chapter starts by introducing the main lines of the problem of universals as debated in the seventeenth century, situating Hobbes's and Leibniz's views against this background. It then proceeds to describe how the contrasting views on the problem of universals led the two authors to divergent approaches to the discussion of the state, global regulation, and international law as we know it today. Finally, before offering some conclusions, the chapter discusses how these divergent views of Leibniz and Hobbes shed new light on the universality binaries as they operate in international law.

1. The Concept of the Universal

The philosophical problem of universals emerged because philosophers wondered how it is possible for humans to have universal concepts such as 'tree' or 'man' if what we experience are always only particular manifestations of these concepts. This problem of universals received extensive treatment and further development in scholasticism.[1] Without going into any great detail of the way the problem of universals was addressed in antiquity or scholasticism, I will very briefly sketch the way the problem of universals was traditionally raised so that the context of Hobbes's and Leibniz's ideas on the topic is clear.

During the lifetime of Hobbes and Leibniz most scholars agreed that universal things (eg a physical universal tree) do not exist. However, they still debated the question of how humans arrive at such a concept as 'a tree' without ever experiencing something like a universal tree. For some scholars the answer resided in the

---

[1] For a general overview of the way the problem of universals was addressed in early modernity, including its links to antiquity and scholasticism, see Stefano Di Bella and Tad M Schmaltz (eds), *The Problem of Universals in Early Modern Philosophy* (OUP 2017), especially their introduction at 1–12, and also Martha Bolton, 'Universals, Essences, and Abstract Entities' in Daniel Garber and Michael Ayers (eds), *The Cambridge History of Seventeenth-Century Philosophy* (CUP 1998) vol 1, 178–211.

affirmation of the existence of universal concepts or ideas. The concept of a tree, for example, would exist for them objectively contrary to the physical universal tree. How exactly they conceived of the actual existence of these universal concepts is a complicated topic which does not need to be answered for our purposes. However, some elements of this answer as they emerge from Leibniz's heritage are provided later in this section because Leibniz was among those scholars who affirmed the existence of universal concepts or ideas in one specific regard: he believed in the existence of universal truths. Hobbes on the other hand rejected the existence of any universals, whether things or ideas. The only universal Hobbes accepted as existent are names (or words we use to designate concepts or ideas, like the word 'tree'). Such a position was called nominalism.

Despite the many intricate ways in which Hobbes's and Leibniz's views in relation to the problem of universals were connected, they still held contrasting views on one key point. The most obvious and well-known opposition between Leibniz and Hobbes on the issue of universals is apparent in Leibniz's rejection of Hobbes's extreme nominalism which is best illustrated with the following statement by Hobbes: 'There is nothing universal but names.'[2] This position was labelled by Leibniz as 'super-nominalism'.[3] The extreme character of Hobbes's opinion is best appreciated against the backdrop of prevailing opinions at the time. The nominalist position as such and rejection of the reality of universal *things* was quite common. However, Hobbes's extremism led him to the rejection of the existence not only of universal things, but also of universal *ideas*: '[T]he name "universal" is not the name of some thing existing in nature, nor of an idea or of some phantasm formed in the mind, but is always the name of some vocal sound or name.'[4] For Hobbes, this did not mean a complete arbitrariness. For instance, Hobbes effectively admitted that the agreement among humans to use a universal name for a group of individual things is based on similarity people observe in things: 'One universal name is imposed on many things for their similitude in some quality or other accident.'[5] However, Hobbes does not equate similitude with the essence or nature of things, thus preventing in many instances the very possibility of knowing the essence of things and concepts.[6] Hobbes's extreme form of nominalism effectively places language and linguistic conventions of usage at the forefront not only of his discussion of universals but also his views on law and politics. Before demonstrating how Hobbes's view of universals impacted his opinions on law and

---

[2] Thomas Hobbes, *Human Nature or the Fundamental Elements of Policy. De Corpore Politico: Or the Elements of Law* (first published 1650, Thoemmes Press 1994) 22.
[3] Gottfried W Leibniz, 'Preface to an Edition of Nizolius' in Leroy E Loemker (ed), *Philosophical Papers and Letters* (2nd edn, Kluwer 1969) 121, 128.
[4] Thomas Hobbes, *De Corpore. The English Works of Thomas Hobbes of Malmesbury* (William Molesworth ed, John Bohn 1839) vol 1, I.2.9, 20.
[5] ibid vol 3, 4.7, 23.
[6] ibid vol 1, I.2.4, 16.

politics, and most importantly international law, it is necessary to say a few more words about Leibniz's view on the problem of universals.

Contrary to Hobbes, Leibniz admitted the existence of eternal universal and necessary truths. It is very difficult to discern how precisely he conceived this existence. On the one hand, Leibniz clearly affirmed that real things are only concrete, not abstract entities so concepts or ideas cannot be said to *exist* in the same way in which a real concrete tree exists. Abstract entities for Leibniz are just modes of thinking.[7] On the other hand, Leibniz made several statements that can be interpreted as affirming the *existence* of eternal truths and ideas.[8] In the present context it is not necessary to resolve all these conundrums, but to connect them to another important feature of Leibniz's thought, namely his monadology.

In Leibniz's philosophy, a monad as a simple substance is a foundational structuring element of everything existent.[9] The main activity of every monad is perception. Leibniz defines perception as a representation of relationships between monads as situations of phenomena. This representation is always perspectival. Each monad represents the whole universe from its own perspective. Despite representing the whole universe, the representation of each monad does not produce a true and full picture of the universe precisely because it remains constrained by the specific perspective of each monad. A complete and true picture of the universe arises only if various existing perspectives of monads can be seen or understood at the same time. If only one monad's perspective is left out, the picture will remain incomplete or deficient in some regards. Thus, in Leibniz's monadology the idea of the universal emerges out of a multiplicity of particulars, out of a variety of perspectives. This also led Leibniz to highly value diversity. Diversity is important because the more different perspectives one can understand, the better understanding of the world one acquires. In sum, for Leibniz the world is structured according to a set of predefined rules embedded in the picture of the universe as emerging from the multitude of monadic perspectives related to each other. By discovering and understanding more and more of these different perspectives and their relations as well as rules governing them, human beings can access universal truths. This human mind's capacity to discover items of eternal knowledge is essential to the possibility of introducing universals as part of functioning human societies.

---

[7] For a powerful defence of this thesis, see Benson Mates, *The Philosophy of Leibniz: Metaphysics and Language* (OUP 1989) 171–73.

[8] See eg Gottfried W Leibniz, *Theodicy. Essays on the Goodness of God the Freedom of Man and the Origin of Evil* (EM Huggard tr, Open Court 1985) 135: 'eternal verities which are in the understanding of God, independently of his will'. For more examples associating the 'are' in this type of statement with presence or existence, see Fabrizio Mondadori, 'Review of The Philosophy of Leibniz by Benson Mates' (1990) 99 The Philosophical Review 613, 622–26.

[9] The short summary in this paragraph is based mostly on Leibniz's monadology: Gottfried W Leibniz, 'The Principles of Philosophy, or, the Monadology' in *G.W. Leibniz. Philosophical Writings* (Roger Ariew and Daniel Garber tr, Hackett 1989) 213.

Leibniz's insistence on the actual existence of universal truths due to the monadic structure of the universe which embeds these truths in reality, coupled with his belief in the capacity of the human brain through certain reasoning procedures to discover eternal universal truths and then embed them in the operation of human societies, makes true universals possible. As the next section demonstrates, the acknowledgment of this possibility affects how Leibniz conceived norm-setting at the global level. This contrasts with the consequences of Hobbes's position on the problem of universals. If the only universals are names given to things, then for Hobbes: '*[T]rue* and *false* are attributes of speech, not of things. And where speech is not, there is neither *truth* nor *falsehood*; *error* there may be ...'[10] And again: 'truth consisteth in the right ordering of names in our affirmations.'[11] Thus, truth is a simple convention arising out of exchange of words between humans. For Leibniz truth is not a simple convention, at least not the universal eternal truths to which Leibniz also equated precepts of justice comparing them to numbers.[12] These truths do have a certain objective existence and are discoverable by human reasoning.

These two contrasting positions on the problem of universals and the ensuing beliefs on the nature of truth led both scholars to different conceptualizations of law generally and international law specifically.

2. State, Sovereignty, and International Law

Hobbes's main focus when it comes to political and legal aspects of his philosophy is on discussions of the concepts of state and sovereignty. This is different for Leibniz, who was more focused on the general idea of justice and the relationship between law and justice. These two positions follow from their views on the problem of universals and led them into different directions as far as the nature of regulation at the global level is concerned, as this section demonstrates. Below I identify the main tenets of Hobbes's position on the nature of states and sovereignty, contrasting them with the available information from Leibniz's works, and situating them against the differences between Hobbes and Leibniz on the problem of universals outlined above. I conclude by explaining how this leads both authors to contrasting perspectives on the idea of international law.

For Hobbes, who reduced truth to a property of speech, the central question in relation to the political organization of life became how to make discourse reflecting truth part of functioning human communities. Hobbes's answer to this

---

[10] Hobbes (n 4) 23.
[11] ibid.
[12] See eg Gottfried W Leibniz, 'Reflections on the Common Concept of Justice' in Leroy E Loemker (ed), *Philosophical Papers and Letters* (2nd edn, Kluwer 1969) 561, 563–64.

question can only be fully understood if we add another point regarding Hobbes's view of truth. Hobbes held that while truth as a discourse is possible in some areas of life where causes of things can be fully known, such as geometry or politics, it is not possible in other areas. Most notably, he held that such notions as 'meum and tuum, just and unjust, profitable and unprofitable, good and evil, honest and dishonest and the like'[13] are fundamentally undefinable. If humans are given a complete freedom, the undefined nature of these notions coupled with Hobbes's view of human nature results in perpetual anarchy and conflict. Therefore, in relation to the role of these notions in human communities Hobbes's main interrogation became not how to produce discourse reflecting truth, but how to control discourse. Hobbes's answer to this interrogation is his widely known articulation of the transition from the state of nature to a sovereign state (or commonwealth as he named it). The Hobbesian commonwealth had two essential characteristics: sovereignty (or the office of the sovereign) and territorially based and delimited nature. Within this territorially delimited unit the office of the sovereign occupied either by a single individual or a group is the entity entitled to define the contents of such undefinable, according to Hobbes, notions as 'just' and 'unjust', 'good' and 'evil', and the like. The definition of these notions by the sovereign and their imposition on the population within the delimited territory occurs through the mechanism of legislation and its implementation. Such a control and imposition are indispensable for Hobbes because, following from his position on the problem of universals, it is impossible to discover objectively existing universal values of 'good' and 'evil' or 'just' and 'unjust'. They simply do not exist objectively. Law as a command of the sovereign becomes the mechanism which, allowing for control of discourse, produces orderly and peaceful existence through a uniform definition of these notions for a given society. Normativity of law is an external force originating from the sovereign, which pushes subjects to compliance. In Hobbes's scheme, which begins with his answer to the problem of universals and is fully explainable by this answer, the relationship between law and universality reveals itself as a strategy of artificial creation and imposition of 'universal'[14] meanings of objectively undefinable notions within territorially delimited units.

As far as the global realm is concerned, from Hobbes's perspective, the question becomes whether the same process—of discourse control and central definition and impositions of meanings of objectively undefinable notions—is possible

---

[13] Thomas Hobbes, *De Cive. The English Works of Thomas Hobbes of Malmesbury* (William Molesworth ed, John Bohn 1841) vol 2, VI.9, 77. See also Hobbes (n 4) 29.

[14] The term 'universal' is in inverted commas because it is used here in a figurative sense in which many philosophers and sociologists talk about the imposition of universal values, rules etc by the state (see eg the work of Pierre Bourdieu on the concept of the state: Pierre Bourdieu, *On the State: Lectures at the Collège de France, 1989–1992* (Polity 2014)). Of course, this is not a universal in the Leibnizian sense, but one can talk about an artificially created universal here in the sense in which the same type of imposition occurs within states across the globe and this is the only universal possible in Hobbes's view: universals are but names imposed by humans.

at the global or interstate level. Is law in the above-defined sense possible between states? In order to understand Hobbes's answer to this interrogation, it is first important to discard the widespread view, according to which Hobbes equated the international realm with anarchy. Usually this view is attributed to Hobbes based on a few statements taken out of context. For example, many reproduce Hobbes's statement from *Leviathan* comparing the attitude of sovereigns to that of gladiators and their posture to that of war.[15] However, the next sentence nuancing this comparison is often omitted: 'But because they [kings, sovereigns] uphold thereby, the industry of their subjects; there does not follow from it, that misery, which accompanies the liberty of particular men.'[16] This indicates what more recent scholarship persuasively argues, namely that despite Hobbes's denial of international law as law he did not equate the interstate realm with anarchy but believed that his internal solution to the problem of universals, namely law as a command of the sovereign within individual states, also creates conditions for peaceful coexistence externally, at the international level.[17] In other words, Hobbes believed that a properly ordered commonwealth that exercises internally an appropriate level of discourse control through law acquires such an attitude externally that peace and cooperation with other states follow. This is further confirmed by Hobbes's support for the so-called leagues or voluntary agreements between states. This idea appears in *Leviathan* when Hobbes discusses different types of 'systems', as he calls them, which arise when men join together for a common business or a common interest.[18] A particular type of such a system arises when men come together 'not by obligation of one to another, but proceeding only from a similitude of wills and inclinations'.[19] Hobbes mostly views such types of assemblies of men as either unnecessary or unlawful. However, he expresses a very supportive view of 'leagues', as he calls these assemblages, if they are constituted by commonwealths: 'leagues between commonwealths, over whom there is no human power established, to keep them all in awe, are not only lawful, but also profitable for the time they last.'[20] These agreements between states are very similar to the contemporary concept of a treaty and also indicate the idea of international organizations. However, for Hobbes these temporary agreements based on the will of states cannot be called law because they do not represent an expression of the will of one sovereign and do not function in the same way in which law within states functions, they cannot impose universals.[21]

[15] Hobbes (n 4) 115.
[16] ibid.
[17] This view is presented in detail in eg David S Grewal, 'The Domestic Analogy Revisited: Hobbes on International Order' (2016) 125 The Yale Law Journal 618.
[18] Hobbes (n 4) II.21, 210.
[19] ibid 222.
[20] ibid 223.
[21] Since Hobbes very much in line with the spirit of his time accorded the status of law to natural law and affirmed that natural law reigns both between individuals and between states, some can always use this argument to insist on the existence of law between states too. However, natural law is not true law

Thus, according to Hobbes order and peaceful existence at the interstate level follow from the nature of states as in the Kantian tradition, not from any type of law. For the purposes of this chapter this leads to one fundamental conclusion: if there is no possibility to control discourse at the global or international level, there can be no global universals. From Hobbes's perspective, universals have always to be produced by somebody controlling discourse within a group of human beings. For Hobbes such control is only legitimately possible within territorially delimited units with the office of a sovereign, which can also be a collective democratic body. Hobbes regarded a global sovereign as an impossibility. The next section of this chapter discusses how this Hobbesian view of universals illuminates the contemporary discussions on universality and its binaries. First it is necessary to present the Leibnizian view on states, sovereignty, and international law.

Leibniz does not devote much time to considering the construction of the state and the nature of internal sovereignty. When it comes to civil philosophy, Leibniz's main focus is on the relationship between law and justice within different human communities. This is easily explainable by Leibniz's belief in the objective existence of necessary and eternal truths and their accessibility to the human mind. Since, according to Leibniz, principles of justice are universal, necessary, and eternal truths and humans can discover these truths, two questions become fundamental for Leibniz: how to discover these truths and how to ensure that human-made laws are actually based on these truths. The former preoccupation traverses all Leibniz's heritage and is most clearly visible in his works on general science and universal characteristic.[22] In relation to law, it explains the significant amount of effort Leibniz devoted to the structure and methods of lawyers' education.[23] From this perspective the role of states and sovereigns changes radically because their task is not the imposition of uniform meanings on the population but the organization of life in such a way that people can engage in intellectual activities leading to the discovery of truths and ensure application of these truths in practice. In this regard Leibniz's proposal for an academy and academic societies where educated princes

---

according to Hobbes. For a defence of this point, see Ekaterina Yahyaoui Krivenko, *Space and Fates of International Law: Between Leibniz and Hobbes* (CUP 2020) s 4.2.

[22] See eg Hans Burkhardt, 'The Leibnizian Characteristica Universalis as Link between Grammar and Logic' in Dino Buzzetti and Maurizio Ferriani (eds), *Speculative Grammar, Universal Grammar, and Philosophical Analysis of Language* (Benjamins Publishing 1987) 43; Martin Schneider, '"Leibniz" Konzeption der Characteristica universalis zwischen 1677 und 1690' (1994) 48 Revue internationale de la philosophie 213.

[23] Reportedly Leibniz's major work in this area, namely *Nova Methodus discendae docendaeque Jurisprudentiae* (1667) (translated into English as Gottfried W Leibniz, *New Method of Teaching and Learning Jurisprudence* (Carmelo Massimo de Juliis, tr, Talbot Publishing 2017), upon his death was found open on his desk marked with marginal annotations; see eg Christopher Johns, *The Science of Right in Leibniz's Moral and Political Philosophy* (Bloomsbury 2013) 165.

play the role of benefactors supporting the work of academies financially is a telling example of Leibniz's vision for the role of sovereigns.[24]

Leibniz's focus on the discoverability of eternal truths by the human mind also explains why, for Leibniz, sovereignty acquires a meaning different from that expressed in Hobbes's work and prevalent in his time. In particular, the sovereign state, which is so central to Hobbes's vision not only of domestic law, but also of the international order, becomes secondary in Leibniz's vision. Leibniz simply takes note of states because these are the main political entities of his time, but he is receptive to a wide diversity of human communities and political forms. This is clearly visible in his two major works on subjects of international law, where he accepts a wide variety of gradations of sovereignty and a wide variety of actors fulfilling the criteria of international legal personality (*persona juris gentium*).[25] As long as all these different entities can ensure appropriate conditions allowing human beings to search for universal and eternal truths as well as enabling transition of these truths into the life of human communities, all of them are acceptable to Leibniz. Moreover, as mentioned in the previous section, Leibniz valued diversity highly and regarded any artificially imposed simplification of diversity as harmful.

This section has demonstrated the intimate link between Leibniz's and Hobbes's distinct views on the problem of universals and their respective approaches to law, the concept of the state, and sovereignty. Leibniz's belief in the objective existence of universals and the ability of the human mind to discover these universals led him to focus on procedures for the discovery of universals. To the contrary, Hobbes's denial of any universals but names and of the possibility of the discovery of truth, especially in relation to notions related to law and justice, coupled with his belief in the need for a uniform understanding in this area to ensure peaceful human existence led him to the articulation of the idea of law within a sovereign state as a means for the production of universals.

3. International Law and Universality Binaries

Given the state-centricity of international law as well as its focus on the will of states as a foundational element of its vision, the Hobbesian legacy retains a central

---

[24] See eg Gottfried W Leibniz, 'Grundriss eines Bedenkens von Aufrichtung einer Societät' in Gottfried Wilhelm Leibniz, *Sämtliche Schriften und Briefe* (Akademie Verlag 1983) Reihe IV, Band 1, 531 and 533, where Leibniz discusses the balance between power and reason.

[25] The two works are similar in content but being directed at different audiences present the issues differently: Caesarini Fürstenerii *De jure suprematus ac legationis principum germaniae* and *Entretien de Philarete et d'Eugene sur la question du temps agitée à Nimwegue touchant le droit de Souveraineté et d'Ambassade des Electeurs et Princes de l'Empire*. The former published under a pseudonym, the second anonymously. Both contained in the second volume of series IV (Political writings) of the Academy Edition of Leibniz's works. For details see <https://leibnizedition.de/en/> accessed 1 May 2021. For a detailed defence of this interpretation of Leibniz's view of subjects of international law, see Yahyaoui Krivenko (n 21) s 6.2.

place in the way international law operates today.[26] However, due to its claim to be law, something Hobbes denied, contemporary international law puts into operation a number of conceptual mechanisms defending its status as law and not a simple political agreement. One of them is the way in which international law tradition 'imagines itself as universal',[27] as pointed out in the introduction to the volume. As the previous section clarified, in the Hobbesian tradition universality in relation to law is always created and imposed. Law is in fact that mechanism which ensures the imposition of universals. Hobbes described this process exclusively as internal to states because his account of the transition from the state of nature to the commonwealth provides legitimacy to the office of the sovereign and thus also legitimizes the artificial production and imposition of universals through law. From Hobbes's perspective it is undeniable that universality emerges only as a result of the elevation of one particular view to the status of a universal and the corresponding denial or at least disregard of other particulars. Universality is always artificial, not natural or authentic. In this sense it might be surprising to many to realize that Hobbes shares the view defended by critical legal scholars, and Third World or feminist approaches to international law. However, contrary to these streams of thought, Hobbes viewed such an artificially created universality as valuable and respectable as long as it follows from the process he described, which leads to the creation of the commonwealth or the state. This basis of universality in a process regarded as legitimate and legitimating is essential from Hobbes's perspective to produce a true universal and make the disregard of particulars acceptable. Thus, by laying bare the artificiality of universality but justifying the necessity of universality not simply as 'a void concept'[28] but a substantive commitment, Hobbes went beyond simple criticism. However, as pointed out in the previous section, Hobbes denied the possibility of a global sovereign or a global state. Most importantly, even if Hobbes erred and a global state could be a possibility, our contemporary international law is far from this utopian ideal. Therefore, as Hobbes made clear, international law as an interstate structure can pretend to be law but can never become law because it is unable to produce a legitimate universal. Thus, universality of contemporary international law is nothing but a reflection of a continuing struggle for hegemony between different forces. This finding is of course not new and reflects the insights of contemporary critical scholarship mentioned above. However, as

---

[26] The Hobbesian legacy in international law remains a defining feature despite diversification of actors and some debates about the diminishing role of states. This is visible for instance in a statement from a landmark manual on international law which affirms that, despite diversification of actors at the global level from the point of view of international law, states remain 'the basic units of currency' (James Crawford, *Brownlie's Principles of Public International Law* (8th edn, OUP 2012) 16). The same emphasis on the nation states as the principal subjects of international law can be found in many other instances, eg in Malcolm N Shaw, *International Law* (7th edn, OUP 2014) 1. As explained in the previous section, the emphasis on state-centricity in the global realm is quintessentially Hobbesian and entirely alien to Leibniz's position.

[27] Introduction, this volume.

[28] Introduction.

with the previous point, Hobbes goes a step further and affirms that this struggle is a natural, integral part of the human condition and the only way out of it is the creation at the international level of legitimate and legitimating procedures similar to those existing within states. Thus, Hobbesian advice on universality sheds new light on both the particularity–universality and hegemony–universality binaries discussed in the introduction. Hobbes would insist that it is impossible to have a *legal* system without elevating one particular to the status of the universal. To avoid the charge of hegemony such an elevation must take place through a legitimate procedure which is so far lacking at the international level. Thus, for Hobbes, the proposal of some scholars 'to reform international law through a methodological turn in order to build a legal system that is also concerned with those that have so far been at the periphery'[29] is a vain endeavour because it is impossible to infuse a universal with a variety of meanings but also because international law as law is simply a mirage, not a true law and can only produce temporary agreement on specific issues.

From Leibniz's vision of universals as objectively existing reality discoverable by the human mind follows a completely different understanding of universality as it relates to regulation at the global level. As explained in previous section, Leibniz conceived this world as arranged in ways predetermined by its monadic structure. This monadic structure also embeds certain universally valid truths, some of which concern questions of justice. Leibniz believed in the capacity of humans to discover these universals (universal truths) and for this reason focused his work on the elaboration of methodologies for such discovery. The central focus of Leibniz's work becomes the organization of the life of human communities in a way which enables this discovery and the subsequent implementation of discovered truths. Thus, the political form of human communities is of secondary importance. The central unit of consideration for Leibniz remains the diversity of individual human beings with their complementary ability to discover and implement universals. This centrality of human beings is clearly visible in Leibniz's fidelity to the term '*jus gentium*' and his definition of voluntary *jus gentium* as emerging in the tacit consent of peoples, not states.[30] Thus, according to Leibniz, global norms as an expression of universal truths exist but the traditional contemporary international law focus on interstate relations for their applicability and implementation is an erroneous simplification.

This account of Leibniz's understanding of universals and their connection to law demonstrates that the relationship between universality, particularity, and hegemony takes an entirely different shape compared to that of Hobbes. Universality cannot be separated from particularity, but their relationship emerges as more complex than a simple binary antagonism or opposition: universality requires all

---

[29] ibid 8–9.
[30] Gottfried W Leibniz, 'Codex juris gentium diplomaticus (Preafatio)' in Gottfried Wilhelm Leibniz, *Sämtliche Schriften und Briefe* (Akademie Verlag 1983) Reihe IV, Band 5, 64.

the particulars for its existence. As soon as there is hegemony of one particular perspective over others, universality disappears because the very essence of universality requires equal respect of all particulars. Thus, in Leibniz's thought, we can also identify an agreement with one aspect of the criticisms voiced by critical legal scholars, and Third World or feminist approaches to international law, namely the need to provide 'a space for plurality'.[31] However, for Leibniz such a space is not imaginable if we reject the substantive understanding of universality as these streams of thought do. Universality for Leibniz is not void but full of meaning and allows for a harmonious coexistence of all particulars. However, discovery of this universality requires a strong continuous cognitive effort. Thus, law has to focus on developing appropriate tools and procedures to allow continuing discovery of universals by lawyers and so can never be simply international since this cognitive task can only be performed by humans.

4. Concluding Remarks

The foregoing discussion of the articulation of the problem of universals and its impact on conceptualization of international law by two early modern scholars is revealing in several regards. First, the philosophical problem of universals exposes many unstated presumptions with which contemporary international law operates as well as the contradictions which plague it. In particular, it becomes obvious that it is impossible to denounce universality of international law as void and hegemonic and at the same time envisage efficient mechanisms for the respect of all particular views within the same international law system. If the universal is a truly void concept, then law is necessarily an imposition of one particular view as a universal. One can only strive to design procedures which will make this imposition legitimate and acceptable to all participants or else denounce the legal system as such. Law and universality respecting all particulars are only possible if one accepts that a universal has some discoverable substantive core.

Secondly, the discussion also highlights the importance for international law scholars to explicitly and consciously reflect on their unstated presumptions about the concept of universality itself. The philosophical problem of universals supplied both Hobbes and Leibniz with a fertile ground from which to start their very different conceptualizations of the concept of the universal. One might agree with them or not and theirs are not the only visions of universals available, but this transparency of the concept enables consideration of all the consequences and better choices regarding any possible future development in relation to international law as we know it. In this sense an explicit articulation of the concept of the universal

---

[31] Introduction, p 9.

enables the production of new spaces for contestation and constructive development of international law.

Thirdly, the discussion of Leibniz's views as a counterexample of the traditional Hobbesian perspective prevalent today reveals that those marginal parts of the international law scholarship which imply a belief in true universals as something objectively existing, like parts of human rights scholarship or many adherents of global constitutionalism, need to redirect their enquiry away from the discussion of the substantive content of these universals to procedural questions of knowledge acquisition, which in turn requires profound debates about the metaphysical foundations of our world.

3
Universalizing the Particular; or, Hotel and Carrier Bag

Matthew Nicholson[*]

In this chapter I argue that contemporary international legal thought, through its focus on the maintenance of international law's form and structure, is more concerned with universality than with particularity. I argue that this 'limits a new space for contestation of international law in international legal discourses',[1] and that the universalization of the particular—making international legal arguments out of particulars, in opposition to approaches that fit particulars into preexisting, universal international legal structures—is the preferable path.[2]

Contesting formalism's focus on the durability of international law's form and structure,[3] I argue that international law should be seen as something continually and fundamentally remade through encounters with diverse, ever-changing particulars. International law does not, I argue, exist as a stable form or structure—a set of practices or methods habitually employed by lawyers and judges—but as an

---

[*] Thank you to Ruth Houghton (Newcastle University) and Aoife O'Donoghue (Queen's University Belfast) for commenting on drafts and for helpful discussions and suggestions, and to the anonymous reviewer for helpful comments. Some of the themes addressed here were explored in my presentation at the ESIL 2018 Conference in Manchester. Many thanks to Patrick Capps (Bristol) for chairing the panel, to my fellow panellists and the audience for their engagement, and to the organisers of the conference for their work. All errors and inadequacies in the text are my fault.

[1] Editors' introductory chapter in this book at 15.

[2] Feminist international law scholarship emphasizes the importance of the particular—see Karen Knop, 'Eunomia is a Woman: Philip Allott and Feminism' (2005) 16 European Journal of International Law 315, 327 (noting, with reference to Seyla Benhabib's work, 'feminism's emphasis on the particular'); Faye Bird, '"Is this a Time of Beautiful Chaos?" Reflecting on International Feminist Legal Methodologies' [2020] Feminist Legal Studies 179, 186, reflecting on Margaret Jane Radin's feminist legal theory as a 'theory ... built on particularities ... No singular perspective can be wielded in solving feminist ethical questions ... What is taken into account in assessing strategic options relates to the specific problem at hand and the various moving parts which shape it.'

[3] On formalism, see Jason A Beckett, 'Rebel Without a Cause? Martti Koskenniemi and the Critical Legal Project' (2006) 7(12) German Law Journal 1045; Justin Desautels-Stein, 'Chiastic Law in the Crystal Ball: Exploring Legal Formalism and its Alternative Futures' (2014) 2 London Review of International Law 263; Jean d'Aspremont, 'The Concept and the Rationale of Formalism in International Law' in Jean d'Aspremont, *Formalism and the Sources of International Law: A Theory of the Ascertainment of Legal Rules* (OUP 2011); Matthew Nicholson, 'Walter Benjamin and the Re-imageination of International Law' (2016) 27 Law and Critique 103; Matthew Nicholson, 'Psychoanalyzing International Law(yers)' (2017) 18(3) German Law Journal 441.

Matthew Nicholson, *Universalizing the Particular; or, Hotel and Carrier Bag* In: *International Law and Universality*. Edited by: Işıl Aral and Jean d'Aspremont, Oxford University Press. © Matthew Nicholson 2024.
DOI: 10.1093/oso/9780198899419.003.0004

effort to represent lives and realities.[4] Formalism is my target given its prominence in recent theoretical debate.[5]

I present this argument through a materialist imagery that contrasts hotel and carrier bag. Drawing on cultural and literary theorist Fredric Jameson's work,[6] I associate the formalist emphasis on form and structure with a particular hotel—the Bonaventure hotel in Los Angeles. Inspired by Ursula K Le Guin's feminist literary theory—specifically, her essay 'The Carrier Bag Theory of Fiction'—I oppose formalist withdrawal into a stable hotel that affords a universal viewpoint.[7] I argue for an image of international law as Le Guin's carrier bag, a flimsy receptacle in which to gather particular things:

> If ... one avoids the linear, progressive, Time's-(killing)-arrow mode of the Techno-Heroic, and redefines technology and science as primarily cultural carrier bag rather than weapon of domination, one pleasant side effect is that science fiction can be seen as a far less rigid, narrow field ... Science fiction properly conceived, like all serious fiction, however funny, is a way of trying to describe what is in fact going on, what people actually do and feel, how people relate to everything else in this vast sack, this belly of the universe, this womb of things to be and tomb of things that were, this unending story.[8]

Le Guin opposes heroic narratives. The first hunters were 'the restless ones who didn't have a baby around to enliven their life, or skill in making or cooking or singing, or very interesting thoughts to think' so they 'decided to slope off and hunt mammoths'.[9] The cultural ubiquity of the 'killer story' of hunting, domination, and 'the Hero' crowds out 'the life story':[10]

> [T]he men and women in the wild-oat patch and their kids and the skills of the makers and the thoughts of the thoughtful and the songs of the singers ... have all been pressed into service in the tale of the Hero. But it isn't their story. It's his.[11]

---

[4] See my previous work: Nicholson, 'Walter Benjamin' (n 3); Nicholson, 'Psychoanalyzing' (n 3); Matthew Nicholson, *Re-Situating Utopia* (Brill 2019); Matthew Nicholson, 'On the Origins of Human Rights' (2020) 5 European Human Rights Law Review 512.

[5] For an illustration of this prominence, see Florian Hoffmann, 'International Legalism and International Politics' in Anne Orford and Florian Hoffmann (eds), *The Oxford Handbook of the Theory of International Law* (OUP 2016) 954.

[6] Fredric Jameson, 'The Cultural Logic of Late Capitalism' in Fredric Jameson, *Postmodernism Or, The Cultural Logic of Late Capitalism* (Verso 1991) 1; Fredric Jameson, 'Spatial Equivalents in the World System' in Fredric Jameson, *Postmodernism Or, The Cultural Logic of Later Capitalism* (Verso 1991) 97.

[7] Ursula K Le Guin, *The Carrier Bag Theory of Fiction* (Ignota 2019). On the value of Le Guin's work for international legal theory—and specifically ideas of utopia in international law—see Ruth Houghton and Aoife O'Donoghue, '"Ourworld": A Feminist Approach to Global Constitutionalism' (2020) 9 Global Constitutionalism 38; Nicholson, *Re-Situating Utopia* (n 4).

[8] Le Guin, *Carrier Bag* (n 7) 36 (paragraph breaks suppressed).

[9] ibid 27.

[10] ibid 33.

[11] ibid 27–28.

Le Guin proposes a 'new story' of 'the thing to put things in, the container for the thing contained'.[12] The 'carrier bag' story has priority—it came first: 'Before ... the weapon ... we made the tool that brings energy home'.[13] I argue that this feminist, anti-heroic, 'carrier bag' theory should be applied to international law—that international law is, in a sense, a carrier bag rather than a heroic, formal-universal hotel—supporting that argument through philosopher Theodor Adorno's work.[14]

A few preliminary clarifications are necessary. First, I am arguing that formalist international legal thought has been *more* concerned with universality than with particularity. This is not to suggest that the particular has no role. It is to maintain that formalism is biased towards the universal, and that this limits engagement with the particular.

Secondly, in focusing on formalism I am not suggesting that international legal actors—states or international organizations, for example—are irrelevant. But we can only know which actors are relevant, and what their relevance is, when we know what we are thinking about and the sense in which it exists. My focus here is limited to such questions of theory and ontology. We need, as feminist scholar Donna Haraway urges, to consider methods and practices of storytelling before we can tell stories: 'It matters what stories we tell to tell other stories with; it matters what concepts we think to think other concepts with.'[15]

Thirdly, I offer what follows as a mere 'carrier bag' of ideas, not a heroic vision of how international law is to be done differently. A heroic narrative of how international law(yers) is(are) to be 'saved' from heroic, formal-universal narratives would be just another 'tale of the Hero' and 'I'm not telling that story. We've heard it'.[16]

Section 1 addresses formalism's preference for the universal over the particular. Section 2 considers the limiting effect of this preference on engagement with the particular through architectural analogies, Fredric Jameson's analysis of the Bonaventure hotel in particular. Drawing on Le Guin's and Adorno's work, Section 3 argues for the universalization of the particular through international law, for an image of international law as a flimsy carrier bag rather than a shiny, stable hotel.

---

[12] ibid 29.
[13] ibid 30.
[14] Theodor W Adorno (EB Ashton tr) *Negative Dialectics* ([1966] Continuum 2007); Theodor W Adorno (Rolf Tiedemann ed, Edmund Jephcott tr), *Metaphysics: Concepts and Problems* (Stanford University Press 2001); Theodor W Adorno, 'Marginalia to Theory and Praxis' in Theodor W Adorno (Henry W Pickford tr), *Critical Models: Interventions and Catchwords* (Columbia University Press 2005) 259; Theodor W Adorno, 'Subject and Object' in Andrew Arato and Eike Gebhardt (eds), *The Essential Frankfurt School Reader* (Continuum 2002) 497. On the complementarity of Le Guin's and Adorno's work, see Nicholson, *Re-Situating Utopia* (n 4) 69–70.
[15] Donna Haraway, 'Introduction: Receiving Three Mochilas in Colombia—Carrier Bags for Staying With the Trouble Together' in Le Guin, *Carrier Bag* (n 7) 9, 10.
[16] Le Guin, *Carrier Bag* (n 7) 29.

1. Preferring the Universal

This volume's editors note, with reference to Martti Koskenniemi's work, that 'international law is an exercise of presenting a particular political view as what should be accepted as universal'.[17] In *Gentle Civilizer* Koskenniemi defends international law's preference for the universal, 'insist[ing] that absent the possibility of building social life on unmediated love or universal reason, persuading people to bracket their own sensibilities and learn openness for others, is not worthless'.[18]

International law's function is, apparently, to '[persuade] people to ... learn openness for others' through a process of 'bracket[ing] their own sensibilities'. This is not an unqualifiedly good thing; it 'is [simply] not worthless'. Such realism is a product of the impossibility of 'building social life on unmediated love or universal reason'. This is an '"empty" ... negative' universalism,[19] international law as 'the fragile surface of political community among social agents ... who disagree about their preferences but do this within a structure that invites them to argue in terms of an assumed universality'.[20]

What matters is that disagreements take place 'within [international law's] structure', not the substance of law. Formal international law checks particularity's power:

> [W]hen professional men and women engage in an argument about what is lawful and what is not, they are engaged in a politics that imagines the possibility of a community overriding *particular* alliances and preferences.[21]

The theoretical foundations of this 'empty' universalism lie in political theorist Ernesto Laclau's work.[22] Drawing on Laclau's thinking, and on Sundhya Pahuja's insistence that 'a universal orientation is unavoidable if there is to be law',[23] the editors conclude 'it does not seem possible to articulate any legal discourse, let alone a critique of legal discourses, without a prior universalizing move'.[24] This 'prior'-itization of universality should be resisted, because it de-prioritizes the particular. Equally, the idea (in this volume's introductory chapter) that the relationship between universality and particularity is binary is questionable,[25] given that binary means 'a way of regarding something that divides it (esp. simplistically) into two

---

[17] Editors' introductory chapter in this book at 7 (citation omitted). For a more comprehensive analysis of Koskenniemi's work than is possible here, see Nicholson, 'Psychoanalyzing' (n 3).
[18] Martti Koskennimi, *The Gentle Civilizer of Nations: The Rise and Fall of International Law 1870–1960* (CUP 2001) 502.
[19] ibid 504.
[20] Martti Koskenniemi, 'What is International Law For?' in Malcolm D Evans (ed), *International Law* (5th edn, OUP 2018) 28, 46–47.
[21] Koskenniemi, *Gentle Civilizer* (n 18) 502 (emphasis added).
[22] See Nicholson, 'Psychoanalyzing' (n 3) 476–79.
[23] Editors' introductory chapter in this book at 6 (fn 31, citation omitted).
[24] ibid 6.
[25] Editors' introductory chapter in this book discussing 'binary opposites' at 6.

opposing or contrasting categories'.[26] A binary perspective fails to reflect the dynamic instability of the relationship between supposedly separate elements, a point made in feminist critique which seeks to move beyond the 'gender binary' in international law.[27]

Dialectical thought contests a binary perspective. 'Dialectics is [according to philosopher Theodor Adorno] the consistent sense of non-identity. It does not begin by taking a standpoint.'[28] In *The Left Hand of Darkness* Le Guin expresses the essence of dialectics in the idea that 'light is the left hand of darkness, and darkness the right hand of light'.[29] Neither universal nor particular can be preferred because there is no original binary. There can be no 'universal orientation',[30] insofar as this would exclude an equal, opposite, and simultaneous orientation towards the particular. As feminist international law scholar Gina Heathcote notes, quoting feminist historian Joan W Scott, 'there is no inclusiveness without exclusion, no universal without a rejected particular'.[31]

Whilst 'the total rejection of universality from international legal discourses is not an option',[32] that is, of course, half the story. It is equally important to recognize the particular as the ground out of which international law (a particular legal argument, a decision or judgment, a norm) grows.[33] The editors recognize this, noting that '[u]niversality has to be deduced from a particularity' and that universality involves 'a hegemonic struggle that aspires to project what represents a particularity as what should belong to everyone'.[34] The focus here is on what universality takes from particularity, how the universal validates itself by drawing from the particular.

I argue, by contrast, for an approach focused not on a universal that draws from the particular, but on the universal need to ground every legal argument, decision, and norm in the particular, in lives and realities now. The concern, in much recent international legal theory, has been to demonstrate the continuing potential of a universal international legal structure: 'Overwhelmed by anxieties of control over reality ... international law has retreated into itself to such an extent that Martti Koskenniemi can declare "international law's objective" to be, among other things,

---

[26] *Oxford English Dictionary*, definition of 'binary (n.), sense 4' (OUP, December 2023) <doi.org/10.1093/OED/1249240598> accessed 10 January 2024.
[27] See Gina Heathcote, *Feminist Dialogues on International Law: Successes, Tensions, Futures* (OUP 2019) 24, critiquing 'reliance on the gender binary ... within international approaches to gender law reform'.
[28] Adorno, *Negative Dialectics* (n 14) 5.
[29] Ursula Le Guin, *The Left Hand of Darkness* ([1969] Orbit 1981) 199. For discussion, see Nicholson, *Re-Situating Utopia* (n 4).
[30] See quotation at n 23.
[31] Heathcote (n 27) 23, quoting Joan W Scott, *The Fantasy of Feminist History* (Duke University Press 2011) 73.
[32] Editors' introductory chapter in this book at 6 (citations omitted).
[33] On this theme, see my previous work: Nicholson, 'Walter Benjamin (n 3); Nicholson, 'Psychoanalyzing' (n 3); Nicholson, *Re-Situating Utopia* (n 4); Nicholson, 'On the Origins' (n 4).
[34] Editors' introductory chapter in this book at 7.

"always ... international law itself'".[35] The editors express the conviction that international law is rooted in universality: 'One could say that the question of universality may even be the starting point of any international legal discourse that seeks global outreach and global authority.'[36] Maintaining the ability to heroically drop international law's structure—treaties, customary international law, *jus cogens*, and obligations *erga omnes*, for example—onto whatever crisis, human rights violation, or conflict comes next, crowds out the idea that the structure itself may need to be remade every time it engages with a particular situation.[37] In Le Guin's terms, 'the tale of the Hero' needs to be replaced with the carrier bag.[38]

I am arguing for a shift from a theoretical-ontological approach focused on the maintenance of form or structure, to one that emphasizes the representation of particulars in and through international law.[39] On this view international law's formal language of treaties and customary international law, for example, is replaced by nothing more substantial than the imperative to ground every argument and decision in the particular:

> [T]here is no set of texts or concepts which the practitioner must use; the responsibility for constellating texts, concepts, aspects or fragments of reality to be included in or excluded from the representation rests with the practitioner.[40]

This does not mean that international law's methods and concepts (treaties, customary international law) are completely abandoned; they remain particular aspects of the realities that must be engaged. But they become exactly that— *particular* parts of those realities—rather than universal frames or forms through which reality is seen.

Why would this shift be necessary? How does a bias towards the universal impose 'limits [on the] ... space for contestation ... in international legal discourses'?[41]

2. An LA Hotel (and a Californian House)

In an effort to answer these questions, the next few paragraphs deliberately break from direct discussion of international law and focus on heroic architecture. My

---

[35] Nicholson, 'Walter Benjamin' (n 3) 104, quoting Martti Koskenniemi, 'What is International Law For?' in Malcolm D Evans (ed), *International Law* (3rd edn, OUP 2010) 32, 52.
[36] Editors' introductory chapter in this book at 1.
[37] See Nicholson, 'Walter Benjamin' (n 3).
[38] See quotations from Le Guin at nn 11–14.
[39] For the fully developed version of this argument—which is grounded in the work of Walter Benjamin—see Nicholson, 'Walter Benjamin' (n 3). On 'representation', see Walter Benjamin (John Osborne tr), *The Origin of German Tragic Drama* ([1963, written 1925], Verso 1998) 27: 'It is characteristic of philosophical writing that it must continually confront the question of representation.'
[40] Nicholson, 'Walter Benjamin' (n 3) 119–20.
[41] See quotation at n 1.

hope is that the abruptness of this break affords a fresh perspective on international legal theory, a means of visualizing the limitations of a formalist approach by imagining it in concrete, architectural form. To do that I want to consider, first, the Westin Bonaventure hotel in Los Angeles, via Fredric Jameson's analysis of it.[42]

What distinguishes the Bonaventure for Jameson is its desire to stand alone: '[T]he Bonaventure aspires to being a total space ... it does not wish to be a part of the city but rather its equivalent and replacement or substitute.'[43] The hotel's exterior is a 'great reflective glass skin',[44] presenting the hotel as 'the distorted images of everything that surrounds it'.[45] The Bonaventure's attempt to simultaneously deny and dominate the outside world is, Jameson suggests, best represented by the fact that the hotel is home to:

one of those revolving cocktail lounges, in which, seated, you are passively rotated about and offered a contemplative spectacle of the city itself, now transformed into its own images by the glass windows through which you view it.[46]

For Jameson the Bonaventure is a 'postmodern hyperspace' that 'has finally succeeded in transcending the capacities of the individual human body to locate itself'.[47]

Jameson analyses the Frank Gehry house in Santa Monica, California as another example of postmodern architecture as self-contained, isolated space.[48] This 'new' house is 'the reconstruction of an older, very conventional frame dwelling' in which 'the original structure pokes up from inside the new structure'.[49] In an interview with Gehry, from which Jameson quotes, the interviewer suggests that 'the old house was the core, and the new house is the wrapper', noting that 'the house looks unfinished and rough'.[50] This is a place of 'numerous contradictory perspective lines going to numerous vanishing points above and below a wide variety of horizons':[51]

For Gehry the world vanishes to a multitude of points, and he does not presuppose that any are related to the standing human being. The human eye is still of critical importance in Gehry's world, but the sense of center no longer has its traditional symbolic value.[52]

---

[42] Jameson, 'Cultural Logic' (n 6).
[43] ibid 40.
[44] ibid 42.
[45] ibid.
[46] Jameson 'Cultural Logic' (n 6) 43.
[47] ibid 44.
[48] Jameson, 'Spatial Equivalents' (n 6).
[49] ibid 108, quoting Barbara Diamonstein, *American Architecture Now* (Rizzoli 1980) 43–44.
[50] ibid 109, quoting Diamonstein (n 49) 43–44.
[51] ibid 115, quoting Gavin Macrae-Gibson, *Secret Life of Buildings* (MIT Press 1985) 12.
[52] ibid 116, quoting Macrae-Gibson (n 51) 16.

Whilst there may be no 'center', no universal perspective and no 'the world', there is 'Gehry's world', contained within 'the wrapper'.[53] On Jameson's view of 'wrapping' as an architectural practice this establishes a 'spatial quarantine or cordon sanitaire' that makes external complexities observable and tolerable.[54] The Bonaventure's hotel lounge effects something like this 'spatial quarantine', converting Los Angeles' complex realities into a sanitized, saleable 'dazzling new perspective on the "City of Angels"'.[55]

I am suggesting that international law—by preferring an 'empty', formal universal to the particular—has situated itself in a 'postmodern hyperspace' much like that of the Gehry house or the Bonaventure.[56] I argue that international law uses 'empty' universalism like a 'cordon sanitaire' that makes heroic engagement with inestimably complex particulars tolerable and, in a limited sense, viable, 'limit[ing the] space for contestation ... in international legal discourses' in a spatial,[57] bordering way. International law and international lawyers are, I suggest, required to stay within the formal 'cordon sanitaire' of methods, concepts, and practices—treaties, customary international law, *jus cogens*, for example—for fear of contamination and a loss of heroic perspective if they step beyond it.[58]

A sense of international law as a hotel or house from which to safely view realities is, I suggest, implicit in Koskenniemi's insistence that:

> In the absence of agreement over, or knowledge of, the 'true' objectives of political community—that is to say, in an agnostic world—the pure form of international law provides the shared surface—the only such surface—on which political adversaries recognize each other as such and pursue their adversity in terms of something shared, instead of seeking to attain full exclusion—'outlawry'—of the other. In this sense, international law's value and its misery lie in its being the fragile surface of political community among social agents—States, other communities, individuals—who disagree about their preferences but do this within a structure that invites them to argue in terms of an assumed universality.[59]

This connects with Koskenniemi's wider defence of universality in international law in terms of an '"empty" ... negative' universal that 'represents the possibility of the universal' by 'resist[ing] reduction into substantive policy, whether imperial or

---

[53] See text at n 50.
[54] Jameson, 'Spatial Equivalents' (n 6) 101.
[55] <www.opentable.co.uk/bonavista-revolving-lounge-at-the-westin-bonaventure-hotel> accessed 10 January 2024.
[56] I am grateful to Ruth Houghton (Newcastle University) for helping me to develop my thinking on this point.
[57] See quotation at n 1.
[58] On these themes, see Nicholson, 'Walter Benjamin' (n 3); Nicholson, 'Psychoanalyzing' (n 3).
[59] Koskenniemi, 'What is International Law For?' (n 20) 46–47.

particular'.[60] This perspective exists above or apart from the particulars of human lives and experiences.

To maintain 'universal terms' in the Cold War era international lawyers could not, Koskenniemi suggests, allow international law to become a substantive instrument of US anti-communism.[61] That would have involved the loss of the 'empty' universalism that sustains and validates their practice, a descent into particulars and partiality. For Koskenniemi international lawyers must avoid 'the ultimate transgression, the cynicism of letting the ideal of universality fall the moment when something about the realization of one's particular preferences is obstructed by it'.[62]

Koskenniemi defends '[f]ormalism's utopian moment' because it involves 'a practice of decision-making that persists in time and through which the aspirations of self-determining communities remain alive—even as (or perhaps precisely because) the universal they embody remains only a "horizon"'.[63] Laclau is more explicit about the regulatory overtones of 'empty' universalism: '[A]s the demands of various groups will necessarily clash with each other, we [?] have to appeal—short of postulating some pre-established harmony—to some more general principles in order to regulate such clashes.'[64] This formal, 'empty' universalism, and the 'we' it invokes, lives, I suggest, in Gehry's house, behind a 'cordon sanitaire', inside a 'wrapper' that preserves the future of international law's apparently 'civilized' (recalling the title of Koskenniemi's book, *The Gentle Civilizer of Nations*) regulatory system. This is the thinking of the regulators rather than the regulated, of a 'we' that looks out, perhaps from a revolving hotel lounge, on the lives of 'various groups', and seeks to order them.

Ruti Teitel's 2011 book *Humanity's Law* offers a further example of 'empty', formal, heroic universalism.[65] Teitel invokes 'The Global Universal' to argue for the existence of a post-Cold War global legal order 'converg[ing] on a rule of law that is aimed at the recognition and preservation of humankind in global politics'.[66] 'Humanity law', for Teitel, 'affords a language and a framework that are capable of recognizing the claims and interests of multiple actors in preservation and security, both individual and collective.'[67] It offers 'a substantive and determinate but open-ended and contextually applied normativity'[68]—something akin to Koskenniemi's 'assumed universality'.[69]

---

[60] Koskenniemi, *Gentle Civilizer* (n 18) 504.
[61] ibid 504, and see ibid 497–509. For analysis, see Nicholson, 'Psychoanalyzing' (n 3).
[62] ibid 508–09.
[63] ibid 508, citing Ernesto Laclau, 'Subject of Politics, Politics of Subject' in Ernesto Laclau, *Emancipation(s)* (Verso 1996) 47.
[64] Ernesto Laclau, 'Universalism, Particularism and the Question of Identity' in Laclau, *Emancipation(s)* (n 63) 20, 26. On the connections between Koskenniemi's and Laclau's work, see Nicholson, 'Psychoanalyzing' (n 3).
[65] Ruti G Teitel, *Humanity's Law* (OUP 2011).
[66] ibid 203.
[67] ibid 216.
[68] ibid 216–17.
[69] See text at nn 20 and 59.

Discussing the invocation of humanity and military intervention in the context of US-led action in Afghanistan (2001) and Iraq (2003), Teitel concludes that 'just wars [should] be waged justly, in ways that are in keeping with the very humanity rights that inspire the use of force in the first place'.[70] The question of whether, for example, Iraq should or should not have been invaded in 2003 is, it seems, too substantive.

Given the 'empty[ness]' of his universalism, it is perhaps surprising that Koskenniemi critiques Teitel's argument for what he sees as a lack of concern with realties: 'What is *done* by ... speech [that employs 'the vocabulary of humanity'] ... eludes her. Questions as to whom it empowers, or whose preferences are implicit within it, are broached hardly at all.'[71] Teitel responds that she 'set out not to praise humanity law but to understand the phenomenon that Koskenniemi admits ... is real—that is, the ascendency of humanity-based discourse "in diplomacy and international institutions"'.[72] Koskenniemi quotes Proudhon ('whoever invokes humanity wants to cheat'),[73] and Teitel replies 'the phenomenon ... is real'. What is the 'reality' of the universalism being discussed here?

Teitel sees humanitarian universalism as 'a way of framing political conflict', a 'discourse' (Teitel describes her book as 'my account of the rise of human-centered discourse in international law').[74] The frame or 'wrapper' that holds the various fragments together is the focus:

> While the book does not espouse a formal fusion of rules or doctrines, I argue that humanity law provides a framework that both legal and political actors employ in today's world ... Most international legal scholarship focuses on individual regimes or tribunals, as if they operated in a relatively self-contained way. But under that approach, it is easy to miss the evolution of a jurisprudence that is being generated by a normative and interpretive framework that operates across these divides, and connects the mandates and decisions of diverse tribunals and institutions.[75]

Capturing a global reality or definitively answering questions about the possibility of universal governance is, it seems, impossible. Perhaps recognizing this, Teitel does not attempt anything so modern or all-encompassing. Taking familiar

---

[70] Teitel, *Humanity's Law* (n 65) 218.
[71] Martti Koskenniemi, 'Humanity's Law by Ruti G. Teitel' *Ethics & International Affairs* (13 September 2012) <www.ethicsandinternationalaffairs.org/2012/humanitys-law-by-ruti-g-teitel/> accessed 10 January 2024.
[72] Ruti G Teitel, 'A Response to Martti Koskenniemi's Review of Humanity's Law' *Ethics & International Affairs* (31 May 2013) <www.ethicsandinternationalaffairs.org/2013/a-response-to-martti-koskenniemis-review-of-humanitys-law/> accessed 10 January 2024.
[73] Koskenniemi, 'Humanity's Law' (n 71).
[74] Teitel, 'A Response' (n 72).
[75] Teitel, *Humanity's Law* (n 65) 6.

elements of international legal discourse—*jus ad bellum, jus in bello*, international human rights law, international criminal law[76]—Teitel supplies a 'wrapper', incorporating those elements into a wider frame labelled 'humanity law'. This is not simply '*jus ad bellum* + *jus in bello* + international human rights law + international criminal law', but it is not *not* that, just as the Gehry house is not 'a house' but also not *not* a house. Gehry wraps kitchen + lounge + bedroom + bathroom, and Teitel does something structurally similar with the post-9/11 international legal order.

Teitel's 'humanity law' offers a heroic, 'hyperspace' vision.[77] Like the Bonaventure hotel's lounge, this is an exercise in creating an unreal reality/real unreality. Teitel offers a study of 'the rise of human-centred *discourse* in international law';[78] a study of the reality of a formal language, rather than a study of the realities it seeks to regulate. This is presented in phrases that sound as if a product is being sold: 'Born at a moment of great uncertainty and flux in global affairs, humanity law supplies a new discourse for politics';[79] 'what we see is the emergence of transnational rights, implying the equal recognition of peoples across borders. Such solidarity exists across state lines and in normative terms, constituting an emerging global human society.'[80] Who are Teitel's 'we'? Where are 'we' sitting? How much did it cost to get in?

3. Carrier Bags (and 'the Whole Problematic History of Ontology')

Behind these questions of formal, 'empty' universality, or Teitel's discourse of 'humanity law', versus a focus on the particular, on lives and realities, sits what Theodor Adorno describes as 'the whole problematic history of ontology ... the history of the relation of the universal to the particular, or of possibility to reality'.[81] This connects with the opposition—which Adorno explores through Aristotle— between form (on the side of the universal) and matter or reality (on the side of the particular):[82] '[I]t is precisely the notion that the idea or the noumenal, the intelligible sphere, is more real than the empirical, which really forms the core of the metaphysical tradition.'[83] For Aristotle 'the universal or the form (they are the same thing in Aristotle) is, just as it was for his teacher Plato, the higher reality'.[84]

---

[76] ibid 4–6.
[77] 'hyperspace'—see text at n 47.
[78] Teitel, 'A Response' (n 72) (emphasis added).
[79] Teitel, *Humanity's Law* (n 65) 216.
[80] ibid 225.
[81] Adorno, *Metaphysics* (n 14) 38.
[82] ibid 37–38.
[83] ibid 37.
[84] ibid 35.

A sense of the form, the discourse, as 'the higher reality' underpins Koskenniemi's and Teitel's thinking. Their thinking, with its preference for the universal, for form, echoes the logic of the Bonaventure hotel's lounge with its 'contemplative spectacle of the city itself',[85] or the Gehry house with its 'cordon sanitaire'.[86] International law's form, its discursive structure, becomes the frame, the place, from which international lawyers view the world. My argument is that this formal preference for the universal should be reversed; that it is time, to borrow a phrase from Adorno, to recognize 'the primacy of the object';[87] the primacy of the things thought about rather than the subject doing the thinking or the form within which she thinks.

This implies a vision of international law not as a discourse, form, or structure, but as a means of representation:

> [N]o longer a set of forms or methods ... but, to borrow Walter Benjamin's term, an 'idea'—something constantly remade by every attempt to represent present reality ... a [Benjamin's term] 'pure means' of representation ... a means of presenting an image of what is, what was, and what should be to an audience.[88]

In place of a prioritization of 'the universal ... the form ... [as] the higher reality',[89] this approach conceptualizes form or structure as something created in and by a process of representation.[90] This rests on a dialectical view of the relationship between form and matter, between universal and particular. Adorno explains the two key positions in Western philosophy in terms of an opposition between 'the idea that what is directly given, the immediate facts of consciousness, should be posited as primary' and the idea that 'primary status is given to the pure concept'.[91] Rejecting both of these positions, Adorno adopts the dialectical position that '[t]he only possible answer is that each of these principles ... always implies the other, or that, in Hegel's language, the two principles are mediated by each other'.[92]

I am arguing, then, for a mediated understanding of the relationship between the universal and the particular in international law, in place of the preference for the universal that has, in the ways sketched above, dominated formal international legal thought. Adorno opposes the idea of 'the autonomy of form',[93] insisting, in its place, on 'the mediateness of form'.[94] At present, I suggest, international

---

[85] See Jameson quotation at n 46.
[86] See Jameson quotation at n 54.
[87] Adorno, 'Marginalia' (n 14) 265: 'The primacy of the object must be respected by praxis'; Adorno, 'Subject and Object' (n 14) 502: 'The object's primacy ... is the corrective of the subjective reduction, not the denial of a subjective share.'
[88] Nicholson, 'Walter Benjamin' (n 3) 106 (citations omitted).
[89] See Adorno quotation at n 84.
[90] See Nicholson, 'Walter Benjamin' (n 3) for the full argument.
[91] Adorno, *Metaphysics* (n 14) 42.
[92] ibid 43.
[93] ibid 73.
[94] ibid.

law is biased towards an autonomous concept of its form—a form that has a de-contextualized character, something like the Bonaventure's lounge, the preserve of a particular 'we', of international lawyers, who seek to 'regulate' the world from behind a 'cordon sanitaire'.[95] In place of this concept of its form international law should, I argue, pursue a mediated concept of form—a form formed, and continually re-formed out of the objects, the lives and situations that it seeks to represent, a form formed and re-formed by the lives and realties that it would 'regulate'.[96]

International law is, then, a flimsy carrier bag, a means of conveying things, a thing with little utility until particular things are placed in and conveyed by it, a thing that is stretched, re-shaped, and re-purposed each time it is filled.[97] It can be picked up and filled by anyone, regardless of training or expertise, and it can carry whatever anyone wants to put in it.[98]

This 'carrier bag' argument matters in international law because 'we've all heard all about the sticks and spears and swords'—the 'Gentle Civilizers' or 'men of 1873'[99]—'but we have not heard about the thing to put things in'.[100] This is an idea of international law as something more concerned with carrying and showing stuff to audiences than with 'heroic' ideas of civilization and humanity. The fostering of such heroic outcomes by international law is, after all, difficult to imagine in view of current realities. Flimsiness and the openness of showing and conveying seem somehow more 'now'.

Adorno insists that 'the truth of ideas is bound up with the idea of their being wrong'.[101] He maintains that it is important 'to free yourselves from a collection of clichés and ideas which have been foisted on you'.[102] In this spirit 'we' should, I suggest, cast off the injunction to remain behind the 'cordon sanitaire' of international law's existing form—its formal language, its existing concepts and methods—and move beyond scholarship that studies the 'reality' of international legal discourse. What is important, now, is to think about ways to represent now, not ways of maintaining existing forms.[103] We need flimsy carrier bags, not stable, shiny hotels.

If that means something to you, if you think this argument has value, then you might want to pick up this carrier bag of an intervention—containing formalist literature on international law (Koskenniemi and Teitel), Gehry's house, the Bonaventure hotel, and, most importantly, Le Guin's feminist concept of the carrier bag—and add what you want to convey to it. If this looks useless to you, if this bag

---

[95] On 'regulate' see Laclau quotation at n 64; 'cordon sanitaire'—see Jameson quotation at n 54.
[96] See Nicholson, 'Walter Benjamin' (n 3).
[97] Le Guin, *Carrier Bag* (n 7).
[98] On these themes, see the quotation at n 40 and Nicholson, 'Walter Benjamin' (n 3).
[99] Koskenniemi, *Gentle Civilizer* (n 18) 502—see Nicholson, 'Psychoanalyzing' (n 3) for analysis.
[100] Le Guin, *Carrier Bag* (n 7) 29.
[101] Adorno, *Metaphysics* (n 14) 144.
[102] ibid 137.
[103] See Benjamin (n 39) 29: '[T]ruth-content is only to be grasped through immersion in the most minute details of subject-matter.' On the value of this perspective for international law, see Nicholson, 'Walter Benjamin' (n 3).

cannot hold the stories you have been told/that you choose to tell yourself, you can throw it away or bury it at the back of the cupboard and carry on with more 'important', 'heroic' projects. Perhaps, when you come home from your quest, you will find it, and maybe you will need it to carry something.

'[W]e've all heard all about all the sticks and spears and swords ... the long, hard things',[104] but 'there are seeds to be gathered.'[105] The seeds of a 'new story' are out there,[106] in the particulars, buried in the soil of realities. We won't find them if we keep telling the same formal, heroic, universal stories.[107]

---

[104] Le Guin, *Carrier Bag* (n 7) 29.
[105] ibid 37.
[106] ibid 29. On methods for telling a 'new story' in and about international law, see Houghton and O'Donoghue (n 7).
[107] See Le Guin, *Carrier Bag* (n 7) 33.

4
International Legal Universalism
A Reactionary Ideology of Disciplinary Self-Aggrandizement

Akbar Rasulov

This chapter is an exercise in critique. Its object is the ideology of international legal universalism (ILU). As I propose to use them in these pages, the term *universality* is meant to convey the concept of a certain 'condition' or 'state of affairs', *universalism*, the practice of valorizing or advocating the achievement of this condition. To speak of universality is to speak of how things are or can be with international law—a feature, an attribute, or an objective characteristic which the international legal system can have or acquire. A typical example would be a phrase like 'the universality of the international human rights regime' or 'the universal reach of international health regulations'. To speak of universalism, by contrast, is to speak of a project, an aspiration, or a vision that someone working with international law may want to pursue—a body of beliefs, discourses, and practices that spring from the notion of urging and promoting the attainment of universality. A typical illustration would be a phrase like 'the universalism of the international human rights agenda' or 'the universalist outlook of international health governance'. Naturally, not every discussion or engagement with universality falls under the rubric of universalism, and not every universalist project will necessarily have in mind the same idea of universality.

As conceived for the present purposes, ILU is essentially understood to be *an intra-disciplinary ideology*, that is to say an ideology operational within the internal space of the international legal discipline. The basic concept of ideology which this argument presumes is rather conventional. Ideology here is defined primarily in terms of *discourse* and *rhetoric* and the *political effects* that attach to them, rather than, say, false consciousness, alienation, or libidinal engineering.[1] My aim in these pages is to begin a critical exposition of the ILU rhetorical complex, not to complete the project of critical deconstruction in its entirety. A more comprehensive analysis of this kind will have to wait for a different occasion.

---

[1] For an overview of the different conceptions and models of ideology, see generally Terry Eagleton, *Ideology* (Verso Books 1991).

The basic methodology on which I will draw in these pages is a version of critical discourse analysis, with a particular emphasis on narratology[2] and Althusserian 'symptomatic reading'.[3] The main inspiration behind the exercise is Felix Cohen's attack on 'transcendental nonsense'[4] and what used to be called 'critical legal theory (without modifiers)'.[5]

Last but not least: as these concepts are understood here, the basic difference between ideology and discourse is the same as that between 'spirit' and 'matter'. International legal universalism is a political project pursued through the medium of the international legal discourse. It is not the actual discursive materials—tropes, lexicons, concepts—that are used in that context.

1. A Map of the Universality Discourse

Generally, the discourse about international law's relationship with universality arranges itself today into three relatively distinct narrative clusters:

Universality as reach. In narratological terms, this is the part of the contemporary international law discourse where the idea of international law's relationship with universality typically gets encoded using the tropes and concepts of *space* and *power*. International law here is understood to be basically a system of power relations; universality is a part of that system's spatial manifestation; to speak of international law and universality is to speak of the extent of international law's legal geography.

In its general contours, the basic narrative goes something like this: however imperfect or underdeveloped any one of its individual elements may be, *taken as a whole* international law today obviously constitutes a universal legal system because its rules and institutions apply *equally and uniformly* to all states. Note the twin emphasis: the idea of international law that is presumed by this narrative is intended to remain operational not at the level of any specific legal regime, process, or institution but something much more abstract—'international law as such', 'international law as a social form', 'international law as a union of primary and secondary rules'. In a similar fashion, the concept of universality, though never explicitly defined in exactly these terms, is also envisaged to be synonymous with the ideas of equality and uniformity. Neither of these assumptions, of course, is

---

[2] For a general introduction to narratology, see eg Mieke Bal, *Narratology* (2nd edn, University of Toronto Press 1997).

[3] See Louis Althusser, 'From *Capital* to Marx's Philosophy' in Louis Althusser and Etienne Balibar (eds), *Reading Capital* (New Left Books 1970) 11, 28–34.

[4] Felix Cohen, 'Transcendental Nonsense and Functional Approach' (1935) 35 Columbia Law Review 809.

[5] Mark Tushnet, 'Critical Legal Theory (without Modifiers) in the United States' (2005) 13 Journal of Political Philosophy 99.

self-evidently right or self-evidently problematic. What is important about them, however, is that they are both, in one way or another, also present in the two other narrative clusters. Indeed, in a certain sense, one may say that these two patterns—the tendency to think of law as an abstract entity and to equate universality with equality and uniformity—form the strongest connecting thread that holds the entire body of the contemporary international law discourse about universality together.

Note the third important building block: the trope of 'obviousness', a framing device that allows the proponents of the respective argument to dispense, if need be, with the need to compile, present, and defend whatever 'empirical evidence' the argument otherwise may require. What makes international law *obviously* universal, according to the universality-as-reach narrative, is one or the other of the two basic scenarios. Either the way the international legal system has been structurally set up makes international law always-already universal by virtue of its very design. Or the way the international legal system has developed historically has made it inevitably universal by virtue of its career trajectory.

A classical illustration of the structural version of the argument is provided by Hersch Lauterpacht and Antony Anghie.[6] 'International Law,' writes Lauterpacht, by its very logic 'is based on the assumption that there exists an international community embracing all independent States and constituting a legally organised society. From this assumption there necessarily follows the acknowledgment of a body of rules of a fundamental character universally binding upon all the members of that society.'[7] 'The association between international law and universality,' writes Anghie, 'is so ingrained that pointing to this connection appears tautological': 'International law is universal [because] it is a body of law that applies to all states regardless of their specific cultures, belief systems, and political organizations.'[8] 'Wherever international law goes,' notes Sundhya Pahuja, because of the way its normative order is set up, 'it claims to [always-]already have jurisdiction to act as the law and extend to everyone.'[9]

A typical illustration of the historical version of the argument is given by Arnulf Becker Lorca and Peter Malanczuk. It may have started as *jus publicum europaeum*, writes Malanczuk, but '[i]n the historical process of the transition from the classical

---

[6] A critical caveat: the analytical exercise that is carried out in this chapter belongs mostly to the genre of structuralist (as opposed to phenomenological) inquiries. That is to say, it focuses mainly on understanding the operative organization of the ILU discourse, not the subjective experiences or perceptions of this discourse by the respective scholars who may very well view their work and understand its significance in entirely different terms. Were one to write their individual intellectual biographies, this last fact, of course, would be of paramount significance. In the context of a structuralist critique, however, it is not.

[7] Hersch Lauterpacht (ed), *Oppenheim's International Law*, vol I (8th edn, Longmans, Green 1955) 51.

[8] Antony Anghie, 'Finding the Peripheries: Sovereignty and Colonialism in Nineteenth-Century International Law' (1999) 40 Harvard International Law Journal 1, 1.

[9] Sundhya Pahuja, 'The Postcoloniality of International Law' (2005) 46 Harvard International Law Journal 459, 462.

system to the modern system, international law definitely lost its European character [as it] was extended from a limited club of nations to a global system now covering some 185 states'.[10] The idea 'that there should be ... a single set of legal rules, principles, and institutions governing interstate behaviour on a global scale', writes Becker Lorca, has not always been regarded as self-evident, but at least since the nineteenth century the concept of 'a universal international law' has become an unquestionable reality.[11]

The narrative that grounds the discussion of international law's universality in considerations of international law's spatial scope in many ways is as old as the discipline of international law itself. Its operative reasoning seems to be a combination of some form of basic empiricism and an implicit equation of law with *geography* and *power*, rather than, say, culture, values, or processes. Just look at international law's geography, goes the argument: its reach is obviously universal. Look at whom it binds and to whom it applies: it obviously binds and applies to everyone.

A classical illustration of this kind of argument template is provided by Hersch Lauterpacht in the eighth edition of Oppenheim in the mid-1950s: 'International law is the name for the body of ... rules which are considered legally binding by States in their intercourse with each other. Such part of these rules as is binding upon all States without exception ... is called *universal* International Law'.[12] Closer to the present day, one finds the exact same formula in play in Bruno Simma's keynote address at the 2008 ESIL Conference: it is a simple fact of history that 'there exists on the global scale an international law which is valid for and binding on all states'.[13] To be sure, one can find all manner of regional or specialized legal regimes in the international arena, '[b]ut all of these particular rules remain "embedded", as it were, in a fundamental universal body, or core, of international law'.[14]

One may rue, in other words, the inevitable fragmentation of some parts of the substantive legal regime, raise questions about the tension between regionalism and globalism, and lament the relatively primitive character of international law's sources. But one cannot, in good faith, deny that *as a system* international law is universal because, in terms of its 'validity and applicability', '[it] is all-inclusive',[15] ie because the spatial scale of its legal geography covers the entire globe equally and uniformly.

Universality as representation. The second narrative cluster relies on a notably different set of tropes and conceptual frameworks. The discussion of international

---

[10] Peter Malanczuk (ed), *Akehurst's Modern Introduction to International Law* (Routledge 1997) 11, 30.
[11] Arnulf Becker Lorca, 'Universal International Law: Nineteenth-Century Histories of Imposition and Appropriation' (2010) 51 Harvard International Law Journal 475, 475–76.
[12] Lauterpacht (n 7) 4–5.
[13] Bruno Simma, 'Universality of International Law from the Perspective of a Practitioner' (2009) 20 European Journal of International Law 265, 267.
[14] ibid.
[15] ibid.

law's relationship with universality in this case is coded far less in terms of matters of power and legal geography and a lot more in terms of procedure and participation. According to this reading, the question whether or not international law constitutes a universal legal system has to be answered not so much by examining the spatial extent of international law's effective reach as a system of power relations, but solely in terms of *how many actors* get to participate in its various constituent *processes*, with legislation as the most obvious focal point.

Note the unspoken change in focus from the idea of law as power (hegemony) to law as process (form) and the accompanying themes of representation, participation, and legal standing.

Historically, most international lawyers who would have made use of this narrative template would tend to develop this line of reasoning mostly in reference to concepts like sovereign equality, multilateral diplomacy, and decolonization. The narrative about universality-as-representation according to this approach would be essentially presented as an argument in favour of upholding the rights and expanding the role of non-Western states in different international legal processes and fora. 'To be vindicated as a universal system,' writes Milton Katz at the end of the 1960s, 'international law [has] to take account of the thought and practice of [all] new or transformed states.'[16] It is 'only as a truly universal system in whose formation every State has its word to say', repeats Christian Tomuschat at the end of the 1990s, that international law can retain its legitimacy as a legal system.[17]

In more recent times, a new thematic variation has started to emerge. Pivoting away from the traditional tropes of sovereign equality, multilateralism, and decolonization, it aims instead to propose an argument that connects the question of international law's universal status to its involvement or contribution to the emergence of a single, fully integrated global polity. 'Universalizing international law', writes Christopher Weeramantry, for example, constitutes 'one of the most urgent tasks' of our times: for far too long 'international law [was] compartmentalised ... within a close cabinet of technical rules little known to those outside the ranks of specialists'. Before and above everything else, it is 'essential [then] that its value, effectiveness, and relevance must be brought home to the *general public*'. Put differently, international law 'urgently needs to be universalized in regard to its constituency',[18] and this constituency is—Tomuschat reminds us—nothing less than 'humankind as a whole'.[19]

Although it seems, by and large, to be a product of the post-Cold War era, the tradition that links the discussion of international law's universality to the notion of

---

[16] Milton Katz, *The Relevance of International Adjudication* (Harvard University Press 1968) 3.
[17] Christian Tomuschat, 'International Law: Ensuring the Survival of Mankind on the Eve of a New Century' (1999) 281 Recueil de Cours, Collected Courses of the Hague Academy of International Law 9, 28–29.
[18] Christopher G Weeramantry, *Universalising International Law* (Martinus Nijhoff 2003) xi.
[19] Tomuschat (n 17) 29.

a fully integrated system of global governance that effectively bypasses the nation-state framework draws on a lexicon of tropes that goes back to a much earlier period. The most obvious of these tropes is the concept of 'international law as the common law of mankind'.[20] Another, no less crucial element is the concept of *monism* and the closely related tropes of systemic integration and globalization.[21]

At first glance, the argument that this new version of the universality-as-representation narrative purports to develop seems to begin exactly where the argument outlined by the old version had ended: it is precisely because the earlier objectives of interstatal equality and procedural multilateralism have already been realized that the question of international law's universality now gets to be posed in terms of international law's representativeness and inclusiveness at the level of 'humankind as a whole'. But note an important detail. What differentiates the new argument from the old argument is not just the obvious change in the levels of analysis—the idea that the democratizing dynamic in international law should go lower and wider—but also a much stronger reliance on the ideas of *evolution* and *international law's 'true nature'*. The operative reasoning that drives the new argument, in other words, sees the switch from the old statocentric approach to the new humankind-as-a-whole approach as a reflection not so much of the fact that international law has already achieved universality in the context of the interstate community, but of the fact that becoming the 'common law of mankind' would be the most logical course of evolution for international law considering its essential nature.

'A universalist approach to international law,' writes Simma, 'expresses the conviction that it is possible, desirable, indeed urgently necessary ... to establish a public order on a global scale.' What is more, 'for many [this] process' seems to be 'already under way'. Instead of remaining 'merely a tool-box of rules and principles destined to govern inter-state coordination and cooperation', international law, notes Simma, 'has undoubtedly entered a stage at which it does not exhaust itself in correlative rights and obligations running between states, but also *incorporates common interests ... not only [of] states but all human beings*'.[22] Crucially, in keeping with this programme, he immediately adds, international law has not only demonstrated its general aptitude for development. It has also revealed its truest nature and deepest purpose: as 'it begins to display more and more [of those] features which do not fit into [its traditional statocentric] structure', the international legal system enters on the path *'to being a true public international law'*.[23]

Note two interconnected assumptions. First, the notion that the abandonment of statocentricity forms a logically unavoidable stage on the road to universality.

---

[20] See eg C Wilfred Jenks, *The Common Law of Mankind* (Stevens & Sons 1958).
[21] On monism, see generally Lauterpacht (n 7) 38; Malanczuk (n 10) 63–64.
[22] Simma (n 13) 267–68 (emphasis added).
[23] ibid 268 (emphasis added).

Secondly, the suggestion that the ultimate political constituency which international law should represent is 'humankind as a whole'. It is an inherent part of the basic 'ideal' of international law, writes Anthea Roberts, that the international legal order must be 'constructed by drawing equally' on all views and inputs so as to avoid any form of 'globalized localisms',[24] and few factors historically have contributed more to preventing this ideal from being realized than international law's traditional commitment to statocentricity.[25] 'The wonder of law,' notes Philip Allott, 'is that it links everyday human behaviour to the order of the universe through the self-ordering of society.'[26] 'Law is a participation in the universal order.'[27] '[T]he great task of the coming decades is to imagine a new kind of international social system ... and ... a new kind of post-tribal international law, which extends to *the level of all humanity* the wonder-working capacity of law.'[28]

Universality as culture. The third narrative cluster has even less time for the idea or language of statocentricity. Its starting point, typically, is the notion of structural paradox, its idée fixe is the concept of law as a projection of values, and its central defining feature in tropical terms is the coding of the question of international law's relationship with universality in terms of law's normative and philosophical content.

The structural paradox trope is usually framed either in the language of geopolitics or functional self-transcendence. A classical illustration is found in Emmanuelle Jouannet's 2007 *EJIL* article. Having been birthed in the crucible of Western imperialism, international law, writes Jouannet, aspires today to become the platform for the advancement, and a channel for the expression, of universal human values.[29] How can a vehicle of imperial violence turn into a vehicle of global equality and all-inclusive emancipation? The answer, at first glance, would seem to be that this must be impossible. But that, of course, notes Jouannet, is not so at all. Side by side with its imperialist past there can also be found within international law a great potential for self-transcendence: 'with the advent of a genuinely internationalized and globalized society', 'that which could be—and has been—perceived as legal imperialism [can] become—or be becoming—a genuine legal universalism'.[30] Thus, while it is certainly true that 'international law is both a part of the problem and a part of the solution',[31] the latter can ultimately triumph over the former and international law may 'not only ... internationalize but

---

[24] Anthea Roberts, *Is International Law International?* (OUP 2017) 8.
[25] ibid 13–14.
[26] Philip Allott, 'The True Function of Law in the International Community' (1998) 5 Indiana Journal of Global Legal Studies 391, 398.
[27] ibid 397.
[28] ibid 413 (emphasis added).
[29] Emmanuelle Jouannet, 'Universalism and Imperialism: The True-False Paradox of International Law?' (2007) 18 European Journal of International Law 379.
[30] ibid.
[31] ibid 397.

also ... universalize the values that it conveys'.[32] Even if it has enabled countless acts of imperialist injustice throughout its history, international law, writes Jouannet, has also remained at the same time the one '*paradigmatic space*' within which the quest for a genuinely universal legal order may be pursued,[33] 'simultaneously and indissociably, the [one] legal form in which ... the promise of the political unification of humanity' can be realized.[34]

Unlocking this unrealized potential, however, is not at all an easy task. The challenge that confronts international law, Jouannet explains, is to resist both the standard 'American' model that essentially proposes to compel universality by force and the standard 'European' model that basically seeks to reduce the quest for universality to some vulgar notion of a global town-hall meeting where every given national or regional legal culture or tradition gets to make its contribution, voice its suggestions, and try rationally to persuade others to come to its view of things.[35] What is required is something far more complex and dynamic. International law, argues Jouannet, must put in place *a process of 'reflexive appropriation'*: an ambitious creative exercise that rejects the fetishism of 'odious universal uniformity' in favour of a truly transformative engagement with every existing legal culture and tradition in which some as yet 'we' would not only try '*to better appropriate*' these preexisting legal cultures and traditions but also to '*free ourselves from them*'.[36]

Note the two implicit presumptions that ground Jouannet's reasoning sequence. First, both the idea of appropriation and the idea of synthesis inevitably raise the question of agency: who is that 'we' who is going to 'better appropriate' but also be 'freed' in Jouannet's account? Secondly, the whole universality-as-culture argument line does not just seem to be heavily dependent on abandoning the traditional liberal ideals of formalism and procedural democracy. It also gives off strong grand-scale cultural-engineering vibes.

The roadmap, as Jouannet describes it, not only stretches beyond the mere formalities of liberal process—'negotiation, argumentation or simple imitation'[37]—it actually starts with the act of *subsuming all the existing legal cultures*, treated for these purposes as if it were some kind of raw material, the final goal being, in the end, *to synthesize* on the basis of this subsumed material an entirely novel kind of universal legal consciousness. If all this sounds weirdly Victorian, it is because, essentially, it is. Universality, in this reading of events, is basically a cousin of Esperanto.

Compare this model of universalization with those proposed by Roberts and Tomuschat. The way forward does not lie through ensuring that 'everyone must

---

[32] ibid 379.
[33] ibid.
[34] ibid 407 (quoting Mikhail Xifaras).
[35] ibid 392–93.
[36] ibid 402 (emphasis added).
[37] ibid.

have their say' in this or that institutional process. Institutional processes work with positive legal rules, and '[a]ll positive law of necessity has its roots in culture'. Taking care of the formal side of the international legal process does not address the question of content, ie 'which values should be inscribed in international law'.[38] Nor does promoting a greater degree of multilateralism and interstate integration. Globalization—which is the essential end-point of multilateralism—is not at all the same thing as universalization. The former, notes Jouannet, 'is simply the necessary result of the interplay of the powers that be'; the latter, by contrast, 'refers to *legal values that are common to all*'[39] and thus requires the use of much 'more subtle practices that are sensitive to the context of contemporary globalized society'.[40]

What sort of subtle practices are we talking about here? Like Esperanto, a universal legal consciousness cannot be assembled mechanically. As Abdullahi An-Naim explains, the reason why the champion of universality should aspire to a 'cross-cultural dialogue' is not so that they can identify any preexisting points of consensus. The goal is not to find the most convincing maximum common denominator but rather 'to explore the possibility of [the] *cultural reinterpretation and reconstruction*' of each given national and regional culture and tradition so as to '*enhanc[e] the legitimacy*' within them of whatever content comes to be recognized as the expression of the universal legal values,[41] if need be through the 'process of retroactive legitimation'.[42] Right from the outset, the exercise, in other words, should aim to go beyond mere 'rational discussion'.[43] The final objective is to 'chang[e]' each culture's 'dominant ... cultural position ... from within' and, 'since cultures are constantly changing and evolving [also] through interaction with other cultures, ... to influence the direction of that change and evolution from outside'.[44] Put differently, the road to universality, for the universality-as-culture tradition, does not lie through any form of comparative inductivist exercises, but through global-level cultural engineering.

The job of international law, explains another expositor of the universality-as-culture tradition, Philip Allott, is to articulate and uphold 'the common interest of international society, the society of all societies'.[45] The common interest of a society, however, can never be reduced to 'merely an aggregation' of all the individual interests of its constituent units or members. It is a projection, rather, of that society's own self-interest qua society, and the only way to determine what that self-interest actually requires lies through the 'enlightened' interpretation of that

---

[38] ibid 390.
[39] ibid 394.
[40] ibid 397.
[41] Abdullahi An-Naim, 'Introduction' in Abdullahi An-Naim (ed), *Human Rights in Cross-Cultural Perspectives* (University of Pennsylvania Press 1992) 1, 3 (emphasis added).
[42] ibid 6.
[43] Jouannet (n 29) 396.
[44] An-Naim (n 41) 4.
[45] Philip Allott, *The Health of Nations* (CUP 2002) 297.

society's 'public mind'.[46] Replace the term 'interest' with 'culture' and 'enlightened interpretation' with 'reconstruction' and what emerges, once again, is the idea of universalism as Esperanto-style cultural engineering. Except that this time there is also the express acknowledgement: the '[c]ommon interest ... may conflict with the self-interest of society-members' and every 'society contains systematic means for resolving such conflicts'.[47]

And, thus, in the end, that fundamental paradox which greeted us at the start of Jouannet's argument turns out actually not to be a paradox at all. There is no tension, no irony, no hidden logical contradiction between the fact that international law had its origins in imperialism and the idea that it should become the road to 'genuine legal universalism'. Far less a symptom of some irresolvable 'aporia or an impasse', the question of international law's universality is just a 'reflect[ion of] the enigma of the human condition'.[48] 'Law carries the structures and systems of society through time. Law inserts the common interest of society into the behaviour of society-members. Law establishes possible future for society, in accordance with society's theories, values and purposes.'[49] The only question is: who gets to decide, in the process of this enlightened-reconstruction-slash-reflexive-appropriation, which of these 'theories, values and purposes' are going to be carried forward 'through time'? What is that 'systematic means' by which the common interest of the international society is going to be defined? Luckily, the universality-as-culture tradition has a ready answer to that too.

'[W]e are compelled,' explains Jouannet, 'to take responsibility for the ambivalence of international law' and to 'take cognizance of the forced Westernization of the non-Western world.'[50] 'It is for this reason,' she continues, 'that the role of *internationalist doctrine* should not be limited to systematizing existing law; it must also submit all of the principles and values embodied in international law to—perhaps even subversive—critique [so as] to shed light on how any value, any principle, any legal universal, can mask shameful ventures or projects of exploitation, domination or manipulation.'[51]

Note the curious terminological choice: the heroic agent at the centre of Jouannet's roadmap—the 'we' takes both 'responsibility' and 'cognizance'—is identified using a vocabulary that is typically reserved for inanimate objects: 'the internationalist doctrine'. The phrasing may at first seem confusing but it has an explanation. At least since the mid-1990s, the idea of 'doctrine' in French legal-theoretical scholarship—as can be seen, for example, in the work of scholars like Phillippe Jestaz and Christophe Jamin (whom Jouannet elsewhere cites often and

---

[46] ibid 295.
[47] ibid 295–96.
[48] Jouannet (n 29) 407.
[49] Allott, *The Health of Nations* (n 45) 290.
[50] Jouannet (n 29) 407.
[51] ibid (emphasis added).

not disapprovingly)—rather than representing only 'a collection of works' or a 'body of opinion' has come to represent also the idea of a *scholarly collective*: 'an informal but homogenous group of authors ... akin to a corporation, a learned society and a gentleman's club'.[52]

Note also the grandiose and elastically expandable mandate the proposed vision assigns to this heroic agent. The role of the scholarly collective behind the 'internationalist doctrine' is not limited to taking stock of the existing international legal system, it also extends to reviewing and, if need be, revising every value and every principle embodied in it—exactly what one would expect the concept of a 'reflexive appropriation' that should free us from the existing legal structures should entail in practice.

Note finally the particular style of governance that will be expected of this agent—the source and form of its power—critique of principles, subversion of values, systematic examination. There is a clear trend here and the last word in defining it should probably go to Allott:

> I do not propose institutional change, whether root-and-branch or Fabian. I do not propose that we take up arms to expropriate the expropriators. I do not propose that we use the power of the people to disempower the powerful. What we will take up is not the power of arms but the power of ideas. We will let our best ideas of society and law flow into our imagining and our understanding of the human world. ... We will make them into humanity's ideal. We will choose them as the programme of a revolution.[53]

2. The Place of ILU within the Universality Discourse

Every mapping exercise is meant to serve a purpose. The purpose of that performed in the previous section was to set out the broader discursive landscape in which the ILU project is conducted. Which parts of this tripartite narrative structure does the ILU project inhabit? Which of those tropes and narrative templates does it typically draw on? Is there a particular mode or style of using these tropes and templates that is distinctly ILU?

To answer the last question first: yes, there is, and its main defining features are *black-boxing, conceptual slippage*, and *Hegelian mystification*. To answer the first question: all of them.

Consider a typical early example of an ILU argument from a 1982 edition of Akehurst's: 'It was not until after the First Word War,' writes Akehurst, 'that

---

[52] Phillippe Jestaz and Christophe Jamin, 'The Entity of French Doctrine: Some Thoughts on the Community of French Legal Writers' (1998) 18 Legal Studies 415, 436.
[53] Allott, *The Health of Nations* (n 45) 419–20.

international law ... became truly universal.'[54] Imperialism played an important role in this: 'the separate systems of international law which had once existed between non-European states had been destroyed during the period of European domination [, and] instead of seeking the re-establishment of [these systems], non-European states have accepted the system which had originally been developed by Europeans.'[55] This legacy is certainly not trivial. But it all lies in the past and it is truly 'unfortunate that some Western international lawyers are still ... stressing the early history of international law and its European, Christian, and naturalist origins'.[56] 'Whatever its historical origins, there is scarcely any rule of international law at the present day which can be described as peculiarly European or Christian.'[57] It is true that 'Afro-Asian states often feel that international law sacrifices their interests to the interests of Western states'.[58] But that is a relatively manageable issue: 'One solution of this problem has been the multilateral treaty[, a]nother solution ... has been to try to use the United Nations General Assembly as if it were a legislature.'[59] Neither strategy is perfect, each has its shortcomings, but the important thing that has to be recognized, in any event, is that many 'major changes in international law have occurred since 1945. ... The accusation that international law is biased against the interests of Afro-Asian states is, on the whole, no longer true.'[60]

Note the seamless transitions from the universality-as-reach narrative to universality-as-culture to universality-as-participation. Note the repeating references to law as an abstract essence, a system of power relations, an embodiment of values ('no longer European or Christian'), and an organic process. Note, finally, the curt nod towards Jouannet's paradox-that-is-not-really-a-paradox and the universality-through-history trope.

International legal universalism is an ideology embodied within a rhetorical complex. It is a way of using and mobilizing tropes, terms, and discursive structures. It is not those discursive structures themselves. It is a programme, not a technique. It draws on many of the same conceptual and discursive materials that are also used by non-ILU scholars, and this dual-use indeterminacy is precisely what makes ILU so slippery from the standpoint of its critical detection.

There is no simple litmus test for how one can spot an ILU argument in action. Ideologies do not, generally, develop to become easy to spot. To recognize an ideology in practice requires the recruitment of a very specific kind of critical tools.

---

[54] Michael Akehurst, *A Modern Introduction to International Law* (4th edn, Allen & Unwin 1982) 12.
[55] ibid 13.
[56] ibid 21.
[57] ibid.
[58] ibid.
[59] ibid 22.
[60] ibid.

3. Functionalism and Disaggregation as a Method

Every concept, in principle, can be turned into a black-box construct.[61] In law, this typically tends to happen more to those concepts that are not commonly perceived as legal terms of art, though sometimes it can also happen to those concepts that are. What is the ultimate reason behind that is anybody's guess. But the most important consequence of a legal concept becoming black-boxed is a rapid increase in the likelihood that it will be recruited for the purposes of *conceptual slippage*: the rhetorical technique of changing the implied content without changing the surface terminology. One way to think about the art of conceptual slippage is to think of it as a form of verbal manipulation that results in the covert shifting of the definitional goalposts. Another way is to understand it as a kind of switch-and-bait strategy.

How can the use of conceptual slippage be detected in practice? What can one do to avoid an inadvertent use of conceptual slippage in one's own discourse or to counter its effects when confronted with its use in other people's discourse? Neither of these questions is particularly novel. Nor is the basic answer to them. In law as much as in any other discipline, critical vigilance is essentially a function of training and practising a certain set of *analytical protocols*—a form of theoretical due-diligence exercise, if you will.

In the present context, most of these protocols have been outlined already more than a century ago: first, by analytical jurisprudes like Wesley Hohfeld, then by the so-called legal-realist scholars like Karl Llewellyn. Here they are, in a nutshell:[62]

- disaggregate large-scale unities (Llewellyn);
- replace all monolithic concepts with bundles (Hohfeld);
- abandon empty word-rituals, such as using 'names' to compensate for 'metaphysics' (Jerome Frank);
- avoid the use of 'reified abstractions, omnibus concepts, and metaphors masquerading as facts' (Lon Fuller);
- distinguish between those legal concepts that are meant to be operative and those that are not;
- concepts that are not operative should not be entrusted with doing any analytical or explanatory work;
- as far as possible, use only narrowly constructed operative concepts;

---

[61] A black-box construct is another word for a floating signifier: 'a highly protean notion [that acts as] a rhetorical umbrella for a variety of different conceptions'. Pierre Schlag, 'Politics and Denial' (2001) 22 Cardozo Law Review 1135, 1136.
[62] See Wesley Hohfeld, 'Some Fundamental Legal Conceptions as Applied in Judicial Reasoning' (1913) 23 Yale Law Journal 16; Jerome Frank, *Law and the Modern Mind* (Brentano's 1930) 57–67; Karl Llewellyn, 'Some Realism about Realism—Responding to Dean Pound' (1931) 44 Harvard Law Review 1222, 1237–41; Lon Fuller, 'American Legal Realism' (1934) 82 University of Pennsylvania Law Review 429, 443.

- avoid all forms of 'transcendental nonsense';
- evaluate all legal concepts solely in terms of their effects;

and last but not least

- when working with any set of concepts lower the *operative blocking level*.[63]

Recall Hohfeld's first lesson for property lawyers—asking the question 'who is the owner of this particular item of property?'—from a juridical point of view, is essentially pointless. As a legal category, the idea of ownership is operatively useless—in reality, every property relation is constituted by a whole bundle of structurally distinct elements (rights, privileges, immunities, etc). The way every such bundle is put together follows no predetermined logic, which is to say that its structure cannot be simply deduced or worked out 'from first principles'. It is only by analysing all the applicable positive legal rules and mapping out on their basis every element of every bundle that a lawyer can obtain an accurate enough picture of the respective legal regime governing the particular item of property. The abstract concept of ownership will be of little use in this undertaking.[64]

Recall too Llewellyn's first lesson for the contract lawyers: there does not, in reality, exist such a 'thing' as Contract—a single transcendent essence the avatars of which crop up all over the world of private and commercial legal transactions. What does exist, rather, is a whole multitude of operatively different phenomena that need to be disentangled from one another because each of them attracts a fundamentally different reaction from courts and regulatory authorities.[65] Contracts between merchants, for instance, are treated very differently from contracts between merchants and consumers, 'sales for resale ... from sales for use', 'one-shot or single delivery transactions [from] long-term ... arrangements'.[66]

How should one go about disaggregating omnibus concepts and breaking down false unities? The essential method is the same as that outlined by Hohfeld and

---

[63] 'The idea of the blocking level ... is that all thought deploys concepts that are understood to permit deduction, and other concepts that are meaningful but too vague or abstract to permit anything like that kind of logical rigor. The blocking level is the level of abstraction below which concepts [are understood to have a] deductive "operativeness", and above which they are experienced as no more than ... convenient labels.' Duncan Kennedy, *The Rise and Fall of Classical Legal Thought* (rev edn, Beard Books 2006) xviii.

[64] As Stuart Banner observes, the idea of thinking of property as an 'assemblage of rights' goes back at least to John Austin. It was, however, Hohfeld and his followers who popularized it and developed it into a broader methodological framework. See Stuart Banner, *American Property* (Harvard University Press 2011) 57–58, 72.

[65] A broadly similar argument was also proposed by Lord McNair in respect of the law of treaties: the Covenant of the League of Nations, bilateral fisheries agreements, extradition treaties, and treaties of cession have so little in common in terms of their 'essential juridical character' that only the most irresponsible lawyer would ever propose that, for the purposes of legal analysis, all these different species of international instruments should be lumped under one single rubric. See Arnold McNair, 'The Functions and Differing Legal Character of Treaties' (1930) 11 British Yearbook of International Law 100–01.

[66] See Grant Gilmore, *The Ages of American Law* (Yale University Press 1977) 82–83.

Llewellyn:[67] look for practical legal effects rather than verbal continuities; think of bundles rather than monoliths; atomize, disentangle, and map out. The basic theory behind this technique has received many different designations over the years. The most accurate is probably *functionalism*,[68] though Wittgenstein's 'meaning is use' may come close too.[69] The general model, in any event, remains unchanged: all meaning is conventional; words do not have any inbuilt meaning; every word has precisely that meaning which in the respective discursive formation it is employed to transmit. The more different uses a given word can have in the present discursive formation, the more semiotic functions it can perform, the more different concepts, therefore, it can end up 'channelling'. To identify each of these different concepts requires identifying each of these different functions. That, in turn, requires the disentanglement and the mapping of all the different uses that can attach to the given word in the given discursive context.

Take one of the most infamous examples of an omnibus concept in contemporary legal and political discourse and one that has already cropped up a few times earlier in this inquiry: the concept of democracy. The question 'what is a democracy?' arguably forms one of the most important anchoring points in legal and political theory. From the functionalist perspective, the best way to begin answering this question would be by mapping out all the different semiotic functions the term 'democracy' is typically assigned to perform in the respective discursive context. Looking at things from this angle, one may posit that in the contemporary international legal discourse, for example, the term 'democracy' is generally used in three fundamentally different ways, which means that it carries accordingly three fundamentally different meanings. The first meaning is the idea of institutional accountability: those who govern must be answerable before those who are governed.[70] The second is the idea of the transmission and translation of will: democracy 'make[s] the government responsive to popular initiatives, input, or needs'.[71] The third meaning is representation and participation: in a democracy, those who govern come from the ranks of those who are governed.[72]

Note the basic differences between these three meanings, the disjunctions that turn these concepts, when they are put together, into a bundle of structurally distinct elements rather than a single, internally undifferentiated monolithic essence.

---

[67] Indeed, a hundred years later it still remains the main tool used by most exponents of the critical legal tradition. See generally Fleur Johns, *Non-Legality in International Law* (CUP 2013) 10–14; Susan Marks, *The Riddle of All Constitutions* (OUP 2000); David Kennedy, *International Legal Structures* (Nomos 1987).
[68] See Cohen (n 4).
[69] See Ludwig Wittgenstein, *Philosophical Investigations* (Basil Blackwell 1986) §43.
[70] See eg Steven Ratner, 'Democracy and Accountability: the Criss-Crossing Paths of Two Emerging Norms' in Gregory Fox and Brad Roth (eds), *Democratic Governance and International Law* (CUP 2000) 449.
[71] Brad Roth, 'Evaluating Democratic Progress' in Fox and Roth (n 70) 493, 503.
[72] Thomas Franck, 'Legitimacy and the Democratic Entitlement' in Fox and Roth (n 70) 25.

It is not for nothing that Abraham Lincoln's classical proto-definition[73] of democracy, rather than summarizing it merely as 'popular rule', defined it instead as a 'government *of* the people, *by* the people, and *for* the people'.[74] The 'government of' is not at all the same thing as the 'government for', just as 'government for' is not necessarily synonymous with 'government by'. A monarch can rule in his people's best interest; that does not mean monarchies and elected governments are the same. A management board in a public corporation can be appointable only by the assembly of its shareholders; that does not mean that its decisions will necessarily always reflect the latter's values, wishes, and interests.

4. Disentangling the Bundle: Three Concepts of Universality in the Contemporary International Law Discourse

If it has not become clear already, the purpose of the brief theoretical detour outlined in Section 4 was basically twofold. In the first place, it helped put in context the narrative mapping exercise with which this inquiry started. In the second place, it brought into sharper relief the idea that not only is it generally helpful to note that each of those different narrative clusters described previously presumes its own, entirely distinct concept of universality and that these concepts can therefore be separated and disentangled from one another, but that it is *only by doing that*—by performing this sequence of narrative mapping, functional reconstruction, and analytical disentanglement—that we can start laying the groundwork for a critical challenge to the ILU ideology.

Taking a cue, against this background, from Lincoln's tripartite formula and recalling the earlier-noted tendency among international lawyers to associate the idea of universality with the concepts of equality and uniformity, it seems possible then, as a preliminary operation, to propose the following disentanglement of the basic conceptual bundle created in the contemporary international law discourse about universality:

---

[73] The reason it is a proto-definition is twofold. First, Lincoln himself did not, in that context, actually use the word 'democracy'. The tradition that identifies Lincoln's 'of, by, and for' formula as the basic definition of democracy is a later invention. Secondly, it is unlikely that many people in Lincoln's day would have seen the term 'democracy' as denoting something positive (and what Lincoln tried to convey by the 'of, by, and for' formula was undoubtedly understood as something very positive). As Morton Horwitz notes: 'Until the twentieth-century, the word "democracy" as well as the idea itself carried mostly negative connotations in American political and legal culture.' Morton Horwitz 'Foreword: The Constitution of Change Legal Fundamentality without Fundamentalism' (1993) 107 Harvard Law Review 30, 59.

[74] Abraham Lincoln, 'Gettysburg Address' in Charles W Eliot (ed), *American Historical Documents 1000–1904* (P.F. Collier and Son 1910) 441.

(1) Universality as the 'equality for'—a product of the narrative in which international law is understood to be a legal system whose rules and processes are the same *for everyone in the world*;
(2) Universality as the 'equality by'—a product of the narrative in which international law is understood to be a legal system whose rules and processes are created *by everyone in the world*; and
(3) Universality as the 'equality of'—a product of the narrative in which international law is understood to be a legal system whose rules and processes equally reflect the values, wishes, and interests *of everyone in the world*.

Note again the significance of the conceptual disjunctions: the progression from 'for' and 'by' to 'of' is no more self-evident in the case of universality than it is in the case of democracy. There is a world of difference between the idea that a legal system is or becomes universal because it subjects everyone to its commands and the idea that it is or becomes universal because everyone gets to have a say in its development, just as there is a world of difference between each of these ideas and the idea that a legal system is or becomes universal when it begins to embody the values, hopes, and aspirations of everyone equally.

With these disjunctions in mind, let us now take a closer look at some of the arguments detailed in Section 2:

(a) what Anghie, Pahuja, and Becker Lorca appear to have in mind is essentially a 'universality as equality for' concept: international law is said to be universal but only in the sense that its rules and processes today apply in the same way across the entire globe and are binding on every state;
(b) by contrast, what Katz, Roberts, and Tomuschat have in mind is 'universality as equality by', since each of them, in effect, presumes that the question of international law's universal status should be answered in reference to whether or not it is only some (imperial) powers or all international law subjects that get to have a say in its creation;
(c) Simma's argument appears to start in the same register as Anghie, Pahuja, and Becker Lorca—international law's universal status is initially established for Simma by the fact that its rules bind and apply to all states—before too long, however, it pivots quickly towards a 'universality as equality of' narrative, in which international law becomes universal inasmuch as it 'incorporates the interests of all human beings';
(d) Jouannet's argument starts in the same register as Katz, Roberts, and Tomuschat—her recognition of the importance of the imperialism paradox signals just how central the questions of participation and inclusiveness are supposed to be in her account—but then almost imperceptibly morphs into an argument about 'universality as the equality of': international law, she says, echoed by Allott, will realize its universal potential only when there

emerges a universal legal consciousness that reflects 'the values common to all';

(e) in both of these cases, the conceptual slippages are accompanied by the heavy reliance on dialectical and essentialist tropes: for Simma, becoming a common law of mankind will take international law beyond its traditional form but will also make it 'truly' itself; for Jouannet, the production of the universal legal consciousness is the paradigmatic function of international law but it also a process of self-negation and self-transcendence.

5. Hegelianism as the Theoretical Bedrock of the ILU Argument

The last missing piece of the puzzle in explaining the operative structure of the ILU rhetorical complex is the idea of Hegelian mystification.

In its standard form, the progress narrative typically seeks to present history as a relatively predetermined sequence of events governed by an inexorable logic of improvement that ensures the continuous progression of all social, cultural, and political forms from a more primitive and violent stage to a more sophisticated and peaceful stage, oppression to liberty, folly to reason, etc. The particular version of the progress narrative that sits at the heart of the ILU rhetorical complex differs from this base model because of two twists. The first twist is the attempt to convert what is essentially a *historicist metaphysics* into a *structural metaphysics*: the history of international law is still presented as an essentially predetermined process of continuous advancement and improvement, but the progress element of the narrative has now been converted from a quasi-historicist argument (progress as predestination) into a quasi-ontological one (progress as the realization of the true nature/ inner essence). The second twist is the *naturalist normativism*: because the propensity towards universality is supposed to be a part of international law's true nature/inner essence, promoting universality in international law is, normatively, the right thing to do.

As international law moves through time, the implicit reasoning goes, the general course of its evolution will inevitably end up reflecting the 'logic' of its nature/essence. As this nature/essence works itself to its logical realization, international law will inevitably come to assume exactly that form, structure, and content which this nature/essence presumes. Like the seed that ultimately grows into a tree, so, too, this inner nature/essence will ultimately sprout a new international law. And since it just so happens that it is in the nature of international law to aspire towards becoming a universal legal system, it follows unavoidably that this is what international law inevitably is going to become.

Note the implications of this dual inversion-expansion argument: the crude combination of the evolutionist trope with the vaguely Providential truth-will-ultimately-reveal-itself trope yields an expansion of the classical progress narrative into a predictive device for determining the shape of the future. The guaranteed certainty of the projected future is then used to provide both a 'vote of confidence' for the actually existing present—however compromised it might otherwise be by the legacies of its past, international law is always redeemed by this guarantee of its future progression—and to sanction the suspension of any genuine concerns that what we are doing in the here-and-now could somehow mess things up for us or those who later come after us. For if history runs according to a fixed script, it cannot, by definition, be 'a dark and open struggle'.[75] And if it is not a struggle, then we cannot lose it.

It does not take a particularly extensive knowledge of the Western philosophical tradition to recognize the basic parallel between this line of reasoning and the general concept of history proposed by the great German philosopher GWF Hegel. For Hegel, the entire course of human history constitutes a reflection of what he describes, in a nutshell, as the gradual self-awakening through a process of dialectical self-transformation of an uncompromisingly pantheistic entity called, suitably enough, the World-Spirit (*Weltgeist*).[76] Since the World-Spirit is basically an updated version of the traditional Christian concept of God,[77] and God, by definition, is free from any imperfections, the more the World-Spirit awakens from its slumber, the more perfect the respective social, cultural, and political forms of our society become. Once it awakens completely, the state of perfection will reach its peak, the world and the World-Spirit will become one, reason will triumph, and history, as we know it, will end. So far, so weird, but never mind. Note the essential implications of this hypothesis for the question of agency. In the Hegelian thought experiment, there exists room only for one *real subject*, the World-Spirit. Everyone else—nations, governments, individual geniuses, corporate entities—are nothing more than its ephemeral tools and playthings. The question inevitably arises: how can this hypothesis be reconciled with our everyday experience of ourselves as moral and political agents? The answer Hegel gives to this is refreshingly medieval: we may experience ourselves as independent moral agents possessed of a personal free will, but in the end it is the World-Spirit's will that is always done. Whatever we do, each of us is only a puppet in the hands of the World-Spirit whose grand providential design, because of the clever little principle which Hegel calls 'the cunning of reason' (*List der Vernunft*), inevitably escapes our knowledge.[78]

---

[75] cf Roberto Unger, *False Necessity* (rev edn, Verso Books 2002) xix: 'History, however, is not the unfolding of an idea, nor the upgrading of a machine. It is a dark and open struggle.'
[76] See Anthony Kenny, *The Rise of Modern Philosophy* (OUP 2006) 115–16.
[77] For further discussion, see Louis Althusser, *Essays in Self-Criticism* (Grahame Lock tr, New Left Books 1976) 135–37.
[78] For further discussion, see George Henry Radcliffe Parkinson, 'Hegel, Marx and the Cunning of Reason' (1989) 64 Philosophy 287, 291; Igor S Narskiy, 'GWF Hegel' in Teodor I Oizerman (ed), *Istoriia Dialektiki: Nemetskaia Klassicheskaia Filosofiia* (Mysl' 1978) 216, 307.

And that, in the end, is why, despite every reason to do so, we should not really worry about entrusting the Esperantoesque process of building the common-law-of-mankind-cum-universal-legal-consciousness to a type of collectivity none of us otherwise would readily associate with the idea of competent rulership.

There are only two minor differences that separate Simma and Jouannet's versions of the ILU argument. The first is the difference in execution. In Simma's case, the Hegelian themes and the conceptual slippages are all visibly there (the latter indeed are all but acknowledged in the open). One thus only needs to pay close attention to the actual surface arguments and the occasional slips of the tongue (like that comment about what makes international law the truest version of itself). In Jouannet's case, by contrast, the Hegelian reasoning pattern is played out in a much more covert way. One has to read here, as Althusser would say, the inherent silences of her argument as well as her surface speech. And yet, like Allott and An-Naim, right from the start she assumes a view of international law as a species of collective consciousness, describes the unavoidability of its dialectical self-transformation, and highlights the irreducibility of universality (synthesis) to any already existing rival cultures (theses and their anti-theses).

The second difference is the difference in the immediate political signalling. Simma's take on the ILU argument has much less to say about the privileged role that in this story of redemption should be assigned to international legal scholars. Jouannet's argument, by contrast, all but names international law scholars the ultimate heroes of the new world order of tomorrow.

6. Conclusion: ILU as a Project of Whitewashing and Self-Aggrandizement

It is not difficult to recognize the basic political content that the ILU project advances. What we are looking at is essentially an ideological narrative that simultaneously (1) promises international lawyers an always-already fixed *future* for international law, the journey towards which is supposedly guaranteed by international law's *inner essence*; (2) draws from this guaranteed predisposition an implied legitimation for international law's *present* situation and an excuse for its *past* record; and (3) uses this newly (re-)gained legitimacy to justify whatever self-aggrandizement the international legal profession may end up sliding into under the rubric of executing those 'reflexive appropriations' that are meant to bring about the awakening of the universal legal spirit and help international law become the most perfect version of equality and uniformity possible: a common law of mankind that binds and applies to everyone, channels and incorporates everyone's voices, and conveys and expresses everyone's values and wishes but in a way that is also freed from parochial constraints of any preexisting national legal culture or tradition.

By preventing international lawyers from fixating too much on the present, the ILU ideology also helps entrench a culture of intellectual *false necessity*—the less international lawyers reflect on the deeper content of the actually existing international legal system, the more they are likely to overlook the full extent and conditions of its contestability and malleability—which, on a long enough time scale, always ends up favouring the established status quo and normalizing the established power hierarchies. By shifting the main focus of their attention from international law's traumatic past to the potentiality of its glorious future, it also helps defuse any conversations about historical injustice or corrective reparations, while at the same time promoting a culture of transcendental nonsense-mongering.

Consider again Akehurst's argument: to be sure, the international law of today has its origins in the age of European domination which destroyed every alternative system of international relations that may once have existed among the non-European peoples. But there is no point really in getting preoccupied with this, since whatever may have happened in the past, there is scarcely anything European about international law today, and anyway it is not true that today international law, on the whole, is biased against the interests of non-European states.

Or take again Allott's theory: there is no doubt, writes Allott, that the past of international law was rooted in a whole plethora of 'greatest social evil[s]—colonial oppression, slavery, genocide, methodical terror, war'.[79] It is only right that we should feel bad about it today. But that does not mean for a moment that there should be an additional burden on the international law profession to do anything about that past as lawyers:

> We cannot take responsibility for what we did not do, nor for what was done in the past by, or on behalf of, the society to which we now belong. We can feel shame, *as human beings* [,] *take responsibility for correcting the continuing consequences of the past*[, and] *resolve to do better in the future*. More cannot be expected of us. The past is beyond redemption.... The arrow of human time cannot be reversed. [T]o enact the process of judgement *using conventional legal process ... to achieve retrospective corrective justice* is social evil [-] injustice masquerading as justice.[80]

So what if international law has not yet become a common law of the humankind as a whole? The seeds of it, as Simma shows, are already sprouting: the system has already begun to transcend its traditional statocentric structures. So what if international law's past is rooted in imperialism and oppression? 'Surely,' as Philip Jessup puts it, 'it is not the origin of international law which matters', but its future; and 'just because practices were abused in earlier times', it does not follow that the

---

[79] Allott, *The Health of Nations* (n 45) 66.
[80] ibid 67.

international law of today 'should be swept away'.[81] What is far more important than its imperialist past is the fact that, more than any other social form, international law today is well placed to become the vehicle of genuine universality. All that needs to be done in this process is give more power, respect, and admiration to the properly enlightened and cross-culturally inclined community of international law scholars.

---

[81] Philip Jessup, 'Non-Universal International Law' (1973) 12 Columbia Journal of Transnational Law 415, 419–21.

II
THE INVENTION OF UNIVERSALITY

5
The Assumption, Not Invention, of Universality Is the Problem

Onuma Yasuaki[*]

Introduction

Onuma Yasuaki wrote 'The Assumption, Not Invention, of Universality Is the Problem' for the European Society of International Law (ESIL) Annual Conference 2018. I was his student at the Graduate School of Laws and Politics, the University of Tokyo, and had the honour to present this paper on his behalf.

This paper traces his academic career and his main works in light of the antagonism of the universality and the West-centric features of international law studies. It sharply criticizes the idea which equated European or the United States' norms with general international law. This paper represents his efforts to overcome such biases embedded in the discipline and to find out and establish the commonly valid idea that can be accepted by people with diverse cultural and civilizational backgrounds. His treatises, *A Transcivilizational Perspective on International Law* (Brill/Nijhoff 2010) and *International Law in a Transcivilizational World* (CUP 2017), addressed these problems in detail from theoretical standpoints.

Onuma was a passionate advocate for the rights of minorities and vulnerable people. He worked hard to protect descendents of people forcefully brought to Japan, especially from the Korean Peninsula, people left in Sakhalin Peninsula left after World War II, and 'comfort women'. In addition, he was interested in fighting against the discrimination within Japan against non-Japanese Asians. He was also a pioneer in the study of war responsibility and international law. This paper represents the structure embedded in Japanese society, against which he fought throughout his career.

At the same time, he was a scholar who rigorously and comprehensively studied European and US literature. His edited book, *A Normative Approach to War: Peace, War, and Justice in Hugo Grotius* (Clarendon Press 1993), exemplifies this fact. He often told us that it would not make solid academia if one only claims 'unique' or 'critical' recognition, interpretation, and claims from 'the periphery', 'the weak', and

---

[*] Professor Onuma Yasuaki passed away shortly after the 2018 ESIL Annual Conference. We include the paper that was presented at the Conference by ISHII Yurika on his behalf without major changes.

Onuma Yasuaki, *The Assumption, Not Invention, of Universality Is the Problem* In: *International Law and Universality*. Edited by: Işıl Aral and Jean d'Aspremont, Oxford University Press. © Onuma Yasuaki 2024.
DOI: 10.1093/oso/9780198899419.003.0006

'the marginalized'. Instead, it is necessary to study hard and adequately evaluate the milestones of the 'mainstream' and 'conventional' international law studies before presenting a new perspective. Without such a process, the criticism will be only superficial and unacceptable.

Onuma not only led the Japanese academic community but also achieved a broad international reputation. He served as a Counsellor to the American Society of International Law and was one of the founding figures of the Asian Society of International Law. He also gave lectures in many prestigious institutes. I attended the ESIL Annual Conference 2008 in Heidelberg, where Onuma was a moderator of a panel. Alumni of the Hague Academy of International Law 2007 surrounded him.

Onuma passed away in the morning of 16 October 2018. He worked on his paperback, *Kokusaihō [International Law]* (Chikuma Shobō 2018), until the night before his departure. It is still surreal to me that we will no longer receive his emails and phone calls. We are only fortunate to have his works and learn from them, which are an outstanding legacy of international law studies.

ISHII Yurika
National Defense Academy of Japan

The problem of universality has been one of the central themes of my research since I started to study international law in 1970. In my view, ideas on universality, globally assumed, from the twentieth century up to present have been overwhelmingly US-Euro (or West)-centric. How to overcome this narrowness of the idea, and to find out and establish the universally valid idea that can be accepted by people with diverse cultural and civilizational backgrounds? This question has always been with me, who has spent his life both as a scholar and an activist in social movements.

My interest in this problem of universality was strongly influenced by the three social movements which occurred in Japan from the late 1960s to the early 70s.

The first was the anti-Vietnam War movement. In those days, the United States was engaged in the Vietnam War. The US military forces attacked not only soldiers of North Vietnam but also civilians who assisted the national liberation movement in South Vietnam, where the US supported the corrupt and authoritarian South Vietnamese government. Japan assisted the US in bombing North Vietnam and the national liberation movement in South Vietnam. Although Japan did not send its military forces to Vietnam, Japan supported the US military campaign by allowing the US to use its military bases and providing weaponry and munitions produced by its factories.

The second movement was the 'Student Revolt', which reached its peak in 1968-69. Many students who engaged in this movement criticized not only the power of the government, but also the university authorities and even progressive scholars and other opinion leaders. These critical students believed that the university and those 'progressive' opinion leaders functioned as oppressive social power vis-à-vis invisible, discriminated people. Included among those discriminated against were the Korean and Taiwanese minorities in Japan.

The third was the anti-Immigration System movement. Those who engaged in this movement were concerned with the fate of the people fighting against the South Korean and Taiwanese governments, which ruthlessly suppressed them. Among those people, a number of political and intellectual leaders took refuge in Japan. However, the Japanese government often deported them to those two countries when it was requested by their governments.

What the participants in the three movements regarded as a serious problem was a deeply rooted sense of discrimination against non-Japanese Asians. They believed that this social psychology underlay the policies of the Japanese governments which they regarded as unjust. This psychology dates back to the early Meiji period, when Japan encountered Western Great Powers and was determined to imitate them for maintaining its national independence and making the nation more prosperous and 'civilized'.

This fundamental policy, expressed by the idea of 'Getting out of Asia, Entering into Europe (Liberating from Asia, and Assimilating with Europe)' has persisted throughout the history of modern Japan. The leaders of the three movements reminded me that what is problematic is not only specific government policies. The unconscious and deeply rooted psychology of this 'Getting out of Asia, Entering into Europe' is the problem. Underlying this idea is the discriminatory assumption that Europe or the West is superior to Asia. The values of diverse Asian cultures and civilizations were forgotten and denied. To make the matter worse, such an inferiority complex was not limited to modern Japan. It seemed to be shared more or less by the non-European or non-Western people in general.

From 1979 to 1981, I studied in two major universities in the US as a visiting scholar. In the first year, when I was at Harvard Law School, I found major casebooks or coursebooks of international law were incredibly domestically-oriented and US-centric. In 1981, when I was a visiting scholar at Princeton University, I presented a paper in the 75th Anniversary Convocation of the American Society of International Law. I analysed three major casebooks and coursebooks of international law used in major law schools and political departments of the US universities and demonstrated how materials used in these casebooks and coursebooks are US-centric. Specifically, they include a huge number of US domestic court jurisprudence rather than international treaties and resolutions of the major international organizations.

Underlying this US-centric approach is the *unconscious assumption* that *what is US is what is universal*. I criticized this assumption and argued for the need for a more internationally-oriented and 'intercivilizational' approach to international law.[1] Unfortunately, my presentation was almost ignored by the audience except for Professors Richard Falk of Princeton University and Virginia Leary of the

---

[1] Onuma Yasuaki, 'Promoting Training and Awareness—The Tasks of Education in International Law, Remarks of Onuma Yasuaki' (1981) 75 American Society of International Law, Proceedings 163.

State University of New York, both of whom continued to encourage me in subsequent years.

From the 1990s, I started to publish my view on Euro- or West-centrism in international law in English. The first attempt was an Appendix to *A Normative Approach to War: Peace, War and Justice in Hugo Grotius*, published by Clarendon Press, Oxford, in 1993.

In this book, I concentrated my efforts to grasp the theory of Grotius, expressed in *De jure belli ac pacis*, and to locate him in the history of international law. However, I dared to add the Appendix entitled 'Eurocentrism in the History of International Law'. In this Appendix, I analysed, though elementarily and schematically, how the Euro-centric structure of international law was formed, by exploring the European expansion during the period of 'the Discovery of the New World', and the teachings of Francisco de Vitoria, expressed in his famous lecture *De Indis*.[2]

I continued my study relating to the problem of, and the nature of, universality and international law mainly in the fields of human rights, history of international law, and so-called 'sources' of international law.

In the field of human rights, I published a number of articles from the 1990s, represented by 'Towards an Intercivilizational Approach to Human Rights', *Asian Yearbook of International Law*, vol. 7 (2001).[3] In these writings, I demonstrated that the so-called 'universality of human rights' was advocated mainly by leading Western scholars, who tended to assume that what is Western is what is universal. However, from the perspective of people in the non-Western world, who are the overwhelming majority of humankind, the 'universality of human rights' based on such an assumption is highly questionable. In order to overcome such a problematic assumption, I argued for the need of an 'intercivilizational' or 'transcivilizational' approach[4] to human rights.

In the field of history of international law, I also published several articles related to the problem of universality and international law starting with 'When

---

[2] Francisco de Vitoria, *De Indis et De Ivre Belli Relectiones* (Ernest Nys ed, Oceana Publication 1917).

[3] This article was chosen by Mireille Delmas-Marty, a distinguished comparative lawyer of the Académie française, as one of the ten works which formed her *intellectual persona*. Mireille Delmas-Marty, '10 x 10' (2010) 8 International Journal of Constitutional Law 445.

[4] The working definition of an intercivilizational or trancivilizational approach is a perspective from which people see, sense, (re)cognize, interpret, assess, and seek to propose solutions for the ideas, activities, phenomena, and problems transcending national boundaries by adopting a cognitive and evaluative framework based on the recognition of the plurality of civilizations and cultures that have long existed throughout human history. Onuma Yasuaki, *International Law in Transcivilizational World* (CUP 2017) 10.

What is important when seeing things from the transcivilizational perspective is not to *substantialize* or *essentialize* them but regard them as functional concepts. A number of scholars who have addressed the problem of civilization (such as Arnold Toynbee, Oswald Spengler, and Samuel Huntington) have considered that a human belongs to a particular civilization exclusively. Thus they have tended to substantialize the concept of civilization, which has sometimes been abused to glorify a particular civilization while despising other civilizations and cultures. I have always argued that we should regard the concept of civilization and culture as functional concepts. ibid 20.

was the Law of International Society Born?' *Journal of the History of International Law*, vol.2 (2000). In this article, I demonstrated that the history of international law cannot be written as a history of *law* without exploring *how the non-European people* who had held their own normative systems *accepted the European international law*. Law can be valid as law only when its addressee recognizes it as law. If the so-called expansion of (European) international law occurred without such a recognition, then such a process cannot be the development of law. Only by being accepted, though reluctantly, by people in the non-Western world, could European international law become international *law* which is universally, ie, globally, valid as we see it today.

This article seemed to attract great interest among the experts of the history of international law. In 2004, the *Journal of the History of International Law* organized a journal symposium composed of five leading international lawyers and an international relations scholar, who reviewed this article.[5] Besides this journal symposium, the article has often been cited and referred to by international lawyers, international relations scholars, and historians.

As to the problem of the 'sources' of international law in relation to universality and international law, the first article I published was 'The ICJ: An Emperor Without Clothes?' in N Ando *et al*, eds, *Liber Amicorum Judge Shigeru Oda* (Kluwer Law International, The Hague 2002). In this article, I demonstrated that leading international lawyers addressing the problem of so-called 'sources' of international law assumed that the general practice among major Western powers represents the general practice of states as such. The practice of other nations was hardly considered or taken up. Underlying this approach is the assumption that regards what is general or common among major Western nations as general or universal as such.

In 2007, I gave lectures at the Hague Academy of International Law entitled 'A Transcivilizational Perspective on International Law'. They were published in the *Recueil des Cours*, vol. 342 (2009) and in the pocketbook form from Martinus Nijhoff in 2010. In these lectures and writings, I again sought to demonstrate that most international lawyers have assumed that what is common to the West (or Western Europe and/or the United States) is to be regarded as general or universal. When they refer to the 'general' theory or practice of law, it means the theory or practices of law common to major Western nations. When they refer to the universality of human rights or democracy, it means human rights or democracy common to major Western nations, to be accepted or recognized by other nations.

Finally, I published a treatise on international law entitled *International Law in a Transcivilizational World*, published by Cambridge University Press in 2017. In this treatise, I further sought to demonstrate how theories of international law in

---

[5] These reviewers are RP Anand (India), Antony Anghie (Sri Lanka/the United States), Jorg Fisch (Switzerland), Emmanuelle Jouannet (France), Li Zhaojie (China), and Nicholas Onuf (the United States, an international relations scholar).

general have been strongly influenced by international lawyers of the small number of leading Western nations, and how widely their assumption regarding what is Western is what is general, universal, or global, prevailed.

Based on these researches, I respectfully submit that the fundamental problem with universality and international law is the deeply-rooted and unconsciously shared *assumption* of an idea that equates what is Western with what is universal. It is naturally necessary and important to explore when, where, why, by whom, and how the idea of universality was invented. However, even more important and crucial for us, contemporary international lawyers, is to critically explore through what mechanism the West-centric assumption of universality, which is seriously flawed from the viewpoint of humanity, composed not only of Western people but also non-Western people, came to prevail, and to seek to overcome such a problematic assumption.

In the twenty-first-century world, conflicts over the current international legal order between existing Western powers and the resurging Asian powers represented by China will most likely occur in a frequent and serious manner. An important role international law is expected to play in such a world is to minimize such conflicts. For international law to play this critical role, it must liberate itself from a long-standing West-centric assumption equating what is Western with what is universal. Only by liberating ourselves from this outdated and unjustifiable assumption, can we international lawyers play a meaningful role in the twenty-first-century world. International law of our time is expected to carry out its diverse societal functions *against the background of power allocation among nations completely different from the days when it could assume the supremacy of Western nations over other nations*. We international lawyers must be aware of this critical change and accommodate ourselves to this new reality.

Some may miss the 'good old days', when West-centric international law could function in a relatively stable manner because this international law was the consequence of a 'natural' development of *European* international law. This international law is an indispensable component of Euro- or West-centric modernity. Like other components of West-centric modernity, it provided humanity with a number of benefits. But for non-Western nations, its negative side has been more apparent during the modern period: (1) in the pre-war days, most of them were under colonial rule, being deprived of the capacity to create and manage international law; and (2) even in the post-war period, they have been inferior to Western powers in making and implementing international law, although they represent the overwhelming majority of humanity. In the twenty-first century, now that non-Western nations are steadily becoming superior to Western nations in terms of power, it also becomes apparent that the assumption equating the 'Western' with 'universal', supported by the supremacy of the Western power in the twentieth century, can no longer be maintained.

6
L'Invention de l'Universalité du Droit International

Frédéric Mégret

En faisant le choix de présenter, rédiger et publier cette réflexion en français, je n'entends pas faire l'apologie de la francophonie mais poser de manière performative—en faisant!—la question de la diversité qui se niche au cœur de l'interrogation sur l'universel. L'anglais tend bien à devenir la langue universelle du droit international—on ne m'en voudra pas, j'espère, de « révéler » ce secret de polichinelle—mais par là même il trahit le particularisme de cet universel, désormais porté par la langue de Shakespeare, comme il a pu l'être dans le passé par le français ou le latin. Non pas justement que le français échappât à ce soupçon de particularisme auréolé de prétentions universalistes, bien au contraire, mais qu'il permette peut-être, justement de sa position d'idiome supplanté, de penser la contingence de cet universalisme.

Car, on ne saurait trop le dire, les particularités linguistiques à travers lesquelles le droit international s'exprime sont autant de démentis subtils à sa prétention à l'universalisme abstrait—à moins qu'il ne s'agisse de l'universalisme fertile des malentendus. Dans tous les cas, en réalité, la prétention à l'universalité du droit international émane bien de certains secteurs de la société internationale à des moments donnés de son développement et à des fins qui lui sont propres. Si l'on ne fera pas mine de s'en indigner, c'est que l'histoire *des* « universalismes » du droit international fait partie intégrante de sa filiation intellectuelle et de son devenir. L'universalisme comme projet intellectuel a été porté et continue d'être porté à certaines fins et par certains acteurs de la société internationale.

La question ici ne sera pas donc de savoir si le droit international est bien universel. Trop de réponses à cette interrogation se contentent de reprendre des clichés ou de partir du présupposé qu'elles sont censées démontrer. La question n'a guère de sens qui soit solvable dans les catégories du droit. On ne s'intéressera pas plus à la question de savoir si le droit international *devrait* être universel, question à notre sens trop normative et qui fait une part trop belle à une sorte de volontarisme abstrait. On n'exclura pas pour autant le rôle productif que le débat sur l'universalité puisse jouer dans la genèse, la mutation et même le renouveau du droit international—cela serait aussi intellectuellement malhonnête que faire porter l'entier édifice du droit international sur une affirmation péremptoire de son universalité. Mais on niera à la prétention à l'universalité ce qui lui est trop souvent reconnu sans discussion, à savoir son caractère axiomatique et d'évidence.

Il s'agira plutôt ici de s'interroger sur les conditions d'invention de l'universalité du droit international. De qui vient cette prétention? Quel rôle a-t-elle eu historiquement? A quelles fins a-t-elle été endossée et pour le compte de qui? C'est ici que le passage par le français s'impose peut-être à nouveau mais cette fois-ci pour une raison plus spécifique. La doctrine anglophone s'est, en définitive, assez peu intéressée spécifiquement à la question de l'universalité du droit international, comme si sa réalité s'était imposée à elle sans qu'il soit utile d'en sonder les sous-bassements conceptuels. C'est plutôt à un certain esprit continental que l'on doit l'aspiration à donner ses lettres de noblesse à l'universalité du droit international. Au sein de cette sensibilité continentale, la doctrine francophone a produit en nombre particulièrement généreux des penseurs du droit international pour qui l'universalité a agi comme un référent et même plus, une véritable anxiété.

Les internationalistes non-francophones contemporains de ces débats sur l'universalité du droit international le rendirent bien à la doctrine francophone et à ses obsessions universalistes puisque James Brown Scott[1] ou encore Hersch Lauterpacht[2] choisirent de s'exprimer en langue française spécifiquement sur cette question, de même que toute une génération de juristes latino-américains formés à l'école française dont il sera beaucoup question ici. On se surprend au passage parfois à rêver en découvrant le multilinguisme de ces internationalistes de langue anglaise prêts à apporter la contradiction dans une langue autre que la leur. Où l'on voit bien, en tous les cas, ce que ce genre d'interrogation doit à des trajectoires assez largement nationales puisqu'il est bien question, pour une certaine doctrine française issue des Lumières notamment, de tenter de réconcilier les idéaux universalistes républicains avec un droit international qui, somme toute, s'accommode assez bien d'une application très inégale.

On verra que cet accommodement ne posa pas de problème outre mesure jusqu'à une date assez tardive et qu'il fut matière à des retournements très prompts après que le déni d'universalité du droit international dut se rendre à l'évidence de son démenti. Mais justement, comment et au prix de quels processus doit-on « l'invention » de l'universalité du droit international? Sans doute s'agit-il d'un processus à la cristallisation lent et même cyclique—le droit international s'est imaginé universel à intervalle régulier lorsque, confronté à son altérité, il s'est agi d'étendre son champ d'application à de nouveaux entrants. Ceci n'exclut pas une historicité et même une datation spécifique du phénomène, bien au contraire.

---

[1] 'Discours de Mr James Brown Scott, Session de Lausanne. Août–Septembre 1927' (1927) 33 Annuaire de l'Institut de Droit International <www.idi-iil.org/app/uploads/2017/05/4025-33C_OCR.pdf>.
[2] Hersch Lauterpacht, 'Règles générales du droit de la paix' [1937] RCADI.

Au cœur de notre réflexion on voudra mettre la transformation relativement moderne d'un « droit public européen » à un droit qui se veut proprement international, entendu comme universel, processus enclenché notamment au début du XXème siècle (I). On envisagera ensuite l'émergence d'une réponse « régionaliste » aux prétentions du droit international à s'imposer à tous, américaine d'abord pendant l'entre-deux guerres mais aussi africaine ou asiatique par la suite, et qui mit volontiers l'accent sur les spécificités continentales, peut être au mépris de la revendication d'université du droit international (II). C'est largement en réponse à ces velléités que la réponse du droit international s'est organisée pour défendre son universalité, enfin, selon des modalités désormais bien établies au sein du discours internationaliste (III). Mettre en avant ce processus vieux de plus d'un siècle nous permettra en conclusion de dégager des pistes de réflexion sur ce que pourrait constituer une désinvention/réinvention du droit international entendu comme universel.

1. Si l'universel n'existait pas...

La grande histoire du droit international, du moins tel qu'il est connu et enseigné dans les facultés de manière dominante, est l'histoire de l'externalisation et de la généralisation graduelle d'un droit conçu à l'origine comme avant tout européen. C'est en devenant « extraverti » que ce droit traditionnellement « introverti » va poser certaines de ses questions fondatrices, reconcevoir ses fondements spécifiques et s'offrir au monde comme une approche généralisable et reproductible sinon à l'infini du moins à l'endroit de ceux susceptibles d'émuler l'organisation politique européenne. Il est vrai que l'on peine désormais à imaginer un droit international autre qu'universel dans sa théorie du moins, tant cette universalité est devenue partie constituante de la prétention du droit international à quelque légitimité.

Pour autant, le passage du relatif provincialisme du droit international européen au droit international public que nous connaissons ne va pas sans difficulté. La question de son application en dehors de son berceau civilisationnel resta longtemps une question pour le moins débattue et dont l'issue n'allait a priori guère dans le sens d'une extension, encore moins sur un pied d'égalité. Contrairement à une certaine vulgate internationaliste, l'universalisme du droit international serait même une (ré)invention récente, pour ne pas dire opportuniste. Comment en aurait-il pu être autrement, en effet, dès lors que le droit international était partie prenante d'une domination impériale du monde explicitement fondée sur une application inégale du droit?

Je voudrais pour commencer remonter au XIXème quand la question de l'universalisme commence à se poser dans des termes modernes—fut-ce pour y répondre par un démenti cinglant. Prenons un auteur qui a particulièrement traité de la question de l'universalisme avant la lettre. Henry Bonfils, professeur aux facultés de droit de Toulouse, se prononce dans son Manuel de droit international public dans les termes suivants:

> nous ne croyons pas à l'universalité future du droit des gens. La participation des Etats musulmans, de la Chine, etc, au droit public européen pourra devenir plus intense et plus étendue. Les règles juridiques, réciproquement adoptées, seront de plus en plus nombreuses et importantes. Ce résultat est désirable. Mais l'uniformité intégrale ne s'établira jamais. Un fossé, moins large, mais aussi plus profond et aussi infranchissable séparera toujours les Etats européens et américains, et leurs colonies, des Etats musulmans et de l'Empire du Milieu.[3]

C'est ici le caractère occidental du droit international qui en interdit in fine l'extension à des peuplades non-occidentales. Remarquons au passage que bien entendu l'Afrique ne figure même pas aux candidats à l'inclusion. La non-susceptibilité des extra-occidentaux au droit international est étayée et fondée sur un diagnostic profond de l'incommensurabilité des cultures:

> Les conditions sociales et politiques, dans lesquelles vivent les peuples musulmans ou les chinois, sont incompatibles avec l'idée de pleine communauté internationale. Comme toutes les sciences morales, le droit international dépend essentiellement de l'éducation de l'âme humaine, de ses croyances et de ses aspirations. Il s'est agrandi, il s'est élevé, quand s'est agrandi, quand s'est élevé le respect de la nature humaine—Or, une dissemblance profonde existe entre la conception de la vie d'après les idées chrétiennes et la conception de cette même vie d'après le Coran. L'âme des peuples chrétiens ne ressemble point à celle des sectateurs de Mahomet, de Confucius ou de Bouddha.[4]

Et Bonfils d'enchaîner en citant pêle-mêle le fanatisme religieux, une différente conception du progrès confinant à l'immobilité, une conception non-territoriale et nomadique de l'Etat, ou encore des mœurs différentes, etc. Assurément, cette position n'est pas isolée; dans sa fausse tolérance de l'autre, elle serait même progressiste pour l'époque puisque Bonfils se range parmi ceux qui se refusent à cautionner la mission civilisatrice, même s'ils se gardent de s'opposer à l'impérialisme.[5] En réalité, parler de droit international à l'époque signifie le plus souvent se référer au droit

---

[3] Henry Auteur du texte Bonfils, *Manuel de droit international public (droit des gens): destiné aux étudiants des facultés de droit et aux aspirants aux fonctions diplomatiques et consulaires ([Reprod.]) / par Henry Bonfils,...* (1894) 904 <https://gallica.bnf.fr/ark:/12148/bpt6k93520j> accessed 20 August 2018.
[4] ibid 904–05.
[5] Andrew Fitzmaurice, 'Skepticism of the Civilizing Mission in International Law' in Martti Koskenniemi, Walter Rech, and Manuel Jiménez Fonseca (eds), *International Law and Empire: Historical Explorations* (OUP 2016).

des gens européens. Bien loin de prétendre à l'universalité, le droit international a d'abord et avant tout été conçu comme le droit d'une collectivité particulière, fut elle multiple à son échelle. Jusqu'au tournant du siècle, il est courant de se référer à un « droit international public européen » ou même « américain » entendu au sens de l'Amérique du Nord.[6]

Comment passe-t-on de cette position répandue jusqu'aux premières décennies du XXème siècle à une position de prétention à l'universalité du droit international? Par quel retournement *le déni de l'universalité devient-il le postulat de l'universalité*? Par une sorte de révisionnisme historique un peu court, la prétention à l'universalisme est souvent présentée comme ayant présidé à la naissance même du droit international. Il est vrai que les scolastiques de Salamanque avaient envisagé un projet de droit international empreint d'un cosmopolitisme indéniable, mais il s'agissait de l'universalisme d'un centre imaginant ses relations avec une périphérie.[7] Quant à la paix de Westphalie, évènement souvent présenté comme fondateur du droit international classique, c'est au prix d'un sérieux révisionnisme que l'on en fait un événement d'emblée à vocation mondiale.

On suggèrera ici que la (re)découverte de l'universel revêt en réalité dans un premier temps un caractère assez opportuniste. Du fait de l'économie d'obligations et de prérogatives qui caractérisent le droit international, dénier son application en dehors de l'Europe est aussi se priver d'un outil de contrôle social international et d'extension de l'hégémonie européenne. L'application inégale du droit international devient simultanément de plus en plus difficile à soutenir face à des entités qui s'alignent sur les standards civilisationnels occidentaux et entendent en réclamer le plein dividende. Dans ce contexte, c'est bien à une mutation subtile de la conception fondamentale du droit international que l'on assiste et qui va largement accompagner ce mouvement. Au XIXème, la participation au droit international est encore perçue avant tout comme un privilège. On conserve alors volontiers le bénéfice du droit international à ses Etats d'origine, pour mieux en dénier le bénéfice aux nouveaux venus. On retrouve cette idée dans le célèbre traité de Paris de 1856 dont l'article 2 admet la Sublime Porte "à participer aux avantages du droit public et du concert Européens," sans pour autant d'ailleurs remettre en question le régime des capitulations. Le droit international sert ainsi en même temps à affirmer la souveraineté des Etats européens et à traiter avec d'autres entités sur un pied d'inégalité.

En effet, si l'on dénie aux Etats de la périphérie les avantages d'un statut souverain, on leur en dénie aussi les obligations. Or comme le montre déjà le traité de Paris, les temps changent. L'impérialisme se traduit par une pénétration toujours plus poussée des intérêts commerciaux des puissances européennes qui

---

[6] Paul Pradier-Fodéré, *Traité de droit international public européen & américain: suivant les progrès de la science et de la pratique contemporaines* (G Pedine-Lauriel 1885).
[7] Antony Anghie, *Imperialism, Sovereignty, and the Making of International Law* (CUP 2005).

entendent normaliser leurs rapports avec les jeunes et agitées républiques latino-américaines notamment. Dès lors que ces Etats n'acceptent plus le simple fait de l'impérialisme européen—la diplomatie de la canonnière, ou le type de régime d'extra-territorialité qui règne en terres ottomanes, perses ou chinoises—il s'agira désormais au minimum de leur imposer le droit international. La grande affaire à l'époque est en effet bien d'enchâsser ces premiers candidats extra-européens (encore que, fait qui a son importance, perçus comme descendants d'européens) dans un carcan d'obligations, notamment en ce qui a trait à la protection des investissements et des « étrangers. » James Brown Scott résume avec une formule concise le quid pro quo ainsi enclenché:

> Quand un Etat est reconnu et admis dans la communauté il obtient des droits et est sujet à des devoirs. Quels sont ces droits? La souveraineté et la dignité de nationalité que la communauté n'avait pas accordées ou reconnues jusqu'à son admission. Quels sont les devoirs? Obéissance des principes, lois et usages reconnus par la communauté des Etats civilisés et dont le but est de tempérer, par leur stricte observation, le recours à la guerre et ses misères sans nombre.[8]

En somme, la souveraineté est certes une dignité mais elle est aussi une discipline, à laquelle on espère bien astreindre les nouveaux venus, et ce d'autant que l'Occident entend garder en grande partie le monopole évolutif de la définition des obligations découlant du droit international. Les juristes internationaux passent en quelques générations du déni d'application du droit international en dehors du monde européen, à l'affirmation péremptoire de son applicabilité à tous. Ils le font au nom de la propre crise qu'a subi le modèle européen à l'issue de la Première guerre mondiale mais aussi parce que cet universalisme est un puissant ressort de sa légitimité. Nous ne saurions, en quelque sorte, vous « imposer » le droit international, puisqu'il est, au prix de quelques détours historiques, aussi le vôtre, l'émanation ou d'une conscience collective ou de conditions sociales ou d'un a priori catégorique commun à tous! Par cet habile tour de passe-passe, l'on fait vite oublier que le plein bénéfice du droit international fut longtemps dénié à ce dont on entend en faire les nouveaux bénéficiaires.

Tels sont donc les termes que les internationalistes du tournant du siècle offrent aux « nouveaux venus », du moins ceux qui sont suffisamment proches de ce que le droit international imagine comme étant un niveau de développement suffisant. Or par rapport à cette invitation, deux attitudes se dessinent l'une plutôt docile que l'on associera principalement au Japon et l'autre plus rétive qui émane de l'Amérique latine. La trajectoire nippone d'intégration à la société internationale tend à renforcer l'universalisme du droit international sans lui opposer une très

---

[8] 'Discours de Mr James Brown Scott, Session de Lausanne. Août–Septembre 1927' (n 1) 31.

forte résistance. Le Japon met l'Occident devant le fait accompli de sa civilisation et de son adéquation au système international, provoquant une forte crise au passage mais qui ne remet point en question la nature même du droit international.[9] L'universalité se paie ici d'une absence de contestation de l'ordre existant, ou alors tardive comme avec la tentative de faire adopter une clause d'égalité raciale à Versailles. Elle s'exposera d'ailleurs à un rejet sans appel, preuve que l'intégration du Japon dans la société internationale avait toujours été conçue par les occidentaux sur le mode sinon d'une capitulation du moins d'un abandon.

2. La voie de l'insoumission? A propos des « Droits Internationaux Régionaux »

Face à cette voie de l'assimilation dans la société internationale, d'autres régions vont plutôt tenter de creuser le sillon d'un dissensus par rapport à une universalité dont le bénéfice leur a été trop longtemps dénié ou a servi d'assise à l'iniquité des rapports internationaux. La Société européenne de droit international consacra au thème du régionalisme sa conférence de 2012.[10] Il ne s'agira pas ici de répéter les excellentes réflexions qui furent engagées à cette occasion, mais de noter que le « régionalisme » est l'un des pendants de l'universalisme. Non pas que les deux soient nécessairement incompatibles, comme on le verra, mais qu'au moins dans une certaine acception le régionalisme puisse-t-il aller jusqu'à remettre en cause la prétention à l'universalisme. Il faut sans doute ici distinguer le « régionalisme au sein du droit international » comme simple phénomène de rapprochement entre Etats d'une même région selon des règles propres mais ne visant pas à remettre en cause les règles du droit international général (quitte à prétendre n'être plus une branche du droit international) d'un « régionalisme *du* droit international » lequel entend incarner une conception distincte de celle du droit international universel. C'est cette deuxième conception, parfois liée à la première mais néanmoins distincte, qui nous intéressera ici.

Les républiques sud-américaines les premières s'illustrent par une approche plus insoumise. L'Amérique latine a comme le Japon été victime de la diplomatie de la canonnière et est bien placée pour réclamer son intégration dans la société internationale de plein droit, d'autant que ses élites créoles se conçoivent comme une émanation de l'Occident. En même temps les juristes latino-américains font montre d'une certaine ambivalence par rapport à cette intégration et le prix que leurs pays risqueraient de payer pour leur reconnaissance comme membres de

---

[9] Yasuaki Onuma, *Le droit international et le Japon: une vision trans-civilisationnelle du monde* (Pedone 2015).
[10] Mariano J Aznar and Mary E Footer (eds), *Select Proceedings of the European Society of International Law* (Bloomsbury Publishing 2016).

la société internationale à part entière. Tout se passe comme si ceux à qui on a longtemps dénié le plein bénéfice du droit international ou à qui on a imposé un droit international qu'ils perçoivent comme profondément inégalitaire répugnent désormais à s'y intégrer totalement.

C'est dans ce cadre que certains iront jusqu'à remettre en question l'universalité du droit international, ou en tous les cas du primat et de l'exclusivité du droit international général. On pense notamment à la fameuse controverse sur le « droit international américain » initiée par une série d'éminents juristes chiliens, argentins ou encore colombiens. De Alvarez à Yepes,[11] on voit apparaître une véritable volonté d'émancipation du droit international en Amérique latine, peut être d'autant plus troublante qu'elle vient de pays dont les élites appartiennent à la sphère culturelle européenne. Cette volonté est fondée sur une défense des spécificités de la région, mais aussi sur une critique plus fondamentale de l'universalisme comme si les internationalistes du continent prenaient un malin plaisir à prendre leurs collègues européens au mot lorsqu'ils disent que le droit international n'est pas (vraiment) universel, et à surenchérir dans ce sens, affirmant désormais l'existence de droits internationaux régionaux dont la vocation est d'échapper au moins pour partie à l'emprise du droit international.

Cette controverse est un peu oubliée aujourd'hui[12] mais elle fit date et est intéressante à rappeler à une époque où le « comparative international law » revient sur le devant de la scène.[13] Pour Alvarez, il n'y aurait « aucune utilité ni aucune nécessité à ce que les règles du droit international soient universelles; ce serait se placer à un point de vue très étroit que de vouloir appliquer des règles nées ou posées dans des conditions déterminées à des cas ou situations que l'on ne pouvait prévoir ».[14] Le droit international se devait donc d'être au moins tant particulier qu'universel. Insister sur l'existence d'un droit international américain c'était dès lors insister sur la possibilité d'un droit international différent ainsi qu'une manière de tenir l'Europe à l'écart. En termes de gouvernance il est même suggéré à partir des années 30 que l'Union panaméricaine devra avoir compétence pour certaines questions régionales, et la SdN uniquement pour les questions globales. Provocatrices à l'époque, ces prises de position étaient destinées à être assumées avec une nouvelle vigueur par après, surtout dès lors que certains efforts de régionalisation auront fait naître des formes de droit supranationales dont le rapport avec le droit international demeure ambigu.

---

[11] Jesús María Yepes, *Les problèmes fondamentaux du droit des gens en Amérique*, vol 34 (1934).

[12] Malgré un regain d'intérêt et le fait qu'elle puisse être revisitée selon des modalités plus contemporaines, voir Arnulf Becker Lorca, 'International Law in Latin America or Latin American International Law—Rise, Fall, and Retrieval of a Tradition of Legal Thinking and Political Imagination Symposium: Comparative Visions of Global Public Order (Part 2)' (2006) 47 Harvard International Law Journal 283.

[13] Anthea Roberts and others, *Comparative International Law* (OUP 2018).

[14] Alejandro Alvarez, *Le droit international américain: son fondement-sa nature d'après l'histoire diplomatique des états du nouveau monde et leur vie politique et économique* (A Pedone 1910) 264.

Dans la pratique, les Etats latino-américains ayant obtenu la plus grande partie de ce qu'ils espéraient, les prétentions à un droit distinct se feront cependant petit à petit plus rares, comme si le « droit international américain » avait été plus une menace qu'un réel projet. Si la controverse ne survécut guère à la Seconde Guerre Mondiale, elle traça néanmoins un sillon qui problématisait la nécessaire universalité du droit international, ou en tous les cas de son universalité selon des modalités prioritairement occidentales. D'autres emboîteront le pas, à commencer par certains auteurs africains qui ont entrevu très tôt après les indépendances la possibilité d'un droit international en même temps émanant de caractéristiques africaines et répondant de manière prépondérante à des défis et circonstances régionaux.[15]

Comment évaluer aujourd'hui la pertinence et le caractère réellement novateur de ces tentatives de régionaliser le droit international et donc, d'une certaine façon, de dénier ou bien d'énoncer les limites de l'universalisme? Que reste-t-il intellectuellement du « droit international américain » et de ses héritiers? Pour certains, la revendication d'une approche régionale du droit international aura fait un peu figure de position de négociation, une sorte d'épouvantail pour mieux rediscuter des termes du droit international. A certains égards, Alvarez semble seulement réclamer le bénéfice pour l'Amérique latine de principes qui caractérisaient autrefois le droit public européen (égalité des Etats, respect des frontières). Pour certains commentateurs écrivant de nos jours tels Liliana Obregon[16] ou Carl Laundaeur,[17] Alvarez chercherait d'ailleurs plus à réhabiliter une vision des contributions sud-américaines au droit international général qu'à fournir véritablement le cadre d'un droit distinct. La pensée créole, en quelque sorte, n'aspirerait en définitive qu'à une reconnaissance sur un plein pied d'égalité de sa participation à la civilisation.[18]

La demande de reconnaissance d'un droit latino-américain demeure en outre ambiguë. Certains tenteront d'adoucir le propos d'Alvarez en soulignant la grande complémentarité d'un éventuel droit international américain et du droit international général. A une époque où l'Europe entame les balbutiements de sa propre unification, certains juristes colombiens ont beau jeu d'insister que « ces groupements s'efforcent de resserrer leurs rapports mutuels sans que cela implique

---

[15] Joseph-Marie Bipoun-Woum, *Le droit international africain—problèmes généraux—règlement des conflits* (LGDJ 1970).
[16] Liliana Obregón, 'Noted for Dissent: The International Life of Alejandro Álvarez' (2006) 19 Leiden Journal of International Law.
[17] Carl Landauer, 'A Latin American in Paris: Alejandro Álvarez's *Le droit international américain*' (2006) 19 Leiden Journal of International Law 957.
[18] Liliana Obregón, 'Regionalism (Re)Constructed: A Short History of "Latin American International Law"' in Mariano Aznar and Mary Footer (eds), *Select Proceedings of the European Society of International Law* (Bloomsbury Publishing 2012) <https://papers.ssrn.com/abstract=2193749> accessed 22 June 2020.

qu'ils veuillent constituer une communauté internationale spéciale, séparée de la communauté mondiale."[19] Et de continuer:

> Comme il est fréquent d'entendre dire que l'Union panaméricaine, de même que ce qu'on appelle le droit international américain, constituent une atteinte à l'universalité du droit des gens, nous croyons qu'une mise au point est nécessaire pour dissiper ces malentendus. Personne n'a jamais soutenu, à notre connaissance, qu'il existe un droit international exclusivement américain, c'est-à-dire établi uniquement à l'usage des Etats du Nouveau Monde et entièrement distinct du droit international universel. Mais personne ne nie, non plus, actuellement qu'en Amérique il y a des problèmes, des doctrines, des situations nettement américains et que pour les résoudre on a souvent recours à des principes d'origine américaine. L'ensemble de ces problèmes, doctrines et situations, constitue ce que l'on appelle ordinairement le droit international américain. Ce droit, ainsi compris, n'est nullement une antithèse du droit international universel mais, au contraire, son complément.[20]

Il convient d'ailleurs de souligner que l'idée d'un « droit international américain » fait l'objet d'une réception mitigée auprès d'autres juristes latino-américains, qui reprennent à leur compte l'idée européenne de la nécessaire universalité du droit international.[21] Certains auteurs associés au régionalisme juridique africain sembleront également hésiter sur l'ampleur du phénomène et l'aborder avec une abondance de réserve. Bipoun Woun décrit même le régionalisme « comme le plus sûr moyen de sauvegarder [l']unité du droit international ».[22] De fait, un « régionalisme à caractère universaliste » est bien envisageable comme le souligne Mathias Forteau, dont la finalité serait moins de « se distancier de la société internationale » que de « revendiquer l'égale souveraineté des différents membres de celle-ci de manière à pouvoir y participer pleinement, sans craindre l'interventionnisme européen ».[23]

Il est également vrai, cependant, que l'ambition des droits internationaux régionaux a été pour partie de dépasser le droit international ou du moins d'en faire résonner une conception singulière au sein d'un véritable pluralisme international. Certains principes comme le non-usage de la force ou le respect des frontières ne faisaient pas partie, lorsqu'ils furent en premier proclamés par des

---

[19] Société des nations. Relations entre la société des Nations et l'Union Panaméricaine, Lettre, en date du 26 septembre 1934, de la délégation de la Colombie au Président de l'Assemblée, 1934, p 2. <https://biblio-archive.unog.ch/Dateien/CouncilMSD/C-434-M-189-1934_FR.pdf>.
[20] id 2.
[21] Obregón (n 18).
[22] Bipoun-Woum (n 15).
[23] Mathias Forteau, 'Commentaire sur de Hoogh et Pulkowski' in Mariano J Aznar and Mary E Footer (eds), *Select Proceedings of the European Society of International Law, Volume 4, 2012* (Bloomsbury Publishing 2016) 89.

juristes latino-américains, de l'acquis général du droit international. Par une sorte de mécanisme de vases communicants, certains « passèrent » cependant par la suiteau droit international général. Le régionalisme aurait, en quelque sorte, été coopté dans l'universel. D'autres principes demeurent d'une amplitude plus spécifiquement régionale. On pense par exemple à toute une série d'idées mettant les relations internationales sous le signe d'une solidarité bien éloignée de l'atomisme westphalien. Encore faut-il se demander si la proclamation de ces principes fait l'objet d'un début d'effectivité et de spécificité suffisants pour tracer une voie réellement distincte.[24] Les différences entre divers droits régionaux et le droit international général sont en effet parfois tellement subtiles et contingentes qu'elles semblent ne guère déstabiliser le droit international dans ses fondements. Lauterpacht interpelle en ces termes les juristes américains:

> Il est extrêmement difficile d'obtenir des partisans de cet aspect particulier du régionalisme qu'ils indiquent dans le détail quelles sont les doctrines spécifiques du droit international américain. Ils mentionneront la doctrine uti possidetis, mais c'est là un principe technique relatif à la délimitation des frontières des Etats qui ont succédé à l'Empire espagnol en Amérique. Ils citeront l'arbitrage comme le principe par lequel se règlent les litiges territoriaux en Amérique; mais ce n'est pas là, certainement, un idéal plus respecté des Etats américains que des autres nations. Ils invoqueront la liberté d'expatriation et d'immigration; mais ici encore ces principes ont été adoptés, en partie, par les Etats non américains et abandonnés en partie par les Etats américains eux-mêmes.[25]

Quoiqu'il en soit de leurs faiblesses, ces défis régionaux mobilisèrent comme on va le voir une forte réponse au terme de laquelle les juristes internationaux poseront les fondements de la prétention contemporaine à l'universalité du droit international.

3. Réaffirmation du caractère universel du droit international face aux régionalismes

Le régionalisme en matière de droit international fait l'objet d'une réception mitigée mais non nécessairement hostile de la part des juristes européens, notamment dans des périodes de crise où la prétention à l'universalité du droit international paraît dure à maintenir: on tente alors, en quelque sorte, de sauver ce qui peut encore être sauvé. La démarche sud-américaine de l'entre-deux guerres, par exemple, est accueillie plutôt chaleureusement par les internationalistes et s'inscrit dans une

---

[24] PF Gonidec, 'Existe-t-il un droit international africain?' (1993) 5 African Journal of International and Comparative Law 243.
[25] Lauterpacht (n 2) para 39.

redécouverte de ce qu'un régionalisme tempéré pourrait contribuer à l'édification d'une véritable société internationale.[26] La résolution de 1926 de l'Union juridique internationale reconnaît certes l'« unité du Droit international attesté par la conscience humaine […] et manifestée par des actes répétés et concordants de solidarité qui ont trouvé leur expression la plus haute dans l'institution de la Société des Nations », mais remarque:

> … en même temps que des règles spéciales dues à des conditions géographiques et historiques particulières peuvent se former soit entre Nations d'une même région, soit entre Nations de continent à continent et qu'au lieu de porter atteinte à l'universalité du droit international, base fondamentale de son autorité, ces règles la complètent et la fortifient en donnant une expression nuancée aux particularismes dont la variété harmonieuse fait la richesse de l'unité humaine.[27]

Il est vrai qu'Alvarez ne propose rien de beaucoup plus radical qu'une fierté blessée et ne s'engage guère, par exemple, sur le chemin d'une réévaluation des présupposés profonds du droit international européen, à commencer par sa suffisance raciale, et ce jusque dans les républiques latino-américaines. Les efforts d'institutionnalisation d'une gouvernance régionale américaine s'inscrivent dans un moment d'essoufflement de la Société des Nations, laquelle cherche à renforcer l'assise du droit international en y intéressant des Etats perçus comme périphériques. En outre, cette esquisse de régionalisation du droit international trouve un relai opportun dans le fait que l'Europe elle-même—qui en grande partie se retrouve seule à la Société des Nations—est tentée par une voie régionaliste. Yepès ne fait-il pas mine de redécouvrir avec une ironie certaine, au détour d'une défense du droit international américain, que s'il « existe un droit international particulier aux républiques du nouveau monde, il doit y avoir un droit particulier aux Etats de l'Europe […] »[28]

En réalité, l'Europe de la Société des nations est dans les années 30 dans une position beaucoup trop faible pour imposer une conception rigide de son universalisme. Dans l'entre-deux guerres, Alvarez trouve donc des relais intellectuels chez certains auteurs européens. Georges Scelle par exemple s'interroge sur l'universalisme de la SdN et trouve quelques mérites au régionalisme.[29] L'Europe serait prête à « lâcher du lest », certaines de ses têtes pensantes étant sans doute déjà

---

[26] Jean-Michel Guieu, '« Société universelle des nations » et « sociétés continentales ». Les juristes internationalistes euro-américains et la question du régionalisme européen dans les années 1920' [2015] Siècles. Cahiers du Centre d'histoire « Espaces et Cultures » <http://journals.openedition.org/siecles/2584> accessed 22 June 2020.
[27] Union juridique internationale, 1926, cité dans Jose Ramon de Orue y Arregui, 'Le régionalisme dans l'organisation internationale' (1935) 53 Recueil des Cours Collected Courses of the Hague Academy of International Law 21.
[28] *Recueil Des Cours 1947* (Martinus Nijhoff 1968) 242.
[29] Jean-Michel Guieu, 'Fédérer l'Europe ou subir une nouvelle catastrophe' (2000) 3 Hypotheses 47.

trop conscientes de son déclin. Il s'agit cependant là plus d'une position tactique à un moment où l'Europe est de plus en plus esseulée à Genève et tentée par un repli, ;qis conserverait néanmoins des alliances et des relais en Amérique latine.

Pour autant, l'américanisation du droit international est incontestablement à l'origine d'une sorte d'inquiétude sourde chez les juristes internationalistes, qui y voient une menace pour la SDN mais aussi pour le droit international de façon plus générale. Il est donc notable que malgré le caractère relativement anémique du défi porté par la notion de droit international régional et malgré un contexte géopolitique qui y est plutôt favorable, les juristes internationalistes considèrent que le droit international a trop à y perdre et montent au créneau pour défendre une notion d'universalité somme toute assez récente pour la discipline. L'affirmation de l'unité du droit international se traduit alors par une tentative de présenter le droit international comme un modèle universel indépassable malgré ces contestations.[30] C'est en particulier James Brown Scott qui se trouve à la tête de cet effort de réfutation du régionalisme, notamment dans un discours de 1927 à l'Institut de Droit International:

> Jusqu'à présent, on ne considère pas la géographie comme source du droit des gens et si l'Angleterre, malgré sa position insulaire et sa conception individualiste, ne peut se séparer du continent même par la Manche, on ne pourrait croire que les quelques gouttes d'eau qui forment l'Océan Atlantique peuvent avoir cette conséquence funeste. Malgré la distance et une vaste étendue d'eau, malgré les tempêtes qui rendent souvent la traversée dangereuse, le droit des gens ne s'y est pas noyé. (...) Le droit international ne s'occupe pas des Continents qui ne sont pas comme tels membres de la communauté internationale. Il s'occupe exclusivement des Etats qui sont eux membres de la communauté internationale, abstraction faite du Continent où ils se trouvent au point de vue géographique. La conception du droit international est par sa définition même universelle. Les sources: droit naturel, jus gentium, droit romain, us et coutumes, sont toutes d'origine universelle.[31]

Mais d'où vient, justement, que le droit international serait universel? C'est d'abord à raison des situations que le droit international se doit de résoudre qu'il devrait sa nécessaire constance au-delà des continents—argument qui semble répliquer point pour point une des inspirations d'Alvarez, mais pour mieux la réfuter. La pensée de Scott a de forts relents naturalistes lorsqu'il affirme que:

> Les situations que le droit de gens doit régler sont internationales et les problèmes qui se présentent à l'internationaliste surgissent de la vie internationale. Les

---

[30] Bipoun-Woum (n 15).
[31] 'Discours de Mr James Brown Scott, Session de Lausanne. Août-Septembre 1927' (n 1) 47.

> besoins de la communauté internationale sont universels; le droit l'est aussi, nécessairement, et toutes les nations, malgré la religion, malgré la géographie, malgré leurs prétentions matérielles et spirituelles, s'inclinent ex necessitate devant le droit des gens universel. C'est la vérité fatale de l'histoire.[32]

Plus profondément, Scott et d'autres insistent d'abord sur l'existence en tant que telle d'une communauté internationale: « ubi communitas gentium ibi jus inter gentes—or qui dit communauté internationale, dit droit des gens, rendant un droit international unique une nécessité inéluctable:

> cette coexistence implique un droit supérieur de la conscience universelle, juridique et morale, sous le contrôle de l'intelligence et de la raison humaine. Les lois sont d'après Montesquieu les rapports nécessaires des choses [...] Dans le droit international, comme dans la mathématique universelle, le tout est plus grand que n'importe quelle partie qui le compose. Il y a une primauté du droit international; le droit de la communauté internationale doit être et est, en effet, un droit universel autant que la communauté et qui exclus, par la force des choses et par définition, le droit de n'importe quel groupement des Etats de la communauté. Le droit international doit primer le droit national et dans la communauté des Etats conscients de son existence et de ses responsabilités, il finira par s'imposer à n'importe quel Etat ou quel groupement d'Etats, même à la Fédération des Etats Unis d'Amérique, même à tous les Etats d'un continent[33]

Dans ces conditions, le consentement de tous les Etats est-il même réellement nécessaire? Scott répond par la positive « au point de vue logique » mais note également que « le consentement de presque tous les Etats témoigné par les us et coutumes et la pratique de la communauté internationale de la presque totalité, fait présumer le consentement de tous ». Plus encore:

> Le droit des gens est la conséquence pratique d'une nécessité universelle, à cause de la coexistence des Etats, de résoudre les problèmes qui se sont présentés à chacun des Etats civilisés. C'était le droit de chacun des Etats dont l'existence était reconnue par les membres de la communauté internationale, due à leur simple existence étatique. Pour des conditions universelles, pour des faits universels, pour des problèmes universels, il fallait un droit universel avec des règles universelles.[34]

---

[32] ibid 64. Voir également Lauterpacht (n 2) (« le droit international universel s'entend des « règles de droit international que, en examinant les sources du droit des nations, nous avons décrites comme fondées sur l'existence même d'une société d'Etats et sur la supposition même de l'existence du droit international. Elles complètent le droit international accepté; elles le dominent; elles en forment l'arrière-plan. »).
[33] 'Discours de Mr James Brown Scott, Session de Lausanne. Août–Septembre 1927' (n 1) 36.
[34] ibid 53.

Moins métaphysique, Henri Rolin proposait plutôt lui une vision du droit international comme la sagesse spécifique léguée par l'Europe au reste du monde:

> Il n'est que temps [...] qu'un grand effort soit entrepris pour convaincre ces nouveaux Etats que loin d'être une œuvre artificielle, le droit des gens est né de l'expérience plusieurs fois séculaire des peuples et de la connaissance qu'ils ont acquise au cours de l'histoire des règles essentielles qui doivent nécessairement présider aux relations entre les Etats.[35]

Enfin, en termes doctrinaux, la conception souple et évolutive du droit international s'accommode en réalité assez bien des particularités régionales, dès lors que celles-ci ne viennent pas corrompre l'édifice universel. On y verra pour preuve, par exemple, l'idée que le droit international « particulier » est une évidence largement acceptée en marge du droit international « général. » Il n'en demeure pas moins que, dans une société internationale de plus en plus marquée par la norme péremptoire et la diffusion des pratiques juridiques, de forts phénomènes d'unification se manifestent qui peuvent être contredits par une importance trop grande donnée au fait régional. C'est ce contre quoi met en garde en définitive Lauterpacht:

> l'insistance apportée à défendre le droit international régional devient rétrograde et décevante lorsqu'elle se joint à une appréciation défectueuse du droit international universel ou à une dénégation de sa supériorité ultime. Car ce n'est que par référence au droit international universel qu'il est possible de comprendre le droit international régional. Même si le droit international régional était si complet qu'il couvrit toutes les branches du droit international, on ressentirait encore le besoin impérieux d'un droit international universel afin d'unifier et d'ajuster les différents systèmes de droit international régional.[36]

Dans cette optique, l'universalité revêt elle-même rien moins qu'un caractère impératif, comme une sorte de postulat qui tiendrait à lui seul lieu de promesse d'unité, de caractère obligatoire et d'exemplarité pour le droit international.

4. Conclusion

Quel est le legs de cette « invention » de l'universalisme au XXème siècle? L'universalisme du droit international s'est-il établi de manière définitive à la suite de ces débats? Dans une certaine mesure, le combat pour l'universalisme apparaît

---

[35] Henri Rolin, 'Le droit des gens en 1961' (1961) 14 Chronique de politique étrangère 487, 492.
[36] Lauterpacht (n 2) para 39.

comme un combat gagné d'avance, tant le régionalisme est lui-même défendu avec une certaine ambiguïté. Ce serait donc bien le régionalisme qui a été absorbé par le droit international. Notant la « force d'attraction irrésistible du droit international », Prosper Weil affirmera, à la haute époque des luttes d'indépendance coloniale, que:

> Un Etat, ou un groupe d'Etats, a beau avoir la tentation de faire le droit international à part, cette velléité cède rapidement devant la nécessité—qui est celle précisément qui a conduit il y a plusieurs siècles à imaginer le droit international— de faire vivre côté à côté, sous la protection d'un système unique de normes, des Etats fondamentalement hétérogènes.[37]

L'universalité du droit international est peut-être d'autant plus tenace qu'elle se déploie comme une protection du pluralisme inhérent à la société internationale, ce qui fit remarquer à Dirk Pulkowski que « regional international law may add to the value pluralism within the international legal order but does not thereby qualitatively change international law into something other than it already is ».[38] Les juristes internationaux ont d'ailleurs adopté, de prime abord, une attitude compréhensive par rapport aux velléités régionalistes tant qu'elles s'inscrivent dans le cadre souple du « droit international particulier » et ce bien au-delà de la brève période d'exploration du régionalisme ouverte dans les années 30 à la SDN. A l'inverse, l'universalité des droits humains fera beaucoup plus débat car elle est perçue comme une véritable immixtion d'autorité dans les affaires internes des Etats. Par comparaison, le droit international ne proposerait qu'un universalisme superficiel et peu contraignant—mais par là même assez résistant à sa contestation.

Dans le meilleur des cas, en outre, le droit international aura été modifié au gré de l'incorporation de pans entiers de la société internationale—le régionalisme aura alors rapidement servi son rôle revendicatif, et ne sera plus dès lors d'une grande utilité. Les Etats latino-américains auront ainsi monnayé leur pleine entrée dans le jeu international—agitant la menace finalement assez hypothétique d'un sécessionnisme intellectuel qui eut amputé le droit international d'une grande partie de ce qui était imaginé comme son assise naturelle. La nécessité de promouvoir un droit international spécifiquement américain se sera faite moins pressante dès lors que les Etats européens acceptent la doctrine Drago ou la clause Calvo.[39]

---

[37] Prosper Weil, *Le droit international en quête de son identité: Cours général de droit international public* (Martinus Nijhoff 1996) 85.

[38] Dirk Pulkowski, 'Theoretical Premises of "Regionalism and the Unity of International Law"' in Mariano J Aznar and Mary E Footer (eds), *Select Proceedings of the European Society of International Law, Volume 4, 2012* (Bloomsbury Publishing 2016) 84.

[39] Charles De Visscher, *Theory and Reality in Public International Law* (Princeton University Press 2015) 161.

Sociologiquement, l'Institut de Droit International commence à partir des années 30, sous l'impulsion de Henri Rolin, à diversifier ses membres, pressentant bien que le droit international a besoin de recruter au-delà de l'Europe. Cette diversification est toute relative, il faut bien le souligner, et elle fait la part belle aux descendants de colons européens qui se reconnaissent dans le modèle du Vieux Continent. Mais elle amorce néanmoins un mouvement qui continuera de s'amplifier. Quant aux « régionalistes », ils ne se font pas prier pour faire un pas assumé vers l'universalisme, désormais le plus souvent revendiqué comme cadre de leurs réflexions.[40] Le souci de l'unité du droit international demeure, longtemps, en tout état de cause, un des chevaux de bataille des internationalistes. Pour Lauterpacht par exemple l'universalité bien loin de n'être qu'un attribut comme un autre du droit international revêt une nécessité quasi-ontologique:

> Il n'est pas souhaitable que l'unité et l'universalité du droit international soient obscurcies et mises en péril par les inexactitudes ou les exagérations du régionalisme, de conceptions nationales transitoires, ou par l'allégation de différences fondamentales dans la pensée et les principes juridiques.[41]

Mais en même temps, qui saurait dire aujourd'hui de l'universalisme et du régionalisme ou même du nationalisme qui l'a emporté? Certes, le droit international universel s'est étendu comme l'on sait à une diversité de régimes, qu'il s'agisse des droits humains, du droit de l'environnement ou des droits du commerce et de l'investissement. Son universalité est tant géographique que thématique, et elle se nourrit de cooptation, de socialisation et de l'intérêt de nouvelles élites. Néanmoins, si l'on s'éloigne de la controverse un peu poussive sur la question de savoir s'il existe des droits internationaux régionaux à proprement parler, il existe aujourd'hui incontestablement des droits régionaux sui generis à caractère international ou quasi-international tellement développés qu'ils en viennent à réguler une part toujours plus importante des relations de certains Etats entre eux. Que ceux-ci soient plus ou moins théoriquement enchâssés dans le droit international ne change guère au fait qu'ils sont, pour ainsi dire, souvent autonomes et auto-référents.

La victoire du droit international général sur le droit conventionnel à caractère particulier et régional serait donc toute relative. S'il revient certes au premier d'être le régime par défaut, les régimes conventionnels et/ou régionaux sont tellement constitutifs de la réalité juridique internationale, que le champ du droit international semble considérablement réduit. Déjà en 1943, Georges Scelle constatait:

---

[40] Blaise Tchikaya, 'Les orientations doctrinales de la Commission de l'Union africaine sur le droit international' (2017) 30 Revue québécoise de droit international 113.
[41] Lauterpacht (n 2) 206.

> Le droit international est devenu universel, mais, en même temps, il s'est décentralisé [...] Au sein de la société internationale universelle ou œcuménique, il se forme des groupements de peuples ou d'Etats rapprochés par des phénomènes de solidarité plus étroits tenant à la communauté d'origine ou de race, à la contiguïté géographique et surtout à l'intensité des échanges [...][42]

Que dirait Scelle aujourd'hui face à l'ampleur qu'a pris l'Union européenne, ou bien les systèmes régionaux de protection des droits humains, ou les accords régionaux et inter-régionaux de libre échange ou encore la régionalisation du maintien de la paix? En somme, le plus grand legs de l'universalisme est peut-être l'universalité d'un certain pluralisme, lequel tend de plus en plus à s'inscrire dans des logiques régionales.

Entre étatisme et supranationalisme, cependant, la question reste posée de savoir ce que ce régionalisme, en tant que manière de poser un des enjeux normatifs du droit international, se refuse ou tout simplement ne peut pas voir. L'idée de droit régional est une approche qui identifie malgré tout les Etats comme les principaux vecteurs de la diversité et peine à transcender ce modèle sauf par le haut sur le modèle de l'agrégation régionale. Pour Alvarez, par exemple, cela signifiait passer sous silence ce que la latinité américaine avait dû à son « altérité » indigène au nom d'une volonté de distanciation des anciennes capitales. Mais qu'en est-il, par exemple, de la diversité au sein des Etats, de son encouragement et de sa protection? De la diversité des usages transnationaux qui échappent peu ou prou à la logique publique du droit international public? Et surtout comment pourrait-on imaginer un droit international qui serait revisité à l'aune de la multitude des pensées « inter-communautaires » (et non plus spécifiquement inter-nationales au sens moderne de ce terme) qui ont jalonné l'histoire de l'humanité, et dont les descendants intellectuels de Grotius ne représentent qu'une minorité, fut-elle dominante?

---

[42] Georges Scelle, *Manuel élémentaire de droit international public: (avec les textes essentiels)* (les éditions Domat-Montchrestien 1943).

III
UNIVERSALITY AND RIGHTS

7
Universal Human Rights within Social Particulars

Mark Retter

Human rights claims make an implicit appeal to a universal ethical foundation for the international legal order, which purports to regulate relations between state and person. Although human rights have legal embodiment, this appeal to the ethical domain is critical to their overriding normative force, and to justify why states and their legal authorities ought to progressively realize such rights through domestic and international legal mechanisms. As Onora O'Neill puts it, in practice 'human rights are seen as formulating valid moral claims that human beings can make on one another, and in particular on states and their institutions and officials, even (or especially) when existing institutional structures fail to protect or secure those claims'.[1] So, although it is important to distinguish between legal human rights and moral human rights because there is always the potential for law and morality to diverge, there is a normative justificatory relationship between these, which is implicit in the usage of human rights law. 'If human rights are standards that law and public policy *ought* to secure and enforce', as Onora O'Neill observes, then 'a demand for deeper justification is entirely reasonable'.[2] This is a demand for justification of the universal ethical foundations to international order that moral human rights would presuppose.

What is this universal ethical foundation? As Jacques Maritain observed, the Universal Declaration of Human Rights involved 'a sort of common denominator, a sort of unwritten common law, at the point where in practice the most widely separated theoretical ideologies and moral traditions converge'.[3] But that ethical consensus, framed in subjective rights language, breaks down when returning to concrete application because '[w]here it is a question of rational interpretation and justifications of speculation or theory, the problem of Human Rights involves

---

[1] Onora O'Neill, 'Response to John Tasioulas' in Rowan Cruft, S. Matthew Liao, and Massimo Renzo (eds), *Philosophical Foundations of Human Rights* (OUP 2015) 71.
[2] ibid.
[3] Jacques Maritain, 'Introduction' in UNESCO, *Human Rights: Comments and Interpretations*, UNESCO/PRS/3 (rev) (Paris 25 July 1948) II.

the whole structure of moral and metaphysical (or anti-metaphysical) convictions held by each of us'.[4] So, when explaining the universality and overriding importance of human rights, theorists face the task of not only justifying human rights, but also explaining why there could be practical consensus on their enumeration in international instruments, and yet intractable disagreement about their justification and application.

This justificatory task is connected to a deeper metaphysical problem, concerning the relationship between diverse particulars in human practices and traditions, and universal ethical standards—how is it there can be universal human rights standards that apply across the diverse conditions of human agents and societies? In line with a neo-Aristotelian understanding of universal ethical principles, this chapter seeks to outline a justification for the universality and overriding character of human rights, drawing especially from the work of Alasdair MacIntyre on natural law ethics.[5]

Section 1 develops the core foundations for this theory of human rights. The starting point is an internal teleological structure to social practices motivated by internal goods and supported by cooperative standards and virtues. The pursuit of the goods of social practices is integrated within a narrative life structure to the human agent's overall good. Together, this structure to human flourishing provides a basis to reflect on the common good as *telos* to political practice. Mutual commitments for achieving that political common good presuppose corresponding commitments to friendship and natural justice between citizens, which can incorporate a common concern for human rights. These foundations, set out in Section 1, provide the necessary context for Section 2 to address a challenge facing any natural law account of human rights that embeds the knowledge formation of natural justice within the social networks and traditions of localized social practice. How can the focus on localized practices, traditions, and communities be reconciled with the universal character of human rights, with its exceptionless regard for human dignity beyond the more localized relations of one's political community? An answer to this challenge is particularly important to explain why this theory of human rights extends beyond national communities, to the international community. The answer offered relies on what MacIntyre calls the virtues of just generosity. Finally, Section 3 returns to the key challenge of how this human rights theory can respond to facts of moral pluralism. How can it maintain the claim to universality when there are rival human rights traditions, with opposing conceptions of human rights?

---

[4] ibid III.
[5] MacIntyre's human rights scepticism is addressed in Mark Retter, 'The Road Not Taken: On MacIntyre's Human Rights Scepticism' (2018) 63(2) American Journal of Jurisprudence 189.

1. Social Practice to Human Rights

In this chapter, I rely on MacIntyre's understanding of agency within social practices because it provides a compelling account of the social embeddedness of practical rationality. According to MacIntyre, practical reasoning requires an 'individual to participate in the norm-governed transactions and relationships of a particular institutionalized social order'.[6] That social order is made up of a complex network of different social 'practices'. The concept of a 'practice' serves as an ideal type, but also refers to a diverse range of activities that can approximate the ideal, including chess, farming, architecture, medicine, physics, philosophy, friendship, family life, law, and politics. '[W]hat makes practical rationality possible within each practice', MacIntyre says, 'is the way in which the practice is directed towards the achievement of certain goods, specific to and internal to each particular practice, which provide both activity and enquiry within each practice with their *telos*'.[7] These goods are internal to the achievements, motivations, and justifications for the collaborative activity itself; and contrast with rivalrous and excludable external goods—like power, money, and honour—only contingently related to reasons for collaboration.[8]

Within social practices, participating agents learn to distinguish between what *seems* good based on their desires, and what *is* good by reference to standards of collaboration and excellence internal to the practice. Participating agents learn to exercise practical rationality not simply as autonomous individuals, but as self-directing participants within the collaborative enterprise. If they nevertheless act for competing desires, they instrumentalize and impair collaboration for the internal goods at stake. Thus, the distinction between internal and external goods isolates those ends of social practice that are good for participating agents as a social group, while also providing individual motivation for cooperation. Essentially these are common goods because they are 'only to be enjoyed and achieved [...] by individuals qua members of various groups or qua participants in various activities'.[9] Achieving them requires mutual commitments to standards of conduct and cultivation of relevant virtues, involving the educative transformation of desires.[10]

The human capacity for voluntary action, in pursuit of an overall good, is important to the integration of social practices within individual and communal life. Human agents are embedded within a web of social practices. Competing demands on action implicate us in questioning: 'What is my good?'; 'How is it to

---

[6] Alasdair MacIntyre, 'Practical Rationalities as Forms of Social Structure' in Kelvin Knight (ed), *The MacIntyre Reader* (Polity 1998) 123.
[7] ibid 123.
[8] Alasdair MacIntyre, *After Virtue* (3rd edn, UND Press 2007) (hereinafter MacIntyre, AV) 187–91.
[9] Alasdair MacIntyre, *Ethics in the Conflicts of Modernity* (CUP 2016) (hereinafter MacIntyre, ECM) 168–69.
[10] Alasdair MacIntyre, *Three Rival Versions of Moral Enquiry* (Duckworth 1990) (hereinafter MacIntyre, TRV) 61–63; MacIntyre, AV (n 8) 190–91.

be achieved?' The search for answers captures what MacIntyre calls the 'narrative quest' of each person for an overall good.[11] That narrative quest is conditioned by a social locus to human fulfilment through heterogeneous social practices; and by the capacities, dispositions, and dependencies of our human condition. Thus, while affirming the value of independent practical agency, MacIntyre embeds the pursuit of that free agency within conditions of dependence in which the capacity for practical reasoning is developed, exercised, and sustained.[12] So, the narrative quest identifies a teleological character to human life extending beyond social practices in pursuit of an overall good, but crucially depending on them for constituents of this good.

Since the *telos* to human life integrates the goods of various practices, individuals are mutually committed to an overall communal good for the sake of their personal good. The question 'What is my good?' implicates 'What is our good?' The human need to sustain friendly relations within social practices and integrate different practices as part of a political community engenders a corresponding need for joint practical reasoning if answers to these questions are to be pursued collaboratively, not manipulatively. This provides a justificatory basis for political practice and institutions, with a *telos* (the 'political common good') constituted by the need for common action ('co-action') to achieve integrative common ends, for the good of a political community, and for personal human flourishing.[13]

Mutual commitments to a political common good are presupposed by commitment to personal human flourishing, and this will involve corresponding dedication to nurturing the virtue of justice. To some extent, what that virtue of justice requires in different situations will be articulable as rules that define moral obligations owed between persons.[14] However, there is significant under-determination of the requirements of justice, and there can be serious difficulties ascertaining what the common good requires on particular matters. As a result, there is significant room for reasonable dispute and ongoing political discourse, except in relation to the most fundamental moral precepts:[15]

> I will be unable to consider and to respond to your arguments impartially and impersonally, if I have good reason to fear present or future harm from you or from others, should I disagree with you. And for us to be able to engage in shared

---

[11] MacIntyre, AV (n 8) 204–25; MacIntyre, ECM (n 9) 231–42.

[12] Alasdair MacIntyre, *Dependent Rational Animals* (Open Court 1999) (hereinafter MacIntyre, DRA).

[13] Alasdair MacIntyre, 'Politics, Philosophy, and the Common Good' in Knight (ed) (n 6); MacIntyre, DRA (n 12) 113–46.

[14] Alasdair MacIntyre, *Whose Justice? Which Rationality?* (UND Press 1988) (hereinafter MacIntyre, WJWR) 198–202; MacIntyre, DRA (n 12) 109–11.

[15] Alasdair MacIntyre, 'Intractable Moral Disagreements' in Lawrence Cunningham (ed), *Intractable Disputes About the Natural Law* (UND Press 2009) 23. See also MacIntyre, TRV (n 10) 133–37; MacIntyre, ECM (n 9) 88–89.

enquiry, so that my arguments and yours contribute to our common end, you too must have good reason to be assured that you are secure from harm or threat of harm from me. It follows that a precondition of rationality in shared enquiry is mutual commitment to precepts that forbid us to endanger gratuitously each other's life, liberty, or property.

Through dedication to their personal good, a person is likewise committed to these moral precepts, as constitutive means to the concord necessary for achieving their good. Essentially, it is these moral precepts, arising from the embedded commitments of human agents within social practices, which define the theory developed in this chapter as a 'natural law' ethics. These precepts articulate prohibitive moral obligations between all human agents implicated in a joint enquiry into the political common good. When articulated in explicit terms, these rules can guide human judgement and conduct, by defining moral debts owed between persons. They also constitute an extra-positive source for peremptory norms within legal domains.[16]

The critical importance of natural justice informs MacIntyre's criticism of contemporary rights discourse.[17] Suppressing the demands of natural justice undermines the intelligibility to the obligatory moral debts owed based on human dependency within political community. That reduces subjective moral rights to unexplained primitives in practical reasoning, making them susceptible to an 'individualist fallacy', whereby the potential value of the right for the individual right-holder is presumed to ground an adequate reason to impose duties on others, without due consideration of the constitutive social commitments necessary to make that value a matter for co-action. Describing that interest or capacity as 'sufficiently important' does not address the problem.[18] It fails to identify the relevant sense of 'importance' at stake when proceeding to practical conclusions about the actions required of others. These concerns support MacIntyre's belief that 'conclusions about what rights humans beings have or should have [...] are to be derived [...] from premises about the common good and about what both justice and generosity, virtues that are directed towards the common good, requires in this or that particular situation'.[19]

---

[16] Mark Retter, 'Before and After Legal Positivity: Peremptory Norms in Global, Transnational and National Legal Practice' in Luca Siliquini-Cinelli (ed), *Legal Positivism in a Global and Transnational Age* (Springer 2019).

[17] See eg MacIntyre, ECM (n 9) 77–78; MacIntyre, AV (n 8) 66–70; Alasdair MacIntyre, 'Community, Law and the Idiom and Rhetoric of Rights' (1991) 26 Listening: Journal of Religion and Culture 96; Alasdair MacIntyre, 'Are There Any Natural Rights?' (Charles F Adams Lecture, Bowdoin College, 28 February 1983).

[18] See eg John Tasioulas, 'On the Foundations of Human Rights' in Rowan Cruft, S Matthew Liao, and Massimo Renzo (eds), *Philosophical Foundations of Human Rights* (OUP 2015) 51.

[19] Alasdair MacIntyre, 'What More Needs to be Said? A Beginning, Although Only a Beginning at Saying It' (2008) 30 Analyse & Kritik 261, 272.

On this view, subjective moral rights play a supporting role to natural law precepts:[20]

> [R]ights would not primarily provide grounds for claims made by individuals against other individuals or groups. They would instead have to be conceived primarily as enabling provisions, whereby individuals could claim a due place within the life of some particular community, and the question of what rights individuals have or should have would be answerable only in terms of the answers to a prior set of questions about what sort of community this is, directed towards the achievement of what sort of common good, and inculcating what kinds of virtues.

As *enabling provisions*, subjective rights allow individuals to claim remedy for past or prospective wrongs relative to what is due from others by natural law. Given justice measures the adequacy of remedies, the cooperative facilitation of certain moral claims may be required by natural justice. Indeed, depending on the importance of the natural law duties, it may be incumbent on political institutions to provide means through co-action for realizing some moral claims. By inference, such an obligation on co-action can give rise to an inalienable correlative moral power inhering in the would-be victim to claim enforcement of remedies by a political authority. That obligation is justified by the fact that each member is self-implicated in the flourishing of other members to the extent that the achievement of their personal good presupposes the achievement of a political common good.

From this natural law foundation for moral rights, we can contemplate what justifies identifying particular rights as 'human rights'. An answer is found in the need for such rights to protect and promote human capacities sufficiently important for human flourishing. Human rights hold institutions and members of the political community responsible to its *telos* in the human flourishing of all members, through co-action. The human person depends on the community to protect and sustain their life and health, and to enable their development as an independent practical reasoner. And beyond what is most fundamental to personal integrity of mind and body, the enumeration of human rights intelligibly extends to aspects of human well-being pursued through different social practices, fundamental for responsible self-direction. By consequence, human rights track the contours of ethical demands between human persons in social life, as well as between human persons and the common agency of communities. In my view, this can account for the range of manifesto rights in international human rights conventions, through the human capacities and inclinations for learning, association, family life, movement, political participation, religion, work, and so on.[21]

---

[20] Alasdair MacIntyre, 'The Return to Virtue Ethics' in Russell Smith (ed), *The Twenty-Fifth Anniversary of Vatican II: A Look Back and A Look Ahead* (Pope John Center 1990) 247–48.

[21] See eg Jacques Maritain, *Christianity and Democracy & The Rights of Man and Natural Law* (Ignatius 1986) 152–89.

In considering the specification of human rights, we touch on the tension between their purported universality and the variance in their merits of application to practical circumstances. That tension can be explained through the historically extended and dialectically tested human experience of what forms of conduct are fundamentally contrary to the moral respect owed to each human being, as a subject of intrinsic moral importance within communal relations by virtue of their humanity (ie having 'human dignity'). Although affirmation of human dignity is presupposed across different societies and times, the discernment of what actions, duties, and entitlements it requires within different socio-historical circumstances can vary as a function of the fallibility/progress of human judgement/enquiry, and any material changes to context. This raises an important distinction between: (1) the best articulation to date of human rights *in abstraction*, applying as generalized principles about what claimable moral rights should be recognized to respect human dignity, as a requirement of the common good; and (2) the dynamics of applying these mutually limiting rights in concrete circumstances, through the exercise of practical judgement and authoritative decision-making, and with an implicit appeal to a scale of value in the common good.[22] That distinction allows us to affirm human rights as universal principles applicable to all human beings, whilst accounting for their limitation and variance when applied to concrete socio-historical particulars. Within a tradition of enquiry, we can also distinguish from a dialogical standpoint what is understood to be a real development in respect of an understanding of human rights; whilst also explaining why other societies have fallen short of such standards and may not even recognize them as developments, let alone provide for their authoritative enforcement.[23]

2. Just Generosity and Universal Human Rights

The argument so far relies on the radical dependency in human development as independent practical reasoners to extend the demands of natural justice and human rights to relations between all human beings for the sake of a political common good. But there is an important challenge. Who is a fellow participant in practical deliberation about the common good? MacIntyre's answer is 'everyone'. No human being should be ruled out in advance from the joint practical reasoning presupposed by our quest for human flourishing.[24] The common good of any localized level of politics is orientated to a more limited common good of a globalized

---

[22] Jacques Maritain, *Man and the State* (CUA Press 1998) 101–07.
[23] These distinctions provide answers to the objection that human rights are not universal as it is ridiculous to think Stone Age cave-dwellers possessed such rights: Joseph Raz, 'Human Rights without Foundations' in Samantha Besson and John Tasioulas (eds), *The Philosophy of International Law* (OUP 2010) 321.
[24] MacIntyre, DRA (n 12) chs 10–12.

political community. Although MacIntyre advocates the pursuit of that common good predominantly through local communities, due to the shortcomings of large-scale political institutions and state-based politics, he does not identify the local with the perfected community.[25] Local communities are not self-sufficient for the good life and need to participate in broader forms of political discourse in a global community.[26]

Implicit here is the ideal of a universal ambit to civic friendship, which is subject to an apparent dilemma within the Aristotelian tradition.[27] On the one hand, realizing justice in the *polis* presupposes a form of virtue friendship embodying mutual commitments between citizens to a common good. On the other hand, virtue friendship is rare for two reasons. First, the life of virtue sustaining that friendship is difficult. Secondly, friendships of this kind require enduring mutual association to form acquaintance with the good held in common. That dilemma provides an explanatory background to MacIntyre's turn to localized politics. Although the ideal form of political community may be too large for comprehensive face-to-face relations, it is nonetheless 'composed of a network of small groups of friends', embedded in a shared life of virtue within and across localized practices.[28]

Experience of concord with fellow participants in practices provides a pedagogical foundation to justice and concord in a global political community.[29] In circumstances where mutual accountability to common goods is not as apparent, there is greater likelihood of a breakdown in the virtues of acknowledged dependence required to sustain just relations. A disconnect can develop between individual motivations and the commitments necessary for flourishing practice. The danger of this disconnect is particularly acute for political practice when the community is relatively large and complex, and political discourse is influenced by false ideology, preventing a mutually accountable tradition of enquiry into the common good. But, if moral enquiry needs to be orientated by local practices and friendly concord to think about justice adequately, how is the ideal political community to be instantiated beyond local community?

MacIntyre's response considers why practical rationality requires us to apply standards of natural justice to strangers.[30] In ancient societies, moral concern for strangers was conceivable as part of the pursuit of goods and virtues valued in local community. Strangers were protected by a way of life supporting their hospitable treatment as guests. This requires an act of imagination whereby strangers are

---

[25] ibid 142; MacIntyre, 'Politics and Common Good' (n 13) 246–52.
[26] Thomas Hibbs, 'MacIntyre, Aquinas and Politics' (2004) 66(3) Review of Politics 357, 372–83; Thomas Osborne, 'MacIntyre, Thomism and the Contemporary Common Good' (2008) 30 Analyse & Kritik 75, 80–88.
[27] Aristotle, *Nicomachean Ethics* VIII:1, 1155a22–28; VIII:3, 1156b7–32.
[28] MacIntyre, AV (n 8) 156.
[29] MacIntyre, WJWR (n 14) 179–81, 193–200; MacIntyre, TRV (n 10) 60–63; MacIntyre, DRA (n 12) 160–61.
[30] MacIntyre, AV (n 8) 122–26, 214–21; MacIntyre, DRA (n 12) 125–26, 149–51.

understood as part of the communal enterprise, as being in a relationship of mutual accountability to common goods. The difficulty is that local communities can be narrow-minded and lack this 'cosmopolitan' imagination. Nevertheless, there is a dire need to develop the virtue of justice in relations with strangers precisely because the good in common is less transparent. We cannot know who will be a future partner in joint practical reasoning about some goods intrinsic to our flourishing.[31] Most importantly, we cannot know in advance who we will depend on as a stranger, and who will be a stranger to us and need our generosity. We need to learn to treat everyone as actual or potential participants in our social networks of mutual giving and receiving. This radical dependency extends the ambit of justice to cover generosity towards human distress and need. We should be disposed to show hospitality to strangers and develop the virtue of *misericordia*, inclining us to take 'pity' on the needs of others for the sake of their humanity.[32] That *misericordia* is not simply a sentiment. It involves a rational sensitivity to the distress of others which apprehends that distress as one's own, regardless of preexisting relations. Given solidarity in human distress, the virtues of just generosity dispose us to freely give on the basis of perceived need.

This extension of justice to human need entails a globalized political community, encompassing all human beings in a common good. Generosity to the needy becomes a requirement of justice and can explain the universality of human rights. The vulnerability of human capacities, important for human flourishing, engenders a need for their protection and promotion, which becomes a requirement of just generosity. Human rights provide the enabling mechanism for individuals to claim remedy for wrongs committed against these demands of justice. However, such rights are only enforceable through the co-action of political community. So, why does the practical rationality of just generosity give sufficient reason for co-action to enforce these rights for *all* human beings? This question raises the issue of whether there is a possibility of exceptions. To answer it, I will focus on two important cases relating to the most vulnerable in the human community.

The first concerns those not indebted to the community because its social networks have failed them. Perhaps they developed as independent practical reasoners despite obstacles from the community. The networks on which they depended for care and education may have been deficient due to individual or systemic moral failures. So how can we say the networks of just generosity extend to them when they have been excluded? MacIntyre points out that their situation is necessarily characterized 'in terms of just those norms of giving and receiving that are embodied in the relationships by which characteristically and generally independent practical reasoners are formed and sustained'.[33] So, it is precisely due to human

---

[31] MacIntyre 'Intractable Disagreements' (n 15) 24; MacIntyre, DRA (n 12) 160; MacIntyre, 'Politics and Common Good' (n 13) 248.
[32] MacIntyre, DRA (n 12) 124–26.
[33] ibid 101.

dependency that these wrongs are damaging. The capacity to recognize them as failures presupposes an understanding of healthy social relationships, with sensitivity to human need. The virtue of just generosity becomes the dispositional basis in the moral life of the community for redress. Depending on the type of wrong, human rights may enable the aggrieved person to seek remedy for their exclusion as a rightful participant in those communal networks, in virtue of their common humanity.

The second case concerns inclusion of people with severe mental or physical disabilities who are unable to properly participate in networks of giving and receiving. Some may be unable to be more than passive members of community. If caregiving networks are supported by recognition of mutual dependence and accountability, why should they extend to those unable to give? MacIntyre's answer hinges on the value of *misericordia*. That virtue supports giving and receiving networks by disposing us to consider the needs of other human beings as having a claim on our action and the co-action of political community. Due to the potential urgency of those needs, '[t]he care that we ourselves need from others and the care that they need from us require a commitment and a regard that is not conditional upon the contingencies of injury, disease and other afflictions'.[34] We need to develop the empathetic disposition to help the needy by contemplating that, since they are human, their misfortune might have been ours; our good fortune might have been theirs. If this compassion is fundamental for developing the necessary commitment to care-giving networks, there is good reason to see the disabled as moral teachers.[35] They re-present the inescapable facts of radical human dependence, challenging us to grow in virtue.

In both these cases, what is critical is the importance of unconditional regard for the intrinsic value of each human being. MacIntyre approaches that value from the moral pedagogy of human agents, asking why it is practically rational to recognize human dignity through civic friendship. His answer is that human dependency requires us to develop virtues enabling us to consider the needs of others as our own, simply because of their humanity. Human dependency implicates a universal virtue friendship which establishes equal moral status between human beings. The problem is that we are often tempted to value others instrumentally for what they contribute to us, particularly in terms of external goods. This is especially the case for strangers or those with whom we find it difficult to be friends. Although respect for perceived qualities in other human beings can motivate deeper friendship, we need to learn how to value human beings per se, regardless of these qualities. The paramount need for universal virtue friendship, despite the difficulty, makes it a matter for natural justice. In that sense, friendship completes justice.[36]

---

[34] ibid 128.
[35] ibid 135–40, 147–50.
[36] Aristotle (n 27) VIII:1, 1155a22–28; VIII:9, 1159b25–1160a7.

The justice of the global human community directs us to take for granted that every human being is worthy of the inalienable moral regard of civic friendship, to sustain the common life of virtue constitutive of human flourishing. That universal scope of natural justice explains not only why human rights are universal, but why protecting and promoting the most vulnerable is central to their function. The vulnerable human being becomes the focal case through which we affirm universal human dignity with *misericordia*.

3. Rival Human Rights Traditions

From the standpoint of this chapter, the focal agenda for human rights theory is to render human rights claims intelligible as good reasons for the action they require of others and political authority. All other functions to human rights language should be grounded on this justifiable normativity if we are to avoid transforming them into reified universal claims, standing in juxtaposition to concrete particulars. Nevertheless, many would reject the natural law approach adopted here because they cannot accept the presuppositions on which it rests, and by which human enquiry is understood. And those presuppositions are not amenable to demonstrative proof. This leads us to another critical question. If this natural law justification for universal human rights is not supported by sufficient consensus, how can it maintain its claim to universality?

The first point to make is that the likelihood of rejection does not undermine the justificatory foundations of the theory if it can intelligibly account for its rejection as an understandable error and can explain on its own terms why the criticisms do not impugn it.[37] Indeed, the widespread rejection of this form of natural law foundation to human rights is well-explained on the terms of the natural law tradition as a result of error in moral theory. This error understandably arises from the difficulty of moral enquiry, and the dependence of good moral concepts and theorizing on the virtue of *prudentia*, formed by moral life within localized practice and communities. In fact, close attention to the self-implicating nature of ethical enquiry, and the interdependence between practical and theoretical knowledge, enables the Aristotelian to explain persistent and intractable disagreement about human rights. From this perspective, the intractability of such disagreements is exacerbated by the theoretical fragmentation of contemporary understandings of moral life. Many rival theories have sought to explain the universal and overriding character of human rights claims by reconciling different conceptual fragments, such as fundamental individual interests and freedoms, human capabilities, human well-being, human dignity, political discourse, emergent human rights practice,

---

[37] MacIntyre, WJWR (n 14) chs XVIII–XX.

political equality, and freedom. Those fragments need to be integrated by a form of theory instantiated in a good way of life—a mode of human rights practice orientated by good reasons, supporting the rights and duties applied in practice.

Furthermore, despite prospects for theoretical rejection, the fundamental precepts of natural law remain perennial to practice, as *practical preconditions* to collaboration in moral enquiry, rather than as theoretical artifices of that enquiry. They have normative priority to the debates themselves because participants are committed to them by virtue of their practical need, from circumstances of radical dependency, to collaborate with others to achieve a range of common ends for the sake of their personal good. The human rights theory outlined in this chapter can explain how a practical unarticulated knowledge of basic natural law precepts is available to plain persons, by apprehension of what is fundamentally contrary to the common ends at stake. This helps to illuminate that curious phenomenon of the 'practical human rights consensus' underpinning the Universal Declaration, despite intractable disagreements on theoretical foundations and on difficult applications that require explicit extrapolation from theoretical foundations. As Maritain argued:[38]

> The phenomenon proves simply that systems of moral philosophy are the products of reflexion by the intellect on ethical concepts which precede and govern them, and which of themselves display [...] a highly complex geology of the mind where the natural operation of spontaneous reason, pre-scientific and pre-philosophic, is at every stage conditioned by the acquisitions, the constraints, the structure and the evolution of the social group.

Confronting such complexity to moral enquiry, intractable disagreement is far from surprising; and yet, few moral theories can explain such disagreement without losing a grip on foundations for intelligibility in moral enquiry.

Although this natural law theory of human rights may be vindicated based on metaphysical commitments shared within the Aristotelian tradition, this does not alleviate the political problem of intractable disagreement about human rights law. Indeed, the foregoing discussion heightens awareness of the potential for a plurality of rival human rights traditions, the proponents of which seek to vindicate their own understanding against their rivals in political and legal discourse. Maritain was wary about the prospects for international codification of the Universal Declaration precisely because the movement from mid-level consensus on manifesto rights to concrete application would implicate legal authority in deciding, at least implicitly, between rival understandings of human rights—in some of the most combative moral debates of the community.[39] With their legal

---

[38] Maritain 'Introduction' (n 3) IV.
[39] ibid VII–IX.

codification, human rights courts can become battlegrounds for opposing ethical traditions, with different moral presuppositions and scales of value underpinning rival understandings of human rights. The contentious nature of such decision-making, across a plurality of moral communities and traditions, may ultimately undermine the authority of international human rights law. On one hand, human rights law continues to protect a core practical consensus around fundamental moral precepts, which incorporates recognition of obvious instances of violations. On the other, it can serve to displace authentic ethical discourse and reinforce the juxtaposition of a dis-encapsulated individualism and a bureaucratic rationality in human rights decision-making, which proceeds as if human right norms are ethical first principles.

Averting the sceptical challenge, arising from these tensions, requires attention to the value of subsidiarity. In particular, more attention should be devoted to how a legal principle of subsidiarity can be embodied in human rights law, allowing for conditions in which an unforced ethical consensus may fruitfully develop between overlapping but differentiated moral traditions and communities, orientated by the ethical preconditions to joint deliberation about common ends.[40] That subsidiarity should allow space for rival understandings to be embodied in different politico-legal communities; and should enhance the role for judicial deference between different human rights courts and decision-makers, and in favour of good faith ethical decision-making through local deliberative processes. In renegotiating the politico-legal boundaries of human rights determination, a balance needs to be discerned between a core content to human rights, for which a common sense for justice demands standardization across communities; outer limits of contestation in human rights law, apt for a plurality of politico-legal traditions due to the conditions of moral enquiry; and applications beyond the outer limits, which cannot be justified as having an overriding ethical force fundamental to the pursuit of common ends in community. Of course, the very articulation of these categories, as well as the boundaries between them, is subject to contestation. And yet, for that contestation to remain constructive, it needs to take its bearings from the embedded ethical preconditions to cooperative human deliberation in social practice, or risk supplanting ethical foundations to human rights altogether.

---

[40] Charles Taylor, 'Conditions of an Unforced Consensus on Human Rights' in Daniel Bell and Joanne Bauer (eds), *The East Asian Challenge for Human Rights* (CUP 1999).

8
Human Rights Nationalism as Universality Challenge

Tilmann Altwicker

The ECtHR has a mediator-like role regarding human rights universality. In a similar vein, Judge Pinto de Albuquerque recently argued that the ECtHR is 'the first interpreter' of the principle of human rights universality.[1] This may be surprising at first sight. Universality appears to be a theoretical or philosophical topic. Indeed, the ECtHR has so far carefully avoided even mentioning the concept of universality (at least in majority reasonings).[2] The Court rightly views its task to be the adjudication of complaints, not to resolve theoretical controversies on human rights. However, as shown below, ECtHR has developed an *implicit* universality jurisprudence. Universality is used here in a normative sense, not in the common geographical sense. In the context of human rights, three claims associated with universality in a normative sense can be distinguished: abstractness, inclusiveness, and rationality.[3] All of these relate to the quality of human rights norms (as emerging from their design/wording and their interpretation). The universality qualities of human rights norms can be generically developed from the preambles of international human rights instruments and the rights contained therein: first, universality as abstractness relates to the universal applicability of human rights (eg their applicability irrespective of the ethnic or national context or belonging); secondly, universality as inclusiveness demands that all rights holders enjoy an identical set of human rights; and, thirdly, universality as rationality reflects the idea that these rights can be given a universal, shared understanding (eg that conflicting interpretations can be solved by appeal to legal principles of higher status or authority).[4]

---

[1] Partly concurring, partly dissenting opinion of Judge Pinto de Albuquerque in *GIEM Srl v Italy* App nos 1828/06, 34163/07, and 19029/11 (ECtHR, 28 June 2018) para 94.

[2] Rare examples for a reference to universality in the majority reasoning are: *Çam v Turkey* App no 51500/08 (ECtHR, 23 February 2016) para 64 (universality mentioned as a 'fundamental principle' in the context of the right to education); similarly, *Enver Şahin v Turkey* App no 23065/12 (ECtHR, 30 January 2018) para 55. All ECtHR decisions are available at <http://hudoc.echr.coe.int/> accessed on 31 May 2021.

[3] See, for details, Tilmann Altwicker, 'Non-Universal Arguments under the European Convention on Human Rights' (2020) 31 European Journal of International Law 103–04.

[4] For details on normative universality see Altwicker, 'Non-Universal Arguments' (n 3) 103–04 and Section 2.

Like other value-laden concepts (such as justice or dignity), universality can be employed to reconstruct or to make sense of the ECtHR's case law, even if the term itself is not used by the Court.[5] For its implicit universality jurisprudence, the ECtHR could only rudimentarily rely on the text of the Convention itself. The reason is that references to the idea of universality in the plain text of the ECHR are scarce. The Preamble situates the ECHR in the wider context of ensuring the 'universal recognition' of human rights envisaged by the Universal Declaration of Human Rights of 1948. This is the single explicit reference to the universality concept in the text of the ECHR. Therefore, the ECtHR had to develop an implicit universality jurisprudence by interpretation. In fact, its pronouncements on several current doctrinal 'hotspots'—its interpretation of non-discrimination (Article 14 and Article 1 of Protocol 12 ECHR), its recent vulnerability conception, its margin of appreciation doctrine, and the subsidiarity jurisprudence—can all be reconstructed as interpretations of particular aspects of human rights universality.[6]

This contribution argues that the greatest challenge the ECtHR's human rights universality jurisprudence currently faces stems from the recent wave of human rights nationalism experienced by several contracting states (eg the United Kingdom,[7] Russia,[8] and, partially, Switzerland[9]). This is an attack on the rationality dimension of normative universality outlined above. Certainly, criticism of the Convention and individual judgments by the ECtHR is nothing new. What is new, however, is a form of principled resistance to human rights interpretation beyond the state which is called human rights nationalism here. This new form of resistance manifests itself in 'counter-dynamics' at the political level and/or the judicial level in several contracting states.[10] Sometimes, these 'counter-dynamics' culminate in calls for a denunciation of the ECHR, in the refusal to give effect to certain judgments by the ECtHR, or in the assertion of conceptions of domestic judicial superiority over international adjudication, as shown below.

In the following discussion, human rights nationalism is introduced as a challenge to the idea of universality by prioritizing domestic interpretations of human

---

[5] On the use of the justice concept for reconstructing the ECtHR's case law on non-discrimination, see Tilmann Altwicker, *Menschenrechtlicher Gleichheitsschutz* (Springer 2011) 423–88.

[6] For details, see Altwicker, 'Non-Universal Arguments' (n 3) 109–19.

[7] See Roger Masterman, 'The United Kingdom: From Strasbourg Surrogacy Towards a British Bill of Rights?' in Patricia Popelier, Sarah Lambrecht, and Koen Lemmens (eds), *Criticism of the European Court of Human Rights: Shifting the Convention System: Counter-Dynamics at the National Level and EU Level* (Intersentia 2016) 450 and 476–77 (discussing the Human Rights Act 1998 as the driving force behind the shift towards the common law as the 'natural starting point' for the analysis of a rights issue and a push-back against Convention rights).

[8] See Aaron Matta and Armen Mazmanyan, 'Russia: In Quest for a European Identity' in Popelier, Lambrecht and Kemmens (eds) (n 7) 502 (on the opposition to the Convention and the ECtHR by the judiciary).

[9] See Tilmann Altwicker, 'Switzerland: The Substitute Constitution in Times of Popular Dissent' in Popelier, Lambrecht, and Lemmens (eds) (n 7) 410.

[10] For this distinction, see Sarah Lambrecht, 'Assessing the Existence of Criticism of the European Court of Human Rights' in Popelier, Lambrecht, and Kemmens (eds) (n 7) 514, 534.

rights over universalizing interpretations at a supra-state level. It encompasses a variety of approaches introduced by a variety of actors (judges, political parties). At one end of the spectrum, human rights nationalism comprises strong versions, exemplified by the 'Protecting Human Rights at Home' Approach (endorsed by the Conservative Party in the United Kingdom) or the 'Self-Rule Initiative' (brought by the Swiss People's Party).[11] Both these approaches ultimately aim to establish a systemic supremacy of domestic human rights law over international human rights law (IHRL), openly contemplating withdrawal from international human rights mechanisms in case of irreconcilable conflict.[12] At the other end of the spectrum there are more moderate, pragmatic versions of human rights nationalism, calling for the control of national institutions over international human rights adjudication on a case-by-case basis: some argue for the possibility of a 'judicial override' (eg the German Federal Constitutional Court in the case of *Görgülü*; individual judges of the Russian or Hungarian Constitutional Court),[13] and some legal scholars have suggested a form of legislative veto or 'democratic override' in individual cases.[14] What unites all of these approaches is their principled prioritizing of the domestic over universalizing, supra-state level interpretations of human rights—either on a general level or on a case-by-case level. It will be shown below that human rights nationalism approaches rely on a new binary, to use the helpful analytical concept introduced by the editors of this volume, namely 'national relativism–universality'.

The argument is presented as follows: having introduced the concept of human rights nationalism, Section 1 outlines the ECtHR's human rights universality jurisprudence. Then, it is argued that human rights nationalism adds a new binary,

---

[11] On the United Kingdom approach, see Masterman, 'The United Kingdom' (n 7) 459–66. For Switzerland, see Altwicker, 'Non-Universal Arguments' (n 9) 398–401.

[12] For example, in its earlier Party Programme (2011-15), the Swiss People's Party discussed a withdrawal from the ECHR in case the popular initiatives adopted (on the construction of minarets and on deportation) were to be found incompatible with the Convention; see <www.svp.ch/partei/positionen/positionspapiere/2011-2/parteiprogramm-2011-2015-januar-2011/> accessed 31 May 2021.

[13] See BVerfG, Order of the Second Senate of 14 October 2004, 2 BvR 1481/04, para 62 (stating that '[a]s long as applicable methodological standards leave scope for interpretation and weighing of interests, German courts must give precedence to interpretation in accordance with the Convention. The situation is different only if observing the decision of the ECHR, for example because the facts on which it is based have changed, *clearly violates statute law to the contrary or German constitutional provisions*, in particular also the fundamental rights of third parties' [my emphasis]). On Russia, see Elisabeth Fura and Rait Maruste, 'Russia's Impact on the Strasbourg System, as Seen by Two Former Judges of the European Court of Human Rights' in Lauri Mälksoo and Wolfgang Benedek (eds), *Russia and the European Court of Human Rights: The Strasbourg Effect* (CUP 2017) 247. See also Constitutional Court of the Russian Federation, Judgment of 19 April 2016, No 12-П/2016, unofficial English translation available at <www.ksrf.ru/en/Decision/Judgments/Pages/2016.aspx> accessed 31 May 2021 (claiming a 'right to objection' against a judgment by the ECtHR in respect of prisoners' voting rights). For the case of Hungary, see Eszter Polgári, 'Hungary: "Gains and Losses": Changing the Relationship with the European Court of Human Rights' in Popelier, Lambrecht, and Lemmens (eds) (n 7) 317–19.

[14] For a defence of the idea of a 'democratic override', see Richard Bellamy, 'The Democratic Legitimacy of International Human Rights Conventions: Political Constitutionalism and the European Convention on Human Rights' (2015) 25 European Journal of International Law 1019, 1034. For criticism, see Alice Donald and Philip Leach, *Parliaments and the European Court of Human Rights* (1st edn, OUP 2016) 146–53.

'national relativism–universality', and the ECtHR's handling of the new binary is discussed in Section 2. Section 3 concludes by casting a critical look at the 'turn to the domestic sphere' envisaged by human rights nationalism.

1. Adjudicating Binaries: Contours of a Universality Jurisprudence

Human rights universality is a complex, multidimensional concept. A recent article has distinguished broadly between a *descriptive* universality dimension (relating to the geographical reach and the bindingness of international human rights norms) and a *normative* universality dimension (relating to distinct qualities or claims concerning these rights).[15] Several norms of the ECHR relate to descriptive universality: the geographical reach (or *ratione loci* element) of universality is reflected in Article 56 ECHR and Article 1 ECHR. It is basically limited to the territory of the contracting states and the judicially accepted exceptions of extraterritorial application.[16] Article 1 ECHR also regulates the Convention's bindingness *ratione personae*.

Universality as abstractness—the idea of rights ownership irrespective of the ethnic, national, socio-economic, political, cultural, or religious context or belonging—is mirrored in the non-discrimination provision of Article 14 ECHR, a cross-cutting legal norm that permeates the application of all other Convention rights.[17] Universality as inclusiveness—the idea that all humans enjoy the identical set of human rights—is reflected in the text of the individual rights most of which are guaranteed to 'everyone'.[18] Universality as rationality—the idea that a shared understanding of the practical implications of human rights is possible and, consequently, that conflicting human rights interpretations can be solved by appeal to legal principles of higher status or quality—is alluded to in the Preamble of the ECHR.[19]

As shown in more detail elsewhere, the ECtHR has devised tools to modify or adjust these normative universality claims in individual cases.[20] The normative

---

[15] See, for details, Altwicker, 'Non-Universal Arguments' (n 3) 103–04.
[16] For an overview on the scenarios of extraterritorial application of the ECHR, see Tilmann Altwicker, 'Transnationalizing the Interpretation of Rights: International Human Rights Law in Cross-Border Contexts' (2018) 29 European Journal of International Law 581, 588–94.
[17] Art 14 ECHR reads: 'The enjoyment of the rights and freedoms set forth in this Convention shall be secured without discrimination on any ground such as sex, race, colour, language, religion, political or other opinion, national or social origin, association with a national minority, property, birth or other status.' See partly dissenting opinion of Judge Keller in *Otegi Mondragon v Spain* App nos 4184/15 and others (ECtHR, 6 November 2018) para 21.
[18] Inclusiveness, here, reflects a presumption of formal equality as the starting point.
[19] See the ECHR Preamble which speaks of maintaining a 'common understanding ... of the human rights' laid out in the Convention.
[20] Altwicker, 'Non-Universal Arguments' (n 3) 109–19.

universality claims and their modifications in the case law of the ECtHR together form the Court's universality jurisprudence. The universality jurisprudence can be presented relying on some of the binaries helpfully suggested by the editors of the present volume. The binary of 'cultural relativism–universality' which is extensively debated in the literature seems, thus far, to have had few repercussions on the Court's case law.[21] Doctrinally, cultural relativism could, in principle, be accommodated, for example by accepting a public morals justification or by granting the state a margin of appreciation.[22] However, and in the author's view correctly so, the ECtHR has only very rarely been prepared to accept aspects of culture as a difference-making fact.[23] A sole example so far is the protection of the 'lifestyle' of the Roma people.[24] Thus, if living in caravans is part of the lifestyle of the Roma people (fact), this is considered to have consequences for the interpretation of the domestic planning law (difference-making fact). Furthermore, the Court accepted culture as a difference-making fact in the interpretation of limitation clauses of certain Convention rights. In *SAS v France*, a case concerning the blanket ban on face-covering in public, the ECtHR interpreted the limitation clause of 'protection of the rights and freedoms of others' of Article 8 ECHR (right to private life) and Article 9 ECHR (freedom of religion) in light of the established tradition of social interaction and lifestyle in France.[25] By occasionally allowing aspects of culture to be a difference-making fact, the Court adjusts the abstractness claim of universality.

Another binary made out by the editors, 'gendered inequality–universality', has had more influence on the case law of the ECtHR, as is visible in its case law on 'vulnerable persons' (relating to, among others, victims of domestic violence).[26] Furthermore, the ECtHR has indicated that it is ready to accept instances of 'positive discrimination' or 'affirmative action' in respect of formerly disadvantaged women.[27] By recognizing the need for asymmetric protection under certain circumstances, the ECtHR has modified the (formal) inclusiveness claim endorsed by human rights universality.

Finally, also the binary 'fragmentation–universality' has made its way into the case law of the ECtHR. To facilitate the coexistence of the overlapping legal orders of ECHR and EU law, the Court famously relies on its so-called *Bosphorus*

---

[21] For a helpful overview on the debate, see Neil Walker, 'Universalism and Particularism in Human Rights' in Cindy Holder (ed), *Human Rights: The Hard Questions* (CUP 2013). See also Altwicker, 'Non-Universal Arguments' (n 3) 115–16.

[22] On the margin of appreciation doctrine, see text accompanying note 45.

[23] A difference-making fact provides a causal explanation that simultaneously represents a normative cause for action, see Yun-chien Chang and Peng-Hsiang Wang, 'The Empirical Foundation of Normative Arguments in Legal Reasoning' (2016) 745 Coase-Sandor Working Paper Series in Law and Economics 1. Their example of a difference-making fact is 'Smoking causes health damage': this is a fact that, at the same time, provides a normative reason for action ('quit smoking'), see ibid 4.

[24] See *Chapman v United Kingdom* App no 27238/95 (ECtHR, 18 January 2001) para 96.

[25] See *SAS v France* App no 43835/11 (ECtHR, 1 July 2014) para 122.

[26] See, for details, Altwicker, 'Non-Universal Arguments' (n 3) 110–13.

[27] See *Stec v United Kingdom* App no 65731/01 (ECtHR, 12 April 2006) para 51.

jurisprudence which is essentially an equivalent protection test.[28] Thereby, the idea of coherent legal obligations can be preserved, catering to the rationality element of universality outlined above.

2. A New Binary: National Relativism–Universality

Currently, the biggest challenge to the universality jurisprudence comes from human rights nationalism. Positions subscribing to human rights nationalism employ legal narratives prioritizing domestic over universalizing, supra-state interpretations of human rights. This is sometimes associated with a preference for 'home-grown' solutions over 'legally engineered' solutions to human rights problems or with the acknowledgement that in 'a globalized world, global and local values compete for allegiance, but local authorities are bound to have more influence in shaping the ordinary virtues'.[29] With striking similarities, such narratives have been used by several actors from various European states (judges of highest domestic courts, political parties), all pushing back against the idea of human rights universality: for example, some variants of human rights nationalism draw on the ideas of 'constitutional identity',[30] 'national identity',[31] 'sovereignty' (as the basis for a superior democratic legitimacy narrative),[32] differences in the 'socio-legal consciousness',[33] or differences in the (normative) 'expectations of

---

[28] See *Bosphorus Airways v Ireland* App no 45036/98 (ECtHR, 30 June 2005) para 155.

[29] Tom Zwart, 'Using Local Culture to Further the Implementation of International Human Rights: The Receptor Approach' (2012) 34 Human Rights Quarterly 546, 559–64; Michael Ignatieff, 'Human Rights, Global Ethics, and the Ordinary Virtues' (2017) 31 Ethics & International Affairs 3, 9.

[30] The conflict of the 'constitutional identity' narrative with human rights universality is particularly visible in statements by members of the Russian Constitutional Court. See Mikhail Antonov, 'Philosophy behind Human Rights: Valery Zorkin vs. the West?' in Lauri Mälksoo and Wolfgang Benedek (eds), *Russia and the European Court of Human Rights: The Strasbourg Effect* (CUP 2017) 183 (stating that, according to the Chief Justice of the Russian Constitutional Court, 'each country establishes its own "constitutional identity," and national courts are better fitted for coining this identity than any supranational judicial organs, given the cultural particularities and institutional constraints in every country').

[31] On the 'national identity' rhetoric as a challenge to the 'interpretative authority' of the ECtHR, see partly concurring, partly dissenting opinion of Judge Pinto de Albuquerque in *GIEM Srl v Italy* (n 1) paras 87–90.

[32] For the superior democratic legitimacy narrative, see Zoë Jay, 'Keeping Rights at Home: British Conceptions of Rights and Compliance with the European Court of Human Rights' (2017) 19 The British Journal of Politics and International Relations 842, 846 (tracing the recent trend to human rights nationalism in the United Kingdom to the tradition of 'political constitutionalism' embodied in the idea of parliamentary sovereignty). cf Masterman, 'The United Kingdom' (n 7).

[33] The different 'socio-legal consciousness' narrative has been used to shield off human rights universality by Polish scholars, judges, and politicians; see Krystyna Kowalik-Banczk, 'Poland: The Taming of the Shrew' in Popelier, Lambrecht, and Lemmens (eds) (n 7) 203, 233 (citing criticism that some judgments by the ECtHR do not 'fully correspond to Polish "legal" reality'); Polgári (n 13) 307–08 (citing criticism that the ECtHR 'failed to take into consideration the Hungarian reality'). Discussing the case *Markin v Russia* App no 30078/06 (ECtHR, 22 March 2012), Lauri Mälksoo stated that 'certain ultraprogressive opinions expressed in European human rights discourse ... do not correspond to sociological realities in European countries where postmodernity has not yet arrived in the form of that

society'.[34] The effect of these legal narratives is to shield off the domestic sphere against some or all universalizing interpretations of human rights by supra-state organs.

There are differences between human rights nationalism and the familiar discourse on universality versus cultural relativism.[35] First, human rights nationalism does not primarily rely explicitly on the concept of culture as a legitimizing ground for criticizing the universalist narrative. It is not possible to ground objections to universal human rights in a concept of culture when states are evidently part of a common human rights culture. For example, Switzerland can hardly deny being part of the European human rights culture; the suggestion of a clash of human rights cultures would be considered a misguided line of argument. Secondly, some variants of human rights nationalism are not per se incompatible with (weak forms of) universality. Human rights nationalism may, for example, endorse a 'programmatic' vision of universal human rights (suggesting certain policy goals or means to the legislature) while demanding that national courts adjudicate legal disputes invoking human rights.[36]

The rise of human rights nationalism leads to a new binary, 'national relativism–universality'. National relativism presents a double challenge to the idea of human rights universality: in its stronger versions, human rights nationalism takes issue with the abstractness claim of human rights universality, ie the idea that human rights apply (and, consequently, that their meaning can and should be identified) irrespective of the national context. At this end of the spectrum, human rights nationalism makes an epistemic claim: some interpretations of human rights cannot be universalized. In its weaker forms, human rights nationalism makes an institutional claim by demanding the priority of domestic human rights interpretation over interpretations by an international adjudicatory body in individual cases.[37] This variant of human rights nationalism concerns the issue of who should exercise the ultimate interpretive power in respect of IHRL. The problem regarding the ultimate authority of interpretation of IHRL does not target the abstractness claim but concerns the rationality claim: human rights nationalism, in its weak form,

---

kind of thinking', Lauri Mälksoo, 'Markin v. Russia' (2012) 106 American Journal of International Law 836, 841–2.

[34] Dissenting opinion by Judges K Hajiyev, J Laffranque, and D Dedov in *Sõro v Estonia* App no 22588/08 (ECtHR, 3 September 2015) para 8 ('expectations of society and the legislature's choices in different countries inevitably differ in such matters, depending on their unique historical experience').
[35] For a helpful overview, see Walker (n 21).
[36] See Lord Hoffmann, 'The Universality of Human Rights' (Judicial Studies Board Annual Lecture, 19 March 2009) <www.judiciary.uk/wp-content/uploads/2014/12/Hoffmann_2009_JSB_Annual_Lecture_Universality_of_Human_Rights.pdf> accessed 31 May 2021.
[37] For a useful general overview, see Mikael R Madsen, Pola Cebulak, and Micha Wiebusch, 'Backlash against International Courts: Explaining the Forms and Patterns of Resistance to International Courts' (2018) 14 International Journal of Law in Context 197.

claims that in cases of conflicting interpretations of IHRL, the ultimate authority to decide rests with domestic organs.

The conflict between human rights nationalism and human rights universality is neither merely of an institutional nature (although, in practice, it is often accompanied by criticism of specific international human rights adjudication bodies), nor is it simply a case of conflicting legal interpretations about what is demanded by human rights in an individual case. Instead of criticizing individual decisions, human rights nationalism—voiced by some judges of the highest domestic courts and some political parties—is characterized by a systemic critique or a pattern of criticism of the international adjudication of human rights issues.[38] Instead of mere institutional criticism, the critique is aimed at a deeper layer of international human rights protection: these approaches question the possibility to universalize solutions in the field of human rights protection and they cast doubt on the legitimacy of giving a supra-state organ the 'final word' on human rights issues.

How has the ECtHR responded to human rights nationalism? To some degree, the Court is able to accommodate the new binary, national relativism–universality, by allowing for decentralized interpretations of the Convention rights. According to Article 19 ECHR, it is the ECtHR that—in cases of conflict or doubt—ultimately determines the scope, nature, and content of the obligations undertaken by the contracting states. This general rule, however, does not preclude the ECtHR from redistributing the interpretative power to state organs by way of deference. This aspect pertains to the rationality claim of human rights universality. As outlined above, the rationality condition holds that converging interpretations of human rights are possible and that conflicting interpretations of rights can be solved by reference to common, higher legal principles.[39] The ECtHR allows for decentralized interpretations by argumentatively deferring to the interpretive authority of a domestic court or by deferring to domestic legislative choice, resorting to the Court's margin of appreciation doctrine.[40] Justifications on the decentralization of the power of interpretation by the ECtHR mostly revolve around the ideas of the subsidiarity[41] (and, conversely, the

---

[38] See references in nn 11–14.

[39] See text accompanying n 19.

[40] For an example of deference to domestic legislative choice, see *Correia de Matos v Portugal* App no 56402/12 (ECtHR, 4 April 2018) para 117 (regarding the domestic requirement to be legally represented). See generally Başak Çalı, 'Coping with Crisis: Whither the Variable Geometry in the Jurisprudence of the European Court of Human Rights' (2018) 35 Wisconsin International Law Journal 237, 256–63.

[41] Including the following: 'margin of appreciation', 'fourth instance' doctrine, 'primarily a matter for regulation under national law', 'non-formalist approach', quality of domestic legal process, 'respect for national constitutions' (dissenting opinion by Judge Kūris in *Király and Dömötör v Hungary* App no 10851/13 (ECtHR, 17 January 2017) para 42); 'domestic courts are better placed to examine and interpret facts' (*Lindstrand Partners Advokatbyrå AB v Sweden* App no 18700/09 (ECtHR, 20 December 2016) para 85); 'falls first to the national authorities to redress any alleged violation of the Convention' (*Mikhno v Ukraine* App no 32514/12 (ECtHR, 1 September 2016) para 116); 'supervisory role' of the Court (*AK v Latvia* App no 33011/08 (ECtHR, 24 June 2014) para 86).

autonomy[42]) of the Convention's human rights mechanism. Sometimes, the ECtHR has also justified its deferential approach with a novel variant of the 'better placed' formula: originally, the Court used this formula for situations involving 'better access to information' by domestic authorities: domestic authorities may be better placed to adjudicate alleged human rights violations due to their epistemic lead regarding the needs of society or their direct contact with witnesses. Recently, however, the ECtHR has started to broaden the application of the 'better placed' formula and justified judicial deference to national authorities by pointing out that 'national authorities have direct democratic legitimation in so far as the protection of human rights is concerned'.[43] Since 2003 (and increasingly after 2014), the ECtHR has relied on this 'direct democratic legitimation' formula in order to justify a more deferential approach.[44] Doctrinally, the ECtHR resorts to the margin of appreciation doctrine when it allows for a decentralized interpretation of Convention rights.[45] Through the application of the margin of appreciation the ECtHR is in control of when and how much (non-)universality comes into its case law.[46] It seems that decentralized interpretations are more acceptable with respect to certain Convention rights, and less acceptable with respect to others. For some rights, for example the right to life (Article 2 ECHR) or the prohibition against torture, inhuman or degrading treatment or punishment (Article 3 ECHR), the ECtHR has accepted little room for a national '*Sonderweg*'.[47] It can be argued that universalizing interpretations of these rights are more appropriate due to the fundamental nature of the interest they protect (as indicated by the non-derogability of the right) and/or the existence of a European consensus regarding the interpretation of the right.[48]

---

[42] Including the following: 'autonomy of the Convention' (dissenting opinion by Judge Bernhardt in *Öztürk v Germany* App no 8544/79 (ECtHR, 21 February 1984) para 2).
[43] *Van der Heijden v the Netherlands* App no 42857/05 (ECtHR, 3 April 2012) para 55.
[44] *Hatton v United Kingdom* App no 36022/97 (ECtHR, 8 July 2003) para 97. A HUDOC search reveals seven entries (in February 2020).
[45] For an overview, see Andreas Føllesdal, 'Exporting the Margin of Appreciation' (2017) 15 International Journal of Constitutional Law 359, 363-64 (margin of appreciation doctrine is needed for 'applications to specific local circumstances').
[46] See James A Sweeney, 'Margins of Appreciation: Cultural Relativity and the European Court of Human Rights in the Post-Cold War Era' (2005) 54 International and Comparative Law Quarterly 459, 461. For criticism, see Eva Brems, 'Margin of Appreciation and Incrementalism in the Case Law of the European Court of Human Rights' (2018) 18 Human Rights Law Review 495, 501 (arguing that references to the margin of appreciation 'are rather empty').
[47] See Steven Greer, 'Universalism and Relativism in the Protection of Human Rights in Europe: Politics, Law and Culture' in Petr Agha (ed), *Human Rights between Law and Politics: The Margin of Appreciation in Post-national Contexts* (Hart Publishing 2017) 31-32; for a more nuanced view, see Lech Garlicki, 'Cultural Values in Supranational Adjudication: Is there a "Cultural Margin of Appreciation" in Strasbourg?' in Michael Sachs and Helmut Siekmann (eds), *Der grundrechtsgeprägte Verfassungsstaat: Festschrift für Klaus Stern zum 80. Geburtstag* (Duncker & Humblot 2012) 738-41 (on the role of the margin of appreciation in art 2 ECHR cases).
[48] Føllesdal (n 45) 364; Yuval Shany, 'Toward a General Margin of Appreciation Doctrine in International Law?' (2006) 16 European Constitutional Law Review 907, 927. For empirical evidence, see Altwicker, 'Non-Universal Arguments' (n 3) 119.

3. Conclusion: A Principled Approach to the New Binary?

The pressure on the ECtHR to accommodate human rights nationalism seems to be high at present. This is especially so given the current political agenda in some European states towards pushing back the international protection of human rights. However, it is hard for the Court to devise a principled judicial approach to the new binary, national relativism–universality. In particular, the general justifications offered by the Court for deference to domestic authorities—the principle of subsidiarity and the direct democratic legitimation formula—both offer little normative guidance when it comes to accommodating human rights nationalism. The reference to subsidiarity is only of little help here due to its primarily *institutional* focus. The principle essentially means that the primary responsibility to safeguard the observance of the Convention rights lies with the contracting states. This understanding is reflected in the recent Copenhagen Declaration adopted by all forty-six contracting states.[49] Normatively, the Copenhagen Declaration can be read as pushing the Court towards the stricter application of the principle of subsidiarity, and, thus, to strengthen the domestic, non-universal dimension of IHRL.[50] Subsidiarity is also the central focus of the recent Protocol No 15 to the ECHR (not yet in force).[51] Protocol No 15 to the ECHR will formally incorporate the principle of subsidiarity and the margin of appreciation doctrine into the Preamble of the Convention.[52] In all these instances, subsidiarity essentially focuses on *institutional* questions by opening up the argumentative space on the question of 'who should have the final say'. It is silent, however, upon the issue of human rights universality: reference to subsidiarity does not help when the abstractness claim of human rights universality is at stake. In other words, subsidiarity as such does not turn the national context into a difference-making fact. It does not provide normative guidance on the question of 'what conduct should be protected regardless of the national context', and respectively the question of 'in which cases is a national *Sonderweg* in the interpretation of Convention rights acceptable'.

---

[49] Copenhagen Declaration, adopted at the High Level Conference in Copenhagen, 12–13 April 2018, para 28 <http://rm.coe.int/copenhagen-declaration/16807b915c> accessed 31 May 2021 (stressing, in particular, that the Court 'does not act as a court of fourth instance', that states enjoy a margin of appreciation, that domestic authorities are in principle 'better placed' to 'evaluate local needs and conditions', that there 'may be a range of different but legitimate solutions which could each be compatible with the Convention depending on the context', and that the Court will generally 'not substitute its own assessment for that of the domestic courts').

[50] See ibid para 31 (welcoming the 'further development of the principle of subsidiarity and the doctrine of the margin of appreciation by the Court in its jurisprudence').

[51] <www.coe.int/en/web/conventions/full-list/-/conventions/treaty/213> accessed 31 May 2021. On the drafting history (the Brighton Declaration), see Ian Cram, 'Protocol 15 and Articles 10 and 11 ECHR—The Partial Triumph of Political Incumbency Post-Brighton?' (2018) 67 International and Comparative Law Quarterly 477, 480–84.

[52] Art 1 of Protocol No 15 to the ECHR.

The other justification of deference, the 'direct democratic legitimation' formula, may indeed be viewed as suggesting a difference-making fact. The fact that, for example, a statutory norm was adopted following a democratic legislative process of a contracting state constitutes prima facie legitimacy. Nevertheless, it is doubtful whether a principled approach to the new binary, national relativism–universality, can be founded on the direct democratic legitimation formula. First, the formula is overbroad (situations in which domestic authorities could not claim a more direct form of legitimacy are difficult to conceive).[53] Secondly, a slippery slope problem is arising that may ultimately threaten the idea of the international protection mechanism itself: relying on the direct democratic legitimation formula runs the risk of playing out the powerful idea of democratic control against the idea of international judicial protection of human rights.

The accommodation of the new binary, national relativism–universality, must follow a principled approach. A way forward may be found in what was identified in the literature as a shift by the ECtHR from a substantive to a 'process-based review':[54] the ECtHR is increasingly willing to defer to domestic interpretive authority if the quality of the domestic democratic and judicial processes meet the Convention standard.[55] The pressure to accommodate national relativism may thus eventually lead to a proceduralization of the idea of human rights universality: rather than assessing the outcome of domestic decision-making under universalizable interpretations of Convention rights (following the idea of universality as abstractness and rationality), the Court will limit itself to assessing the domestic decision-making or the domestic judicial proceedings under universalizable human rights principles.

---

[53] Including the following: a case concerning a government policy on night flights (*Hatton v United Kingdom* App no 36022/97 (ECtHR, 8 July 2003)); a new law barring the applicants from compensation claims regarding negligence in establishing a prenatal diagnosis (*Maurice v France* App no 11810/03 (ECtHR, 6 October 2005)); matters of social-economic policy (*Valkov v Bulgaria* App nos 2033/04 and others (ECtHR, 25 October 2011) para 92); the problem of compellability of witnesses (*Van der Heijden v the Netherlands* App no 42857/05 (ECtHR, 3 April 2012)); matters of housing reform in a post-socialist setting (*Berger-Krall v Slovenia* App no 14717/04 (ECtHR, 12 June 2014)); the relationship between state and religions (*SAS v France* App no 43835/11 (ECtHR, 1 July 2014) para 122); a law prohibiting health professionals from attending home births (*Dubská and Krejzová v the Czech Republic* App nos 28859/11 and others (ECtHR, 15 November 2016)); restrictions in choosing the place of residence (*Garb v Netherlands* App no 43494/09 (ECtHR, 6 November 2017)); refusal of leave to conduct one's own defence in domestic court proceedings (*Correia de Matos v Portugal* App no 56402/12 (ECtHR, 4 April 2018)).

[54] Robert Spano, 'The Future of the European Court of Human Rights—Subsidiarity, Process-Based Review and the Rule of Law' (2018) 18 Human Rights Law Review 473, 480–94.

[55] See Thomas Kleinlein, 'Consensus and Contestability: The ECtHR and the Combined Potential of European Consensus and Procedural Rationality Control' (2017) 28 European Journal of International Law 871 (with references to the case law).

IV

UNIVERSALITY AND THE NON-HUMAN

9
Universalisms of Human Dominion

Alejandro Lorite

International law is born of the destruction of worlds. Its universalism is tied to the suppression of all other universes that have disappeared, and keep disappearing, since the start of European colonial expansion. As part of its work in globalizing a local construction of everything, international law carries a specific universalizing code of reference for human relations to animals, including a variety of ways of redefining animals in their position and worth relative to humans. The human–animal division upon which various segments of international regulation covering animal life are implicitly founded is specific and contingent, but is entrenched, globalized, and naturalized by legal rules that implement it. The object of this contribution is to stage and name that binary relation. In the following I attempt therefore a characterization of international law's universalism in relation to animals with the use of two structural homologies, that is, the parallelism in form of two relations of domination in which the dominated are constructed as effects of the system of domination, as well as dependent extensions of the dominant: imperial erasure of native worldview and self-determination, on the one hand, and totalitarian control in the political space of camps, on the other. Proposing that animals are found in a structurally homologous situation, which has consequences for the critique of current regulation and legal reform, requires mobilizing and assemblage of interdisciplinary input that will render exotic what international law makes natural and obvious. I proceed in four steps, which draw inspiration from different domains of inquiry.

In Section 1, I start with a definition of the human–animal binary as a dualism and situate it as such among other dualist constructions tied to structures of oppression. I mention the imperial displacement of other worlds and other knowledges, and more specifically the reconstruction of imperial subjects as instruments of imperial agents and effects of imperial normative systems. I draw here on Antony Anghie, for his reading of the construction of the barbarian Other by the European self in the context of the birth of modern international law. Then, for a specific framing of binary oppositions, such as that between human and animal, I rely on Valerie Plumwood, for her analysis of dualisms and what she posits as their association with domination. This approach yields a particular understanding of the objects of domination as deprived of both an autonomous existence and an autonomous representation of the universe.

In Section 2, I suggest that the human–animal dualism as it is conveyed and entrenched by international law is the expression of a historically contingent schematization of the experience of the world by living beings. The existence of alternative cultural dispositions to human–animal and human–nature binaries imposes a relativization of the worldview carried by international regulation. I suggest that the human–animal relation envisioned by international law is therefore part of a project of political domination and is grounded in a view of humans that is not only relative, but also competing (victoriously) against alternatives, most notoriously represented by reconstructed Indigenous cosmologies and epistemologies. Properly relativizing the globalized worldview carried by international law is necessary to characterize it as structurally problematic, and, more specifically, to describe it as a totalizing frame of domination akin to what has been said of colonialism and totalitarianism among humans. For the complicated effort at relativizing the given worldview, I draw on a certain strand of cultural anthropology, exemplified here by Philippe Descola and Eduardo Viveiros de Castro.

In a third step, I briefly depict the expression of this relative worldview of human–animal relations in international law, by alluding to some examples of the normative reconstruction of animals as dependent instrumental or functional extensions of humans without autonomous representations of the world, along the lines of what Valerie Plumwood suggests of dualisms and domination. I focus more specifically on a central piece of the international legal architecture of 'global animal law',[1] the World Animal Health Organization (or OIE), which I depict as an institutional expression of the global construction of animals in those derivative terms. I focus on the adoption of animal welfarism as the legitimating ethics for this imperial construction of animal life as a dependent extension of separate and autonomous human needs.

In a fourth step, I suggest that the worldview on human–animal relations that is conveyed by international, or global, animal law, such as it is represented by the OIE, is mistakenly evaluated with reference to so-called speciesism, that is, the notion of a discrimination based on species belonging. Animals are not victims as subject to the dynamic of illegitimate discrimination as it is understood within Liberal legal orders; they are victims as objects of the inner rationality of Liberalism, which projects them as the unreasoning insiders-outsiders that we appropriately call 'non-human animals'. The extensive and extreme violence against animals that is legitimated by (international) law is indeed rational, and even defines reason and morality itself in many ways (as when we resent humans being treated 'like animals'). That violence keeps being perfected within the Liberal domain of reason,

---

[1] See eg Anne Peters, 'Global Animal Law: What It Is and Why We Need It' (2016) 5 Transnational Environmental Law 9; Thomas G Kelch, 'Towards Universal Principles for Global Animal Advocacy' (2016) 5 Transnational Environmental Law 81. More generally see Anne Peters, *Studies in Global Animal Law* (Springer Nature 2020).

which expels animals to the borderlands of mercy and kindness, on the outskirts of an ethics rooted in human dignity and social contractualism. The proper point of reference is therefore, from the speculative viewpoint of animals, not discrimination as an affront to Liberalism, but totalitarian domination as a legitimated reconstruction of individuals, collectives, and assemblages into dependent extensions of the imperial master. I suggest that we call this Dominionism. For this proposal I draw on an often used and abused, but rarely engaged with, quote by Isaac Bashevis Singer, who depicts the animal condition as an 'eternal Treblinka' and all human beings as Nazis to animals. I decide here to take Singer's passage as evoking a structural homology between two relations of total political, epistemological, and ultimately ontological domination, in order to lay out foundations for a critical and constructive assessment of international law's universalism as serving this political project of domination on a global scale.

In conclusion, I suggest that international law's appropriate reaction should be to momentarily pause in the full awareness of the technocratic horror at hand, withdraw into contrite silence about the welfare of fellow animal earthlings, even if it is only to move on to a better administration of the global slaughterhouse.[2]

1. Universes of Dualism and Destruction

Universalism in international law is rooted in the historical deployment of the local universals of natural law to construct the space of colonialism. Antony Anghie's canonical reading of Francisco de Vitoria displays the argumentative structure of universalism as destruction.[3] Europeans and 'the Indians lately discovered'[4] are brought together under a common legal framing of relations between self and other in the forms of sovereignty and property, humanity and divinity. That extension of the Christian and jusnaturalist universe, to encompass the Others within the realm of normative argument, thus subjects 'them' seemingly to the same rules as 'us'. That allows in turn for the systematic exploitation, spoliation, and subjugation of them by us, precisely on account of their differences from us within that supposedly common normative frame of humanity.[5] From the imperial point of view, the *barbari* natives of the New World do have government and property, which allows us to deal with them, but then again they may also be 'inept' and 'stupid',[6] with imperfect sovereigns, or with improperly shared private property, and as such may

---

[2] Alejandro Lorite Escorihuela, 'A Global Slaughterhouse' (2011) 2 Helsinki Review of Global Governance 25.
[3] Antony Anghie, 'Francisco De Vitoria and the Colonial Origins of International Law' (1996) 5 Social & Legal Studies 321.
[4] Francisco de Vitoria, *De Indis Et de Iure Belli Relectiones* (Ernest Nys ed, Carnegie Institution of Washington 1917) 115, 217.
[5] Anghie, 'Francisco De Vitoria' (n 3) 327.
[6] Vitoria, *De Indis* (n 4) 336.

ultimately 'exist only as the objects against which Christian sovereignty can exercise its power to wage war'.[7]

Anghie calls Vitoria's imagined New World natives 'schizophrenic',[8] because they are universal by reason, and particular by socialization. Binarity is unavoidable in the narrative structure of the birth of sovereignty and international law: Spaniards and Indians, Christians and heathens, centre and periphery, universal and particular, property and sovereignty. Given the association of such binarity with violence and destruction, one is led to assume critically that such binaries are deployed in a way that makes the most of a background of power differentials. The epistemological dimension of the binary construction of the Other (as a necessary extension of the imperial Self) is matched with a normative, political, and moral dimension of binarity: the Other is constructed against the modelling of the self, and thus immediately and relationally defined by its *own* lacks, flaws, and shortcomings with reference to the model (of proper reasoning, proper aesthetic judgement, proper mores). As such the oppositional pairs cannot be seen simply as mere descriptive divisions and contrasts, or ethereally logical dichotomies. Those must be seen more properly as dualisms.

1.1 Dualisms Are about Domination

Valerie Plumwood clarified in the most searching way the nature and function of dualisms in the context of feminist debates on the critique of formal logic. She suggested that we approach dualisms in terms of specific associations between particular binary oppositions, on the one hand, and relations of domination, on the other hand:

> A dualism, I argue, should be understood as a particular way of dividing the world which results from a certain kind of denied dependency on a subordinated other. This relationship of denied dependency determines a certain kind of logical structure, as one in which the denial and the relation of domination/subordination shapes the identity of both the relata.[9]

Plumwood proposed that 'Western thought' is 'characterized by a set of interrelated and mutually reinforcing dualisms which permeate culture, forming a fault line which runs through its entire conceptual system'.[10] The notion that Western civilization is marked by the ubiquitous organizational influence of binary oppositions

---

[7] Anghie, 'Francisco De Vitoria' (n 3) 330.
[8] ibid 327.
[9] Valerie Plumwood, 'The Politics of Reason: Towards a Feminist Logic' (1993) 71 Australasian Journal of Philosophy 436, 443.
[10] ibid 443.

has by now become common; but Plumwood's structured reading offers a dual take on dualisms as organizing forms of thought. They are, on the other hand, culturally contingent and interconnected, and, on the other hand, systemically entangled with the operationalization of structures of domination in those contexts (civilized/savage, male/female, culture/nature, human/animal etc). Dualisms, she suggested, were 'not universal features of human thought, but conceptual responses to and foundations for social domination',[11] so that the articulation of chains of dualisms (the origin of which is admittedly subject to debate and speculation) has been evolving over time alongside the history of the domination itself.

The period of colonial conquest, for instance, brought 'to the fore civilised/primitive as a variant of reason/nature and of reason/animal and mind/body, and the rise of science brings to the fore subject/object dualism'.[12] Beyond contextual variations across time and space, a general proposition is that dualisms are generally characterized by common features associated with domination, as well as with the denial of the dependency that domination creates for both dominant and dominated. Those features form the bases for the interconnection, or echoing, between discrete dualisms associated with domination in a given context (human/animal; man/woman; master/servant; colonized/colonized).[13] Valerie Plumwood's argument suggests five such features, such as incorporation (ie making the dominated one into a mere part of the dominant one) or objectification/instrumentalism (ie making the dominated one into only an instrument of the dominant one's desires and needs).[14] Those features converge in constructing the dominated element of the duality as inferior to the dominant element, but also as ontologically separate yet existentially dependent on the dominant. The dominated element is made into an object for the dominant's instrumental reason and (most importantly for what will follow on the human–animal relations) a generalized particular, whereby dominated individuals are defined essentially by the fact that they are part of a dominated class and thus essentially replaceable units:[15]

> The other is not seen as a unique individual bound to the self by specific ties, and is related to as a universal rather than as a particular, as a member of a class of interchangeable items which can be used as resources to satisfy the master's

---

[11] ibid 444.
[12] ibid 444.
[13] Valerie Plumwood uses a variety of terms to depict the dualistic form, and in particular the dominated element in it, against a discussion of Hegel's master/servant and Memmi's colonizer/colonized: 'the dominated', 'the dominated class' 'the dominated group', 'the lower side', 'the oppressed group'. Valerie Plumwood, *Feminism and the Mastery of Nature* (Routledge 1993) 49, 53, 78, 81, and 115.
[14] The other features are: backgrounding, radical exclusion (also called hyperseparation), and stereotyping, ibid 47–55.
[15] This is of course a crude rewording of Plumwood's spectacular conceptual exposition. See Plumwood, 'The Politics of Reason' (n 9) 447–53.

needs. Elimination of reliance on any particular individual of the relevant kind also facilitates denial of dependency and backgrounding.[16]

Dualisms operate to inform or constrain the social, political, and ultimately conceptual visibility of an object. Inhabitants of the African continent or the New World are made forcefully visible, thinkable within the imperial reach, by being constructed as the subordinate and (ontologically and then also politically) dependent element in the pair. They cannot escape from the metaphysical condition of being a mere extension of the dominant. A variety of critical projects in law and elsewhere have thus suggested undoing those constructions, made visible to a universalized Western civilizational gaze in the course of imperial expansion, which constructs otherness by way of universalizing sameness. The Other is 'different' according to the standards of differentiation that are imposed by imperial expansion of the dualisms (the 'Indians' are different among themselves and also from us Europeans, at least according to European notions of sameness and difference). Within that inner logic of imperial expansion accompanied by law, once brought into the universalist fold by force, 'Indians' are 'kind of' like us, so we the Europeans can justify, not only to us but also to them, that they are inferior and must bow to our superior access to universal truth, so that the truth can be brought down forcefully upon them by us.

1.2 Dualisms Are about an Inside and an Outside

When seen through the lens of Plumwood's 'logic of domination',[17] the form of all dualisms, as they are generalized and exported in a history of violence, is that of a division between an inside and an outside. The space of the inside is occupied by those who have access to the knowledge that allows for the determination of the very border between inside and outside; that epistemological separation, between those who know and those who do not, turns into a political hierarchy between those who are in the know and those who are not. Those in the know have the authority and legitimacy to rule over those who do not know. In all cases the outside is a by-product of the constitution of a centre encountering a periphery, which is precisely constructed as the outside by the centre. This is reminiscent of Anghie's more precise discussion of the invention of sovereignty in the encounter with the New World natives, which constitutes the foundation for subordination, if not subjugation: 'sovereignty doctrine expels the non-European world from its realm, and then proceeds to legitimise the imperialism that resulted in the incorporation of

---

[16] Plumwood, *Feminism* (n 13) 54.
[17] Plumwood, 'The Politics of Reason' (n 9) 445.

the non-European world into the system of international law.'[18] The distinction between inside and outside implies exclusive knowledge of the universe within which the inside and the outside make sense. The state of nature and its savages is a projection of society's and reason's Others, by the inhabitants of the social inside, onto inhabitants of a (projected) natural outside; the latter are defined as waiting for subjugation on the basis of the dualist logic of existential dependency of the dominated (outsider) on the dominant (insider).

Universalism itself can be seen structurally as the expression of a dualism that opposes the universal and the particular, while indicating (as dualisms do) a normative tilt towards the former.[19] It must then also be approached contextually, as anchored in a history of violence in which a particular universe has been made universal by force. Alternative universes have been lost as a result of their colonial suppression by European universalism, that of international law as carrier of a progressively Liberal enlightenment and of capitalist expansion. As such, then, universalisms are relative and have always been made by the domination of the inside over the outside that it creates, by way of imperial imposition of the criteria of insiderness and their normative, political, and economic consequences.

International law reflects and expresses a particular universalism of human–animal relations, which is foundational of an anthropocentric vision of universal order. The legal construction of animals in contemporary international law evinces a dualist structure of the human–animal relation, within which the subordinate category of 'animal' checks all the boxes of Valerie Plumwood's list of features of the dominated pole of the binary (animals being unsurprisingly one such dominated group of entities in her own descriptions).[20] The human–animal dualism carried by our contemporary internationalist universalism is arguably in fact the archetype of the insider/outsider distinction that fuels the imagination of a bounded liberal political order inside, standing in opposition to the waging of war against the disorder of nature and savagery on the outside.[21] Animals are brought in from the outside by rules that subjugate them, because animals have been defined and constructed out of the polity in the first place, by way of the erasure of any animal viewpoint that is not mediated by human minds and needs. International law carries on an imperial mission within which animals are, again self-evidently, mere extensions of humans by way of their construction as outsiders, defined by the criteria set by the human

---

[18] Antony Anghie, 'The Evolution of International Law: Colonial and Postcolonial Realities' (2006) 27 Third World Quarterly 739, 740.

[19] Plumwood, Feminism (n 13) 181.

[20] ibid 29: '[D]ifferent kinds of domination act as models, support and reinforcement, for one another, and the way in which the same conceptual structure of domination reappears in very different inferiorised groups: as we have seen, it marks women, nature, "primitive" people, slaves, animals, manual labourers, "savages", people of colour—all supposedly "closer to the animals".'

[21] In associating her analysis of dualistic domination with Liberalism, Plumwood herself emphasizes the notion of Liberalism's original self-interested individual subjecting the environment to instrumental reason from a perspective that denies all autonomous perspective or worth to the projects of others. See ibid 151–52.

insiders from the viewpoint of their own position towards the universe. This momentum of international law is completed by moral extensionism, which sanctions imperial rule by adding the veneer of human justice. In an epistemologically and politically delicate interplay of homologies and comparisons, the notion of 'relative universalisms' revealed by cultural anthropology in the ashes and debris of genocide allows us to consider international law's peculiar universalist reach over animals, from the perspective of the animal outsider, as a form of political control that merges imperialism and totalitarianism. I will suggest that we call it Dominionism.

2. Relative Universalisms and Animal Selves

Cultural anthropology shows, according to Philippe Descola, that binaries as such are in fact not Western inventions ('*inventions de l'Occident*') but are extensively used by all peoples in many circumstances ('*par tous les peuples dans bien des circonstances*').[22] The specific content of binaries, as opposed to the binary form itself, is however not universal. Descola famously proposes that a specific pair of universal binaries (self/other; interiority/physicality) allows for a closed classification of 'general schemas that govern the objectivization of the world and of others'[23] ('*schèmes généraux d'objectivation du monde et d'autrui*'[24]). The universalizing gesture of anthropology therefore relativizes universalism characteristically by specifying and localizing modes of apprehension of the universe. Binaries are rescued as a useful tool in thinking the possibility of an epistemological and ontological outside, beyond the reach of the judgements of modernity, and evoking alternative social and moral arrangements that set a boundary to the Eurocentric worldview. Descola suggests that the cultural West is committed to what he calls 'modern naturalism', a broad epistemological framing and sensibility of the relation of the human subject to natural objects, and that 'modern naturalism' is only one of four (and only four) existing schemas of objectivization, alongside animism, totemism, and analogism.[25]

2.1 Universal Relations and Relativity of Universalisms

With a view to replacing an arrogant universalist/relativist dichotomy, which presumes in ethnocentric fashion precisely so much about the given unicity of the natural universe and the corresponding univocality of cultural particulars, Descola

---

[22] Philippe Descola, *Par-delà nature et culture* (Folio 2015) 220.
[23] Philippe Descola, *Beyond Nature and Culture* (University of Chicago Press 2013) xviii.
[24] Descola (n 22) 16.
[25] ibid 220.

lays out the notion of a loose meta-universalism, which he calls 'relative universalism'. Relative universalism is a universalism of relations that, while acknowledging the radical difference of epistemologies and ontologies across 'cultures', maintains the hope of universal human communication through the universalism of formal relations (inside/outside; self/other). That allows crucially for some representation ('diplomatic representation', as Viveiros de Castro puts it) of the Other's descriptive practices.[26]

The Western world, or Western modernity, is very deeply committed to 'modern naturalism',[27] a mode of objectivization marked by an ontological dualism within which, to simplify a complex argument, humans stand separate from nature and act on it through observation and control, that is, through culture.[28] On the one hand there is nature in its universality and factuality, and on the other hand there is the variety of cultural reactions to objective nature. The positioning of such a relation between nature and culture, with the assertion of the universality of nature, amounts however to a clandestine 'particular universalism', in Bruno Latour's expression, most obviously carried along by the sciences. This includes social sciences, like anthropology, that carry the temptation of universalizing from the particulars of Western civilizations.[29] But the Others, those beyond naturalism, engage with 'nature' and natural objects from within alternative frames or schemas—'animism', 'totemism', 'analogism'—that result concretely in, among other things, alternative understandings of what animals really are in their relations to humans, how they differ from us, what their place is alongside us in the universe, and what the rules of engagement are supposed to be.[30]

Stated in different ways, the project of exploring the outside of modern naturalism yields a concrete notion that animals are 'social constructs', in the general sense of not being given as raw and transparent material of the outside world, but are appendices (or by-products) of entire social and cultural systems (which include such things as modern sciences). Elsewhere, outside the reach of modern naturalism, human–animal relations may be based on the fundamental idea that there is no universal convergence of reference, as Viveiros de Castro calls it, there is no common or shared reliance on the existence of one common reality by the most diverse thinking perspectives (human, animals, machines).[31] Rather, different Indigenous communities live on the notion that uniformity of spirit across a

---

[26] ibid 522–23. Eduardo Viveiros de Castro, *The Relative Native: Essays on Indigenous Conceptual Worlds* (Martin Holbraad, David Rodgers, and Julia Sauma trs, HAU 2016) 48.
[27] Descola (n 22) 70.
[28] ibid 122.
[29] Viveiros de Castro (n 27) 237.
[30] Eduardo Viveiros de Castro, 'Cosmological Deixis and Amerindian Perspectivism' (1998) 4 The Journal of the Royal Anthropological Institute 469; Eduardo Kohn, *How Forests Think: Toward an Anthropology Beyond the Human* (1st edn, University of California Press 2013); Descola (n 22) 23–65.
[31] Viveiros de Castro, *The Relative Native* (n 26) 18.

variety of (dis)embodiments (humans, animals, spirits) yields many natures,[32] what Viveiros de Castro names 'multinaturalism' (in opposition to 'multiculturalism').[33]

Radical difference is manifested in the fact that in an alternative objectivization scheme or, in Viveiros' terms, a different perspective, such as that of a given Amerindian cultural context, the boundary between humans and animals, which allochthonous European people, such as myself, accept as a given, does not seem to obtain. Alternative schemes, observable in so-called Indigenous epistemologies, express radically distinct modes of objectivation, characterized for instance by the acknowledgment that animals (ie those that non-Indigenous moderns like myself call 'animals') have themselves representations of the world different from our own,[34] that animal minds or spirit are of a kind with human spirit but distanced from us by the physical discontinuity of bodies.[35] More simply, in that perspective there is no such thing as a category of 'animals' opposed to 'humans'.[36] There are only discrete communities of beings in a world of 'immanent humanity'.[37]

2.2 Relativism and the Construction of Animals

This is not an instance of 'cultural relativism', in the sense of how Western universalisms condescendingly regard exotic variations in the apprehension of a given physical nature. Alternative modes of approaching the universe, exemplified by Indigenous social organization and in particular Indigenous communities' relations and coexistence with animals and other beings, display a radical difference in relating to animals from what modern naturalism seems to promote. The difference is however simply one dimension of a generally different understanding of what humans are, of what a human community may be, and of what our relation to the material and the spiritual world is. Animals appear to be treated differently in that mode of existence or universe, because those that we (ie individuals like me who are rooted in our own naturalist universe) see as 'animals' are in fact part of a more general economy of relations in a differently shared universe, where exchanges with other beings have different meanings, functions, and rules. Animals are not objects or property because those are not the relevant categories. Subject/object relations in alternative epistemological universes, such as Indigenous communities observed by Descola, Viveiros, and others, do not translate into objectification and

---

[32] ibid 18.
[33] Viveiros de Castro, 'Cosmological Deixis' (n 30) 472.
[34] Eduardo Kohn, 'How Dogs Dream: Amazonian Natures and the Politics of Transspecies Engagement' (2007) 34 American Ethnologist 3.
[35] Descola (n 22) 497–98.
[36] Viveiros de Castro, *The Relative Native* (n 26) 226.
[37] ibid 187.

exploitation, because this is not the proper framing of the relationship, either to guide behaviour or to understand it.

The alterity of those universes comes through in the realization that it is simply, or nearly, impossible to access that universe for the imperial outsider, except through a self-construction and self-translation by the insiders, which is then itself translated into conceptual schemes that make sense in relation to the language of science.[38] As Viveiros de Castro presents it, the confrontation is not with different opinions or beliefs, but, if anything, with a different 'theory of the mind', a different way of deploying the 'mental states of different beings in the world'.[39] The chief concern in approaching such alterity is the risk of subjecting it to a foreign logic or rationality that erases local social meaning, as is deliberately done as part of the process of cultural genocide. Descola's 'relative universalism' points to the fact that alterity lies not in belief, perception, or opinion, but at a very fundamental and categorical level of thought and experience. In other words, to follow also Viveiros de Castro, the experience of both alterity and the universals of relations comes from the confrontation with the objects of 'Indigenous reason', where 'reason' is itself relative to a given universalism.[40]

All of this is to say that glimpses of the alternative allow for the fundamental relativization of social relations, in the quintessential critical gesture of triggering a crisis,[41] that is, entering the logic of decidability, a mode of relation to the given universe as something that was decided upon, by the fiat of some humans or the course of history.[42] A modern European universalist relationship to animals, as it is expressed among other things by international legal regulation (in ways that I will sample below), is situated within a grander '*schème d'objectivation*' that can be imagined itself as a possible exotic object for anthropological investigation. Regulation that implements a worldview of subject/object, dominant/dominated relation between humans and animals must be seen as part of a contingent political project of human domination.

For instance, the global economic system kills millions of male chicks every year after having produced them industrially, as part of 'chick-culling', simply because they are deemed useless to the next steps of food production. They are literally treated like refuse to be discarded, which as such, however, is a meaningful practice within our framing of chick–human relations. There are methodic ways of reconstructing alternative worldviews (such as the ones deployed by anthropologists), and from the perspective of those alternative worldviews the given practice of mass destruction of animals may not be comprehended as reasonable or meaningful. The system of domination in which the destruction occurs must then be

---

[38] ibid 18.
[39] ibid 26.
[40] ibid 19.
[41] Roland Barthes, *Le bruissement de la langue (Essais critiques IV)* (Seuil 1984) 361.
[42] Jacques Derrida, *Du droit à la philosophie* (Galilée 1990) 179.

characterized from an outside point of view, as an exotic violent ritualistic practice of destruction that expresses the deep structure of animal–human relations also found in other practices of that exotic (Western) worldview. In other words, the type of violence done to chickens (or pigs, or cows, or deer, or dolphins, or mice), which is organized and rationalized by law, policy, and culture, can be imagined from the outside, and can thus be seen as part of a sociopolitical project drawing on the deeper epistemological and ontological foundations of our anthropocentric universalism. Doing the work of reconstruction is imperative to understand what is done to animals, what the nature of the harm is, and what the law's part in it is.

3. Human Law's Empire and Animal Objects

3.1 How to Construct Animal Objects

According to Valerie Plumwood, in the dualist construction of domination the dominated one manifests a series of features. The one she calls 'incorporation' is of an ontological nature and points to the loss by the dominated one of their existential independence and their reconstruction with reference to the dominant: 'The Other is recognised only to the extent that it is assimilated to the self, or incorporated into the self and its systems of desires and needs: only as colonised by the self. The master consciousness cannot tolerate unassimilated otherness.'[43] Another feature, 'instrumentalism', or 'objectification', refers to the loss of independent purpose and ultimately autonomous worth:

> [T]hose on the lower side [...] are made part of a network of purposes which are defined in terms of or harnessed to the master's purposes and needs. The lower side is also objectified, without ends of its own which demand consideration on their own account. Its ends are defined in terms of the master's ends. The dualizing master self does not empathically recognise others as moral kin, and does not recognise them as a centre of desires or needs on their own account. Hence on both counts he is free to impose his own ends. [...] The identity of the underside is constructed instrumentally, and the canons of virtue for a good wife, a good colonised, or a good worker are written in terms of usefulness to the centre.[44]

Carol Adams' invocation of an 'absent referent' to animal life in the language of meat consumption and production, which suppresses the notion of an autonomous existence behind the processed object of consumption (pork and not pig, chicken and not hen, beef and not cow, and so on) may be a specific and particularly deep

---

[43] Plumwood, *Feminism* (n 13) 52.
[44] ibid 53.

expression of the logic of domination by reconstruction of the dominated self in the image of the dominant's needs.[45]

Legal regulation of human–animal relations implements the enforcement and entrenchment of such a dualist logic, within which animals are reconstructed as dependents and instruments. The facts and the justice of that unequal relationship are implicitly normalized, naturalized, and legitimated by law to ensure the reproduction of the relationship in beneficial ways for the centre. Antony Anghie calls 'dynamic of difference' the process by which legal imperialism creates otherness in ways that then allow for subjugation in terms that are justified by the very existence of the difference just created by the conqueror:

> [J]urists using the conceptual tools of positivism postulated a gap, understood principally in terms of cultural differences, between the civilized European and uncivilized non-European world; having established this gap they then proceeded to devise a series of techniques for bridging this gap, of civilizing the uncivilized.[46]

Further, Anghie says of the permanence of international law's Western universalism (associated as it is with the instrumentalization of animality for the conquest of Others)[47] that 'the universalizing mission of international law ... could adapt itself to changed circumstances and anticolonial political sentiments and still continue its task of ensuring that the Western model of law and behavior would be seen as natural, inevitable, and inescapable'.[48] Law serves the entrenchment of a worldview and its reproduction by crowding out alternative ways of being and representing the world (whether non-Western or non-human), as well as reconstructing the carriers of those ways as deficient participants in the dominant (Western) worldview. In the case of animals, beings seemingly without culture or language or history, the process is more obvious and even more deeply naturalized. The structural homology that I am alluding to here follows Plumwood's warning of the existence of lines of convergence and chains of equivalence between discrete dualisms and the arcs of domination.[49]

The signature imperial move is that of accompanying the deployment of violence with, first, the legal regime that grants it meaning and direction and, secondly, the

---

[45] Carol J Adams, *The Sexual Politics of Meat (20th Anniversary Edition): A Feminist-Vegetarian Critical Theory* (A&C Black 2010) 66.
[46] Antony Anghie, *Imperialism, Sovereignty and the Making of International Law* (CUP 2007) 37.
[47] Vitoria, *De Indis* (n 4) 161.
[48] Antony Anghie, 'Colonialism and the Birth of International Institutions: Sovereignty, Economy, and the Mandate System of the League of Nations' (2001) 34 New York University Journal of International Law and Politics 513, 566.
[49] See eg Plumwood, *Feminism* (n 13) 45. The human–animal dualism has a particular place in Plumwood's discussion of the (non-exhaustive) chain of seventeen dualisms that characterize 'Western thought' (ibid 43). The human–animal dualism is significant because it maps onto fundamental oppositions between nature and culture, body and mind, or emotion and reason, all of which support each other to characterize the lower side of oppressive dualisms as inferiors (ibid 108).

expression of concern and care for the well-being or 'welfare' of those dispossessed of their world. Here, we will thus turn first to the legal system, and particularly international law, to highlight the operationalization of a system of domination within which animal subjectivity and representation are reconstructed as an extension of human needs and social functions; in it we will also encounter the extension of ethical legitimation of violence by way of applying a moral framing derived from human needs to animals, resulting thus is a logic of exclusion and further violence and destruction. This constitutes the use of a first structural homology, or comparison of relations,[50] to circumscribe the nature of human–animal relations entrenched in law and globalized by international legal regimes. To clarify further, it is not that animals are 'like' the colonized peoples of European imperialism. Rather, the *relationship* of animals to humans bears homologous familiarity with the *relationship* of Vitoria's Indians to European princes. The contents, agents, and objects of violence and domination being radically different, what stands out in this proposed homology is the dualist structure of domination depicted by Plumwood as part of the implementation of human/European universalism by way of imperial rule: the dominated subject occupies a formal position that is relationally defined, stereotyped, objectified, and so on.

Vitoria's colonial sin is his imagining of international law as the frame of universal justice in the encounter with the Other, in a way that makes justice an element of the system of imperial oppression and spoliation itself; international law does not express a view from nowhere (or a divine viewpoint) or even an independent frame of reference for judging the moral grounds of the encounter with the New World natives: international law in the birth of sovereignty performs a normative annexation into the 'inescapable' Western model of law, as Anghie puts it. Once the legal framing of sovereignty and property are imposed on the New World natives, radical alterity has been erased in favour of a gradation of differences within the imposed worldview. ('The master consciousness cannot tolerate unassimilated otherness', says Plumwood.[51]) Vitoria and Las Casas can thus push for basic rules of humanity based on both (Christian) presumptions of universal humanity and (European) prejudices of moral worth of those already deemed 'savages'. This is epistemic violence,[52] the violent displacement of knowledge and modes of knowing, accompanied of course as well by unfathomable amounts of physical violence. The echoing effect between the two contexts of domination, colonial and animal, is multiple. *First*, the echo is created by the analytic grid that I am using here, and which is itself universalist in imposing a sense of similarity between two contexts of domination that could be seen as completely unrelated; but

---

[50] Barry Brummett, *Rhetorical Homologies: Form, Culture, Experience* (University of Alabama Press 2009).

[51] Plumwood, *Feminism* (n 13) 52.

[52] Gayatri Chakravorty Spivak, 'Can the Subaltern Speak?' in Cary Nelson and Lawrence Grossberg (eds), *Marxism and the Interpretation of Culture* (repr edn, University of Illinois Press 1998).

there is here precisely the affirmation of a structural homology between relations of domination, based on the notion that dualism itself is a universal form of domination carried by 'Western thought', which is carried now by international law and the forces of globalization since colonialism. *Secondly*, and precisely because this universalism of domination is a projection from within a particular worldview, the echoes between human–animal and colonizer–colonized are also a symptom of the fact that the suppression of other universes by European colonialism has been done by framing the Other in terms that extend the human–animal dualism (natives are like animals, as Juan Ginés de Sepúlveda would say to justify their subjugation[53]). Finally, as suggested earlier by cursory appeal to cultural anthropology, the possibility of framing from the outside the human–animal relation conveyed by the development of global animal law and ethics today is rendered possible by the reconstructed outside perspective of alternative (most notoriously Indigenous) universes that were not fully destroyed by colonialism. In some of those universes animals have representations and perspectives that are independent of our own, and most importantly, as mentioned above, ways of being in the world that do not depend on human purposes, needs, or even acknowledgement.

3.2 International Law's Animal Objects

Within the imperial space where colonial subjugation was made comprehensible and universally legitimate, international law expresses a similar structure of imperially epistemic conquest with regard to 'animals' at a global level: a projection of modern naturalism's basic presumption of the radical alterity of beasts, as well as the reduction of radical alterity to classifiable hierarchical difference, thus paradoxically also limiting the radicality of the difference between them and us when that appears suitable to our needs. Animals are outsiders to the social order but can be selectively and variously brought back inside by legal (or scientific) determination. This is done based on a spectrum of possible determinations that oscillate between the fact that they are homogenous in their difference from us ('the animals', 'the beasts') and the fact that they are also infinitely different from one another and varied in their relation to us; this in turn is deemed either important or insignificant in context depending on human assessment and regulation. (Are they food? Are they a nuisance? Are they part of the workforce? Are they a medium of entertainment? Do we share a significantly common biological nature?) Animals find then a place in the international legal order (as in domestic legal orders) as objects of regulation, either in the form of specific functional categories, classes,

---

[53] See relevant passages of Supúlveda's *Democrates Alter* (1547) in Felipe Castañeda, 'La imagen del indio y del conquistador en la Nueva Granada: el caso de Bernardo de Vargas Machuca' [2006] Eidos: Revista de Filosofía de la Universidad del Norte 40.

and species, or as 'living resources' to be managed, for the purpose of commerce in international trade law, or else more general international transactions, such as in the Law of the Sea.[54] Animals come into international law quite prominently also as part of nature conservation efforts in international environmental law, within which there is room for tension about the field's anthropocentrism,[55] but which is in any case extensively committed to seeing animals as resources for something or someone else, be it future (human) generations, or Gaia herself.[56]

Law's construction of animals as functional resources for humans implies that legal regimes may not always consider even relevant whether the animal is alive or dead.[57] Since animals (as the dominated) are constructed in relation to humans and 'not encountered fully as an independent other, and the qualities attributed or perceived are those which reflect the master's desires, needs and lacks',[58] life (or health, or reason, or anything else) is a quality that may or may not be functionally relevant in a specific legal regime. In such a fashion, which could be illustrated by countless examples, international regulations simply approach animals as functional extensions of humans and humans' social relations, within which animals find their imposed meaning, and from which they are collectively separated while remaining diverse and functionally, if not existentially, connected. The international classification of goods for the purpose of trademarks considers that animal skins are in the same category as umbrellas and whips (class 18), that animal hair is in the same class as sawdust and bivouacs (class 22), that animal claws and horns are in the same class as armchairs, while live animals themselves are in the same class as woodchips (class 31).[59] In the given cultural and epistemological context of international trademark protection and economic exchange those distinctions and

---

[54] See eg the canonical decision of the WTO Appellate Body Report, *United States—Import Prohibition of Certain Shrimp and Shrimp Products* (12 October 1998) WT/DS58/AB/R [134]. See also United Nations Convention on the Law of the Sea (adopted 10 December 1982, entered into force 16 November 1994) 1833 UNTS 3 (1982) 21 ILM 1261 art 61.

[55] Philippe Sands, *Principles of International Environmental Law* (CUP 2003) 293.

[56] Some examples are: the Convention on Wetlands of International Importance Especially as Waterfowl Habitat (adopted 2 February 1971, entered into force) 996 UNTS 245 (Preamble); the Convention on the Conservation of Migratory Species of Wild Animals (adopted 23 June 1979, entered into force 1 November 1983) 1651 UNTS 358; or the Agreement on the Conservation of Cetaceans of the Black Sea, Mediterranean Sea, and Contiguous Atlantic Area (ACCOBAMS) (adopted 24 November 1996, entered into force 1 June 2001) 36 ILM 780 (Preamble) [3]; Memorandum of Understanding for the Conservation of Cetaceans and Their Habitats in the Pacific Islands Region (adopted 15 September 2006) UN Doc UNEP/CMS/PIC-1/Inf/3.

[57] International Bovine Meat Agreement (adopted 12 April 1979, entered into force 1 January 1995) 1186 UNTS 344. The Agreement was terminated on 31 December 1997. Of relevance here are the international coding systems for commodities, which operate functional groupings that also disregard life or sentience as relevant characteristics of animal commodities. See International Convention on the Harmonized Commodity Description and Coding System, of 14 June 1983 [1987] OJ L198/3-34.

[58] Plumwood, *Feminism* (n 13) 53.

[59] Nice Agreement Concerning the International Classification of Goods and Services to Which Trademarks are Applied (adopted 15 June 1957, entered into force 8 April 1961) 550 UNTS 46. The list of items per class can be found on the website of the World Intellectual Property Organization. See 'Nice Classification' online: World Intellectual Property Association <www.wipo.int/classifications/nice/en/> accessed 28 July 2021.

indistinctions are meaningful and rational. That is what Plumwood calls 'incorporation'. When (quasi) international regulation turns to pets, a similar legal phenomenon is visible in the narrative construction of the animal. We humans state their specific relative status by labelling them pets ('cats and dogs are considered to be pet animals...') and derive from that status a position in society ('... and therefore it is not acceptable to use their fur or products containing such fur'). In the case of cats and dogs, they are not acceptably associated with other sources of fur, that is, there is no commercial cat fur. At the same time, however, pet animals remain characterized as instruments of human well-being and destiny. Their protection is ultimately less about them than it is about avoiding trade disruptions, generated here very specifically by economically harmful confusion among the consumers of fur: 'in order to eliminate obstacles to the functioning of the internal market and to restore consumer confidence in the fact that the fur products which consumers buy do not contain cat and dog fur.'[60] This is what Plumwood calls 'instrumentalism'. Overall, the international legal system here behaves imperialistically in ways that are reminiscent of Anghie's description of international law's contribution to empire in the civilized/uncivilized divide: assuming that they are outsiders and bringing in the law to manage their treatment as outsiders.[61]

International law manifests in those examples the dual relation of proximity and distance (self/other; inside/outside) that is foundational of a specific understanding of humans in their relationship to animality in general, or animality as a general trait.[62] When relating concretely to animality, however, the difference of approach and treatment between the regulation pertaining to 'straddling stocks' and that dealing with 'pets' is comprehensible only because of the very relational nature of 'animals' as entities socially (and then legally) constructed as functional extensions of humanity. This is a fairly straightforward echo of Plumwood's depiction of dualistic rhetoric. 'Animals' are both the subordinated element of the human/non-human animal dualism, and a collective of functionally distinct entities that are selectively constructed by law as part of a local economy of social relations. As so-called 'non-human animals', they are normatively governed by the fact that they are precisely both, that is, 'non-human' and animals. The former makes them outsiders, and the latter will point, for philosophy and law, to the type of functional relationship that each species or group has with us or our institutions (pet, pest, service animal, wildlife, farm animal, straddling stock) and that functional relationship will determine appropriate rules.[63] Hobbes said that there is no contract with beasts, because we cannot reason with them and they are therefore

---

[60] Regulation (EC) No 1523/2007 of the European Parliament and of the Council, banning the placing on the market and the import to, or export from, the Community of cat and dog fur, and products containing such fur, of 11 December 2007 [2007] OJ L343/1.
[61] eg Anghie, *Imperialism* (n 46) 66.
[62] See generally Giorgio Agamben, *The Open: Man and Animal* (Stanford University Press 2004).
[63] Sue Donaldson and Will Kymlicka, *Zoopolis: A Political Theory of Animal Rights* (OUP 2013).

left out of the social compact;[64] we produce therefore rules relating to their functional submission to the service of our compact as rules of empire.

3.3 International Animal Regulation, Welfarism, and Domination

Imperial extension of human rules and regulations, to cover animals as functional resources or objects destined for human ends, is most manifest in the legitimation of physical violence on animals, such as for the purpose of food production or scientific and medical experiments. Such predation (which is what we would call it if the consumer were non-human) and torture (which is what we would call it if the victim were human) are regulated in detail as meaningful practices within a normative system that interpellates animals as discrete resources. Out of the Hobbesian exclusionary political sovereign (which takes on very meaningfully the name of a Biblical monstrous animal)[65] the imperial moment[66] of bringing the outsider under the rule of law for the purpose of oppression is best exemplified by legislation that announces the objective of 'animal welfare', only to then immediately define farm and lab animals out of the realm of animality.[67] But the more manifest ideological momentum of that imperial dynamic comes, as the structure of Vitoria's universalist vision shows, in the expansion of moral concern itself to complete the submission of the Other.

In national and subnational legal systems across the world, the so-called 'animal turn',[68] or 'animal question',[69] has yielded a variety of regulatory reforms concerning the treatment of animals. Most notoriously some jurisdictions have amended the overall legal status of animals, to the effect that they are specifically not to be considered mere things. Prominent among those endeavours are revisions of civil codes in France ('*Les animaux sont des êtres vivants doués de sensibilité*'),[70] Switzerland ('*Les animaux ne sont pas des choses*'),[71] Germany and Austria ('*Tiere sind keine Sachen*'),[72] or Québec ('*Les animaux ne sont pas des biens*').[73] Those

---

[64] Thomas Hobbes, *Hobbes: Leviathan: Revised Student Edition* (CUP 1996) 187.
[65] Jacques Derrida, *The Beast and the Sovereign*, vol I (University of Chicago Press 2010) 26–30.
[66] This is not about the theory of the *Leviathan*'s relationship to imperialism. For that, see Hannah Arendt, *The Origins of Totalitarianism* (Houghton Mifflin Harcourt 1973) 139–43.
[67] See eg United States, Animal Welfare Act, 7 USC 2132(g). While the US law excludes farm and lab animals, the equivalent law in the Province of Québec, Canada, defines specifically what animals are covered by the Welfare Act, and thus manages to exclude the same categories. See Québec, *Loi sur le bien-être et la sécurité de l'animal*, RLRQ c. B.3-1 [2015].
[68] Harriet Ritvo, 'On the Animal Turn' (2007) 136 Daedalus 118.
[69] Yoriko Otomo and Edward Mussawir, *Law and the Question of the Animal: A Critical Jurisprudence* (Routledge 2013).
[70] French Code Civil, art 515-14.
[71] Swiss Civil Code, art 641a.
[72] German Civil Code, art 90a; Austrian Civil Code, art 285a.
[73] Code civil du Québec, art 898.1.

provisions designate animals for special legal care, or 'protection', (which some Codes base on their possession of sentience/sensitivity) while however subjecting them by default to the legal regime of property. Criminal codes have generally followed, if not preceded, those reforms by taking into consideration the possibility of animals being (unlike things) harmed in specific ways, in the sense of being possibly subjected to cruelty. This momentum in legal reforms is fuelled by what commentators have generally called 'welfarism', cleanly referred to by Sue Donaldson and Will Kymlicka as a moral disposition seeking or advocating 'the humane use of animals',[74] a perspective generally distinguished from 'animal rights' or else 'abolitionist' perspectives, as part of complex scholarly debates over morality, law, and policy regarding the very notion of the use of animals by humans.[75]

International law has experienced similar impulses towards a reconsideration of the status of animals, albeit in a much less visible and grandiose-sounding fashion than civil code reforms. Although the manifestation of an interest in the well-being of animals is diverse in international regulation, a significant example from the perspective that I am taking here is that offered, quite appropriately in the context of this discussion (and the fact that it takes place in times of a pandemic allegedly triggered by animals), by the universal international organization tasked formally with the question of animal health. The World Organization for Animal Health (WOAH) was created in 1924 as the *Office international des Epizooties* (OIE) and worked de facto as a technical agency of the League of Nations. It is now the world agency of reference in everything that concerns animal health control at the global level, and produces, among other documents of reference, the Terrestrial Animal Health Code (or simply 'Terrestrial Code'), a compilation of recommendations and guidelines to be used by national veterinary administrations and relating to the health of internationally traded animals.[76]

From the above, one will expect that as a regulatory framework addressing the health condition of animals, international animal health law will define into legal existence both the animals and what their health means. What comes through from the Terrestrial Code is that animal health is unsurprisingly functionally considered, from a perspective that assigns to animals a derivative ontological quality, that of commodities. The Terrestrial Code is presented immediately as a guide for veterinarians, and more specifically as a guide for them in the early detection of animal diseases for the purpose of 'preventing their spread via international trade in animals and animal products, while avoiding unjustified sanitary barriers to trade'.[77] In its foreword, the Terrestrial Code was moreover presented in a previous

[74] Donaldson and Kymlicka (n 63) 3.
[75] Gary Lawrence Francione and Robert Garner, *The Animal Rights Debate: Abolition or Regulation?* (Columbia University Press 2010).
[76] Terrestrial Animal Health Code, vol 1 (31st edn, World Organization for Animal Health 2023). The WOAH makes the Code available online through its library of codes and manuals: <https://www.woah.org/en/what-we-do/standards/codes-and-manuals/ > (accessed 10 January 2024).
[77] ibid ix.

edition as 'a key part of the WTO legal framework for international trade', because an important treaty of the World Trade Organization system, the Agreement on the Application of Sanitary and Phytosanitary Measures (SPS Agreement),[78] which is key to regulating barriers to trade justified by sanitary concerns, designates the WOAH (then still OIE) as the official standard-setter for those sanitary measures.[79]

In that light, when the WOAH is concerned about animal health, it is concerned about animal disease as a problem for trade among humans. As indicated in 2011 at the World Congress of the OIE, recommended policy was presented as part of a series of measures in the Codes, both Terrestrial and Aquatic, that 'aim at facilitating commodity based trade',[80] following on the assumption that '[t]he goal of the OIE is to maximize animal health and trade benefits, while minimizing negative effects on other populations'.[81] As such, the health of animals is necessarily considered as a quality pertaining to the specific object constructed by regulation, that is, a tradable object, and more precisely a 'commodity'. The Terrestrial Code determines that, for the purpose of the Code, a commodity can be defined as 'live animals, products of animal origin, animal genetic material, biological products and pathological material'.[82] Animal health is health relative to the needs of the trading system. In the case of pandemics related in one way or another to animal-borne diseases, such as foot-and-mouth disease, H1N1, or the 2019 SARS-CoV2 pandemic, the reaction of the OIE has been to provide recommendations directed at the continuance of trade, including in all cases the question of risk-based actions such as culling.[83] One can note that as an international organization whose object is epizooties, the 'World Organization for Animal Health' oversees by way of regulation and guidelines an astonishing amount of animal death. It is however now very interested in 'animal welfare', which the Organization's website announces as follows:

> Animal welfare is a complex and multi-faceted subject with scientific, ethical, economic, cultural, social, religious and political dimensions. It is attracting growing

---

[78] Agreement on the Application of Sanitary and Phytosanitary Measures (SPS), 1867 UNTS 493
[79] Terrestrial Animal Health Code (29th edn, World Organisation for Animal Health, 2021) ix.
[80] See the abstract of Dr Thiermann's presentation at < https://www.woah.org/fileadmin/Home/eng/Conferences_Events/sites/WILDLIFE_ACTES_2011/Abstracts/Thiermann.pdf> (accessed 10 January 2024).
[81] See the presentation slides and summary of the presentation by Dr Alejandro Thiermann, President of the OIE Terrestrial Animal Health Code Commission, 'Managing the Interface: Zoning, Compartmentalisation and Commodities' (OIE Global Conference on Wildlife Animal Health and Biodiversity, Paris 23–25 February 2011) <https://www.woah.org/fileadmin/Home/eng/Conferences_Events/sites/WILDLIFE_ACTES_2011/Presentations/S6_3_AlejandroThiermann.pdf> (accessed 10 January 2024).
[82] Terrestrial Animal Health Code (n 76) xiv.
[83] In the case of the Covid-19 pandemic, see OIE Considerations on the Application of Sanitary Measures for International Trade Related to COVID-19 (26 December 2020) <https://www.woah.org/fileadmin/Home/eng/Our_scientific_expertise/docs/pdf/COV-19/A_COVID-19_Considerations_OIE_Sanitary_Measures.pdf> (accessed 10 January 2024).

interest from civil society and is one of the priorities of the World Organisation for Animal Health (WOAH)..[84]

Given that statement, it is unsurprising as such that the OIE added to its Terrestrial Code a chapter on 'Animal Welfare' and moreover adopted a 'global strategy on animal welfare' in 2017. One may legitimately wonder what the function of welfare is in animals considered from the narrow perspective of trade, given that animals are encased in an ontological niche where it does not really matter whether they are dead or alive. An indication comes from the amended version of the above definition of animal welfare that we encounter in the 'global animal welfare strategy': 'Animal welfare is a complex, multifaceted, international and domestic public policy issue with scientific, ethical, economic, legal, religious and cultural dimensions *plus important trade policy implications*'.[85]

In a rhetorical form that will soon appear as characteristic of the OIE vision (ie veterinary care is subservient to political framing of animal use decided somewhere else), the global strategy states matter-of-factly that '[a]nimals may be kept as working animals, companion animals, for production of food, fibre and other animal products, for scientific and educational purposes and are transported and traded internationally', followed by the policy statement that '[t]he OIE recognises all these purposes as legitimate, while carrying an associated ethical responsibility to ensure any such use is humane as defined through the OIE's international standards for animal welfare, in recognition of the sentience of animals'.[86] The OIE's 4th Global Conference on Animal Welfare in 2016 recommended that member states participate in the development of welfare standards and their implementation, while making clear that the promotion of animal welfare is justified as a means towards socio-economic goals for human communities and the larger environment (as understood in contemporary international law), framed in this case in terms of sustainable development.[87] The OIE is thus 'requested to ... develop and promote the OIE animal welfare standards, as the key reference for national, regional and international trade'.[88]

What do the animal welfare standards of the OIE actually say? A rapid trajectory through the language of the Code clarifies the gesture of imperial interpellation by the law, which may be already apparent in the fact that 'Animal Welfare' is

---

[84] 'Animal Welfare', on the World Organization for Animal Health website, <https://www.woah.org/en/what-we-do/animal-health-and-welfare/animal-welfare/> (accessed 10 January 2024).
[85] World Organization for Animal Health, Global Animal Welfare Strategy, May 2017, 3 <https://www.woah.org/fileadmin/Home/eng/Animal_Welfare/docs/pdf/Others/EN_OIE_AW_Strategy.pdf> (accessed 10 January 2024) (emphasis is mine).
[86] ibid 4.
[87] Recommendations of the Fourth OIE Global Conference on Animal Welfare—Animal Welfare for a Better World (Guadalajara, Mexico, 6–8 December 2016) <https://www.woah.org/app/uploads/2021/03/a-recommendations-aw-guadalajara.pdf> (accessed 10 January 2024).
[88] ibid 2.

Chapter 7 of the Code, three subsections of which are dedicated to killing animals. The trajectory in question starts with the 'Guiding Principles on Animal Welfare' (Article 7.1.2 of the Code), the first among them being that 'there is a critical relationship between animal health and animal welfare'. That suggests then, against the rest of the Code, that welfare contributes to health, or health to welfare, and both to international trade not being disrupted. The relationship between health and welfare is the first principle concerning the Animal Welfare approach of the OIE (which then is the approach of all worldwide veterinary activity that is put in the service of trade), and it is followed by a reference to the 'five freedoms' (from hunger and thirst, from pain and disease, from discomfort, from fear, and the freedom to pursue and express normal patterns of behaviour) as appropriate guidance for animal welfare (Article 7.1.2 §2), as well as a reference to 'the 3 Rs' (replacement, reduction, refinement) for the use of animals in science (Article 7.1.2 §3). Science, it will be repeated quite often in OIE literature, will be the measure of animal welfare, including of 'the measure of the strength of animals' preferences, motivations and aversions' (Article 7.1.3 §3).

Following the standards, and still under the heading of Animal Welfare, the Code states in the next three 'guiding principles' that 'the use of animals in agriculture, education and research, and for companionship, recreation and entertainment, makes a major contribution to the wellbeing of people' (Article 7.1.5 §5).[89] This mirrors a similar (and similarly out-of-expert bounds) assertion by the OIE in the already mentioned 'global animal welfare strategy', based on no immediately clear connection to animal welfare, that the 'use' of animals is legitimate. The statement is obviously significant in axiomatically positing that use itself is unquestionable, as a foundation to then proceed to a discussion on the manner of use. The guiding principles add here that 'the use of animals carries with it an ethical responsibility to ensure the welfare of such animals to the greatest extent practicable' (Article 7.1.5 §6) and 'improvements in farm animal welfare can often improve productivity and food safety, and hence lead to economic benefits' (Article 7.1.5 §7).

In other words, the Code describes the use of animals (including in areas over which it does not seem to have obvious subject-matter jurisdiction) as legitimate and important and asserts that there is an ethical duty to ensure 'to the greatest extent practicable' the welfare of animals, which we know incidentally to be defined with reference to the overall objective of free and unimpeded trade. First, 'animal welfare' is thus invoked as part of a general legitimation of the use of animals in a variety of fields, while, secondly, it allows also for the enlisting of veterinarians,

---

[89] The 2021 version of the Terrestrial Code (n 76), 333 amended the text, to say '[t]hat the use of animals in agriculture, education and research, and for companionship, recreation and entertainment, makes a major contribution to the wellbeing of people'. See Terrestrial Animal Health Code (2023) online <https://www.woah.org/en/what-we-do/standards/codes-and-manuals/terrestrial-code-online-access/> accessed 29 July 2021.

as guardians of 'animal welfare' in the normalization of those activities. If we can fulfil our ethical responsibility, economic activity feeding the globalization of trade must continue; veterinary science is recruited to make sure that our ethical responsibility is met, because animal welfare is part of animal health, and animal health is defined with regards to the objective of unimpeded trade. Animal health has no independent value from the perspective of the World *Animal Health* Organization. Most notably, the reference in the 2017 Animal Welfare strategy to 'sentience' as a foundation for caring about animal welfare in the first place is nowhere to be found in the . Sentience is ultimately only proxy: it does not serve as a reference point for assessing independent value or moral worth (because animals here have none), but as a factual given in the scientific assessment of welfare, which is itself understood as a risk factor in trade.

That helps explain why a significant and detailed segment of Chapter 7 of the Code is dedicated to the actual killing of animals. As commodities, just as their health and their welfare are qualities that are related to tradability, so is their life and their properly administered death. A healthy commodity is here a well-killed animal, just as welfare signals the science-sanctioned normalcy of minutely regulated transport cages (standard of five freedoms) and ultimately scientific experiments (standard of the 3Rs), both of which are normalized by commodification while involving legitimate levels of oppression.

The section of the Code on slaughter is introduced by the following announcement:

> These recommendations address the need to ensure the welfare of food animals during pre-slaughter and slaughter processes, until they are dead. These recommendations apply to the slaughter in slaughterhouses of the following domestic animals: cattle, buffalo, bison, sheep, goats, camelids, deer, horses, pigs, ratites, rabbits and poultry. Other animals, wherever they have been reared, and all animals slaughtered outside slaughterhouses should be managed to ensure that their transport, lairage, restraint and slaughter is carried out without causing undue stress to the animals; the principles underpinning these recommendations apply also to these animals.[90]

This abstract description finds concrete expression, outside of the WOAH, in actual statistics concerning the billions of individual animals that are processed each year in the slaughterhouses—slaughterhouses that quite naturally the Code normalizes as part of the health and welfare of the animal commodities that are processed and transformed according to the purposes of trade. The Terrestrial Code speaks therefore of 'animal welfare and beef cattle production systems' (7.9), 'animal welfare

---

[90] Terrestrial Animal Health Code (n 76) 371.

and broiler chicken production systems' (7.10), 'animal welfare and dairy cattle production systems' (7.11), or 'animal welfare and pig production systems' (7.12).

The destruction of animal life is here described in quite minute and technical detail and normalized by an appeal to considerations of welfare, in addition to (and in combination with) functional constructions of the relationship of animal health to international trade. International regulation here contributes factually to the smooth deployment of a global slaughterhouse.[91] It signals however also that the slaughterhouse is the culmination of an imperial subjection of the animal Other to human rules that are supposed to explain in universal terms why it is justified to exploit and destroy them.

4. The Ethics of Dominionism

4.1 Moral Extensionism and Speciesism

In a first step in this discussion, I relied on Valerie Plumwood to frame the link between dualism and domination, and on Antony Anghie to characterize dualism in colonial conquest as an annexation of erstwhile autonomous worldviews. In a second step, I relied on cultural anthropology to point to the universalism of (binary) relations and the relative nature of the universalism carried by European conquest and contemporary naturalism. This allowed me to signal alternative (and imperially suppressed) framings of human–animal relations, in which animals themselves have autonomous representations defined in the terms of their own relationship to their world. In a third step, I used the example of the OIE's regulatory rhetoric to illustrate how contemporary international law can convey a human–animal dualism that reflects and implements politically the cultural construction of animals as dependent instruments of human destiny. In this final fourth step, I want to characterize the specificity of the relative universals carried by international law as precisely stripping animals of their moral, epistemological, and ontological independence. As indicated, I suggest here the term Dominionism to characterize the regime of our relation to animals, as well as the ideological justification of that regime. The point of such a characterization is to frame the purpose and scope of any future reform project supposedly designed to assist in improving the animal condition in law.

Concern over animals as being more than simply things or objects has led to the development of 'animal ethics' as an array of questions relating to the rights and wrongs of our relationship to animals.[92] The very notion of animal ethics systematizes what we see at work in the construction of 'animal welfare' by

---

[91] Lorite Escorihuela (n 2).
[92] See eg Tom L Beauchamp and RG Frey, *The Oxford Handbook of Animal Ethics* (OUP 2011).

international animal health law in the Terrestrial Code, or the reforms in the legal status of animals in domestic legal systems. Moral extensionism is the ideological disposition that considers ethics as a domain or scope of activity that can be expanded to encompass new agents. In the case of animal ethics, the idea is to extend notions of morality from relations among humans to relations between humans and animals. From a political Liberal perspective, the most notorious argument for the *exclusion* of animals from the realm of moral consideration is their already mentioned assigned lack of reason or common language with humans, which prevents negotiation and the establishment of common rules. The most notorious argument for the *inclusion* of animals in the realm of moral consideration is in turn that animals share with us humans the experience of pain and joy, that is, sentience. If exclusion is based on the assertion of radical difference, inclusion is based on the assertion of radical sameness: like us, they feel. From that perspective, the reason for a dynamic extension of moral rule to animals is the master Liberal prohibition of discrimination, which in the case of animals will be designated as antispeciesism. Speciesism is a prejudice based on species-membership, as an analogy to racism and sexism.[93]

If we accept that understanding of speciesism, then speciesism is not the correct way of framing the oppressive norms of human–animal relations. Animals, constructed as they are as the subordinate term of the human–animal dualism, cannot be imagined as protected against discrimination, whether they feel or not. Discrimination is commonly conceived as being constituted by an illegitimate, that is, irrational distinction in the treatment of individuals, against the background of the rule of equality mandated by reason: if we are all the same, we should be treated in the same way, and skin colour, gender, or sexual orientation, for instance, have no relevance.[94] As anti-speciesism goes, animals share with us the trait of sentience, and on that basis should be treated in many cases in the same way as we humans are. However, the general and metaphysically loose notion of 'animals' is constituted as a specific negative extension of humanity, in the form of humans being both animals themselves and different from all the other animals (as indicated by the peculiar expression 'non-human animals'). In turn, legal and moral construction of animality always ends up fragmenting animality into an array of functional specificities, which incidentally render a general operational idea of 'animal welfare' useless. Legal gesticulations around the welfare of farm animals or lab animals are telling in that respect. In a world of slaughterhouses, animals are not part of the background of equality that allows reason to operate and pinpoint

---

[93] Richard D Ryder, *Speciesism, Painism and Happiness: A Morality for the Twenty-First Century* (Andrews UK 2017) 76; Peter Singer, *Animal Liberation* (repr edn, Ecco 2001) 6.
[94] As Justice Harlan said, in one of the most famous dissents of constitutional law history, discrimination refers to a distinction that 'cannot be justified on any legal grounds'. *Plessy v Ferguson*, 163 US 537, 562 (Harlan, J, dissenting).

the irrationality of putting mice in cages. Mice belong in cages, and we breed, if not generate, them *to that end*.

Animals are not within the limits of the polity and are instead the object of an imperial rule that makes them and names them on the borders of the social compact, the rule of human instrumental reason itself being the blunt instrument of domination. In that sense the master dualism is the human–animal opposition, which projects an irrational outside to the inside realm within which dualisms of reason operate. As Adorno and Horkheimer put it: 'In war and peace, arena and slaughterhouse, from the slow death of the elephant overpowered by primitive human hordes with the aid of the first planning to the perfected exploitation of the animal world today, the unreasoning creature has always suffered at the hands of reason.'[95] Nowhere is this clearer than in the consideration of the limits of moral extension when addressing 'animals'. Peter Singer has hesitations about whether lobsters are properly within the realm of moral consideration,[96] and Martha Nussbaum clearly thinks that the suffering and death of shrimp are not such a big deal, or at least not as big of a deal as the suffering and death of cows.[97] Certainly, there are reasons for such line-drawing, but the reasons are like Vitoria's determination of whether there was such a thing as public and private property by natives before the arrival of Spaniards,[98] or whether natives can be enslaved as a result of war.[99] The rules of natural law regarding dominion over land and movables, the rules applied in wars among the Christian princes, and the rules applicable in the relations of Christians to pagans, are all extended by an exercise of legal analogy to absorb the New World, so that the rights of natives depend on the selective criteria determined by the conqueror, regardless of local self-understanding and representations (of such things as war or property).[100] The obvious question is: do we really know what it means to be a shrimp or a lobster,[101] any more than what the conquerors knew what it was to be in the world as a native of the New World? And what is it that may be lost by harming or sacrificing any kind of being that is not us? The perspective of lobsters and shrimp is inaccessible in its own terms, which historically has been taken as a green light from science to draw the normative conclusion that shrimp and lobsters are less or not important. All this is reverberated in law, which sanctions the hierarchical treatment of species, and ethical reasoning which justifies randomly

---

[95] Max Horkheimer and Theodor W Adorno, *Dialectic of Enlightenment* (Gunzelin Noeri tr, Stanford University Press 2002) 204.
[96] Larry Carbone, *What Animals Want: Expertise and Advocacy in Laboratory Animal Welfare Policy* (OUP 2004) 59.
[97] Martha C Nussbaum, *Frontiers of Justice: Disability, Nationality, Species Membership* (Harvard University Press 2009) 386–87.
[98] Vitoria, *De Indis* (n 4) 127–28.
[99] ibid 181.
[100] Francisco de Vitoria, *Vitoria: Political Writings* (CUP 1991) 283.
[101] Thomas Nagel, 'What Is It Like to Be a Bat?' (1974) 83 The Philosophical Review 435.

the sacrifice of individuals on account of belonging to a species (or to a race, or to a culture, or anything else).

Humans and animals are not equal terms of a dyad, they are uneven poles of a dualism of domination. Yet speciesism, as derived in most versions of it from a basic welfarist disposition, performs the extension of moral consideration with the obvious result that entities subject to that extension are now unprotected, under a normative arrangement sanctioning their abandonment. Following the political assertion that there is precisely no common framing across the nature–culture divide, relative universalism invites us here to depict two radically different viewpoints, that of the dominant human and that of the dominated animal, against the misleading anti-speciesist assumption of a measure of ontological equality or even autonomy granted to animals. The convergence of the two perspectives, that of the dominant and that of the dominated, would express that true nature and measure of the harm done. I suggest that we call the perspective of the human master Dominionism, because the harm done is not irrational distinction, but oppression by foreign rationality. As a result, I will suggest next that we consider the perspective of the animal, and as such I will refer to the structural analogy between totalitarian control of humans over humans, on the one hand, and Dominionist rule over animals, on the other. International law's logic is, I would suggest, a reflection of this translation of modern naturalism into a political framing of global human empire. This is not a comparison, again, it is a structural homology between relations. This is made possible by the fact of the human–animal dualism in the first place, where animals are (again, as the expression 'non-human animals' signals it quite clearly) both the same as and different from us.[102]

4.2 Dominionism: Dualism and Totalitarian Rule

Dominionism, which echoes in this context the history of colonial political constructs,[103] alludes metaphorically to a particular understanding of the original moment of human endowment with political and economic power, imperium and dominium, over the Earth, as it is described in Judeo-Christian scripture.[104] In terms of (political) theology and political debate, the term Dominionism generally

---

[102] Juán Ginés de Sepúlveda suggested that Indians were *like* animals, not that they were actual animals. In characteristically Aristotelian fashion, he suggested that they were 'born to obey and to serve others like beasts and fierce animals whom they resemble'. As cited in Jan Carew, 'Columbus and the Origins of Racism in the Americas: Part Two' (1988) 30 Race & Class 33.
[103] See eg Symposium: New Dominion Constitutionalism (2019) 17 International Journal of Constitutional Law 1166–300. The colonial master says that the colonized servant is like an animal, which refers obviously not to the fact that they are part of the animal kingdom, but rather that colonizing masters are in a similar position towards servants as humans are towards beasts.
[104] Holy Bible, Genesis 1:28.

refers to evangelical Christian theocratic movements in the United States,[105] and more specifically to the strategic implementation of a Christian polity deriving its authority directly from the Biblical grant, or 'dominion mandate'. In short, it is a political theory within the movement of evangelical Christian so-called reconstruction theology, which advocates for the replacement[106] of the existing civil legal architecture with Old Testament Biblical law.[107] The assertion of power over Earth and its inhabitants is both a foundational political act in general, and a more specific framing of humans' position with regard to Earth and fellow earthlings. In general terms, Dominionist framing provides the patriarchal basis for absolute monarchical claims against which John Locke would essentially build up social-contract liberalism (the critique of Dominion-based arguments for monarchy being the subject of John Locke's *First Treatise*). In specific terms, the Dominionist reference lays the ground for the equally conservative assertion of power over nature and animals, as encapsulated succinctly in statements such as this: 'God gave us the Earth ... We have dominion over the plants, the animals, the seas ... God said: "Earth is yours. Take it. Rape it. It's yours."'[108]

Dominionism thus associates the relationship of power between humans and animals with the creation of property and sovereignty that forms the ground of modern European political thinking and in particular the development of political Liberalism. Oppression of animals is not an error or accident of political Liberalism, but refers in essence to the outward disposition of political Liberalism in its dealings with nature in all its projected embodiments, be it animals embodying the state of nature or by extension animalized humans constructed as such.[109] Political Liberalism's ontological commitments to the intimate relation between individual liberty and private property finds ideological roots in Locke's imaginings of Amerindians' relations to their hunting preys,[110] and so Dominionism echoes also the fact that the fabrication of private property, just like the establishment of sovereignty, both derived from divine grant, is done as part of Adam's vice-regency over animals. Most importantly still, the Biblical reference also points to the structural relation between humans and animals being grounded in the naming of animals by humans while the latter are explicitly in a state of ignorance about the world.[111] The imperial gesture of imposing a frame of definition on the reality of the Other is

---

[105] Paul Maltby, *Christian Fundamentalism and the Culture of Disenchantment* (University of Virginia Press 2013).

[106] Michael J McVicar, *Christian Reconstruction: R. J. Rushdoony and American Religious Conservatism* (The University of North Carolina Press 2015).

[107] Michelle Goldberg, *Kingdom Coming: The Rise Of Christian Nationalism* (1st edn, WW Norton 2007) 13

[108] Cited by Maltby (n 104) 119–20.

[109] James Sakéj Henderson, 'The Context of the State of Nature' in Marie Battiste (ed), *Reclaiming Indigenous Voice and Vision* (UBC Press 2000).

[110] On Locke and animals, see Dinesh Joseph Wadiwel, 'The Will for Self-Preservation: Locke and Derrida on Dominion, Property and Animals' (2014) 43 SubStance 148.

[111] Holy Bible, Genesis 2:19.

crystallized in the implementation of the divine grant of dominion over the world based on telling animals who they are. This leads us thus finally to the point where we can imagine the best framing for the opposite perspective, the position of the animal dominated by foreign reason and defined into a functional existence in the service of the human master.

The best framing is provided by the most famous literary quote of the contemporary animal liberation movement, a textual reference that has unfortunately been widely mishandled, instrumentalized, and cheapened. In a passage from a short story, Nobel laureate Isaac Bashevis Singer describes his main protagonist, Herman waking in bed after a prolonged illness, and thinking anxiously about a mouse that he had got into the habit of feeding and had plausibly starved to death during his convalescence:

> In his thoughts, Herman spoke a eulogy for the mouse who had shared a portion of her life with him and who, because of him, had left this earth. 'What do they know, all these scholars, all these philosophers, all the leaders of the world, about such as you? They have convinced themselves that man, the worst transgressor of all the species, is the crown of creation. All other creatures were created merely to provide him with food, pelts, to be tormented, exterminated. In relation to them, all people are Nazis; for the animals it is an eternal Treblinka.'[112]

This excerpt has been quoted extensively, but generally not taken to carry more meaning than that of a descriptive 'comparison', that is, an analogy of pains and deaths alongside other comparisons used to describe the treatment of animals.[113] I choose here another reading of Singer's invocation of Nazi extermination camps, to convey a global understanding of human relations to animals.[114] Preliminarily, I approach Singer's reiterated choice of words (he uses the reference to animals elsewhere, for instance to suggest a parallel between zoos and concentration camps)[115] as deliberate and careful, as careful as that of many others concerned with the fate of animals and whose families and loved ones had close acquaintance with World War II and the Holocaust.[116] Further, I suggest that the magnitude of Nazism as an alternative political framing of the universe, and not simply a phenomenon amenable to judgement in the categories of political Liberalism,[117] is also

---

[112] Isaac Bashevis Singer, 'The Letter Writer' in *The Collected Stories of Isaac Bashevis Singer* (Farrar, Straus & Giroux 1982).

[113] eg Marjorie Spiegel, *The Dreaded Comparison: Human and Animal Slavery* (rev edn, Mirror Books/IDEA 1996).

[114] The expression 'eternal Treblinka' is famously borrowed by Charles Patterson to discuss not only the relations between the Holocaust and the treatment of animals, but also the relations between Holocaust survivors and the cause of animal welfare and rights. Charles Patterson, *Eternal Treblinka: Our Treatment of Animals and the Holocaust* (Lantern Books 2002).

[115] Isaac Bashevis Singer, *Enemies: A Love Story* (Penguin Books 2012) 43.

[116] Charles Patterson, *Eternal Treblinka* (1st edn, Lantern Books 2002) 139.

[117] Carl Schmitt, *State, Movement, People: The Triadic Structure of Political Unity [1933]* (Plutarch Press 2001) 11.

to be considered seriously. On that basis, a close reading of the text suggests a radical inversion from the misreadings that have substituted an analogy for Singer's assertion of homology. First, Singer is not talking about the magnitude of the suffering of the animals by comparing it to the Shoah, he is concerned about the (im)possibility of expressing the true nature of the Shoah itself. Secondly, Singer is not talking about subjects of suffering, but relations of domination. As I said, it is a homology, not an analogy—the latter being absurd, and as such legitimately resented as a hypothetical aberration. Specifically, Singer is here giving justice not to the animals, but to the victims of the Nazi persecution, by evoking the enormity of the Shoah in its internal rationality. He does so by juxtaposing to the uniquely unfathomable horrors of Treblinka the apparently rational, comprehensible, mundane violences of humans on animals. The key lies in the fabrication of normalcy by reason, as it appears in the interplay between the devouring void of nothingness represented by Nazi camps, on the one hand, and the normalcy of the ordinary world in which all of the unfathomable violence occurs. This is also how Imre Kertesz, for instance, evokes the enormity of the Shoah through the flat factual descriptions given of the Buchenwald camp by the protagonist of *Fatelessness*.[118]

The specificity of the homology here, which aims at depicting a totalitarian form of rule constituted by the redefinition of a being into another being attached to the foreign logic of the dominant, is best highlighted by contrast. Another famous literary instance of such juxtaposition between the Holocaust and animals comes in the speeches of JM Coetzee's character Elizabeth Costello, who suggests that 'we are surrounded by an enterprise of degradation, cruelty, and killing which rivals anything that the Third Reich was capable of, indeed dwarfs it...'.[119] That is an analogy. What Costello proposes here is indeed a comparison to highlight the gravity of the situation of animals—and that comparison is precisely taken up as such in outrage by Abraham Stern, Coetzee's fictional friend of Costello's:

> The Jews died like cattle, therefore cattle die like Jews, you say. That is a trick with words which I will not accept. You misunderstand the nature of likenesses; I would even say you misunderstand willfully, to the point of blasphemy. Man is made in the likeness of God but God does not have the likeness of man.[120]

Unlike Costello, who fashions a language of comparison to analogize things that are not comparable, Singer speaks to a structural homology. What is in any event the meaning of such a comparison, and from where is that meaning drawn? What Singer does when he speaks of Treblinka and the mouse is to evoke a binary relationship in which one part is defined in a relation with another part, but more

---

[118] Imre Kertész, *Fatelessness* (Knopf Doubleday Publishing Group 2007) 102.
[119] JM Coetzee, *The Lives of Animals* (Amy Gutmann ed, Princeton University Press 1999) 21.
[120] ibid 50.

precisely defined by that other part and against that other part. One of the parts does not have representation anymore, and its being is redefined to match the representation of the Other in its entirety. We humans and our science do not know anything about animals, Singer says. To animals, from a constructed standpoint that doesn't say anything about the epistemology of the mouse or the animal (because that epistemology is precisely gone), it is an eternal Treblinka, a regime of total domination in which the dominated participates as an object or pure extension of the master's will. What I see as posited in Singer's literary evocation is thus not a comparison, of the type that is displayed in propaganda campaigns for veganism for instance, but rather a statement about the enormity of the Shoah through the evocation of a parallelism of forms. Singer alludes to a structural homology between the Nazis' relation to their victims, on the one hand, and our relation to animals, on the other hand, *from a reconstructed animal standpoint*. The homology is specifically tied to the notion that animals are unknown to us and brought under our rule as something that they presumably are not, something that has been dualistically reconstructed as an extension of human needs and ends.

Because we have some passing familiarity with the facts of animal abuse and industrial mistreatment, the parallel suggests that Nazi persecution serves, like the treatment of animals at our hands, a variety of purposes from inside the Nazi perspective. The unfathomable truth seeping through Herman's delirium is this: it makes sense to us to persecute you, and it made sense to the Nazis to treat other human beings in exactly parallel ways. Singer expresses here through the extraordinarily deep literary image of the silent mouse the limits of representation caused by the Shoah[121] and thus manifests paradoxically the impossibility of comparing anything to the Holocaust by signalling the homology between two worlds of silence. The soul-crushing tragedy that is conveyed is the homological structure of justification itself. The Nazi universe is manifestly endowed with an inner logic, which culminates into Treblinka as a shorthand here for a particular master-servant relation that must be deemed foreign to political Liberalism, except for the colonial context and the historical toleration of slavery, as well as our human–animal relations.

4.3 The Inner Reason of Totalitarian Rule

Nazis do not discriminate against Jews or Roma, they seek to eliminate them according to a logic that makes sense of genocide. In Nazi terms, Heinrich Himmler casts the destruction of Jews as the extermination of pests: 'Antisemitism is exactly the same as delousing. Getting rid of lice is not a question of ideology. It is a matter

---

[121] Saul Friedländer, *Probing the Limits of Representation: Nazism and the 'Final Solution'* (Harvard University Press 1992).

of cleanliness.'[122] It is not an insult or a provocation, but a description of a scientific fact within the Nazi universe, where Jews are carriers of pathogens dangerous to the health of the Aryan nation. As Snyder suggests, Hitler's perspective on the Jewish question is not framed in public health terms, as it is for Himmler, but in ecological terms, which reconstructs Jews as agents of disruption and corruption in a global racial ecology.[123] The magnitude of Hitler's endeavour of destruction is only sizeable if one understands that it obeys an alternative logic, a 'logic' that rejects the very basis of how Modern political Liberalism approaches the world, including the worth of individuals or the political centrality of states. Friedländer famously suggests the notion of a 'redemptive anti-Semitism', which in many ways is the opposite of irrational hatred or demagogic manipulation (in the sense of : the Nazis are simply crazy, or the Nazis are simply criminal). It is the fabric of a worldview that explains everything in terms of the effects of the presence of Jewish people in the universe, while including a form of redemption deriving from the struggle to free the world from the Jews.[124] Here the channelling of resources dedicated to the manic destruction of peoples, the spreading of the systematic extermination operation well beyond Germany, all that betrays a globalist anti-statist disposition informed by the fact that the enemy is considered as a plague. As would appear clearly in the repetition of examples, Jews and Roma are not considered to be things, but individual human beings who are agents of destruction against racial hygiene, what the Nazis will term anti-races.

Following an internal logic of relations organizing the Nazi worldview, experimenting on humans by Nazi scientists and doctors is part of the Nazi scientific and Nazi medical pursuit of truth, framed by Nazi ethics.[125] As appears at Nuremberg, there is again logic, a local logic, to the murderous madness. If a particular 'scientific' mindset frames the infamous Tuskegee syphilis experiment in the United States,[126] a similarly 'scientific' mindset says here of experiments on concentration camp inmates in the context of similarly infamous Nazi research: 'They are absolutely essential for the research on high-altitude flying and cannot, as it had been tried until now, be carried out on monkeys, because monkeys offer entirely different test conditions [...] [T]he problems in question can only be solved by experiments on human beings.'[127] The destruction of the victims of the Nazi persecution simply

---

[122] Speech of the Reichsführer-SS Heinrich Himmler at Kharkow April 1943, in Office of United States Chief of Counsel for the Prosecution of Axis Criminality, *Nazi Conspiracy and Aggression*, vol 4 (The United States Government Printing Office 1946) 574.

[123] Timothy Snyder, *Black Earth: The Holocaust as History and Warning* (Tim Duggan Books 2016) 321.

[124] Saul Friedländer, *Nazi Germany and the Jews: vol 1: The Years of Persecution 1933–1939* (Harper Perennial 1998) 85.

[125] See eg Florian Bruns and Tessa Chelouche, 'Lectures on Inhumanity: Teaching Medical Ethics in German Medical Schools Under Nazism' (2017) 166 Annals Of Internal Medicine 591.

[126] Allan M Brandt, 'Racism and Research: The Case of the Tuskegee Syphilis Study' (1978) 8 The Hastings Center Report 21.

[127] *Trials of War Criminals Before the Nuremberg Military Tribunals Under Control Council Law No 10, Nuernberg, October 1946–April 1949* (US Government Printing Office 1949) 126.

follows the internal instrumental logic of Nazism. The enormity of genocide is that it comes with a justification. It should go without saying, but of course animals are not the object of genocidal persecution across centuries; but, again, the point is not to compare events or phenomena, but relational structures.

Singer is getting to the incomparability of the Holocaust by alluding to a parallel not in importance, magnitude, or significance, but in logic and structure—a parallel of forms that ultimately suggests a continuity, the continuity of reasoned destruction, based on a master–servant dualist construction, where the subordinated element is reconstructed into only what the master needs and wants. Life and death are entirely subsumed in the logic of the dominant, and all norms and rules of behaviour are informed by a core relationship of epistemological erasure and ontological reconstruction. As someone whose stories are peopled with Holocaust survivors, Singer is here as elsewhere pointing to the search of meaning in the logical destruction of all meaning. It is metaphor, rather than comparison; eulogy, as he says, rather than description. Because the issue is ultimately the displacement of normative meaning by normative meaning—parameters of good and evil, helpful and unhelpful, rational and irrational are displacing competing parameters by force. Arthur L Caplan has insisted on the notion that Nazi scientific informing and assistance to Nazi violence itself is central to understanding the Holocaust, and that it is thus foolish and dangerous to leave it unexamined. Nazis are not just mean, or crazy, or idiotic, or cruel, or barbaric. Ignoring the force of reason in the unfolding of evil constitutes the actual cheapening of suffering and sacrifice:

> The myths of incompetence, madness, and coercion have obscured the truth about the behavior of biomedicine under Nazism. Most of those who participated did so because they believed it was the right thing to do. This helps to explain the relative silence in the field of bioethics about both the conduct and justifications of those in biomedicine who were so intimately involved with the Nazi state.[128]

Eternal Treblinka: the invocation of eternity then suggests a human understanding of their relationship to animals as being divinely rooted outside of time in the moment of creation, where the crown was conferred. It is significant that the victims of the Holocaust are not mentioned by Singer. Their perspective is simply evoked as an absence, the silence of destruction, the impossibility of representation, implied in the notion that, however much science pretends to know of animals, we know nothing and yet do everything we want to them. We know nothing of the other side of the destruction of meaning carried out by the Nazis. Because in the universe that they created at Treblinka, Buchenwald, or Auschwitz, the past and future of inmates had no purpose and no value, so no meaning either.

---

[128] Arthur L Caplan, 'Too Hard to Face' (2005) 33 Journal of the American Academy of Psychiatry and the Law Online 394.

The parallel, more than a supposed 'comparison', prompts the notion that animals are the object of a fiction, are thus concealed in their true nature by the deployment of an ideological fairytale that makes them for humans and thus hides them forever in what they are. We know nothing of them—our deployment of knowledge over them increases our knowledge of ourselves and further conceals their reality. The main analogy is between deployments of creative political power, where Treblinka is a universe fabricated by Nazis, and a corresponding universe is fabricated in which our relationship to animals and the rest of 'nature' makes sense. Racialism is the component of Nazism that organizes the relationship between individuals according to an inner logic of racial emancipation, and an outer dynamic of war among racial groups. Dominionism is the component of political Liberalism that organizes the relationship between humans and animals into an exercise of appropriation and use according to an inner logic of human freedom, and an outer logic of war on nature.

5. Concluding the Dominion

International law is entangled in the process of creation and reproduction of a universe out of the destruction of worlds. Highlighting the Dominionist fabric of the modern Liberal state leads to glimpses of the ideological layers that connect the destruction of alternative universes, on the brink of extinction along with their besieged Indigenous guardians, with the naturalization of unfathomable amounts and systems of violence that engulf our fellow non-human earthlings. The evocation of the structures of oppression, following the disturbingly searching lines by Isaac Bashevis Singer, does not serve the purpose of saving animals. It is only about us, and always about us, because animals, after all, what do we know of them? The problem is that international law, as the beckoning of political Liberalism to the whole universe from the plane of international relations,[129] carries in its fibre the arrogance of universal dominion and the secret contempt of nature. Out of the ideological momentum of Liberalism, coupled with the destructive atomizing force of Capitalism that it channels and projects, international law spreads a universe of borders between insiders and outsiders, those in the know and those without, the universe of enmities and genocides where it is only normal to kill the Tutsi mice[130] or the Rohingya fleas[131] because after all fleas and mice are a nuisance

---

[129] Hans J Morgenthau, *Scientific Man Versus Power Politics* (The University of Chicago Press 1965) 67; Martti Koskenniemi, 'The Politics of International Law' (1990) 1 European Journal of International Law 4, 7.

[130] *The Prosecutor of the Tribunal v Georges Anderson Ndrerubumwe Rutaganda, Indictment*, ICTR-96-3-I (12 February 1996) [4].

[131] Laignee Barron, 'U.N.'s Top Court Says Myanmar Must Protect Rohingya' *Time* (23 January 2020) <https://time.com/5770080/myanmar-rohingya-genocide-un-court/> accessed 20 September 2020.

to us humans. International law has, however, surrounded us all by shutting out all other universes. The obvious path of resistance for those of us concerned about international law's complicity in entrenching in the world a totalitarian logic of domination is however without any possibility of innocence or purity because, in the words of Isaac Bashevis Singer, we are all Nazis. Still, the path leads us to engage, as citizens and jurists, in the work of voluntary and progressive withdrawal of Dominionist rule from the world, and towards replacing all of international law's endless discourse about and on animals with silence. Rules of law and ethics about animals concern relations among humans, with reference to animals as effects of, or instruments in, these relations. Proliferation of rules and standards only entrenches and refines totalitarian oppression in the world and lends it a warm corner in international law to fester and ultimately contaminate human relations. Silence may moreover be the only point of reference common to all worlds, the speculative inner worlds of the animals and the weltanschauung of the dominating humans that international law imagines. Welfarism, as indicated by the grand European colonial invasion of the world, may be the best ideological fuel of oppression. In that sense, the only way of being fair is not to define what is fair.[132] That is because in the terms of the relativity of universalism, our legal and ethical standards of treatment are not more reliable to our animal subjects than Nazi law and Nazi ethics are to victims of Nazi totalitarianism.

International law's flight forward into the proliferation of regulation, especially today in the forms of animal welfare and liberal rights, is just an acceleration of imperial control and further entrenched legitimation of a surrounding system of commodity exchanges. The flight forward generates increasing amounts of horror for animals and further normalizes the existence of absolute violence on the borderlands of the polity for all abandoned humans. The task is now to legally engineer the walls of silence against the words of humans. In their long shadow we may imagine, side by side with efforts to better address humans' permanent aggression on their own climates and natural environments, progressive efforts to undo the legal architecture of global Dominionism and reach out to the horizon of naturalism, across the traces of alternative human universalisms. We may encounter, in humility and wonder, ways of expressing respectfully dualist, or maybe wondrously triadic, framings of the world and all our fellow earthlings. In those frames we may finally hear the last echoes of the master mythical narratives of insiders against outsiders, and of humans caught in a war of conquest with nature and animals, which has brought us humans to constituting the most destructive viral parasite on planet Earth.[133]

---

[132] I want to thank Dorian A Monforte for lending me this enlightening formula.
[133] Nicolas Truong, 'Philippe Descola: "Nous sommes devenus des virus pour la planète"' (*Le Monde online*, 22 May 2020) <www.lemonde.fr/idees/article/2020/05/20/philippe-descola-nous-sommes-devenus-des-virus-pour-la-planete_6040207_3232.html> accessed 20 September 2020.

10

The Universal Recognition of Animal Welfare and its Dark Sides

Régis Bismuth

The fate of animals in factory farms, slaughterhouses, and laboratories—and more generally of all animals under human control—has become a challenge of our time and one which has gained momentum in the last two decades, notably among the civil society and policymakers. It has also become an interdisciplinary field of scholarly interest, also known as the 'animal turn' which, to some extent, 'has made its way into international law'.[1] This has given rise to the 'Global Animal Law' project that includes a transnational perspective in addition to the classical public international law angle.[2] One of the key dimensions of this animal turn is the concept of 'animal welfare' which, unlike animal rights or abolitionist doctrines, has gained some form of recognition at the international level. Widely recognized in national legal systems, 'animal welfare' is also regarded by some as a universal value,[3] and even a general principle of law.[4] However, there is a striking dissonance between on the one hand its alleged universal reach and on the other hand the actual cruel treatment of most animals under human control. The question then arises as to whether animal welfare, despite its wide recognition, is simply disregarded in practice.

Although 'animal welfare' seemingly pertains to the protection of animals' individual interests as sentient beings, this contribution aims to highlight that it has been actually, perhaps counterintuitively, the conceptual vehicle that has eventually allowed for the perpetuation and social acceptance of animal exploitation. Indeed, as practised in international institutions such as the World Organisation for Animal Health (also known as OIE for *Office International des Epizooties*), the

---

[1] Katie Sykes, 'Globalization and the Animal Turn: How International Trade Law Contributes to Global Norms of Animal Protection' (2016) 5 Transnational Environmental Law 55, 79.
[2] For a broader perspective, see Anne Peters' *magnum opus* 'Animals in International Law' (2020) 410 Recueil des Cours 95.
[3] Michael Bowman, Peter Davies, and Catherine Redgwell, *Lyster's International Wildlife Law* (2nd edn, CUP 2011) 678.
[4] Katie Sykes, '"Nations Like Unto Yourselves": An Inquiry into the Status of a General Principle of International Law on Animal Welfare' (2011) 49 Canadian Yearbook of International Law 3, 35–36; Charlotte E Blattner, *Protecting Animals within and across Borders: Extraterritorial Jurisdiction and the Challenges of Globalization* (OUP 2019) 76–80. See also Peters, Animals in International Law (n 2) 505–07.

Régis Bismuth, *The Universal Recognition of Animal Welfare and its Dark Sides* In: *International Law and Universality*. Edited by: Işıl Aral and Jean d'Aspremont, Oxford University Press. © Régis Bismuth 2024.
DOI: 10.1093/oso/9780198899419.003.0011

concept of 'animal welfare' is deprived of any ethical dimension and is mostly an economic- and efficiency-driven technical tool that legitimizes the industrial exploitation of animals (Section 2). Moreover, the universal issue of animal welfare recognized in the context of the *Seals* dispute at the World Trade Organization (WTO)—a precedent rapidly canonized by the Global Animal Law project—could be analysed under a more critical lens to highlight that its loose application is tainted with anthropocentrism, and eventually allows for the continuing discrimination between animal species (Section 3). Beforehand, these issues deserve to be explored in light of a broader context in which animal protection has also been perceived as one of the many manifestations of cultural imperialism and Western-centrism (Section 1).

1. Animal Protection in International Law and the Temptation of Western-Centrism

Leaving aside five Council of Europe conventions (on the protection of animals during transport, of animals kept for farming purposes, of animals for slaughter, of animals used for scientific purposes, and of pet animals)[5] and certain provisions of the Convention on International Trade of Endangered Species (CITES),[6] international law does impose direct and explicit obligations upon states for the protection of animals' individual interests as sentient beings.[7] In very general terms, international law mainly deals with animals to the extent they belong to species in conservation treaties (the environmental law perspective) or it regards them as commodities (the trade law perspective).[8]

The environmental law perspective and the ethical dimension underlying the protection of animals as sentient beings are sometimes intertwined. This was demonstrated with respect to the protection of whales in Chopra and d'Amato's

---

[5] The European Convention for the Protection of Animals during International Transport (No 65, 13 December 1968), its additional Protocol (No 103, 15 May 1979) and its revised version (No 193, 6 November 2003); the European Convention for the Protection of Animals Kept for Farming Purposes (No 87, 10 March 1976) and its Protocol of Amendment (No 145, 6 February 1992); the European Convention for the Protection of Animals for Slaughter (No 102, 15 May 1979); the European Convention for the Protection of Pet Animals (No 125, 13 November 1987); and the European Convention for the Protection of Vertebrate Animals Used for Experimental and other Scientific Purposes (No 123, 18 March 1986) and its Protocol of Amendment (No 170, 22 June 1998).

[6] eg its Article III(2)(c) refers to the minimization 'of the risk of injury, damage to health or cruel treatment'. See also Michael Bowman, 'Conflict or Compatibility? The Trade, Conservation and Animal Welfare Dimensions of CITES' (1998) 1 Journal of International Wildlife Law & Policy 9.

[7] See also Denys-Sacha Robin, 'Statut et bien-être des animaux: quelques remarques sur les balbutiements d'un droit international animalier' (2016) 143 Journal du droit international 455.

[8] This is clearly reflected in the *Max Planck Encyclopedia of Public International Law*. To date, it does not include an entry on 'Animals', but the word appears in the sections 'Sanitary and Phytosanitary Measures', 'GMOs', and 'Codex Alimentarius', 'like products' (trade perspective) as well as 'Migratory Species', 'Endangered Species', 'Fisheries', 'fish stocks', and 'marine mammals' (environmental perspective).

prescient article published more than thirty years ago about whales' 'emerging right to life'.[9] This blurred frontier came to the fore in the International Court of Justice case *Whaling in the Antarctic*. Japan argued that Australia's stance with regard to the protection of whales was not grounded in scientifically based conservation objectives but rather 'on the fundamental belief in Australian public opinion that, unlike other inferior members of the animal kingdom, whales are unique, sacred, charismatic mammals that should never be killed'[10]—echoing a former Australian Prime Minister's statement in 1979 which mentioned that 'the harpooning of these animals is offensive to many people who regard killing these special and intelligent animals as inconsistent with the ideals of mankind'.[11]

Japan even went further, accusing Australia of misusing international law with the purpose of imposing its moral values on other states: 'the days of civilizing missions and moral crusades are over. In a world with diverse civilizations and traditions, international law cannot become an instrument for imposing the cultural preference of some at the expense of others.'[12] In other words, Japan intended to use international law as a shield against an international animal rights doctrine seemingly targeting non-Western cultural traditions.

The emerging field of 'global animal law' is aware of the risk that 'international animal rights protection face[s] the critique of cultural imperialism, ... mirroring the critique against the Western human rights movement'.[13] Besides, there is a general perception—and preconception—that Europe is the model student of animal protection. Even the Parliamentary Assembly of the Council of Europe declared some time ago that 'the humane treatment of animals is one of the hallmarks of Western civilization'.[14]

The pervasive penchant for Eurocentrism in this area not only ignores the more progressive stances adopted in some jurisdictions (Argentina, Colombia, India) where courts have recognized habeas corpus or other fundamental rights for certain animals,[15] but is also not a true depiction of the European reality. The five Council of Europe conventions on animal welfare protection have been ratified only by a minority of Council of Europe Member States. It is also in Europe that anyone can attend some of the cruellest practices on animals (eg bullfighting in Spain and France, *grindadráp* in the Faroe Islands). Moreover, while Article 13 of

---

[9] Anthony D'Amato and Chopra K Sudhir, 'Whales: Their Emerging Right to Life' (1991) 85 American Journal of International Law 21.

[10] *Whaling in the Antarctic (Australia v Japan: New Zealand intervening)* (Oral Proceedings) CR2013/12 (2 July 2013) 42 <https://icj-cij.org/files/case-related/148/148-20130702-ORA-01-00-BI.pdf> accessed 6 January 2024.

[11] Cited in D'Amato and Sudhir (n 9) 22.

[12] *Whaling in the Antarctic* (n 10) 63.

[13] Anne Peters, 'Toward International Animal Rights' in Anne Peters (ed), *Studies in Global Animal Law* (Springer 2020) 115; Peters, *Animals in International Law* (n 2) 493–500. See also Sykes (n 4) 35–36.

[14] Council of Europe, Parliamentary Assembly, International Transit of Animals, Recommendation 287 (1961).

[15] Peters, 'Toward International Animal Rights' (n 13) 110–11.

the Treaty on the Functioning of the European Union (EU) recognizes animals as 'sentient beings' and provides that the EU and Member States 'shall ... pay full regard to the welfare requirements of animals' in relevant EU policies, animals are also treated as 'products' in EU law, and the moral standards underlying the EU animal welfare policy appear to be flexible depending on species and economic imperatives.[16]

But the anti-imperialist critique targeting animal rights advocates should not eclipse the fact that, above all, animals have universally experienced all modes of domination which, in some, way echo, replicate, or inspire existing ones targeting individuals or minorities.[17] It is thus not a surprise that studies on systems of oppression and discrimination such as on imperialism, colonialism, slavery, racism, and sexism have found some resonance in animal ethics[18]—while bearing in mind that processes of human and animal exploitation and domination have sometimes worked hand in hand.[19]

And, paradoxically, it is under the cover of an 'animal welfare' concept that the exploitation and domination of animals under human control has been legitimized and eventually perpetuated.

2. Animal Welfare as a Technical Legitimization of Animal Exploitation by the OIE

Leaving aside stances based on animal rights doctrines seeking the abolition of animal use, improvement in 'animal welfare' has become the cornerstone objective of the global animal law movement.[20] But animal welfare is not a monolithic concept. There are significant gaps between, on the one hand, an ideal of animal welfare in which moral considerations would prevail and, on the other hand, animal

---

[16] See Section 3. See also Katy Sowery, 'Sentient Beings and Tradable Products: The Curious Constitutional Status of Animals under Union Law' (2018) 55 Common Market Law Review 55.

[17] In his novel *The Unbearable Lightness of Being*, just after pointing out that Tereza was obliged to behave lovingly because she needed him, Milan Kundera wrote: 'We can never establish with certainty what part of our relations with others is the result of our emotions—love, antipathy, charity, or malice— and what part is predetermined by the constant power play among individuals. True human goodness, in all its purity and freedom, can come to the fore only when its recipient has no power. Mankind's true moral test, its fundamental test (which lies deeply buried from view), consists of its attitude towards those who are at its mercy: animals. And in this respect mankind has suffered a fundamental debacle, a debacle so fundamental that all others stem from it' (Milan Kundera, *The Unbearable Lightness of Being* (Harper & Row 1984) 289).

[18] See eg Marjorie Spiegel, *The Dreaded Comparison—Human and Animal Slavery* (rev edn, Mirror Books 1997); Carol J Adams, *The Sexual Politics of Meat: A Feminist-Vegetarian Critical Theory* (Continuum 2010).

[19] See eg Mathilde Cohen, 'Animal Colonialism: The Case of Milk' in Peters (n 13) 35.

[20] Anne Peters, 'Global Animal Law: What It Is and Why We Need It' (2016) 5 Transnational Environmental Law 9, 10; Anne Peters, 'Introduction to Symposium on Global Animal Law (Part I): Animals Matter in International Law and International Law Matters for Animals' (2017) 111 AJIL Unbound 252, 254.

welfare as practised on a daily basis, in factory farms but also within international institutions. The former is based on values while the latter is mainly a technique subordinated to economic considerations.

Animal welfare could first be regarded as a multidisciplinary field encompassing different areas of expertise with their own concepts and methodological tools (biology, neurobiology, veterinary medicine, immunology, psychology, cognitive sciences, etc). The goals of animal welfare are multiple: improving the life of animals (health, environment, etc); satisfying social demands (of consumers, non-governmental organizations, etc); and/or addressing economic constraints (productivity, quality of final products, etc).

The field of animal welfare faces a fundamental epistemological problem stemming from the different underlying cultural and ethical representations of the various actors involved. As such, it is not possible to precisely define what animal welfare is without determining what constitutes a 'good life for animals'.[21] To the extent that the definition does not only rely on facts (objective scientific assessments), but also on values, animal welfare should be understood as both a natural and moral science.[22] It is within this framework that David Fraser has identified three dimensions of animal welfare—which are not mutually exclusive and which often go hand in hand—that must be taken into account: basic health and functioning (function well), affective states (feel well), and natural living.[23]

Prima facie, the Terrestrial Animal Health Code of the OIE echoes, albeit through a more scientific taxonomy, the three dimensions of animal welfare as envisaged by Fraser.[24] In its section on 'Guiding Principles for Animal Welfare',[25] the Code has endorsed the 'internationally recognized "five freedoms"' which were first adopted by the UK Farm Animal Welfare Council in 1979: freedom from hunger, thirst, and malnutrition; freedom from fear and distress; freedom from physical and thermal discomfort; freedom from pain, injury, and disease; and freedom to express normal patterns of behaviour.

But words should not be misleading. The inherent flaws of the 'Five Freedoms' do not lie in the non-legally binding nature of the Code but lie, rather, in their content. These 'freedoms' are not construed as rights[26] and the animal welfare dimension they promote presents significant ethical shortcomings, mainly because

---

[21] David Fraser, *Understanding Animal Welfare—The Science in Its Cultural Context* (Wiley-Blackwell 2008) 41.
[22] See generally Marian Stamp Dawkins, 'Animal Suffering: The Science of Animal Welfare' (2008) 114 Ethology 937; Fraser (n 21) 238. See also Nicolas Delon, 'La Sensibilité en éthique animale, entre faits et valeurs' in Régis Bismuth and Fabien Marchadier (eds), *Sensibilité animale—Perspectives juridiques* (CNRS Editions 2015) 61.
[23] Fraser (n 21) 241.
[24] ibid 233–34.
[25] OIE Terrestrial Animal Health Code, art 7.1.2.
[26] For an attempt to analyse the Five Freedoms through a rights-based framework, see Clare McCausland, 'The Five Freedoms of Animal Welfare Are Rights' (2014) 27 Journal of Agricultural and Environmental Ethics 649.

they fail to question what is a 'life worth living' and how the negative experiences of animals might be minimized while providing them opportunities to have positive experiences.[27] The—mainstream and prevalent in practice—approach to animal welfare promoted by the OIE through the Five Freedoms is mostly economic- and efficiency-driven. The OIE Terrestrial Animal Health Code even specifies that 'improvements in farm animal welfare can often improve productivity and food safety, and hence lead to economic benefits'.[28]

Indeed, contrary to generally accepted ideas, animal welfare is an essential component of factory farming, but with a technical and managerial dimension, leaving aside major ethical concerns and focusing on how animals could be adapted to industrial conditions. Chicken debeaking, cattle dehorning, or pig castration are painful procedures, but which also minimize the harm these animals inflict on each other in factory farms (freedom from injury). Optimization of processes in slaughterhouses is a strategy for reducing stress of livestock animals awaiting slaughter (freedom from fear and distress) and to preserve the quality and economic value of meat. Nest areas enclosed with plastic curtains help laying hens to hide themselves while laying their eggs and to replicate conditions of a natural nesting behaviour (freedom to express normal patterns of behaviour). In this light, the Five Freedoms endorsed by the OIE are obviously less an international Bill of Rights for animals than an instrument to perpetuate their exploitation on a large scale and make it more socially acceptable.

Eventually, the great divide is not the one between Fraser's and the OIE's conceptions of animal welfare which—even if one is more tainted with ethical considerations—do not call into question but rather legitimize the industrialized and intensive farming paradigm.[29] The genuine divide appears to be between a zootechnician conception (zootechnics being defined as the scientific art of maintaining and improving animals under domestication) and a peasant approach to animal welfare, deeply rooted in a traditional know-how of how farmers live with animals on a daily basis. As explained in the writings of Jocelyne Porcher, this latter dimension does not envisage farming solely as pure economic activity but also as an experience in which both farmers and animals could share a common pleasure in living together.[30]

Eventually, animal welfare, as defined and practised at the international and transnational level, is more likely to legitimize rather than to call into question a

---

[27] David Mellor, 'Updating Animal Welfare Thinking: Moving beyond the "Five Freedoms" towards "A Life Worth Living"' (2016) 6 Animals 1. See also Steven P McCulloch, 'A Critique of FAWC's Five Freedoms as a Framework for the Analysis of Animal Welfare' (2013) 26 Journal of Agricultural and Environmental Ethics 959; Sowery (n 16) 77–78.

[28] OIE Terrestrial Animal Health Code, art 7.1.7.

[29] On this aspect, see Régis Bismuth and others, 'La concurrence des normativités au coeur de la labellisation du bien-être animal' (2018) XXXII Revue internationale de droit économique 369, 379–81.

[30] Jocelyne Porcher, *Vivre avec les animaux—Une utopie pour le XXIe siècle* (La Découverte 2011); Jocelyne Porcher, 'Le "bien-être animal" existe-t-il?' [2005] Économie rurale 1.

system of domination as well as the industrial dimension of current farming activities and their integration in global production networks.

3. A Recognition of Animal Welfare Tainted with Anthropocentrism in the WTO Context

In practice, animal welfare is a loose concept whose contours depend mainly on the person or entity implementing it. Despite its intrinsic vagueness, the concept of animal welfare has received some form of universal acceptance. In that regard, another milestone was achieved in 2013–14 when a WTO panel recognized, in the *Seals* dispute, that 'animal welfare is a matter of ethical responsibility for human beings in general',[31] 'a globally recognized issue',[32] as well as 'an important value and interest'.[33] It is thus not a surprise that some have considered that 'something momentous happened in 2014 in the evolution of global animal law' as 'for the first time, an international tribunal recognized animal welfare as normative matter that has status at the international level'.[34]

The *Seals* dispute is an iconic precedent for global animal law, just as the *Trail Smelter* arbitration is for international environmental law.[35] But iconic precedents are often misunderstood or distorted and sometimes magnified more than they deserve. This is true for the *Trail Smelter* arbitration.[36] It is also true for the *Seals* dispute. Its canonization should not indeed eclipse more questionable aspects of that precedent, which indirectly endorses the perpetuation of discrimination between species and emphasizes the prevalence of economic values over moral ones.

In the *Seals* dispute, Canada and Norway challenged an EU regulation prohibiting the importation and the placing on the European market of seal products—except where these products result from hunts traditionally conducted by indigenous communities, where these products contribute to indigenous communities' subsistence, where the import of such products is occasional and consists exclusively of goods for personal use, and where these products result from by-products of hunting conducted for the sole purpose of the sustainable management of marine resources.[37] As an explanation for the adoption of the regulation, the preamble refers to the 'concerns of citizens and consumers about the animal

---

[31] *European Communities: Measures Prohibiting the Importation and Marketing of Seal Products—Panel Report* (25 November 2013) WT/DS400/R, WT/DS401/R [7.409].
[32] ibid [7.420].
[33] ibid [7.632].
[34] Sykes (n 4) 55.
[35] David D Caron, 'Foreword' in Rebecca M Bratspies and Russell A Miller (eds), *Transboundary Harm in International Law—Lessons from the Trail Smelter Arbitration* (CUP 2006).
[36] Duncan French, 'Trail Smelter (United States of America/Canada) (1938 and 1941)' in Eirik Bjorge and Cameron Miles (eds), *Landmark Cases in Public International Law* (Hart 2017) 159.
[37] Art 3(1) and (2) of Regulation (EC) No 1007/2009 of the European Parliament and of the Council of 16 September 2009 on trade in seal products [2009] OJ L286/36.

welfare aspects of the killing and skinning of seals' and 'the possible presence on the market of products obtained from animals killed and skinned in a way that causes pain, distress, fear and other forms of suffering'.[38]

Without going into detail on the panel and Appellate Body reports, it is important to note that, for the first time, animal welfare concerns such as those underlying the EU regime have been recognized as falling within the scope of the 'public morals' exception of General Agreement on Tariffs and Trade Article XX(a) and potentially justifying a trade restriction. Canada questioned the consistency of the EU approach to animal welfare, leading to very stringent trade restrictive measures for seal products, while being significantly more flexible with respect to slaughterhouses and wildlife hunts. In other words, Canada argued that a member state 'must regulate similar public moral concerns in similar ways for the purposes of satisfying the requirement "to protect" public morals under Article XX(a)'.[39] The Appellate Body rejected Canada's contention and stressed that 'Members may set different levels of protection even when responding to similar interests of moral concern',[40] and that the EU was not required 'to address such public moral concerns in the same way'.[41] The Appellate Body stressed that such an objective of consistency is only explicitly mentioned in the Agreement on the Application of Sanitary and Phytosanitary Measures (SPS Agreement).[42] Therefore, consistency in domestic regulation is required for measures relating to animal killing only to the extent they have a sanitary or phytosanitary dimension. Moreover, WTO member states are free to implement a trade restrictive measure to address animal welfare concerns to the extent that the rationale behind the measure at stake is a matter of public morals, but regardless of animal welfare regulations applicable to other species.

According to Howse, Langille, and Sykes, this is a positive development that 'allows for the gradual evolution of domestic law on issues with a moral aspect'[43] since it would be impossible to regulate animal welfare 'in a perfectly simultaneous and consistent fashion'.[44] They added that 'there is a wide range of differences in the ways different societies value different animals, and it is not the WTO's place to second guess the appropriate level of protection for each species'.[45]

---

[38] ibid, Preamble, para 5.
[39] *European Communities—Measures Prohibiting the Importation and Marketing of Seal Products*, Appellate Body Report (22 May 2014) WTO Docs WT/DS400/AB/R, WT/DS401/AB/R, [5.200].
[40] ibid.
[41] ibid.
[42] ibid, fn 1254. (Art 5.5 of the SPS Agreements provides: 'With the objective of achieving consistency in the application of the concept of appropriate level of sanitary or phytosanitary protection against risks to human life or health, or to animal and plant life or health, each Member shall avoid arbitrary or unjustifiable distinctions in the levels it considers to be appropriate in different situations, if such distinctions result in discrimination or a disguised restriction on international trade.')
[43] Robert Howse, Joanna Langille, and Katie Sykes, 'Pluralism in Practice: Moral Legislation and the Law of the WTO After Seal Products' (2015) 48 George Washington International Law Review 81, 114.
[44] ibid.
[45] ibid 115.

The argument could, however, be examined under a more critical lens, highlighting the anthropocentric dimension of the WTO ruling. The Appellate Body's position implies that member states preserve their 'discretion ... to protect the same general moral concern about animal welfare at a higher level for some animals compared to others'.[46] It is thus more a 'discretionary' standard that applies (states have the discretion to apply divergent animal welfare standards across species depending on their preferences) rather than a 'margin of appreciation' standard that would enable WTO panels and the Appellate Body to assess, not the absolute and perfect consistency of animal welfare measures that would be impossible to reach, but at least their overall convergence. A closer look at the broader context clearly indicates that the EU approach to animal welfare is more subordinated to economic imperatives than grounded on sincere moral concerns. A caveat: the following should not at all be interpreted as a defence of seal hunting but rather as an attempt to highlight the insincerity, or at least the morally deficient dimension, of the EU animal welfare policy—an element which ought to be taken into account to temper the anthropocentric dimension of the public morals exception in the WTO context.

The most stringent trade measure (prohibition of placing on the market) has been applied to seal products for the 'pain, distress, fear and other forms of suffering' that seal hunting actually causes. Obviously, the EU has a far less rigorous approach when it comes to animals raised and/or killed on EU territory. Seals experience an intense and cruel suffering at the moment of their killing, but they are wild animals and have at least enjoyed a life of freedom without human intervention and restrictions. This is not the case of millions of animals in European factory farms, living a miserable existence as well as an often too short life, and rarely experiencing a 'humane killing',[47] if any. This is also the case for fur farming where animals (foxes, minks, chinchillas, etc) that are reproduced, raised in small cages, killed—sometimes gassed in killing boxes—and skinned solely for the production of clothes. While the necessary purpose of every animal use should be at the heart of a genuine ethical animal welfare assessment, this dimension is clearly missing in the EU framework. Besides, a report of the European Commission on that matter even admitted that its objective was not 'to recommend whether or not continued fur farming is ethically acceptable'[48] but to carry out 'only a scientific assessment of the welfare of animals kept for fur production'.[49] The EU has perhaps an animal

---

[46] Simon Lester, Bryan Mercurio, and Arwel Davies, *World Trade Law: Text, Materials and Commentary* (3rd edn, Hart Publishing 2018) 394.
[47] Referring here to the vocabulary of the OIE Terrestrial Animal Health Code, ch 7, General Considerations ('Good animal welfare requires ... humane slaughter or killing').
[48] European Commission, 'The Welfare of Animals Kept for Fur Production—Report of the Scientific Committee on Animal Health and Animal Welfare' (2001) 6 <https://food.ec.europa.eu/system/files/2020-12/sci-com_scah_out67_en.pdf> accessed 6 January 2024.
[49] ibid.

welfare policy but its allegedly moral dimension is obviously superseded by economic considerations,[50] a dimension ignored by WTO courts.

Far from an animal welfare policy with a genuine moral compass, some EU Member States also allow some of the cruellest practices on animals. An example of this is bullfighting, which is still practised in France and Spain. This is not an activity taking place out of sight on the ice floes of Canada, but a show open to the public and families that intends to magnify the aesthetics of violence and suffering, and that certain municipalities in Spain have declared as protected cultural heritage. The UN Committee on the Rights of the Child recommended to Spain that it should 'prohibit the participation of children under 18 years of age as bullfighters and as spectators in bullfighting events'[51] in order to prevent the harmful effects of this practice on the youngest. Admittedly, there is no EU competence to prohibit such activities, but it is noteworthy that a share of Common Agricultural Policy funds is knowingly allocated to breeders of fighting bulls,[52] thereby showing the EU's contribution to this practice.

Ultimately, several animal species in the EU experience as much—and perhaps sometimes even more—pain, distress, fear, and other forms of suffering as seals do, not only during their killing but also during their entire lives, and in some cases for the satisfaction of recreational activities. The moral standards behind the EU animal welfare policy are of variable geometry and suddenly appear to become inflexible when it comes to the treatment of other species on a foreign soil. It is thus hard to explain the EU animal welfare policy from a moral standpoint. Some have suggested that the Seal regulation scrutinized by WTO courts is based on emotional motives (the 'cuteness' of baby seals).[53] It is also true that some EU animal welfare regulations are based on the subjective preferences of the population more than on a genuine and consistent assessment of the suffering and pain they experience. Another example is the EU directive on the protection of animals used for scientific purposes which intends to limit the use of great apes, the latter being described 'as the closest species to human beings with the most advanced social and behavioural skills'.[54] The EU probably has an animal welfare policy but its moral dimension varies in intensity according to species and is tainted with emotional or anthropocentric motivations, which are mostly superseded by economic considerations, particularly when it comes to factory farming.

---

[50] See also Sowery (n 16).

[51] UN Committee on the Rights of the Child, 'Concluding Observations on the Combined Fifth and Sixth Periodic Reports of Spain' (2018) CRC/C/ESP/CO/5-6, 7, para 25.

[52] Eurogroup for Animals, 'Spanish Bullfighting Financed with €130 Million from the EU's CAP' (24 June 2020) <www.eurogroupforanimals.org/news/spanish-bullfighting-financed-eu-130-million-eus-cap> accessed 6 January 2024.

[53] Tamara Perišin, 'Is the Seal Products Regulation a Sealed Deal? EU and WTO Challenges' (2013) 62 International and Comparative Law Quarterly 373, 375.

[54] Directive 2010/63/EU of the Parliament and of the Council of 22 September 2010 on the protection of animals used for scientific purposes [2010] OJ L276/33, Preamble, para 18.

While the WTO Appellate Body's stance in the *Seals* dispute leaves some room for a gradual improvement of animal welfare—a development that should not be overlooked—it also may have the effect of structurally preserving discriminatory treatments between species, even in the same country. It might also reinforce the impression of cultural imperialism[55] and the impression that some economically powerful states or groups of states have the capacity to impose on other states animal welfare standards that are more stringent than those they impose on themselves with regard to the treatment of other animal species.

4. Concluding Remarks

As counterintuitive as it may seem, the concept of animal welfare—as practised in the OIE and as a universal value recognized by the WTO Appellate Body—is also in the international arena an instrument of legitimization and perpetuation of animal exploitation. Experts at the OIE have indeed developed a zootechnician conception of animal welfare as the cornerstone of factory farming and one which is aimed at the optimization of animal use for industrial production in the upstream of the food chain. Downstream, the predominance of the concept seemingly having an ethical dimension in the discourse of producers and distributors has constituted an instrument of consumer acceptance. In the same vein, in the *Seals* dispute at the WTO, animal welfare has been used by the EU as a public moral defence to justify trade restrictive measures targeting cruel practices on certain animals occurring abroad while the EU model of factory farming relies on the same zootechnician conception and one which is more oppressive on other sentient beings. Far from guaranteeing interspecies justice, the way the animal welfare justification is used at the WTO may exacerbate the feeling that the protection of animals may lead to a sense of cultural domination.

Ultimately, the concept of animal welfare is just another illustration among many of how a universally recognized issue, paved with good intentions from the outside but with at best fragile moral foundations from the inside, subordinated to economic interests and subject to manipulation by experts, could be perceived by others as an instrument of hegemony and could perpetuate deeply rooted modes of domination on the weakest. Perhaps, at some point, the Global Animal Law movement will burn some of its old idols.

---

[55] Anne Peters, 'Liberté, Égalité, Animalité: Human–Animal Comparisons in Law' (2016) 5 Transnational Environmental Law 25, 37.

V
UNIVERSALITY BEYOND EUROPE

11
Regionalism, Hegemony, and Universality in the International Order of the Far East

Mohammad Shahabuddin

Any history of international law in Japan begins with nineteenth-century European encounters, often symbolized by the arrival of Commodore Perry's gunboats in 1853.[1] The normative connection between Japan's various responses to the premodern international order, on the one hand, and its engagement with the nineteenth-century European international law, on the other, is not adequately spelled out. This chapter demonstrates that what appears as a straightforward application of European international law as a universal norm in Japan's late-nineteenth century imperial projects was in fact shaped by a long-standing process of Japan's historical engagement with a system of cultural hierarchy in the regional order.[2]

Therefore, to properly appreciate Japan's emergence as an imperial power in the Far Eastern regional order, its military aggression in successive World Wars, and the role of international law in such imperial projects—all using the European language of the standard of civilization[3]—it is imperative to understand Japan's premodern engagements and responses to various hegemonic orders defined by the notion of cultural superiority. This is neither to claim any causal or linear relationship between various prewar Japanese ideologies and Japan's late-nineteenth and

---

[1] See eg Yasuaki Onuma, 'When Was the Law of International Society Born? An Inquiry of the History of International Law from an Intercivilizational Perspective' (2000) 2 Journal of the History of International Law 1–66; Yasuaki Onuma, *A Transcivilizational Perspective on International Law: Questioning Prevalent Cognitive Frameworks in the Emerging Multi-polar and Multi-civilizational World of the Twenty-first Century* (The Hague Academy of International Law 2010); Susumu Yamauchi, 'Civilization and International Law in Japan during the Meiji Era (1868–1912)' (1996) 24(2) Hitotsubashi Journal of Law and Politics 1–25; Masaharu Yanagihara, 'Introduction: The Role of Prominent Jurists in Japan's Engagement with International Law, 1853–1945' (2013) 56 Japanese Yearbook of International Law 95–121; Masaharu Yanagihara, 'Japan's Engagement with and Use of International Law, 1853–1945' in Heinhard Steiger and Thilo Marauhn (eds), *Universality and Continuity in International Law* (Eleven International 2011) 447–70; Masaharu Yanagihara, 'Japan' in Bardo Fassbender and Anne Peters (eds), *The Oxford Handbook of the History of International Law* (OUP 2012) 475–99; Kinji Akashi, 'Japan-Europe' in Fassbender and Peters, 724–43.
[2] For a more detailed elaboration of this argument, see Mohammad Shahabuddin, 'The "Standard of Civilisation" in International Law: Intellectual Perspectives from Pre-War Japan' (2019) 32(1) Leiden Journal of International Law 13–32.
[3] Note that during the interwar period, Japanese foreign policies gradually moved towards pan-Asianism (*Asia-shugi*), but the underlying notion of 'civilizing mission' continued to justify Japan's leadership role in Asia.

Mohammad Shahabuddin, *Regionalism, Hegemony, and Universality in the International Order of the Far East*
In: *International Law and Universality*. Edited by: Işıl Aral and Jean d'Aspremont, Oxford University Press.
© Mohammad Shahabuddin 2024. DOI: 10.1093/oso/9780198899419.003.0012

early-twentieth century imperialism,[4] nor to argue that Japan's imperialism vis-à-vis its Asian neighbours was the product of any particular aspect of Japanese culture. Instead, this chapter highlights the structure within which Japan constantly engaged with, challenged, and deconstructed the dominant ideas in various prewar epochs and the way such engagements offer a useful framework to understand Japan's encounter with the nineteenth-century European notion of the standard of civilization.

This contextualization of the Japanese encounter with the European concept of the standard of civilization thus offers an analytical framework to rethink the notion of universality in international law. Contemporary debates on universality and Eurocentrism in international law set the premise for my investigation in this chapter. At one level, the chapter acknowledges that despite its claims to universality, international law since the nineteenth century has remained largely Eurocentric, as critical scholarship in the discipline has already powerfully demonstrated.[5] At another level, it is also evident that in critiquing Eurocentrism, critical international lawyers often do not look beyond Europe as the point of departure.[6] Eurocentrism is understood here as a pattern that Chakrabarty explains as the dominance of Europe as the subject of all histories. This dominance is part of a very profound theoretical condition under which historical knowledge is produced, and Europe remains the sovereign, theoretical subject of all histories.[7]

Thus, using the example of Japan, this chapter offers a framework that not only looks beyond Eurocentrism in critiquing the purported universality of international law and its imperial projects but also helps identify various other regional systems of hegemony and the way they engaged with European imperialism. In this sense, I rely on the notion of universality in this chapter more as a language of power than as a mode of propagating international law at a global scale.

In what follows, the chapter first offers the historical context of Japan's response to regional hegemony in the Far Eastern regional order as well as its attempts to redefine hierarchical norms to its advantage. In doing so, the chapter relies extensively on various secondary sources or translations of Japanese language primary literature of leading intellectuals from the premodern period. Against this backdrop of the intellectual history of premodern regional hegemony in the Far East, the chapter then explains how this regional experience shaped Japan's engagement with the nineteenth-century European hegemonic notion of universality as ingrained in international law discourse.

---

[4] Although such connections are commonly made. See eg Masao Maruyama, *Thought and Behaviour in Modern Japanese Politics* (Ivan Morris ed and tr, OUP 1969 [1963]).

[5] See eg Antony Anghie, *Imperialism, Sovereignty, and the Making of International Law* (CUP 2005).

[6] ibid. cf Arnulf B Lorca, *Mestizo International Law: A Global Intellectual History 1841–1933* (CUP 2014).

[7] Dipesh Chakrabarty, *Provincializing Europe—Postcolonial Thought and Historical Difference* (Princeton University Press 2000) 27–34.

1. Hegemonic Regional Order in the Far East: A Prelude to Encounters with European 'Universality'

Since its articulation by Confucius (552–479 BC), the philosophy of Confucianism gradually emerged as the most dominant normative force in the Far Eastern regional order.[8] In Confucian philosophy, the ruler is the only son of heaven, with heaven's mandate to lead the people of the world, and the centre of civilization for all humanity.[9] Rulers throughout the world must therefore obey the Chinese emperor.[10] However, given that the emperor's influence in reality had certain geographical limits, people outside the sphere of such influence were known as 'barbarians', in contrast to the 'central flowering' of Chinese culture.[11] There was no question of equality between the emperor and other rulers: all relations were subject to rules, customs, and rituals set by the Middle Kingdom, not to treaties between the parties.[12] Rulers in other jurisdictions could not designate themselves as emperor, though some did so domestically.[13]

Confucianism was introduced to Japan in the fifth century[14] and with it came the Sinocentric tribute system.[15] Successive rulers of Japan, appointed by the Chinese ruler, paid tribute to China in order to strengthen and sanctify their authority.[16] Nevertheless, in the seventh century, Japanese rulers began to challenge the notion of Chinese superiority, albeit for domestic political convenience. Around the same time, Japanese rulers also refused to be appointed by the Chinese emperor. When Yoshimitsu Ashikaga was appointed monarch of Japan by the Chinese emperor, the matter was seen rather as an exception; political and intellectual elites criticized Ashikaga as being too submissive to China.[17] The formal relationship between China and Japan ended in the middle of the sixteenth century when Japan demanded equal status in diplomatic relations and China, viewing the rest of the world as subordinate, refused.[18] Japan did, though, accept Confucianism as the normative framework for its relations with other neighbouring countries such as Korea and the Ryukyu Kingdom (Present-day Okinawa), because this

---

[8] Hiroshi Watanabe, *A History of Japanese Political Thought 1600 –1901* (David Noble tr, International House of Japan 2012 [2010]) 9–26.
[9] ibid 24.
[10] Onuma, 'When Was the Law of International Society Born? (n 1) 12. See also Yanagihara, 'Japan' (n 1) 476–77.
[11] Watanabe (n 7) 25.
[12] Onuma, 'When Was the Law of International Society Born?' (n 1) 12.
[13] ibid 17.
[14] Wei-Bin Zhang, *Fukuzawa Yukichi: The Pioneer of East Asia's Westernization with Ancient Confucianism* (PublishAmerica 2010) 26.
[15] Yasuaki Onuma, ' "Japanese International Law" in the Pre-war Period—Perspectives on the Teaching and Research of International Law in Pre-war Japan' (1986) 29 The Japanese Annual of International Law 23, 23–24.
[16] ibid 24.
[17] ibid 24, 26.
[18] ibid 24.

'small-Sinocentrism' perfectly paved the way for Japan to make similar claims against them.[19]

Despite the practical relevance of Confucianism, Tokugawa rulers saw its demand for morality-based rule as a potential threat to their entire social and political order, which was based on hereditary status and military might.[20] The military affairs scholar Yamaga Sokoo (1622–85) argued that excelling in martial arts is the raison d'etre for practising Confucianism; thus, being a martial nation, Japan has also acquired the necessary degree of Confucian civilization. Indeed, Sokoo at one point claimed that 'Japan was actually the centre of the world', and 'even if it wasn't exactly in accordance with the Confucian teachings, it was fine for Japan to do things in its own way, nor should it feel inferior to China'.[21] By the seventeenth century, Japan not only challenged China's position as the centre of the universe but was openly questioning the superiority of Confucianism.

The resistance of the Japanese intelligentsia to the notion of 'Middle Kingdom' based on Confucian ideology entered a new phase with the emergence of National Learning or *Kokugaku*.[22] Beginning in the seventeenth century, the already-fragile foundation of Confucianism in Japanese society began to collapse before a more nationalist ideology primarily based on the ancient Japanese Way of the Divine Kingdom and the unbroken lineage of the imperial family. *Kokugaku* criticized the Confucian worldview as 'too normative oriented, too oppressive to human emotions and sentiments, and too submissive to China'.[23] *Kokugaku* scholars such as Hirata Atsutane (1776–1843) claimed that Japan's unbroken imperial line (*bansei ikkei*) demonstrated that this island empire was the 'Land of Gods'.[24] This made Japan the Middle Kingdom and superior to China, where dynastic changes and 'Tartar rule' were frequent,[25] and laid the foundation for Japan's claim to leadership in Asia.

According to Motoori Norinaga (1730–1801), the ancient Way signified the great and honourable customs of august Japan and comprised all aspects of human living of the age of the gods and the first legendary emperors of Japan.[26] Norinaga asserted that the early emperors governed by the ancient Way of the gods and made decisions by inquiring 'after the minds of the gods through divination'. To Norinaga's chagrin, the Confucian teachings imported from China overshadowed the ancient Way of managing state affairs, and rationality and individual thinking

---

[19] See Akashi, 'Japan-Europe' in Fassbender and Peters (eds) (n 1) 727.
[20] Watanabe (n 7) 86–88. See also Zhang (n 13) 27.
[21] Yamaga Sokoo, *Chuuchoo jujitsu*, cited in Watanabe (n 7) 90–91.
[22] Watanabe (n 7) 285.
[23] Onuma, '"Japanese International Law" in the Pre-war Period' (n 14) 26.
[24] Sven Saaler, 'Pan-Asianism in Modern Japanese History' in Sven Saaler and J Victor Koschmann (eds), *Pan-Asianism in Modern Japanese History: Colonialism, Regionalism and Borders* (Routledge 2007) 3
[25] ibid.
[26] Watanabe (n 7) 238.

gradually permeated public opinion. Norinaga blamed Japan's fall from grace into corruption and degradation on the spread of Confucian thought and 'Sinicization' in contemporary society,[27] and 'in the end, there was no difference at all between the evil customs of the Chinese barbarians and our own'.[28]

For Norinaga, the essential reason Chinese Confucian learning was incompatible with the Japanese Way was Confucianism's underlying assumption about the source of legitimacy of power. A Confucian ruler is to be obeyed because of his virtue and correctness; eventually someone will usurp the throne, asserting that he himself is correct and virtuous. With this analogy, Norinaga concluded that 'the Way in China is nothing but devices to seize someone else's country, and schemes to protect it from being seized',[29] characterizing the Confucian sages as mere rebels.[30] By this logic, the uniqueness of the Japanese imperial continuity and its resultant superiority over China resided in its culture of loyalty towards the emperor irrespective of his virtue.[31] Confucianism was irrelevant; Japan's claim to superiority was based on the eternal unbroken imperial lineage.

Given that Japanese superiority was based on its own ancient Way, Norinaga had no difficulty in seeing this as the universal standard. This ancient Way, for him, was 'the Way of mankind'—a model for the entire human race.[32] Whereas the Neo-Confucian scholar Asami Keisai (1652–1715) argued that one's own country is always the Middle Kingdom and other countries are the 'barbarians', thus Japan was the Middle Kingdom regardless of any standard of superiority or inferiority,[33] Norinaga believed in the inherent superiority of the Japanese Way beyond cultural relativism. Norinaga held that if one truly believed in the teachings of the imperial land (*Kookoku*, ie Japan), then one should also accept that the teachings of other lands are indisputably false, hence people from there should also believe in the teachings of the imperial land.[34] The immense popularity of *Kokogaku* thinkers deeply influenced the Mito School of Confucianism. Mito School was a pro-imperial movement informed in part by the teachings of the *Kokogaku* scholar Motoori Norinaga. The popularity and influence of *Kokugaku* thinkers compelled Mito scholars to rethink Confucian learning. As a result, Mito scholars in reviving Confucian moral culture not only infused elements of *Kokugaku* myth but also

---

[27] ibid 248.
[28] John S Brownlee, 'The Jeweled Comb-Box: Motori Norinaga's *Tamakushige*' (1988) 43(1) Monumenta Nipponica 35, 59.
[29] Sey Nishimura, 'The Way of Gods: Motoori Norinaga's *Naobi no Mitama*' (1991) 46(1) Monumenta Nipponica 21, 29.
[30] ibid 33–34. See also Maruyama (n 3) 150.
[31] Motoori Norinaga, *Kuzubana*, quoted in Watanabe (n 7) 245.
[32] Brownlee (n 27) 45.
[33] See Watanabe (n 7) 280.
[34] Motoori Norinaga, *Toomonroku*, quoted in Watanabe (n 7) 242.

asserted that Japan's native Way was primary and esteemed Chinese moral norms were merely a supplement.[35]

Mito scholars in the late eighteenth and early nineteenth centuries encountered a more drastic force—early signs of European imperialism. With the arrival of new technologies and the improved knowledge of world geography supplied by Western learning, most assumptions of the Sinocentric world order were dispelled. By the early nineteenth century, Mito thinkers, most prominently Seishisai Aizawa (1781–1863), had to respond to this emerging threat of European imperialism towards Japan. Aizawa's *New Theses* served mainly as a policy work for the Tokugawa feudal system (*Bakufu*) to endorse its anti-foreigner policy (*jooi*) and prescribe a long-term strategy to defend Japan against the imminent threat of European imperialism.[36] Aizawa saw *jooi* as sweeping away or eradicating what is culturally barbarian, 'an attempt to build barriers between Japanese commoners and foreigners'.[37]

Aizawa and other nineteenth-century Mito thinkers saw that Europeans would first win a reputation for benevolence with small acts of kindness, capture people's hearts and minds, propagate Christianity, and having set the premise find a convenient moment to conquer those people. Aizawa's solution thus went beyond banning Christianity to transforming the untrustworthy commoners themselves, through a sense of national-spiritual unification—*kokutai*. While Tokugawa and Ch'ing writers used the term *kokutai* or *kuo t'i* to mean 'the nation's honour' or 'dynastic prestige', Wakabayashi argues that Aizawa's use in his book *New Theses* (1825) was significantly different, connoting 'the unity of religion and government' used by a ruler to create spiritual unity and integration among his subjects and, thereby, transform a people into a nation.[38] In *New Theses*, Aizawa attempted to unite the people with the Divine through a purpose-built religion and series of social ceremonies. These would address the prevalent lack of spirituality—which could breed Christianity—and renew the commoners' consciousness about their ties to the Divine Land.

These currents of thought caused 'the beginnings of national consciousness— over and above simple ethnic pride—in nineteenth century Japan', with *New Theses*, coupled with the government's policy of expulsion by force, signalling the emergence of proto-nationalism in Japan and a shift from the notion of a universal empire (ie Confucian China) to a nation-state (imperial Japan).[39] However, the perception of international relations remained predominantly hierarchical, in that

---

[35] Bob Tadashi Wakabayashi, *Anti-Foreignism and Western Learning in Early-Modern Japan* (Harvard University Press 1986) 138.
[36] However, some foreigners were exempt: 'four gates' were held open for international trade. See Hok-chung Lam, 'Learning the New Law, Envisioning the New World: Meiji Japan's Reading of Henry Wheaton' (2013) 56 Japanese Yearbook of International Law 4, 34–36.
[37] Wakabayashi (n 34) 54.
[38] ibid 13.
[39] See Wakabayashi (n 34) 9, 15, and 139. cf Maruyama (n 3) 323–67.

neither the Confucians nor the *Kokogaku* or Mito scholars accepted a worldview based on the equality of nations.[40]

The foregoing three examples of Japanese engagements with the dominant ideas of the Middle Kingdom, the Divine Kingdom, and the 'national-spirit' underscore the way Japan historically responded to regional hierarchical systems or imperial powers by constantly challenging and deconstructing the dominant ideas and asserting its own cultural superiority. This dynamic process of engaging with the regional hegemonic order offered the normative structure within which Japan managed, first, its encounter with the nineteenth-century European notion of the standard of civilization imposed as a universal norm and, later on, its imperial relationship with Asian neighbours.

2. The Regional Order Meets the Hegemonic Universality of International Law

The late Tokugawa rulers' approach to foreigners had changed in the face of Commodore Perry's warships due to the realization that Japan could not stand the European invasion that would come if it did not open up ports for foreign trade.[41] Aizawa himself discarded the rhetoric of expulsion of foreigners after the late 1850s.[42] In fact, Japan not only opened itself to Europe, but almost totally transformed its state and society, facing new challenges and new notions of civilization and its standards, after the Meiji Restoration of 1868. In 1887, Foreign Minister Inoue Kaoru's policy was 'Westernisation symbolised by balls and garden parties in the Rokumeikan that were designed as an aid to procuring treaty revisions from the Western powers'.[43] As Itoo Hirobumi, a key political figure of the Meiji regime and the first prime minister of Japan, emphasized, Japan's aim from the very beginning was to be considered a civilized nation and to become a member of the comity of European and American nations.[44] From the Japanese point of view, this was essential in order to renegotiate unequal treaties, which Japan had to sign with Western nations before the Meiji Restoration.

However, it was never clear if Japan's civilization would be recognized. Given that there was no fixed standard of civilization, Japan was subject to the changing

---

[40] Onuma, '"Japanese International Law" in the Pre-war Period' (n 14) 26.
[41] See Hirohiku Otsuka, 'Japan's Early Encounter with the Concept of the "Law of Nations"' (1969) 13 Japanese Yearbook of International Law 35, 35–41; William G Beasley, *Japanese Imperialism 1894–1945* (OUP 1987) 14–26.
[42] See Donald Keene and Aizawa Seishisai, 'A Plan for Tasks at Hand: Aizawa Seishisai's "Jimusaku"' (2007) 62(1) Monumenta Nipponica 75, 75–86; Wakabayashi (n 34) 137.
[43] Sukehiro Hirakawa, *Japan's Love-Hate Relationship with the West* (Global Oriental 2005) 117.
[44] Ryusaku Tsunoda, W Theodore de Bary, and Donald Keene (eds), *Sources of Japanese Tradition*, vol II (Columbia University Press 1964) 678.

interests and fears of the civilized nations.[45] As Jansen notes, '[e]quality and membership in the circle of great powers were not easily gained and when Meiji Japan thought itself ready to enter international politics' on a basis of respect, 'it proved to have more to learn'.[46] Even sympathetic foreigners doubted whether any non-European people could establish a stable constitutional government of its own accord.[47] As Anand eloquently demonstrates, Meiji architects of modernization were equally aware of the inherent cultural bias of European international law that was instrumental for treaty renegotiation.[48] After all, Henry Wheaton's *Elements of International Law* (1836), the first book on international law to come to Japan—as a Chinese translation in 1864—defined this law as something 'understood among civilized, Christian nations'; the precondition 'Christian' was deleted only in the third edition of 1846.[49] The racist underpinning of European international law was hardly overlooked by the Meiji politicians and thinkers.[50] However, rather than unveiling their agitation about this European attitude, the ruling elites of Japan continued to advocate Westernization and assimilation to become Europe's equal, for they were not courageous enough to refute it 'coldly and fearlessly'.[51]

Japan could not then fight back the Europeans, but it could demonstrate military strength and thus its civilized position in world affairs through the 'othering' of its neighbouring countries. As a matter of fact, historically Japan's claim to superiority, rhetorical as it sometimes was, was always defined in relation to subordinate Korea. By the 1870s, Japan had learned to translate cultural superiority into European-style imperial practices. The most prominent intellectual of Meiji Japan, Yukichi Fukuzawa (1835–1901), argued in his newspaper *Jiji Shinpo* that while Japan was advancing on the road to civilization, Korea and China were falling behind and thereby risking European invasion. Thus Japan should, in its own interest, try to civilize these countries. In his famous 1885 article 'On Departure from Asia' (*Datsu A-ron*), he explained why Japan should disassociate itself from uncivilized neighbouring countries and move towards the West.[52] China and Korea were destined for ruin and European invasion unless great leadership guided them towards civilization.[53] How, then, should Japan deal with these countries, which would

---

[45] Erica Benner, 'Japanese National Doctrines in International Perspective' in Naoko Shimazu (ed), *Nationalism in Japan* (Routledge 2006) 29. cf Thomas J Lawrence, *The Principles of International Law* (DC Heath & Co 1895) 55–60.
[46] Marius B Jansen, 'Modernization and Foreign Policy in Meiji Japan' in Robert E Ward (ed), *Political Development in Modern Japan* (Princeton University Press 1968) 183.
[47] Benner (n 44) 29.
[48] See Ram P Anand, *Studies in International Law and History: An Asian Perspective* (Martinus Nijhoff 2004), 24–102.
[49] Henry Wheaton, *Elements of International Law* (3rd edn, Lea & Blanchard 1846) 46. See also Lam (n 35) 22.
[50] See Takeshi Osatake, *Bakumatsu Hishi Shinbun Waiso* (Iwanami Shoten 1995) 3–4, cited in Yamauchi (n 1) 2.
[51] ibid.
[52] Fukuzawa, 'Datsu-A Ron', *Jiji Shimpo*, 16 March 1885, Sinh Vinh tr, 'On Departure from Asia' (1984) 11 *Fukuzawa Yukichi Nenkan* [The Yearbook of Yukichi Fukuzawa] 1, 1.
[53] ibid 4.

nevertheless continue to be, geographically at least, neighbours? Fukuzawa, rather predictably, advised the Japanese authorities to deal with China and Korea 'exactly as the Westerners do'[54] and actively advocated for military intervention in Korea.

The Western attitude towards Japan changed with Japan's increasingly aggressive foreign policy vis-à-vis China and Korea: only Japan's emergence as an imperial power signalled its 'progress' to the satisfaction of the West. Japan's decisive victory in the Sino-Japanese War of 1895 signalled Japan's emergence as a superpower in Asia. Political and military elites in late-nineteenth-century Japan were convinced that imperialism equated civilization. Britain and the United States endorsed this depiction of imperialism as civilization, largely for their own imperial convenience. Britain's agenda was to prevent Russia from expanding its influence in East Asia; the United States intended to check Britain.[55] With British protection, Japan was in a better position to deal with the Russian occupation of Manchuria in China. Following the Russo-Japanese War beginning in 1904, and ensuing mediation offered by the US President, Japan sealed its first-ever victory in a war against a European power in 1905.[56]

International lawyers played an active role from the very beginning of this imperial project. When fifty-four shipwrecked Ryukyans were murdered by the Taiwanese in 1874, Japan sent an expeditionary force to attack Taiwan. China protested, demanding their immediate withdrawal, but Japan, on the advice of the French professor Gustav E Boissonade justified the expedition under the theory of occupation of *terra nullius*. Citing Vattel, Martens, Heffter, and Bluntschli, Japan argued that territorial sovereignty over land could be recognized only where the state claiming it effectively exercised governmental functions, and that eastern Taiwan, where the Ryukyuans were killed, was outside the Chinese jurisdiction. Hence, the Japanese occupation did not infringe Chinese sovereignty under international law. China eventually agreed in the Peking Agreement (1874) that Japan's enterprise was 'a just and rightful proceeding to protect her own subjects'.[57]

During wars with China and Russia, Japan had two legal advisors, Sakue Takahashi for the Navy and Nagao Ariga for the Army, both professors at the Naval Academy. Their mandate was to observe the law of war 'in the samurai spirit or according to the traditional spirit of brotherhood'.[58] Both later published monographs[59] demonstrating how Japan had incorporated European international law

---

[54] ibid.
[55] For a detailed account of diplomacy leading up to the Russo-Japanese War, see Beasley (n 40) 80–82.
[56] ibid.
[57] Taijudo Kanae, 'Japan's Early Practice of International Law in Fixing Its Territorial Limits' (1978) 22 The Japanese Annual of International Law 1, 15. See also Lam (n 35) 33.
[58] Shigeru Kuriyama, 'Historical Aspects of the Progress of International Law in Japan' (1957) 1 Japan Annual of International Law 1, 3.
[59] Takahashi joined Cambridge University and published *Cases on International Law during the Sino-Japanese War* (1899) and *International Law applied to the Russo-Japanese War with the Decisions of the Japanese Prize Court* (1908). Westlake wrote the introduction to his book on the Sino-Japanese War and Holland contributed a preface. Ariga produced similar books in French: *Law guerre sino-japonaise*

from the inception of its modernization and observed international law during the war, while China remained barbaric—killing non-combatants, destroying ships, offering a reward for the head of a Japanese general, engaging privateers to detain neutral merchant vessels, and killing prisoners, even sometimes hacking them to pieces.[60] Takahashi contrasted 'civilized' Japan with 'barbarous' China and concluded that Japan had the right of reprisal.[61] Likewise, Kanzo Uchimura depicted Japan's victory in the Russo-Japanese War as 'the upward progress of the human race'—free government, free religion, free education, and free commerce for 600,000,000 souls in Asia and, therefore, the war itself as a 'holy war'.[62] These imperial wars thus justified Japan's civilized position, as approved by European international lawyers[63] and proved by its seat at the Paris Peace Conference in 1919 as a Great Power.

Japanese scholar and art enthusiast Kakuzo Okakura (also known as Tenshin) (1863–1913), in his 1905 book *The Awakening of Japan*, candidly depicted imperialism as civilization:

> It was a hard task for us to convince the West that an Eastern nation could successfully assume the responsibilities of an enlightened people. It was not until our war with China in 1894–95 had revealed our military strength as well as our capacity to maintain a high standard of international morality that Europe consented to put an end to her extra-territorial jurisdiction in Japan. It is one of the painful lessons of history that civilization, in its progress, often climbs over the bodies of the slain.[64]

In his more popular *The Book of Tea*, published a year later, he maintained: 'He [the West] was wont to regard Japan as barbarous while she [the East] indulged in the gentle arts of peace: he calls her civilized since she began to commit wholesale slaughter on Manchurian battlefields.'[65] Similarly, writing in 1907 the politician and journalist Yosaburō Takekoshi portrayed Japanese imperialism as a source of pride, a symbol of equality with the West, and a contribution to modern

---

au point de vue du droit international (1896) and *La guerre russo-japonaise au point de vue du droit international* (1908). For other scholarly works concerning the Russo-Japanese War, see Fujio Ito, 'One Hundred Years of International Law Studies in Japan' (1969)13 The Japanese Annual of International Law 19, 23.

[60] See Yamauchi (n 1) 13.
[61] ibid.
[62] Uchimura Kanzo, 'Justification of the Corean War' (1894) 25 *Kokumin no Tomo* (A friend of the nation) 116–23, quoted in ibid 8.
[63] See eg John Westlake, 'Introduction' in Sakuyé Takahashi, *Cases on International Law during the Chino-Japanese War* (CUP 1899) xv–xvi; Thomas Erskine Holland, *Studies in International Law* (OUP 1898) 114–15.
[64] Kakuzō Okakura, *The Awakening of Japan* (John Murray 1905) 182.
[65] Kakuzō Okakura, *The Book of Tea* (Dover Publications 1964 [1906]) 2–3.

civilization: 'Western nations have long believed that on their shoulders alone rested the responsibility of colonizing the yet-unopened portions of the globe and extending to inhabitants the benefits of civilization; but now we Japanese, rising from the ocean in the extreme Orient, wish to take part in this great and glorious work.'[66]

3. Conclusion

This story of Japan's engagement with the nineteenth-century European notion of the standard of civilization against the backdrop of its long-standing practice of dealing with dominant forces in the regional context helps us better understand the ideological structure of Japan's engagement with European powers and also with its Asian neighbours. While Japan's engagement with the nineteenth-century European idea of the standard of civilization took various forms—from self-defence to imperialism—the pattern of this engagement makes better sense in the context of Japanese responses to the preexisting hierarchical regional order of the Far East. As we have seen, as part of a hegemonic regional order based on cultural superiority, Japan historically deconstructed and reconstructed the meaning of that cultural superiority that shifted from Sinocentrism to the unbroken imperial lineage to the national-spirit (*kokutai*). It is against this historical backdrop that, following the Meiji Restoration, Japanese intellectuals gave the European idea of the standard of civilization various new meanings, in line with Japan's military strength and political convenience. The political and military elites in late-nineteenth-century Japan were indeed convinced that imperialism equated civilization. This policy of imperial pursuits saw fruition as the Western powers finally agreed to renegotiate unequal treaties—only after Japan secured victory in an imperial war against China.

In general, this contextualization of the nineteenth-century encounter between Europe and such an insular island-nation as Japan—within the framework of a pre-nineteenth-century hierarchical regional order and the dynamic process of normative contestation therein—underscores the limits of Eurocentric universality in international law scholarship. Recent efforts to acknowledge contributions of semi-peripheral elites to the development of international law since the mid-nineteenth century are therefore also limiting and do not fully break with Eurocentrism, in that they explain such contributions essentially as responses to the European international legal order.[67] Japan's normative response to the nineteenth-century European civilization, or the development of Japanese international law ostensibly

---

[66] Yosaburō Takekoshi, *Japanese Rule in Formosa* (George Braithwaite tr, Longmans, Green, and Co. 1907) vii.
[67] See eg Lorca (n 5).

since then, or Japan's imperialism towards its Asian neighbours later in that century—none of these took place in a vacuum. Far from being merely a result of the encounter with Europe in the mid-nineteenth century, regional hierarchy and hegemony have been omnipresent in the Far Eastern regional order, in which Japan engaged with its neighbours. While this chapter does not claim any linear causal connection between any particular premodern Japanese ideology and Japanese imperialism since its modernization, we have however demonstrated that Japan's relationship with Europe and its hegemony towards its neighbours were informed and shaped by a preexisting hierarchical regional order in the Far East.

By highlighting not only rich varieties of rules and vocabularies governing international relations in the non-European world but also the hegemonic underpinning of those non-European orders, this narrative thus highlights the relevance of non-European regional orders in the discourse on international legal history but simultaneously exposes asymmetric power relations within those orders with reference to the local varieties of civilizational discourse. In this sense, this contextualization of the engagement with the nineteenth-century notion of the standard of civilization from Japanese perspectives raises a more general question about the inherent relationship between hegemony and international law.

12
Universality in International Law Beyond the European

An Islamic Law Perspective

Mashood Baderin

When we think of international law today, especially in the Global North, what instinctively comes to mind is the notion of a single-value set of established legal norms, principles, and institutions governing interstate relations globally. This creates a perception of settled universal norms that all states must or are expected to observe in their relationships with one another, giving rise to the concept of universality in international law. The reasonableness of universality in international law is grounded in the need for international cooperation towards achieving global agreement in addressing issues of common interests between states, ranging from less controversial issues such as international postal regulations to more difficult issues such as regulation of the use of force and protection of human rights. Despite its reasonableness, debates about the scope of universality in international law continue to be topical with regard, particularly, to the interpretation of international norms relating to human rights, international criminal law, and the use of force, amongst others.[1] From the 1970s, the strongest contestation in anti-colonial international law scholarship has been against its Eurocentric universality, which is criticized as promoting a 'single value approach to international law' as opposed to the acceptance of 'moral pluralism' in international law.[2] Today, states and other stakeholders in the international law venture, particularly of the Global South (including Muslim-majority states), are of the view that while universality in international law is desirable, the concept is substantively Eurocentric without appropriate appreciation and consideration of the contributions that other civilizations can make to strengthen its universal acceptability and effectiveness.

In view of Islamic law being a major legal system based on one of the major civilizations of the world today, this chapter argues that the principles of Islamic

---

[1] See eg Jack Donnelly, 'International Human Rights: Universal, Relative or Relatively Universal' in Mashood A Baderin, and Manisuli Ssenyonjo (eds), *International Human Rights Law: Six Decades after the UDHR and Beyond* (Ashgate Publishing 2010) 32–48.

[2] James T Gathii, 'International Law and Eurocentricity' (1998) 9 European Journal of International Law 184–211.

international law should be acknowledged and utilized for the realization of inclusive universalism in contemporary international law and thereby strengthen its universal acceptability and effectiveness, especially in the Muslim world. Sequentially, the chapter starts with the discussion and critique of the current Eurocentric essentialism of international law and argues for the universality of international law beyond the European. It then analyses the concept of universality in Islamic international law, and finally advocates for complementary universality between European and Islamic perspectives of international law. Four major factors identified as aiding the perpetuation of Eurocentric universality of international law are then critically analysed and addressed in the context of Islamic international law.

Both contemporary international law and classical Islamic law sources are employed to construct the arguments advanced in the chapter. Thus, the chapter presents a dialogical analysis that draws inspiration from UN General Assembly Resolution 53/22 adopted unanimously at its 53rd Session in November 1998 declaring the year 2001 as the United Nations Year of Dialogue Among Civilisations.[3] Although, after more than twenty years, Resolution 53/22 is almost forgotten, its principles remain germane to the question of the need to promote universalism in international law beyond the European,[4] in response to the continuing contentions against the Eurocentric universalism in international law from the last to the present century.

1. Contentions against Eurocentric Essentialism in International Law

Despite their acknowledgement of and necessary participation in modern international law, many states and publicists from the Global South tend to perceive it suspiciously as a trojan horse with a hidden baggage of imperialism, hegemony, control, and imposition of Western civilizational superiority. For example, in the last century during the 1993 Vienna World Conference on Human Rights, representatives of African, Asian, and Arab states questioned the Eurocentric essentialism in international human rights law as being insensitive to non-Western cultures and values. In their final regional declaration issued after the conference, the Asian countries noted the need for a universalism that recognizes the

---

[3] UN Doc A/RES/53/22 (4 November 1998).
[4] Significantly, the first and second preambular paragraphs of the Declaration respectively reaffirmed 'the purposes and principles embodied in the *Charter of the United Nations,* which, inter alia, call for collective effort to strengthen friendly relations among nations, remove threats to peace and foster international cooperation in resolving international issues of an economic, social, cultural and humanitarian character and in promoting and encouraging universal respect for human rights and fundamental freedoms for all', and 'recognized the diverse civilizational achievements of mankind, crystallizing cultural pluralism and creative human diversity'.

contribution that Asian cultures and traditions can make to international human rights norms.[5] Even in this century, different voices continue to challenge the international human rights system as being embedded with neocolonial, hegemonic, and complicit political nuances of the powerful developed states of the Global North. Balakrishnan Rajagopal has critiqued international human rights as language often used by the powerful states of the Global North for 'military intervention, economic reconstruction and social transformation'.[6] This is against the background of the past colonial and continuing hegemonic experiences of many nations of the Global South from European imperial domination, both politically and legally. Today, most African states harbour legitimate concerns about the Eurocentric universality in international law due to their past experience of colonial legal systems and norms that were imposed on them by colonizing powers who speciously branded them as 'received laws' through so-called 'reception statutes' that have tied them to the aprons of their colonizing powers enduringly long after their independence from colonization.[7] There is a similar historical experience by Asian countries, as reflected in the observation of Muthucumaraswamy Sornarajah that:

> The Asian perspective to international law was the result of a shared experience of colonialism of the Asian people. It was born of an arduous struggle in the twentieth century to throw off the yoke of colonialism, shared by all Asian people. China and Thailand did not experience colonialism but the system of extraterritoriality which was imposed upon them through force generated sufficient resentment against colonial powers to ensure that they too shared the historical experience of hurt that other Asian states felt. Colonialism was maintained through force that was buttressed by the shaping of an international law that justified subjugation of the peoples of Asia and Africa. There was an innate racial superiority evidenced by notions relating to the standards of civilisation.[8]

Generally, the origins of contemporary international law as a system based on imperialism and domination have been well acknowledged in the literature.[9] Based on these historical colonial experiences, while most states of the Global South

---

[5] See 'Report of the Regional Meeting for Asia of the World Conference on Human Rights' (Bangkok, 29 March–2 April 1993) UN Doc A/Conf.157/ASRM/8.

[6] Balakrishnan Rajagopal, 'Counter Hegemonic International Law: Rethinking Human Rights and Development as a Third World Strategy' (2006) 27(5) Third World Quarterly 767–83, 770. See also Makau Mutua, *Human Rights Standards: Hegemony, Law, and Politics* (State University of New York 2016).

[7] JH Pain, 'The Reception of English and Roman Dutch Law in Africa with reference to Botswana, Lesotho and Swaziland' (1978) 11(2) The Comparative and International Law Journal of Southern Africa 137–67, 137.

[8] M Sornarajah, 'The Asian Perspective of International Law in the Age of Globalization' (2001) 5 Singapore Journal of International and Comparative Law 284–313, 284.

[9] See eg Antony Anghie, *Imperialism, Sovereignty, and the Making of International Law* (CUP 2004).

acknowledge the need for universality in international law, they often contest its non-inclusiveness by calling for genuine universalism[10] in the interpretation and application of its norms. Thus, apart from the need to inject 'moral pluralism' into international law, the call for the universality of international law beyond the European has an underlying decolonization paradigm. This is reflected in counter-hegemonic claims against the current Eurocentric universality of international law, leading to scholarly propositions of new universalizing conceptualizations of international law, such as 'trans-civilizational'[11] universality, 'cross-cultural'[12] universality, 'solidaristic'[13] universality, and 'inclusive'[14] universality, all aimed at achieving a reconstruction of universality and genuine universalism in international law. Apparently, such propositions are not meant to undermine the universality of international law but to foster a search for an enduring inclusive universalism beyond the European, through a civilizational dialogue that would lead to some form of overlapping consensus amongst the different civilizations and stakeholders in contemporary international law.

This author's sustained view is that the universal nature of international law should be understood from two connotations, namely, *'universality of international law'* and *'universalism in international law'*. On the one hand, *'universality of international law'* signifies the universal quality or conceptual acceptance of international law as a necessary international cooperative venture,[15] which has become fully established over the past seventy-five years since the creation of the United Nations (UN). Thus, no state today would unequivocally accept that it is a violator of international law, thereby establishing its universality, ie its universal quality. On the other hand, *'universalism in international law'* implies a common universal consensus in the interpretation and application of international law norms globally,[16] which, unlike its *universality*, continues to be contested both academically and politically today, especially in respect of issues relating to human rights, military interventions, etc. While significant progress has been made, the full realization of *'universalism in international law'* is still an aspiration, which can only be

---

[10] I establish a distinction between 'universality' and 'universalism' in international law as explained later below.

[11] Yasuaki Onuma, *A Transcivilizational Perspective on International Law* (Martinus Nijhoff 2010).

[12] Abdullahi Ahmed An-Na'im (ed), *Human Rights in Cross-Cultural Perspectives: A Quest for Consensus* (UPP 1995).

[13] R St J MacDonald, 'Solidarity in the Practice and Discourse of Public International Law' (1996) 8 Pace International Law Review 259–302.

[14] Bruno Simma, 'Universality of International Law from the Perspective of a Practitioner' (2009) 20(2) European Journal of International Law 265–97.

[15] This is deduced from the fact that linguistically the suffix 'ity' denotes the quality, condition, or degree of a phenomenon. See Judy Pearsall and Bill Trumble (eds), *The Oxford English Reference Dictionary* (2nd edn, OUP 1996) 746.

[16] This is deduced from the fact that linguistically the suffix 'ism' denotes system, principle, result, or practice. See ibid.

achieved through the appreciation of other worldviews and civilizations beyond its current Eurocentric universality.

The one-time Vice-President of the International Court of Justice (ICJ), Professor Christopher Weeramantry, is one of the leading advocates of inclusive universalism in international law beyond its current Eurocentric universality. Being a Sri Lankan, his position on universalizing international law may not be surprising, but his global expertise and reputation as an international law jurist should eliminate any suggestion of prejudice regarding his juristic views on the subject. In his 2004 book, *Universalising International Law*, Justice Weeramantry critiques the Eurocentric universalism of international law and argues the need for a universalizing vision of international law 'that takes in the vast panorama of global cultures, as a source of enrichment of its principal concepts and underlying philosophies'.[17] This provides a pertinent framework for the main argument advanced in this chapter that Islamic law contains relevant norms and principles that can contribute to enhancing the universality of international law beyond its current single-value European perspective.

2. Beyond European Universality in International Law

The contentions against Eurocentrism in the universality of international law may be broadly grouped into geographical, ideological, and religious contentions. Examples of the geographical contentions are reflected in regional claims such as the African[18] and Asian[19] perspectives of international law, the ideological contentions are reflected in political claims such as the Socialist[20] and Marxist[21] perspectives of international law, while the religious contentions are reflected, for example, in the Islamic[22] and Hindu[23] perspectives of international law.

Evidently, the Islamic perspective, which is the focus of this chapter, advances a strong religious contention reinforced by elements of geographical and ideological assertions against current Eurocentrism in the universality of international law.

---

[17] Christopher G Weeramantry, *Universalising International Law* (Martinus Nijhoff 2004) xi.
[18] See eg Jakob Zollmann, 'African International Legal Histories—International Law in Africa: Perspectives and Possibilities' (2018) 31(4) Leiden Journal of International Law 897–914.
[19] See eg Sornarajah (n 8).
[20] Raluca Grosescu and NR Little, 'Revisiting State Socialist Approaches to International Criminal and Humanitarian Law: An Introduction' (2019) 21(2) Journal of the History of International Law 161–80.
[21] Robert Knox, 'Marxist Approaches to International Law' [2018] Oxford Biographies <www.oxfordbibliographies.com/view/document/obo-9780199796953/obo-9780199796953-0163.xml> accessed 9 June 2020.
[22] Mashood A Baderin (ed), *Islamic Law and International Law* (Ashgate Publishing 2008).
[23] KRR Sastry, 'Hinduism and International Law (Volume 117)' in *Collected Courses of the Hague Academy of International Law* <http://dx.doi.org/10.1163/1875-8096_pplrdc_A9789028615427_06> accessed 9 June 2020.

This is underpinned by the general perception in the Muslim world that, despite its apparent secular outlook, international law is essentially a Euro-Christian venture that is, at worst, aimed at undermining Islamic values, and at best, does not appreciate the importance of adhering to Islamic values in the Muslim world. This perception is reflected not only in the statements of individual Muslim-majority states but in official resolutions of the Organisation of Islamic Cooperation (OIC), which represents the Muslim world's largest intergovernmental body. For example, in its Resolution No 1/38-REG of 2011 the OIC expressed 'its deep concern over the attempts [by the powerful states of the Global North] to exploit the issue of human rights to discredit the principles and rules of Islamic Shariah (laws) and to interfere in the affairs of Islamic States' and reaffirmed 'the right of States to adhere to their religious, social, and cultural specificities which constitute heritage and streams of thought that contribute towards enriching the common international conceptions of human rights'. Consequently, it called 'for the non-use of the universality of human rights as a pretext to interfere in the states' internal affairs and diminish their national sovereignty'.[24] It is well documented that the epoch of international law from the thirteenth to the eighteenth century was an epoch of the 'international law of Christianity'[25] deeply rooted in Christian religious principles. Heinhard Steiger states that 'Christianity formed the major intellectual foundation of the legal order for the entire epoch', which, inter alia, 'brought Europe together, not only into an intellectual-religious unit, but also under the political idea of *res publica* Christiana', a term he identified as still being 'used in treaties as late as the 18th Century'.[26] Also, a Muslim publicist, Muhammad Hamidullah, writing in the preface of the first edition of his book *The Muslim Conduct of State* published in 1941, noted that:

> There was no *international law* in Europe before 1856. What passed as such was admittedly a mere public law of *Christian nations*. It was in 1856 that for the first time a non-Christian nation, Turkey, was considered fit to benefit from the European Public Law of Nations, and this was the beginning in internationalising the public law of Christian nations of Europe.[27]

Obviously, by the late nineteenth century Christian influence on international law had declined substantially, and contemporary international law subsequently materialized as a positivist secular construct under both the Covenant of the League

---

[24] OIC Res No 51/25-P of 1998 in Resolutions on Legal Affairs adopted by the 38th Session of the Council of Foreign Ministers (Session of Peace, Cooperation and Development) in Astana, Republic of Kazakhstan on 26–28 Rajab 1432H (28–30 June 2011).
[25] Heinhard Steiger, 'From the International Law of Christianity to the International Law of the World Citizen' (2001) 3 Journal of the History of International Law 180–93, 183.
[26] ibid 184.
[27] Muhammad Hamidullah, *The Muslim Conduct of State* (rev 7th edn, Sh Muhammad Ashraf 1977) vii.

of Nations of 1919 and the UN Charter of 1945. Nevertheless, the Muslim world still perceives contemporary international law as very much influenced by Euro-Christian nuances. Geographically, the Muslim world today encompasses countries in Asia, Africa, and the Middle East with Islamic law as a principal legal system in many of the countries, and Islam constitutionally declared as the state religion that strongly influences their international political ideology. Writing in 1962, late Ibrahim Shihata, the-then Vice-President and General Counsel for the World Bank and Secretary General of the International Centre for the Settlement of International Disputes, had argued that:

> in order to eliminate a major excuse for the violation of international law, there should be greater participation by other legal systems in the formation and development of international law. For by reflecting to a greater extent on the principles of non-European legal systems in the rules of international law, the validity and fairness of international law will be more widely recognized and more strongly supported ... Through this approach, contemporary international law will probably prove to be a more readily accepted system to [the] vast part of the international community vaguely referred to as the 'Muslim world'.[28]

A recognition of the important need to encourage the participation of other legal systems in the formation and development of international law may be inferred from Article 38 of the Statute of the Permanent Court of International Justice (PCIJ) under the League of Nations, which was subsequently adopted as Article 38(1) of the ICJ Statute, acknowledging the general principles of law recognized by civilized nations as part of the sources of international law. The phrase 'civilised nations' in that provision has, however, been controversial and critiqued as intended to 'distinguish European Christian States from States not thought to possess similar legal systems or values'.[29] Yet, Article 9 of both the PCIJ Statute and the ICJ Statute further provided that, in electing judges to the Court, 'the electors shall bear in mind not only that the persons elected should individually possess qualifications required, but also that in the body as a whole the representation of the main forms of civilization and of the principal legal systems of the world should be assured'. Similar provisions are today found in Article 31(2) of the International Covenant on Civil and Political Rights (ICCPR)[30] and Article 8(1) of the International Convention on the Elimination of All Forms of Racial Discrimination (ICERD).[31]

---

[28] Ibrahim Shihata, 'Islamic Law and the World Community' (1962) 4 Harvard International Club Journal 101–13, 101–02.
[29] See eg James Sloan, 'Civilized Nations' [2001] Oxford Public International Law <https://opil.oup law.com/view/10.1093/law:epil/9780199231690/law-9780199231690-e1748> accessed 22 July 2020.
[30] UN Treaty Series, vol 999, 171.
[31] UN Treaty Series, vol 660, 195.

In his course entitled 'The Principles of International Law in the Light of Islamic Doctrine' delivered at the Hague Academy of International Law in 1966, Sobhi Mahmassani referred to the earliest formal Islamic representation against the Euro-Christian universality of international law advanced through a memorandum presented on behalf of Muslim-majority states to the League of Nations in September 1939 and to the UN Conference in San Francisco on 17 April 1945, submitting that Islam constituted one of the main forms of civilization and Islamic law one of the principal legal systems of the world in the sense of Article 9 of both the PCIJ Statute and the ICJ Statute.[32] Such representation reflected, at that early stage, a collective quest by the Muslim world to be recognized as an important religious and ideological block in the international order and for Islamic law to be internationally recognized as a relevant legal system that could contribute to the development of contemporary international law. That agitation continues today, as is reflected in different international resolutions/instruments adopted, and different parallel supra-regional institutions established, by the OIC to assert recognition for Islamic norms and law in the universality of international law. This is underscored by the historical fact that a classical notion of Islamic international law—known as *al-siyar* in Islamic legal parlance—had emerged around the eighth century, and was also universalizing in nature. Muhammad Hamidullah had asserted notably in 1941 that international law 'with its modern connotation' existed formally in the Islamic legal system as early as the eighth century[33] and was evidenced by the writings of Muslim jurists and publicists such as Muhammad al-Shaybānī at that time. Muhammad al-Shaybānī is often referred to as the Hugo Grotius of Islamic international law, even though he preceded Grotius by some eight centuries.[34] Thus, beyond the European conception of international law, there is the Islamic conception of international law, the norms of which are often advanced by Muslim-majority states to contest or complement the Eurocentric universality of contemporary international law. This chapter therefore advocates a proper understanding of the similarities between contemporary international law and Islamic international law and an exploration of the areas in which Islamic law has contributed and can continue to contribute to the development of contemporary international law and thus bring the two systems closer in a way that can greatly enhance the universality of international law beyond its traditional European perspective. This is against the background, as identified by Lori Fisler Damrosch in 2006, that the 'Islamic

---

[32] Sobhi Mahmassani, 'The Principles of International Law in the Light of Islamic Doctrine' (1966) 117 Recueil des Cours, Collected Courses 201–328, 222.
[33] Hamidullah (n 27).
[34] Mashood A Baderin, 'Muhammad al-Shaybani (749/50-805)' in Bardo Fassbender and others (eds), *The Oxford Handbook on the History of International Law* (OUP 2012) 1081–85; John Kelsay, 'Al-Saybani and the Islamic Law of War' (2003) 2(1) Journal of Military Ethics 63–75.

influence on international law has received less attention than it undoubtedly deserves' in Western scholarship.[35] The position has not changed much since then.[36]

3. The Concept of Universality in Islamic International Law

Islamic international law—*al-siyar*—is derived from the normal sources, methods, and principles of Islamic law, supplemented by the practices developed by the early Muslim rulers in their relationship with other polities. The system was well established from as early as the eighth century based on the legal expositions of the Islamic jurist Muhammad al-Shaybānī on the subject, prompting Justice Christopher Weeramantry to acknowledge al-Shaybānī as the author of the most detailed early treatise on international law and noting that *al-siyar* was a precursor to the development of modern international law and that Hugo Grotius' work on international law might have been influenced by earlier Islamic scholarship, including the works of al-Shaybānī on the subject.[37] Thus, I have argued elsewhere that if Grotius is acknowledged as the 'father of international law', al-Shaybānī would rightly qualify as the 'grandfather of international law'.[38] Al-Shaybānī dealt generally with issues relating to international law in his different works on Islamic jurisprudence. He however devoted two books exclusively to Islamic international law, namely *kitāb al-siyar al-saghīr* (*The Shorter Book on International Law*) and *kitāb al-siyar al-kabīr* (*The Longer Book on International Law*), both of which were written in the eighth century. The latter was written in response to a critic of the former by another leading jurist of *al-siyar* at the time, Abd al-Rahmān al-Awzā'ī, and is considered as al-Shaybānī's *magnum opus* on Islamic international law.

While al-Shaybānī's works on Islamic international law principally systemized the rules of conduct in war and peacetime that the Muslim realm (*dār al-Islām*) must uphold in its relationship with the non-Muslim realm (*dār al-harb*), it nevertheless covered many other issues of modern international law, such as the general rules on treaties, territorial jurisdiction, diplomatic relations, and neutrality. For example, he established in his writings that there can be permanent treaty relationships between Muslim and non-Muslim states and that there should be no misappropriation, treachery, mutilation of the dead, or killing of children during warfare. In a recent article on the history of international law, Randall Lasaffer observed notably that 'the precursors of Grotius and Westphalia need to be studied

---

[35] Lori Fisler Damrosch, 'The "American" and the "International"' in the American Journal of International Law' (2006) 100(1) American Journal of International Law 2–19, 9.
[36] See Nahed Samour, 'Is there a Role for Islamic International Law in the History of International Law?' (2014) 25(1) European Journal of International Law 313–19.
[37] Christopher G Weeramantry, *Islamic Jurisprudence: An International Perspective* (Macmillan 1988) 132, 149–58.
[38] Baderin, 'Muhammad al-Shaybani' (n 34) 1082.

sincerely if we are ever to understand the formation of this law of nations' and that Grotius' 'main source of inspiration remains a blank spot on the historical map'[39] of international law. There is no doubt that al-Shaybānī and his works on *al-siyar* should form part of that study of modern international law for a full understanding of his immense contribution to the formation of international law as a jurist that preceded Hugo Grotius by some eight centuries in that field.

Similar to contemporary international law, the rules of Islamic international law were intended to apply universally. The concept of universality under Islamic international law is derived from the Qur'anic concept of '*ma'rūf*', which literally means 'well-known'. This concept connotes 'Common Good' or 'Universal Good' and is strongly enjoined as a universal norm that must be upheld by everyone in Islamic law generally. Its opposite is the concept of '*munkar*', which literally means 'despised' and connotes 'Common Evil' or 'Universal Evil', which should be avoided by all. Obviously, the scope of this concept of universality related to the specific ideals of Islam and the perceptions of 'goodness' and 'evil' at the time. However, they resonated with ideals such as the binding nature of agreements and respect for human dignity specifically enjoined by the sources of Islamic law even then, which were perceived as important universal norms that must be respected by all. The traditional scope of *ma'rūf* is expandable by relevant principles of Islamic law such as *maslahah* (human benefit) and *darūrah* (necessity) to cover the widening scope of 'Common Good' under contemporary international relations.

4. Towards Complementary Universality between European and Islamic Perspectives of International Law

Based on the above analysis, this chapter advocates the need for a complementary universality between the European and Islamic perspectives of international law. That approach will go a long way in facilitating the universality of international law beyond the European, especially in the Muslim world. To achieve this, the traditional exclusively Eurocentric approach to universality in international law has to be reversed. Over the years, the exclusively Eurocentric approach has been reflected and perpetuated through four main channels, namely: (1) the textbook historical narrative of international law, (2) norm recognition and formation in international law, (3) judicial interpretation and recognized principles of international law, and (4) political manipulations of international law. For the realization of genuine universalism in international law beyond the European, it is imperative to change the exclusively Eurocentric approach in each of these four main aspects as briefly analysed and advocated below with particular reference to Islamic law.

---

[39] RCH Lasaffer, 'International Law and its History: The Story of an Unrequited Love' in Matthew Craven and others (eds), *Time, History and International Law* (Martinus Nijhoff 2007) 27–42, 40.

4.1. The Textbook Historical Narrative of International Law

The traditional historical narrative of international law is inherently Eurocentric and usually defined by the Peace of Westphalia of 1648, which is often depicted by most Western international law historians as the beginning of international law. Early influential Western international law jurists such as James Lorimer (1818–90) had advanced the view that antecedent practices of non-Euro-Christian civilizations did not form part of the heritage of international law.[40] That historical narrative promoted a Euro-Christian civilizational superiority in the heritage of international law that has continued to a large extent up to the present day. It is submitted that the universal history of international law is highly prejudiced if reference to earlier relevant practices of other civilizations, such as Islam, are excluded from the narrative. Conversely, a historical narrative of contemporary international law that acknowledges relevant antecedent practices of non-Euro-Christian civilizations is necessary to enhance the universal validity of contemporary international law and, consequently, improve global compliance with international law norms. There has recently been some effort in academic scholarship aimed at correcting the historical anomaly of an exclusively Euro-Christian historical narrative of international law.[41] In the introductory chapter of *The Oxford Handbook of the History of International Law*, which advocates for 'a truly global history of international law',[42] the editors noted the Eurocentric historical narrative of international law as reductive and incomplete and that it 'ignores too many other experiences and forms of legal relations between autonomous communities developed in the course of history'.[43]

Regrettably however, most conventional international law textbooks have preserved that traditional Eurocentric historical narrative. Textbooks are important, as they form the foundation of learning in most disciplines, so there is a significant need to correct that incomplete historical narrative of international law in international law textbooks. With regard to making a reference to the Islamic civilization in a textbook historical narrative of international law, one notable exception is Malcolm Shaw's *International Law* textbook, which, while maintaining that '[t]he foundations of international law (or the law of nations) as it is understood today lie firmly in the development of Western culture and political organisation',[44] provides

---

[40] James Lorimer, *The Institutes of the Law of Nations: A Treatise of the Jural Relations of Separate Political Communities*, vol 1 (1883) 12–13. See also Henry Wheaton, *Elements of International Law* (1836) 17–18.
[41] See eg Bardo Fassbender and Anne Peters (eds), *The Oxford Handbook of International Law* (OUP 2012); Ignacio de la Rasilla and Ayesha Shahid (eds), *International Law and Islam: Historical Explorations* (Brill 2019); Baderin, *Islamic Law* (n 22).
[42] Bardo Fassbender and Anne Peters, 'Introduction: Towards A Global History of International Law' in Fassbender and Peters (eds) (n 41) 1–27, 2.
[43] ibid.
[44] See eg Malcolm Shaw, *International Law* (8th edn, CUP 2017) 10.

a short Islamic perspective in its analysis of the historical development. The passage however opens with a negative statement that Islam's 'approach to international relations and law was predicated upon a state of hostility towards the non-Moslem world and the concept of unity, Dar al-Islam, as between Moslem countries'.[45] As the promotion of peaceful relations between states is a fundamental objective of contemporary international law, the negative view that Islamic international law 'was predicated upon hostility towards the non-Moslem world' needs clarification in relation to the history of contemporary international law. Most Western scholars tend to problematize the comparison between Islamic international law and contemporary international law by reference to the division of world order into the 'territory of war' (*dār al-harb*) and the 'territory of Islam' (*dār al-Islam*) under classical Islamic international law. This division is often (mis)understood and (mis)interpreted out of context to negatively depict Islamic international law as a system that is historically hostile to non-Muslim polities and thus not amenable to the principle of peaceful coexistence of states and the promotion of international peace and security as advocated in contemporary international law.[46] That (mis)understanding neglects the fact that when the principles of Islamic international law were being formally formulated by the classical Muslim jurists in the eighth century, the whole world at the time was, by default, a territory of war (*dār al-harb*) in which warfare was recognized as a legitimate instrument of imperial relations, and conquest was recognized as a legitimate means of territorial expansion amongst nations. Aggressive warfare and conquest in international relations were only renounced in the twentieth century through their formal restriction under the Covenant of the League of Nations in 1919, followed by the adoption of the Kellogg-Briand Pact of 27 August 1928[47] before being legally abolished in contemporary international law through Article 2(4) of the UN Charter in 1945.

Having no obvious control over the default warring situation that prevailed globally then, the classical Muslim jurists defined the territories under Islamic rule as the territory of Islam (*dār al-Islam*), ie a territory of peace unified against the preexisting territory of war outside the control of Islamic rule, which was appropriately defined as the territory of war (*dār al-harb*). This hinged on the theory that the nations within the territory of Islam (*dār al-Islam*) would be united in peace and not go to war against one another as enjoined in different Qur'anic provisions such as Q49:10— 'Certainly the believers are brethren, therefore maintain peace

---

[45] ibid 13–14.
[46] See also Majid Khadduri, 'Islam and the Modern Law of Nations' (1956) 50 American Journal of International Law 358–72 and a rebuttal of that view in Mashood A Baderin, 'The Evolution of Islamic Law of Nations and the Modern International Order: Universal Peace through Mutuality and Cooperation' (2000) 17(2) American Journal of Islamic Social Sciences 57–80.
[47] See RCH Lesaffer, 'Kellogg-Briand Pact (1928)' in Rüdiger Wolfrum (ed), *Max Planck Encyclopaedia of Public International Law* (OUP 2011) <https://opil.ouplaw.com/view/10.1093/law:epil/9780199231690/law-9780199231690-e320?rskey=89nbRG&result=1&prd=MPIL> accessed 10 November 2020.

between your brethren and be careful of your duty to God, so that you may receive mercy'. In this sense, the division of the world order then into *dār al-Islam* and *dār al-harb* under classical Islamic international law does not necessarily mean a division of the world into friends and foes, but a division denoting territorial demarcation in terms of the war-prone tendencies of the times. It meant that *dār al-Islam* was territory in which war was barred between Muslims due to the unifying factor of Islam in that territory; as a consequence of Islamic control, that territory was the realm of peace. This is similar to, but predated, the doctrine of perpetual peace advocated by Immanuel Kant in his 1795 essay *Perpetual Peace: A Philosophical Sketch*,[48] which was a precursor to the modern democratic peace or liberal peace theory, which posits that democracies would not go to war against each other but could go to war with others.[49]

Perceived in this way, the concepts of *dār al-Islam* and *dār al-harb* reflect an attempt by the early Muslim jurists to exclude the prevalent warfare of those times from the Islamic realm and not to initiate or perpetuate hostility with the non-Muslim world as is often erroneously portrayed. There is evidence within classical Islamic jurisprudence to the effect that the classical Muslim jurists were not establishing a principle of permanent hostility between the Islamic and non-Islamic realms, as is commonly suggested, but were making a distinction mainly for administrative exigencies. For example, Hamidullah quotes one of the classical jurists, Al-Dabūsīy, who stated that 'the distinguishing factor between the Muslim and non-Muslim territories is the difference of authority and administration'.[50] I have argued elsewhere that the classical rules of Islamic international law do not mandate the Muslim world to maintain a permanent state of hostility towards the non-Muslim world in contradiction to the current rules of contemporary international law.[51] In fact, the classical Muslim jurists also recognized territories of accord (*dār al-sulh* or *dār al-'ahd*) through which peaceful coexistence could be created by treaty between the *dār al-Islam* and those parts of the *dār al-harb* that were willing to maintain peaceful relations with the *dār al-Islam*. Thus, the concept of peaceful coexistence amongst willing states was recognized under classical Islamic international law long before it became a fundamental norm of contemporary international law currently enshrined in the UN Charter. A proper understanding of this historical narrative of Islamic international law and the similarities between it and contemporary international law would engender complementarity between the two systems that can contribute positively to the genuine universality of international law beyond the European, as advocated herein.

---

[48] See M Campbell Smith (tr), *Perpetual Peace: A Philosophical Essay by Immanuel Kant 1795* (Allen and Unwin 1903).
[49] See eg Michael E Brown and others (eds), *Debating the Democratic Peace: An International Security Reader* (MIT Press 1996).
[50] Hamidullah (n 27) 88.
[51] Baderin, 'The Evolution of Islamic Law of Nations' (n 46).

4.2. Norm Recognition and Formation in International Law

Traditionally, norm formation in contemporary international law also developed from Eurocentric perspectives on the basis of the perceived superiority of European civilization. From inception, some form of 'normative power' was traditionally ascribed to European civilization in respect of norm recognition and formation in international law, which continues to have significant influence in international law. Today, the legal basis for norm recognition and formation in international law is contained in Article 38(1) of the ICJ Statute, which is generally considered as the most authoritative enumeration of the sources of international law, and which provides that:

> The Court, whose function is to decide in accordance with international law such disputes as are submitted to it, shall apply:
> a. international conventions, whether general or particular, establishing rules expressly recognized by the contesting states;
> b. international custom, as evidence of a general practice accepted as law;
> c. the general principles of law recognized by civilized nations;
> d. subject to the provisions of Article 59, judicial decisions and the teachings of the most highly qualified publicists of the various nations, as subsidiary means for the determination of rules of law.

There is universal recognition of treaties as possible norm-creating instruments between states parties in international law based on the deemed consent of the states who ratify such treaties. In relation to Islamic law, the norm-creating role of treaties has been well recognized since the earliest period of Islam in the seventh century. This is reflected in Q5:1—'O you believers, fulfil [all] obligations', which places both a moral and legal obligation on Muslim-majority states to comply in good faith with their international treaty obligations under Islamic law.[52] This is consistent with the normative principle of *pacta sunt servanda* under Article 26 of the Vienna Convention on the Law of Treaties 1969, as was earlier acknowledged in the *Saudi Arabia v Aramco* case in 1958, that Islamic law recognizes that agreements and pacts must be fulfilled in good faith.[53] However, there is no similar universal certainty about the other normative concepts listed in Article 38(1)(b)–(d) of the ICJ Statute, namely, 'international custom', 'civilized nations', and 'the most highly qualified publicists'. These concepts were and continue, largely, to be influenced by Eurocentric understandings and standards.

---

[52] See Labeeb Ahmed Bsoul, *International Treaties (Muʿāhadāt) in Islam* (University Press of America 2008).
[53] (1963) 27 ILR 117.

Writing in 1955, Georg Schwarzenberger had noted that there is a strong nexus between civilization and international law.[54] Thus, we will start with the contestations about the concept of 'civilized nations' and its continued impact on the Eurocentric nature of contemporary international law. The reference to 'civilized nations' in Article 38(1)(c) of the ICJ Statute is acknowledged as a remnant of European 'Westphalian civilization' portrayed as the 'standard of civilization' under international law,[55] whereby other states were obliged to conform to Western norms as international custom.[56] Thus, European states constituted the 'civilized nations', while others, particularly the Muslim-majority states, were considered uncivilized barbarians in traditional international law discourse. In his *Institutes of Law of Nations* published in 1883, James Lorimer had distinguished between 'the progressive and non-progressive races' in the formation of international law, arguing, inter alia, that it is with the 'progressive races', namely Europeans, 'alone that the international jurist has directly to deal' and that the international jurist 'is not bound to apply the positive law of nations to savages, or even to barbarians, as such', arguing with particular reference to the Turks that 'we have had a bitter experience of extending the rights of civilisation to barbarians who have proved to be incapable of performing its duties, and who possibly do not even belong to the progressive races of mankind'.[57] Similarly, in his *International Law* published in 1904, John Westlake also argued that the concept of 'international society' and its influence on the development of international law 'is composed of all the States of European blood, that is of all the European and American States except Turkey, and of Japan',[58] noting that a rule of international law is formed only if the 'general consensus of opinion within the limits of European civilisation is in favour of that rule'.[59] With particular reference to Muslim-majority states in his *Elements of International Law*,[60] Henry Wheaton depicted the Muslim world particularly as 'internationally uncivilized' and barbaric, asserting that the Muslim-majority states should thus 'renounce their peculiar international usages and adopt those of Christendom',[61] which he considered as the standard of civilization for international law. In the words of Alexis Heraclides and Ada Dialla:

> Lorimer, like almost all of his contemporary publicists, was convinced that international law was Christian and Christianity the highest civilization. Oriental

---

[54] Georg Schwarzenberger, 'The Standard of Civilisation in International Law' (1955) 8(1) Current Legal Problems 212–34.
[55] David P Fidler, 'The Return of the Standard of Civilization' (2001) 2(1) Chicago Journal of International 137–57, 138.
[56] Gerrit V Gong, *The Standard of 'Civilization' and International Society* (Clarendon Press 1984) 14–15.
[57] James Lorimer, *The Institutes of the Law of Nations*, vol 1 (1883) 102.
[58] John Westlake, *International Law* (1904) pt 1, 40.
[59] John Westlake, *Chapters on the Principles of International Law* (1890) 78.
[60] Henry Wheaton, *Elements of International Law* (1836).
[61] ibid 18.

communities were akin to immature or irrational individuals deprived of legal capacity. He believed that non-Christian states based on Hinduism and Buddhism could qualify as civilized states, but this was not the case with Muslim states, for they sought to become universal [even though the European states were themselves seeking to become universal at the time].[62]

This European 'normative power' within international law based on the presumed civilizational superiority of European nations has largely influenced the scope of 'the general principles of law' applicable by the ICJ and other international tribunals. With the exception of a very small number of cases, the ICJ has mostly interpreted its understanding of 'the general principles of law recognized by civilized nations' as general principles of law of European/Western legal systems, and thereby perpetuating the exclusively Eurocentric universality of international law. It would greatly enhance the genuine universality of international law beyond the European if the ICJ were to adopt the practice of acknowledging relevant general principles of law in other legal systems of the world to establish that such principles are not exclusively European but also recognized in other legal systems, and thereby establish their global acceptability and strengthening of relevant customary international law norms. In relation to Islamic law, examples could be cited of the principle of *istihsān*, which is similar to the principle of equity; the principle of *maslahah*, which is similar to public interest or public order; and the principle of *darūrah*, which is similar to the principle of necessity under Western legal systems. This view has also been advanced in the individual opinions of some ICJ judges, as discussed in the next section.

Coming now to 'international custom' under Article 38(1)(b) in relation to the recognition and formation of the norms of customary international law, it is a well-established principle that the two main ingredients are state practice and *opinio juris*.[63] While this is theoretically understood to mean the actual practice and *opinio juris* of the majority of states, it is usually the practices and *opinio juris* of the powerful European/Western states that have, similarly, been relied upon in determining general customary international law on most issues. This influence of Western states on the creation of customary international law is reflected in the controversy about whether UN General Assembly resolutions can create customary international law, as the Western states are outnumbered by developing states in the UN General Assembly. This is manifested in the observation by Shaw that:

---

[62] Alexis Heraclides and Ada Dialla, *Humanitarian Intervention in the Long Nineteenth Century: Setting the Precedent* (Manchester University Press 2018) 35.

[63] See eg the *Legality of Nuclear Weapons* case, where the ICJ confirmed the long-standing principle that customary international law is based 'primarily in the actual practice and *opinio juris* of states'.

it is inescapable that some states are more influential and powerful than other states and that their activities should be regarded as of greater significance. This is reflected in international law so that custom may be created by a few states, provided those states are intimately connected with the issue at hand, whether because of their wealth and power or because of their special relationship with the subject-matter of the practice, as for example maritime nations and sea law. Law cannot be divorced from politics and power and this is one instance of that proposition. The influence of the United Kingdom, for example, on the development of the law of the sea and prize law in the nineteenth century when it was at the height of its power, was predominant. A number of propositions later accepted as part of international customary law appeared this way ... One can conclude by stating that for a custom to be accepted and recognised it must have the concurrence of the major powers in that particular field ... This follows from the nature of the international system where all may participate but the views of those with greater power carry greater weight.[64]

While the wealth and power of European/Western states to influence the recognition and formation of customary international law may be inevitable, it certainly evidences the perpetuating influence of Eurocentrism in norm recognition and formation in international law.[65] This perpetuating influence can be mitigated by reference to relevant contributions from other civilizations in norm recognition and formation in international law in relevant areas of international law. For example, the doctrines of contemporary international law of the sea are commonly believed to have been developed exclusively from Renaissance Europe, and the contribution of Islamic law, especially to the concept of freedom of navigation and passage rights, is not acknowledged in the customary international law rules on the law of the sea. In lamenting the 'gap left by Renaissance and early modern European lawyers... to explore the Islamic contributions to the development of the customary law of the sea', Hassan Khalilieh has noted that:

With the advent of Islam in the Mediterranean world in the seventh century CE, the semienclosed sea, which had been called by the Romans '*mare nostrum* (our sea)' for a millennium, ceased to be a Roman lake. From that time onward, the Mediterranean Sea has continued to be shared by Christians and Muslims, and neither party could consider it to be *mare nostrum*; the eastern, western, and southern shores of the Mediterranean Sea were entirely under Islamic control for

---

[64] Malcolm N Shaw, *International Law* (5th edn, CUP 2003) 75–76.
[65] The ICJ however accepted the possibility of regional or local rules of customary international law in the *Asylum Case (Columbia v Peru)* [1950] ICJ Reports, 266 at 276–278.

several centuries, as have been the Red Sea, the Persian Gulf, and vast littorals of the India Ocean until the penetration of the Portuguese into the eastern area.[66]

As noted above, the concept of custom, known as '*urf*', is well recognized in Islamic law, and in relation to customary international law this is expressed in the Qur'anic concept of '*ma'rūf*', which literally means 'well-known', connoting the 'Common Good' or 'Universal Good' enjoined as a universal norm that must be upheld by everyone. Similarly to the other concepts analysed above, the concept of 'the most highly qualified publicists' in Article 38(1)(d) is, in practice, exclusively applied to classical and contemporary European publicists. With very few recent exceptions[67] as mentioned earlier, Muhammad al-Shaybānī is hardly ever referred to as one of the most highly qualified publicists of international law, similar to classical European publicists such as Francisco de Vitoria, Alberico Gentili, Hugo Grotius, and others, despite the great contributions he is acknowledged to have made in the field of Islamic international law and indirectly thereby to contemporary international law.

In view of the contending debates between advocates of a 'clash of civilizations' and 'dialogue among civilizations' in international law over the past two decades or more, it is necessary to encourage the harmonization of civilizational values and principles in international law discourse in a way that promotes equality of human civilizations and relevant legal systems within international law in contrast to the traditional exclusively Euro-Christian Westphalian standard of civilization that continues to influence the application of Article 38(1)(c) of the ICJ Statute. From an Islamic perspective, the concept of equality of human civilizations is reflected in Q49:13—'O mankind, We have created you of a male and female and made you into nations and tribes that you may know one another, surely the most honourable of you in the sight of God is the most righteous of you; surely God is Knowing and Aware.' This Islamic philosophy of equality of human civilizations should form part of contemporary discourse on the genuine universality of international law beyond the European for promoting the effective universalization of international law. This is reinforced by the provisions of Article 9 of the ICJ Statute which provides that in electing the judges of the Court 'the electors shall bear in mind not only that the persons to be elected should individually possess the qualifications required, but also that in the body as a whole the representation of the main forms of civilization and of the principal legal systems of the world should be assured'.

---

[66] Hassan S Khalilieh, *Islamic Law of the Sea: Freedom of Navigation and Passage Rights in Islamic Thought* (CUP 2019) vii–viii.
[67] eg Fassbender and others (eds) (n 34).

4.3. Judicial Interpretation and Recognized Principles of International Law

Judicial interpretation is an important aspect of the development of international law. Article 92 of the UN Charter designates the ICJ as the principal judicial organ of the UN, thus its pronouncements play a significant role in the development of international law. Writing in 1958, Sir Hersch Lauterpacht had noted that the ICJ's 'essential function is ... to contribute by its decisions to the development of international law',[68] and that it had actually 'made a tangible contribution to the development and clarification of the rules and principles of international law',[69] through its judicial decisions. This view has been reiterated by different scholars.[70] Despite the provision in Article 59 of the ICJ Statute that '[t]he decision of the Court has no binding force except between the parties and in respect of the particular case', there is no doubt that the decisions of the Court in different cases have had a significant effect on the understandings of the scope of different norms and recognized principles of international law, and consequently the development of international law generally. However, a scrutiny of the Court's decisions over the years shows that in its lead judgments the ICJ apparently relies almost exclusively on Western and European legal jurisprudence in its judicial interpretations and reference to the recognized principles of international law. Emilia Powell has noted in that regard that:

> With some notable but rare exceptions, lawyers from the Western hemisphere outnumber the non-Western judges [of the ICJ]. Thus the influence of the Islamic legal tradition or, for that matter, other non-European legal traditions is minuscule and depends on the composition of the bench. If a judge with knowledge or comprehension of Islamic law sits on the Court, then Islamic law-based legal arguments may appear in the jurisprudence. Otherwise, the discourse at The Hague is framed in Western legal language.[71]

It is instructive to note that the Court has been reminded on a number of occasions in separate and dissenting opinions of some of its learned judges, in relevant cases, of the need to consider the principles of other legal traditions in its application of the general principles of international law pursuant to Article 38(1)(c) of the ICJ Statute. For example, the separate opinion of Judge Fouad Ammoun in the *North*

---

[68] Hersch Lauterpacht, *The Development of International Law by the International Court* (Stevens & Sons 1958) 42
[69] ibid 5.
[70] Christian J Tams and James Sloan (eds), *The Development of International Law by the International Court of Justice* (OUP 2013).
[71] Emilia J Powell, *Islamic Law and International Law: Peaceful Resolution of Disputes* (OUP 2020) 207. See generally pp 207–18 for an analysis of references to Islamic law at the ICJ.

Sea Continental Shelf case[72] is a *classicus* on the need for the ICJ to refer to other legal traditions, particularly Islamic law, in relevant cases, to enhance the genuine universality of international law. The learned judge highlighted that in seeking to apply the general principles of law to fill a lacuna that had arose in the case, it was important

> in the first place to observe that the form of words of Article 38, paragraph 1 (c), of the Statute, referring to 'the general principles of law recognized by civilized nations', is inapplicable in the form in which it is set down, since the term 'civilized nations' is incompatible with the relevant provisions of the United Nations Charter [specifically art. 2(1) on the sovereign equality of states], and the consequence thereof is an ill-advised limitation of the notion of the general principles of law.[73]

He asserted that such 'discrimination between [the so-called] civilized nations and uncivilized nations, ... was unknown to the founding fathers of international law, the protagonists of the universal law of nations'[74] and then went on to argue that:

> If it is borne in mind particularly that the general principles of law mentioned by Article 38, paragraph 1(c) of the Statute, are nothing other than the norms common to the different legislations of the world, united by the identity of the legal reason therefore, or the *ratio legis*, transposed from the internal legal system to the international legal system, one cannot fail to remark an oversight committed by arbitrarily limiting the contribution of municipal law to the elaboration of international law: international law which has become, in short, particularly thanks to the principles proclaimed by the United Nations Charter, a universal law able to draw on the internal sources of law of all the States whose relations it is destined to govern, by reason of which the composition of the Court should represent the principal legal systems of the world.[75]

Consequently, the learned judge proposed that a combined understanding of Articles 38(1)(c) and 9 of the ICJ Statute, within the context of the principle of sovereign equality enshrined in Article 2(1) of the UN Charter, require the Court not to restrict its search for equity as a general principle only to European legal traditions, but extend the search to other legal traditions, including the Islamic legal tradition. Lack of a better summary necessitates a full reproduction of his

---

[72] [1969] ICJ Rep 101–53.
[73] ibid para 35.
[74] ibid.
[75] ibid.

well-articulated submission in which he built an inclusive case for the application of equity as a general principle recognized by different legal systems, as follows:

> Incorporated into the great legal systems of the modern world referred to in Article 9 of the Statute of the Court, the principle of equity manifests itself in the law of Western Europe and of Latin America, the direct heirs of the Romano-Mediterranean *jus gentium*; in the common law, tempered and supplemented by equity described as accessory; in Muslim law which is placed on the basis of equity (and more particularly on its equivalent, equality) by the Koran and the teaching of the four great jurisconsults of Islam condensed in the Shari'a, which comprises, among the sources of law, the *istihsan*, which authorizes equity-judgments; Chinese law, with its primacy for the moral law and the common sense of equity, in harmony with the Marxist-Leninist philosophy; Soviet law, which quite clearly provides a place for considerations of equity; Hindu law which recommends 'the individual to act, and the judge to decide, according to his conscience, according to justice, according to equity, if no other rule of law binds them'; finally the law of the other Asian countries, and of the African countries, the customs of which particularly urge the judge not to diverge from equity and of which 'the conciliating role and the equitable nature' have often been undervalued by Europeans; customs from which sprang a *jus gentium* constituted jointly with the rules of the common law in the former British possessions, the lacunae being filled in 'according to justice, equity and good conscience'; and in the former French possessions, jointly with the law of Western Europe, steeped in Roman law. A general principle of law has consequently become established, which the law of nations could not refrain from accepting, and which founds legal relations between nations on equity and justice.[76]

Similarly, in his separate opinion in the *Gabíkovo-Nagymaros Project (Hungary v Slovakia)* case[77] the-then Vice-President of the ICJ, Judge Christopher Weeramantry, highlighted that when dealing with newly developing areas of international law such as the principles of environmental law then, within the context of Article 9 of the ICJ Statute, he saw 'the Court as being charged with a duty to draw upon the wisdom of the world's several civilizations, where such a course can enrich its insights into the matter before it [and the] Court cannot afford to be monocultural, especially where it is entering newly developing areas of law'.[78] He then went on to submit aptly that:

---

[76] ibid para 38.
[77] *Gabcikovo-Nagymaros Project (Hungary v Slovakia)* (Judgment) [1997] ICJ Rep 88–116.
[78] ibid 94.

In relation to concern for the environment generally, examples may be cited from nearly every traditional system, ranging from Australasia and the Pacific Islands, through Amerindian and African cultures to those of ancient Europe.... This survey would not be complete without a reference also to the principles of Islamic law that in as much as all land belongs to God, land is never the subject of human ownership, but is only held in trust, with all the connotations that follow of due care, wise management, and custody for future generations. The first principle of modern environmental law—the principle of trusteeship of earth resources—is thus categorically formulated in this system.[79]

Also in his dissenting opinion in the *Aegean Sea Continental Shelf (Greece v Turkey)*,[80] Judge Salah Tarazi highlighted that the definition of a treaty under Article 2(1)(a) of the Vienna Treaty on the Law of Treaties (VCLT) as 'an international agreement concluded between States in written form and governed by international law, whether embodied in a single instrument or in two or more related instruments and whatever its particular designation', is universally acknowledged. The learned judge noted with reference to Islamic law that the definition under the VCLT was not new as 'Islamic law had already provided that in conventions one must consider the intention of the parties and not the literal meaning of the words and phrases employed'.[81]

Judge Awn Al-Khasawneh had also referred to Islamic law in his dissenting opinion to the judgment on jurisdiction in the *Aerial Incident of 10 August 1999 (Pakistan v India)*,[82] to highlight that the rule of separability of treaty provisions under Article 44 of the VCLT is also acknowledged under other legal traditions including Islamic law by referring to the Islamic legal maxim

that which cannot be attained in its entirety should not be substantially abandoned. A concept remarkably similar to the Roman law principle *ut res magis valeat quam pereat*—a document should be given validity wherever possible ... and ... generally agreed to be one of the basic goals of the law on invalidity, as formulated in the Vienna Conventions of 1969 and 1986, namely 'to preserve, whenever possible, the validity of conventional arrangements rather than to altogether destroy it by considerations alien to that goal'.[83]

---

[79] ibid 104–05. See also Judge Weeramantry's separate opinion in the *Maritime Delimitation in the Area between Greenland and Jan Mayes* case [1993] ICJ Rep 38, para 238, where the learned judge made reference to the Qur'anic injunction on equity.
[80] *Aegean Sea Continental Shelf* (Judgment) [1978] ICJ Rep 55–62.
[81] ibid 57.
[82] *Aerial Incident of 10 August 1999 (Pakistan v India), Jurisdiction of the Court* (Judgment) [2000] ICJ Rep 48–51.
[83] ibid.

These bold references to Islamic law in the separate and dissenting opinions of the learned ICJ judges should be commended and the ICJ should be persuaded to accede to their reasonable calls, which would certainly enhance the genuine universality of international law beyond the European in the context of judicial interpretation and recognized principles of international law. One rare occasion on which the ICJ had, in a lead judgment, made reference to the contribution of Islamic law to a recognized principle of international law was in the *United States Diplomatic and Consular Staff in Iran* case,[84] in which the Court observed that 'the principle of the inviolability of the persons of diplomatic agents and the premises of diplomatic missions is one of the very foundations of [the international law] regime, the evolution of which the traditions of Islam made a substantial contribution'. This was obviously an effort to establish the customary international law nature of the principle of the inviolability of the persons of diplomatic agents and the premises of diplomatic missions, in relation to the actions of the Islamic Republic of Iran in that case. It is submitted that a continuation of such acknowledgement of Islamic law to the development of international law, by the lead judgments of the ICJ in relevant cases, would, from an Islamic law perspective, go a long way in promoting the genuine universality of international law beyond the European.

4.4. The Political Manipulation of International Law

The political manipulation of international law places its universality within the context of power, hegemony, and narrow national interests of the powerful European and Western states of the Global North. The politics of international law is often reflected in how the narratives on the 'big issues' of international law are formulated and assessed and how its successes are proclaimed. These 'big issues' of international law, often influenced by the political clout of the powerful Western states, include the use of force in relation to collective security, humanitarian intervention, self-defence, the imposition of sanctions, and the politicization of human rights.

Over the years, there has been much consternation from the Muslim world about different military interventions, led by powerful Western states, in Muslim-majority states such as Iraq, Libya, and Syria, often justified through politically manipulated interpretations of different international law principles on the use of force. Being one of the most politically manipulated concepts of international law in contemporary times, the concept of collective security will be used as an illustrative example of the failure of Eurocentric international law, occasioning the flawed US-led coalition on the use of force in Iraq in 2003 and the NATO-led

---

[84] [1980] ICJ Rep 3, para 86.

coalition on the use of force in Libya in 2011. It is submitted that a complementary consideration of the concept of collective security from an Islamic law perspective would have demonstrated the genuine universality of that concept under international law beyond the European, which could have contributed to a better international outcome in handling the situations at the time.[85] Weeramantry had made a similar observation during the Iran-US diplomatic hostage crisis of November 1979 to January 1981. The learned judge made reference to this in his *Islamic Jurisprudence: An International Perspective* as follows:

> There will be in the future an increasing need for non-Islamic countries all over the world to negotiate with Islamic countries on a multitude of matters ranging from questions of war and peace to mercantile contracts. Such negotiation will require more understanding of Islamic attitudes, history and culture. An excellent recent example of an opportunity lost through lack of such understanding was the hostage crisis in Iran. The USA, asserting the well-accepted principle of diplomatic immunity and right to protection, kept referring continually to the formulations of this rule in the Western law books. Islamic law is also rich in principles relating to the treatment of foreign embassies and personnel. These were not cited, as far as the author is aware, nor was the slightest understanding shown of the existence of this body of learning. Had such authority been cited by the USA, it would have had a three-fold effect: its persuasive value would have been immensely greater; it would have shown an appreciation and understanding of Islamic culture; and it would have induced a greater readiness on the Iranian side to negotiate from a base of common understanding. It is not often sufficiently appreciated, especially in the Western world, that many of the current rules of international law are regarded by a large segment of the world's population as being principles from the rule-book of the elite club of world powers which held sway in the nineteenth century. In the midst of this general attitude of mistrust, the worthy rules are tarred with the same brush as the self-serving. World cultural traditions need to be involved, where available, to bolster up and reinforce these rules.... The same considerations apply at many other levels. The non-Islamic world neglects them at its own cost.[86]

With regard to the concept of collective security, Alvin LeRoy Bennett and James Oliver have identified that the idea 'is not unique to the twentieth century' and neither is it an unprecedented creation of modern international organizations. They noted that political philosophers in every period of recorded history, in both

---

[85] See Mashood A Baderin, '9/11, The US-Led War on Iraq and the Future of Collective Security Law: With an Insight from Islamic Law' in Matthew J Morgan (ed), *The Impact of 9/11: The Day that Changed Everything?* (Palgrave Macmillan 2009) 267–80.
[86] Weeramantry, *Islamic Jurisprudence* (n 37) 166.

Western and Eastern civilizations, had 'advocated means of controlling conflict that might reasonably be labelled Collective Security measures'.[87] They gave examples of the views of Greek philosophers such as Plato, Christian theologians such as St Augustine, ancient Chinese philosophers such as Confucius, and Roman Stoics such as Cicero to substantiate the antiquity of the idea of collective security.[88] Similar to other Western literature on the subject, there was not even a passing reference to any antecedent in Islamic thought on the concept. However, it is instructive to note that the Qur'an specifically established a relative rule of collective measures as early as the seventh century for dealing with apparent threats to peace and security within the Islamic community by providing that:

> If two parties among the Believers fall into a dispute, then you all should make peaceful settlement (*fa aslihū*) between them; but if one of them transgresses beyond bounds against the other, then you all should fight (*fa qātilū*) against the transgressing party until it complies with the command of God. If it complies, then you all should make peaceful settlement (*fa aslihū*) between the two of them with justice and you all should act equitably (*fa aqsitū*). Indeed God loves those who are equitable.[89]

This principle, which is incorporated into Islamic international law, reflects the recognition of collective measures as a system for maintaining peace and security under Islamic law, similar to the concept of collective security under contemporary international law. The verse indicates six important elements for the application of collective measures under Islamic law, which, if adopted, can help ameliorate some of the problematic political manipulation of collective security under contemporary international law: (1) the collective pronoun '*you all*' is a golden cord that runs through the verse signifying the importance of multilateralism for its effectivity; (2) the verse emphasizes peaceful settlement and only authorizes fighting (military action) in case of complete defiance and continued transgression by the offending party; (3) there is emphasis on peaceful settlement, and the collective is required to act in sincerity and utmost good faith; (4) the general rule in every conflict under Islamic law is based on the principle '*al-sulh khayr*' meaning 'peaceful settlement is better',[90] thus, the door of finding a peaceful settlement is never shut in the process; (5) the importance of adhering to the rule of law in collective measures is reflected by reference to justice and equity in the process; and (6) loyalty and equality of membership is essential for an effective collective security system.

---

[87] Alvin LeRoy Bennett and James K Oliver, *International Organizations: Principles and Issues* (7th edn, Pearson 2002) 145–46.
[88] ibid 4–9.
[89] Q49:9.
[90] Q4:128.

It is evident from the above analysis that the concept of collective security is recognized as a necessary method for the collective maintenance of peace and security under Islamic political and legal thought, subject to the elements of multilateralism, exhaustion of all avenues of peaceful settlement, good faith, rule of law, loyalty, and equality of membership within the system. All these elements are indispensable for any ideal collective security system today, especially the element of good faith, which is fundamental in Islamic law, and very much needed in international law today to restrain the narrow interest of states in their relationships. I have argued elsewhere[91] that, looking back at the Iraqi invasion of 2003, the important lesson to be drawn 'is that the introduction and accommodation of this Islamic perspective of collective measures into the discourse on the enforcement of international collective security law could have enriched the debates on the subject and also enhanced a better understanding and accommodation of international collective security law in the Muslim World' at the time, which could have led to a better outcome than the continuing chaos in Iraq to date. Such an informed dialogue would have promoted a more in-depth reflection on the necessary elements of multilateralism, rule of law, good faith, and exhaustion of all possible means of peaceful settlement as envisaged by the relevant provisions on collective security under the UN Charter. It would also have eliminated the allegations of political manipulation of international law principles made against Western states in the early days of the Iraqi crisis.

There are similar Islamic law principles relating to the concept of self-defence,[92] humanitarian intervention,[93] and human rights,[94] amongst others,[95] that can certainly complement the debates on those concepts in contemporary international law positively to realize genuine universality of international law beyond its current narrow European universality.

5. Conclusion

Looking at both its longer and shorter histories, international law has certainly come a very long way and its indispensability has been established over time in the relationship between modern nation states. While universality is its essential corollary both in theory and practice, it is obvious that this is still reflected as a Eurocentric universality in many ways as this chapter has endeavoured to show with reference to Islamic law. This Eurocentric universality continues to create a climate of understandable distrust for non-Western partners in the international

---

[91] Baderin, '9/11, The US-Led War on Iraq' (n 85) 277.
[92] Q22:39–40.
[93] Q4:75.
[94] Q17:70.
[95] Baderin, *Islamic Law* (n 22).

law venture, which often hampers the global effectiveness of international law at critical times. This edited volume is a bold step in highlighting the need to continually address that challenge of promoting genuine universality of international law beyond the European for the desired global effectiveness of international law.

The issues relating to Islamic law identified in this chapter towards achieving genuine universality of international law beyond the European call three main principal stakeholders in contemporary international law to action. The first is international law scholars and academics, who must rise to the challenge of addressing the problem of the exclusion of relevant Islamic international law perspectives in the current textbook historical narratives of contemporary international law, which has left a yawning gap in the completeness of the historical narratives. The second is international tribunals, especially the ICJ, which must respond to the call of some of its learned judges over the years on the need to acknowledge relevant principles of other legal systems of the world to complement the frequently referenced European principles in relevant cases, when the need arises to fill any lacuna in international law using 'the general principles of law recognised by civilized nations' pursuant to Article 38(1)(c) of its statute. Last, and perhaps the most important, are the political leaders of the powerful states of the Global North, who must demonstrate more good faith in respecting and upholding the principle of equality of states and civilizations in international law beyond narrow national interests that lead to their manipulation of international law principles, and thereby undermine global confidence in the veracity of international law. Until each of these principal stakeholders rises to the respective challenges identified in this chapter, the essential quest for genuine universality of international law beyond the European, to ensure its universal acceptability and global effectiveness, will continue to remain a mere aspirational ideal, especially for the Muslim world.

13
Beyond Co-option and Contestation

The Chinese Belt and Road Initiative and the Universality of International Law

Kanad Bagchi and Milan Tahraoui

Within the discipline of international law, the narrative of universality evokes, simultaneously, both a sense of nostalgia and cynicism. As Geoff Gordon rightly suggests, universalism has served both colonial and imperial aspirations, as it has provided the language and the means for resisting the very same forces.[1] In this sense, inherent in the very concept of universality lies a certain duality that creates but also destroys, liberates but also shackles, nurtures plurality and yet consolidates hegemony. As the editors of this volume illustrate, ontologically the claim to universality works through the creation of 'binaries' by the 'othering' of particularity and then subsuming the latter entirely into the universalist fold.[2] Universalism and particularism therefore are not mutually exclusive narratives, but co-constitutive in the manner that their boundaries remain porous and pervious.

Nowhere are these tensions more apparent than in China's massive and ambitious Belt and Road Initiative (BRI), which some have characterized as one of the most comprehensive 'international program[mes] of cooperation and reciprocal engagement'.[3] As the evolving contours of the BRI unfold, scholarly opinion has been split between, on one hand, scepticism concerning Chinese influence and foreign policy interventions, both in the region and outside. China's engagement with the world economy through the BRI and its considerable weight in global financial markets are seen as symptomatic of a rising hegemon, determined to unsettle the fundamental structures underpinning the current mode of global governance.[4] Naysayers, on the other hand, point to China's seeming endorsement, if not

---

[1] Geoff Gordon, 'Universalism' in Jean d'Aspremont and Sahib Singh (eds), *Concepts of International Law: Contributions to Disciplinary Thought* (Edward Elgar 2019).

[2] Işıl Aral, Jean d'Aspremont, and Iain Scobbie, 'Universality and International Law: A Contestation Around Binaries (draft)'; see also Kinhide Mushakoji, 'Multilateralism in a Multicultural World: notes for a theory of occultation' in Robert W Cox (ed), *The New Realism: Perspectives on Multilateralism and World Order* (United Nations University Press 1997) 83–108, 107, fn 1.

[3] Guilherme Vasconcelos Vilaça, 'Strengthening the Cultural and Normative Foundations of the Belt and Road Initiative: The Colombo Plan, Yan Xuetong and Chinese Ancient Thought' Research Paper <https://papers.ssrn.com/sol3/papers.Cfm?abstract_id=2887892>.

[4] Congyan Cai, *The Rise of China and International: Taking Chinese Exceptionalism Seriously* (OUP 2019).

vehement affirmation, of the traditional doctrines of international law such as the principles of sovereignty, non-intervention, and the like and they claim that much of what the Chinese approach represents, both within and outside the context of BRI, is predominantly nothing new and is certainly not a threat to the current system of international rules.[5] To put it differently, Chinese engagement with international law and the BRI in particular is presented variously as either 'co-opting' or 'contesting' the universality of international law.[6]

Taking the BRI as the central focus of our analysis, we claim that both the normative implications of the project and its finer institutional contours present a more nuanced picture. We contend that behind the enormous economic and infrastructural project that the BRI represents, lies a far-reaching normative and ideational thrust that extant scholarship seems to overlook. The Belt and Road Initiative espouses a certain ambition towards reorienting the values and precepts of international law drawn from a specific historical and cultural heritage that is different from traditional 'Western' ideas.[7] In this sense, the BRI is a concerted attempt not only to challenge the normative underpinnings of the international legal order, but to imagine and endeavour to bring to international law a different 'civilizational'[8] paradigm.[9] This is what we call the 'Universalism of the BRI'—a project articulated in the 'name of humanity as a whole, aimed at the universal values of peace, openness, cooperation, and inclusiveness'.[10] Section 1 of this chapter sketches out in broad terms the larger vision of the BRI and shows how its normative underpinnings cannot be fully captured through a binary lens.

Yet, the BRI is neither monolithic nor does it contain a fully coherent operational framework. Some of this ambiguity is clearly by design. The Belt and Road Initiative's challenge to the current international order is by no means a radical call for its repudiation. To the contrary, BRI reinforces traditional doctrines of

---

[5] See eg Tom Ginsburg, 'Eastphalia as the Perfection of Westphalia' (2010) 17(1) *Indiana Journal of Global Studies* 27–45; Simon Chesterman, 'Asia's Ambivalence about International Law and Institutions: Past, Present and Futures' (2016) 27(4) European Journal of International Law 945–78, 968.

[6] See eg, with respect to the former strand of thought, Li Zhaojie, 'China' in Simon Chesterman, Hishashi Owada, and Ben Saul (eds), *Oxford Handbook of International Law in Asia and the Pacific* (OUP 2019) 299–319, 307.

[7] Human rights law is certainly a field where China expresses its diverging view with positive international law most unambiguously. See eg Human Rights Council, National Report Submitted in Accordance with Paragraph 5 of the Annex to Human Rights Council Res 16/21 China, A/HRC/WG.6/31/CHN/1, distributed generally 20 August 2018 <www.ohchr.org/EN/HRBodies/UPR/Pages/CNIndex.aspx> 2–4 ('C. The concept and theoretical system of human rights with Chinese characteristics'), especially 3–4 and 10.

[8] Onuma Yasuaki, *International Law in a Transcivilizational World* (CUP 2017); Milan Nebyl Tahraoui, 'Book Essay: Yasuaki, Onuma: International Law in a Transcivilizational World' (2018) 78(4) Zeitschrift für ausländisches öffentliches Recht und Völkerrecht 1046–64.

[9] See eg Martin Jacques, *When China Rules the World* (2nd edn, Penguin Books 2012), especially 340–41 and 374–83.

[10] Michael A Peters, 'The Chinese Dream, Belt and Road Initiative and the Future of Education: A Philosophical Postscript' [2019] *Educational Philosophy and Theory* <doi.org/10.1080/00131857.2019.1696272>.

international law such as 'sovereignty' and 'non-intervention' as linchpins of a new order that would be responsive especially to the needs of the 'Global South'. How does one reconcile the two? Through the lens of co-option and contestation we explore 'the many faces of BRI' and argue that it moves constantly between rhetoric and reality. This forms the bulk of the analysis in Section 2.

Finally, in Section 3, we call for the imagining of new spaces of reform and change outside of a strict binary frame. In recent scholarship, BRI has been subjected to tremendous scrutiny, especially from a private and economic law perspective. Yet, reflections on how the BRI participates in shaping, if not creating, a different international public order seems to be less explored. We end with some critical reflections on the question of power and dominance that this evolving public order represents and what this means for the Global South.

Having said that, it is important to emphasize that the BRI with its own evolutionary trajectory is nestled within a larger Chinese approach to international law. It therefore becomes crucial that, while being focused on the ideational and institutional dimensions of the BRI, one does not lose sight of broader Chinese engagement in international law.

1. Universalism of the Belt and Road Initiative

The infrastructural and connectivity dimension of the BRI are well-known and documented.[11] In a nutshell, the BRI envisions an overlapping set of networks that will run through land (Silk Road Economic 21 Belt) and through sea (21st Century Maritime Road). Based on recent estimates, it will span through at least seventy different countries, covering 60 per cent of the world's population and a large portion of the world economy, creating infrastructures, capital expenditure, resource development, modernization, cultural exchanges, industrial investment etc, while providing a stable system of currency and trade. It has been characterized as China's most significant engagement with respect to both regional and non-regional multilateralism.[12] The BRI initiative has found a central place in the Chinese political agenda, and this can be seen from its continuous reinforcement in various international forums,[13] joint statements by Chinese ministries, inclusion in China's 13th five-year plan (2016),[14] and its incorporation into the Constitution of the Chinese Communist Party as an official doctrine.

[11] See eg World Bank, 'Belt and Road Economics: Opportunities and Risks of Transport Corridors' 18 June 2019 <https://openknowledge.worldbank.org/bitstream/handle/10986/31878/9781464813 924.pdf>.
[12] Weifeng Zhou and Mario Esteban, 'Beyond Balancing: China's Approach Towards the Belt and Road Initiative' (2018) 27(112) Journal of Contemporary China 487–501, 487 and 496.
[13] See the various press releases published with respect to the Belt and Road Forum for International Cooperation <www.beltandroadforum.org/english/25/index.html>.
[14] See the 13th Five Year Plan For Economic and Social Development of the People's Republic of China (2016–2020), Translated by Compilation and Translation Bureau, Central Committee of the

It is important to recognize at the outset that the BRI emerges at a time when there is a perceptible shift in the international order characterized by the declining role of the 'West' in international law. More fundamentally, international law in terms of both practice and theory was already encountering varied contestations and resistance from non-Western powers. Clearly, the fact that the 'world [...] is undergoing the greatest changes in a century' is not lost on China but provides, in its own words, 'opportunities [...] altering the international structures of power'.[15] This reflects China's ambition to push for what it perceives as its fair place in international society. It is in this context that the BRI espouses both a normative and an ideational vision for an alternative international public order.

What does this vision entail? First, the BRI is critical of Western international law and perceives the latter as perpetuating a cultural, civilizational, economic, and political system marked by inequality and dominance over non-Western states and peoples. In this sense, BRI's claim for universality distances itself from Western universalism, which China argues was rooted in 'colonialism and imperialism'.[16] Instead, the BRI offers a vision of universality that claims to bring shared prosperity and common development through a system that reflects the interests of all states. The BRI speaks in the language of 'cooperation' 'coordination', and 'multilateralism' that would be built on the ideas of 'openness', 'inclusiveness', and 'peace'.[17] The vision of the BRI couched within an overarching framework of 'community' and 'shared interests' while prescribing the road towards a 'common destiny' or a 'global community of shared future' signals a break from the universal-liberal paradigm of modern international law.

For China, these are not simply hollow aspirations devoid of meaning but are central to the conception of BRI. As Fu Ying puts it, the phrase 'community of shared interests' 'celebrates diversity, inclusiveness and respects the legitimate interests and values of nations, regardless of their social systems or their levels of development'.[18] Through the BRI, China speaks to and on behalf of developing

---

Communist Party of China. Beijing, China <http://en.ndrc.gov.cn/newsrelease/201612/P020161207645765233498.pdf>. For an analysis of the 13th Five Year Plan and its focus on BRI, see Michel Aglietta and Guo Bai, 'China's 13th Five-Year Plan In Pursuit of a "Moderately Prosperous Society"' CEPII Policy Brief No 12 (September 2016) <www.cepii.fr/CEPII/fr/publications/pb/abstract.asp?NoDoc=9474>.

[15] The State Council Information Office of the People's Republic of China, *China and the World in the New Era* (White Paper, September 2019) <https://eng.yidaiyilu.gov.cn/zchj/zcfg/104833.htm> (hereinafter 'China White Paper 2019').

[16] ibid.

[17] People's Republic of China, *Vision and Actions on Jointly Building Silk Road Economic Belt and 21st-Century Maritime Silk Road* (28 March 2015) <www.beltandroad.gov.hk/visionandactions.html> (hereinafter 'Vision and Actions Document 2015').

[18] Fu Ying, 'China's Vision for the World: A Community of Shared Future' *The Diplomat* (22 June 2017) <https://thediplomat.com/2017/06/chinas-vision-for-the-world-a-community-of-shared-future/>.

states in their quest for voice and control over processes of global governance. It is presented as the means to include 'marginalized countries into the mainstream'.[19]

Chinese discourse around the BRI is deeply critical of the West's singular claim to the universal that envisages a particular way of life as both materially superior and culturally advanced. Instead, the BRI starts from the premise that 'there is no such thing as one single path or model that is universally applicable'.[20] History figures prominently in the BRI and China does not shy away from developing legal claims by centring its own 'most ancient' civilization within the narrative of international law. For instance, the BRI constantly draws parallels to the erstwhile Silk Road, which according to China embodies a 'historic and cultural heritage shared by all countries around the world'.[21] The BRI propagates a claim for universality that ought to recognize the equal moral worth of different civilizations and peoples.

The burden of the past is what makes the civilizational paradigm crucial for China. Part of the story of the history of international law that followed and cemented Western hegemony systematically discredited Chinese cultural and philosophical traditions, leading to what is popularly known as the 'century of humiliation'.[22] This was followed by acquisitive wars and the imposition of unequal treaties that dishevelled Chinese suzerainty in the Asian region, which, by several accounts, represented an extremely sophisticated and successful regional political and economic regime. Subsequently, decades of isolation from the international system of rules on the basis of China's internal models of political and economic governance further amplified China's distrust of international law as a means of exclusion and control. This is evident from the BRI's continuous affirmation of the Five Principles of Peaceful Coexistence—a paradigm which was adopted by India, China, and Burma in 1954 and designed specially to send out a strong message against Western interventionism and hegemony.[23] China's engagement with its BRI-partnered countries invariably emphasizes the importance of upholding 'territorial integrity', 'sovereignty', and 'non-interference'.

Questions concerning economic development and the 'right' path towards the same also animate much of the thinking and objectives behind the universalist

---

[19] Long Yongtu, former Chinese vice minister for trade, quoted in 'Belt and Road Initiative Reflects New Trends of Globalization: Former Boao Forum Secretary' (2 April 2016) <www.china.org.cn/world/Off_the_Wire/2016-04/02/content_38166299.htm>.

[20] China White Paper 2019 (n 15).

[21] Vision and Actions Document 2015 (n 17).

[22] Xue Hanqin, 'Chinese Contemporary Perspectives on International Law: History, Culture and International Law' (2012) 355 Collected Courses of The Hague Academy of International Law 41–234; Martin Jacques, *When China Rules The World* (2nd edn, Penguin Books 2012; Alison Adcock Kaufman, 'The "Century of Humiliation", Then and Now: Chinese Perceptions of the International Order' (2010) 25(1) Pacific Focus 1–33; Wang Tieya, 'International Law in China: Historical and Contemporary Perspectives' (1990) 221 Collected Courses of the Hague Academy of International Law 195–369.

[23] For an analysis of the five principles, see Zhenmin Liu, 'Following the Five Principles of Peaceful Coexistence and Jointly Building a Community of Common Destiny' (2014) 13(3) Chinese Journal of International Law 477–80.

ambitions of the BRI. The BRI 2015 Vision and Actions document abounds with musings that re-evaluate the world order as reeling under pressures emerging from 'uneven' global development, 'weak global recovery', and, most importantly, a continuing challenge to the development of certain states.[24] The BRI instead seemingly adopts an approach that brings the specific political, legal, and cultural situatedness of the state concerned to the forefront and ties development to the 'traditions' and cultural predispositions of the country, as charted out by its 'own people'.[25] Crucially, while embracing 'modernization', China and the BRI reject any form of proclaimed westernization that attempts to 'impose its own models on others'.[26]

A similar developmental narrative also features prominently in the rhetoric on human rights, where the latter is essentially seen as 'historical, dialectical and developmental'.[27] This reflects China's long-standing position that the dominant liberal-universal framework, with civil and political rights at its core, is unsuited to the needs of the developing world.[28] Instead, China claims to put forward a historically grounded and culturally sensitive approach to human rights that provides equal weight to both the 'universality and particularity of human rights'.[29] While China continually emphasizes the universality of all human rights, the right to subsistence and development feature prominently as fundamental to the path to prosperity.

What essentially transpires from the above discussion is that the BRI's claim to universality is not predicated upon any objective or neutral conception of what international law is or ought to be. In fact, on close scrutiny it becomes apparent that this claim to universality is indeed a reflection of a particular civilizational legacy and history that is uniquely Chinese. This has led most scholarship on the BRI to adopt a binary lens which views the former as either 'strengthening' or 'challenging' the universality of international law. Yet, the promise of the BRI and its potential for a universalism offers a distinct way to understand China's engagement with international law.

To put it differently, thinking in binaries prevents us from perceiving social orders—international law being one such social order—in their holistic sense, confining our imagination to a 'unitary idea of order' built around a template of a

---

[24] Vision and Actions Document 2015 (n 17).
[25] China White Paper 2019 (n 15).
[26] ibid.
[27] The State Council Information Office of the People's Republic of China, *Progress in Human Rights over the 40 Years of Reform and Opening Up in China* (White Paper, 12 December 2018) <http://english.www.gov.cn/archive/white_paper/2018/12/13/content_281476431737638.htm> 44.
[28] Andréa Worden, 'The CCP at the UN: Redefining Development and Rights: How the Belt and Road Initiative Threatens to Undermine the 2030 Agenda for Sustainable Development' *China in Context and Perspective* (17 March 2019) <https://sinopsis.cz/en/the-ccp-at-the-un-redefining-development-and-rights/#fn27>.
[29] English.gov.cn, 'Full Text: Progress in Human Rights over the 40 Years of Reform and Opening Up in China' (12 December 2019) <http://english.www.gov.cn/archive/white_paper/2018/12/13/content_281476431737638.htm>.

hierarchical and coherent set of rules and principles. But as Armin von Bogdandy and Sergio Dellavalle inform us, in a post-unitary constellation social orders can exhibit several apparent inconsistencies.[30] In this political and social reality, 'order can be universal and particular at the same time',[31] and, we argue, be simultaneously far-reaching and yet circumspect. The BRI intervenes within such a social order that is marked by shifting hierarchies and contains dispersed and disaggregated sources of power and legitimacy. It uses international law to create 'spaces' that offer the message of universality. However, it is true that this universalism is predicated upon the paradigm of particularity that is presented to the world in universalist terms as something that is or ought to be 'shared by all'.

This ought to make us think whether universalism and particularism, as competing paradigms of international law, inherited a bias that refuses to see complexity in the order of society. Universality, with all its claims for an ever-expanding sphere of validity, obscures the individual identities, that then only surface as radical defiance, ultimately de-legitimizing the order itself. Similarly, particularism admits of absolutely no possibility of a shared conception of an order, even if that order aspires to equality and inclusion. In both cases, the limitations of these dichotomies are evident, as the BRI, or for that matter the larger Chinese approach to international law, does not fit neatly into either. In our conception, therefore, there can be several 'universalisms' coexisting in parallel, without any one of those systems being regarded as 'particular'.

2. The Many Faces of the Belt and Road Initiative

If we agree that the BRI espouses a universalistic aspiration and is simultaneously couched within a particularistic narrative, how we do assess its relationship with positive international law? Depending on the legal regime in question, China either embraces the normative ethos of a particular regime or contests its dominant logic. Eschewing a strict binary framework allows us to witness these differing logics as pertaining to the 'many faces of BRI'. In each of the regimes noted below the universal aspirations of the BRI evolve even as China simultaneously 'co-opts' and 'contests' international law in multifaceted ways.

---

[30] Armin von Bogdandy and Sergio Dellavalle, 'Universalism and Particularism: A Dichotomy to Read Theories on International Order' in Stefan Kadelbach, Thomas Kleinlein, and David Roth-Isigkeit (eds), *System, Order, and International Law: The Early History of International Legal Thought from Machiavelli to Hegel* (OUP 2017) 482–507.
[31] ibid 500.

2.1 International Human Rights and the Developmental Perspective

The international human rights discourse as transpiring through the BRI is paradigmatic of how skilfully China pursues a strategy that Bin Li calls a 'mixture of engagement and resistance'.[32] While it engages with international human rights bodies such as the UN Human Rights Council and the UN Human Rights Commission, including participating in Periodic reviews, with what China calls to be in the spirit of 'a positive, confident, inclusive and open attitude',[33] several international NGOs have underscored how China works more to disrupt and hinder than to cooperate.[34] This is done through several means, including pressing for and gathering support[35] around procedural and substantive re-interpretations, broadening or narrowing the scope of existing norms, and through 'normative innovations'.[36]

Fundamental to this contestation lies an explicit agenda towards re-orienting the very basis of the international human rights regime, from it being centred around the universalism of individual rights towards a more community-based system of rights. In this, the rhetoric of the BRI is deeply intertwined with the concept of 'Community with a Shared Future for Mankind' that is reinforced as a 'Chinese Proposal' backed by a 'theoretical system of human rights with Chinese characteristics'.[37] This narrative is centrally located within the Chinese 'developmental' paradigm, that perceives human rights as means to an end rather than an end in itself. In this constellation, human rights ought to serve and be promoted on the basis of specific 'national conditions and the needs of the people'[38] which 'prioritize'[39] rights to subsistence and development. For instance, in its 2008 National Report to the UN Human Rights Council published within the framework of its Universal Periodic review, China claimed that while the universality of human rights is an essential element of the international human rights (IHR) system, 'national realities'

---

[32] Bin Li, 'China's Socialist Rule of Law and Global Constitutionalism' in Takao Suami and others (eds), *Global Constitutionalism from European and East Asian Perspectives* (CUP 2018) 58–98, 90.

[33] Human Rights Council, National Report (n 7) 4, para 13.

[34] Amnesty International, 'China: Global Coalition Urges UN to Address Beijing's Human Rights Abuses' (9 September 2020) <www.amnesty.org/en/latest/news/2020/09/china-global-coalition-urges-un-to-address-beijing-human-rights-abuses/> Human Rights Watch, 'The Costs of International Advocacy: China's Interference in United Nations Human Rights Mechanisms' (5 September 2017) <www.hrw.org/report/2017/09/05/costs-international-advocacy/chinas-interference-united-nations-human-rights#page>.

[35] Alastair Iain Johnston, 'China in a World of Orders: Rethinking Compliance and Challenge in Beijing's International Relations' (2019) 44(2) *International Security* 9–60, 33; Yu-Jie Chen, 'China's Challenge to the International Human Rights Regime' (2019) 51(4) New York University Journal of International Law and Politics 1179–222, 1214–15, especially 1215.

[36] Courtney J Fung, 'Rhetorical Adaptation, Normative Resistance and International Order-making: China's Advancement of the Responsibility to Protect' [2019] Cooperation and Conflict 1–23.

[37] Human Rights Council, National Report (n 7) 2–4.

[38] ibid para 4.

[39] English.gov.cn (n 29) 3.

of specific countries assume equal importance.[40] The universalism of the BRI does not advocate for the redundancy of the present IHR regime. To the contrary, it offers an alternative conception for what the IHR regime ought to pursue. China advances its conception of human rights beyond the popular narrative around rule of law, civil liberties, and democratic participation and centres its imagination on the logic of 'development' as human rights.[41]

2.2 Conditionality Through Other Means: International Economic Governance and the AIIB

It is on the international financial front that the BRI has perhaps received the maximum attention. The establishment of the Asian Infrastructure Investment Bank (AIIB) was heralded as a rather bold step and a huge success of Chinese multilateralism, especially because of significant resistance from the US.[42] The institutional set-up of the AIIB including its Articles of Agreement (AOA) promised much for an overhaul of global economic governance. For instance, unlike West-centric institutions such as the International Monetary Fund (IMF) and World Bank (WB), where the developing nations' share of the vote has always been disproportionate to their size and influence in the global economy, the AIIB would have a more appropriate representation for the developing countries. Moreover, as against the recurring criticism concerning the ill-suited and pervasive conditionality programmes spearheaded by the IMF and WB, the AIIB would be specifically barred from interfering in the political space of the receiving countries.[43] Finally, while the IMF and WB took several decades to develop and recognize the importance of the social and environmental impact of its conditionality measures, and only after repeated protests, the AIIB makes social and environmental impact a priority, so much so that it is included in its constitutive document.[44] In furtherance of this mandate, the AIIB released its 'Environmental and Social Framework' which prescribes a stringent regime of environmental and social impact assessments to be

---

[40] Human Rights Council, National Report Submitted in Accordance with Paragraph 15(A) of the Annex to Human Rights Council Resolution 5/1: China, A/HRC/WG.6/4/CHN/1, distributed generally 10 November 2008, 5.
[41] See, in this regard, Surya P Subedi, 'China's Approach to Human Rights and the UN Human Rights Agenda' (2015) 14(3) Chinese Journal of International Law 437–64.
[42] Mike Callaghan and Paul Hubbard, 'The Asian Infrastructure Investment Bank: Multilateralism on the Silk Road' (2016) 9(2) China Economic Journal 116–39.
[43] AIIB Statute, art 31(2): 'The Bank, its President, officers and staff shall not interfere in the political affairs of any member [...]. Only economic considerations shall be relevant to their decisions.'
[44] Art 13(4): 'The Bank shall ensure that each of its operations complies with the Bank's operational and financial policies, including without limitation, policies addressing environmental and social impacts.' See also Forbes.com, 'The 'Lean, Clean And Green' AIIB Is Ready For More Ambitious, Independent Projects' (10 July 2017) <www.forbes.com/sites/sarahsu/2017/07/10/the-lean-clean-and-green-aiib-is-ready-for-more-ambitious-independent-projects/>.

conducted at the time when a project is commissioned and during its implementation. It entails the Environmental and Social Policy (ESP) as well as Environmental and Social Standards (ESS), which, inter alia, provide standards for involuntary resettlements for indigenous peoples.[45]

The reality of the AIIB's operational dynamics, however, reveals a different yet all too familiar story. The contradictions within the AIIB can be observed in several ways. While the AIIB is high on the rhetoric of inclusiveness and equality, China still holds a significantly dominant position on the governing board. With a voting share of around 26 per cent, China effectively holds a blocking veto. The AIIB and other financial institutions under the BRI impose their own version of 'conditionality' attached to financial assistance, that on some accounts are extremely intrusive and highly political.[46] Moreover, the governing rationality of the BRI financing institutions remains fundamentally aligned with that of the IMF and the WB, such that in most of the projects that have been undertaken by the AIIB, it has partnered with the WB, the Asian Development Bank, and the European Bank for Reconstruction and Development.[47] While economic and financial governance remains a key plank for China and also the BRI, what becomes clear is that there is a simultaneous strategy of co-option and contestation.

2.3 Cyber Governance and Digital Sovereignty

Finally, through what China labels as the digital/cyber silk road, Chinese influence in cyber and digital governance activities is already being felt in a relatively 'new field' of global governance. China continues to champion the cause of cyber sovereignty and is one of the main proponents of informational cyber sovereignty. The latter forms part of several policy documents relating to cyber matters and internet governance[48] and is also a recurring theme in its contribution to the development of the application of international law to cyber space.[49] The concept of cyber

---

[45] AIIB, 'Environmental and Social Framework', approved in February 2016 <www.aiib.org/en/policies-strategies/framework-agreements/environmental-social-framework.html>.

[46] Mikael Mattlin and Matti Nojonen, 'Conditionality and Path Dependence in Chinese Lending' (2015) 24(94) Journal of Contemporary China 701–20. They document four different sorts of conditionality inherent in Chinese lending, namely: (1) political conditionality, (2) embedded conditionality, (3) cross conditionality, and (4) emergent conditionality. For instance, political conditionality entails maintaining diplomatic relations with China, adhering to the One-China policy, and supporting the Chinese position on global issues, such as human rights and governance. Embedded conditionality on the other hand requires recipient countries to employ Chinese contractors, technology, equipment, etc.

[47] Gerard J Sanders, 'The Asian Infrastructure Investment Bank and the Belt and Road Initiative: Complementarities and Contrasts' (2017) 16(2) Chinese Journal of International Law 367–71.

[48] The Information Office of the State Council of the People's Republic of China (White Paper on The Internet in China, 8 June 2010) <www.chinadaily.com.cn/china/2010-06/08/content_9950198.htm> under 'V. Active International Exchanges and Cooperation'.

[49] See eg People's Republic of China, China's Submissions to the Open-Ended Working Group on Developments in the Field of Information and Telecommunications in the Context of International

sovereignty relies on the premise that every state should be enabled to control information that is 'disseminated' from 'abroad' within its sovereign sphere of jurisdiction. This corresponds more or less to its own territory, which translates into a low threshold of applicability of the principle of non-intervention with respect to digital activities.[50] Cyber sovereignty requires that a state enjoy a minimum level of control over at least its core infrastructures used for digital content and cyber activities.[51] In this regard, the BRI entails 'bilateral' cooperation on technical standards, positioning Chinese standards on network security as benchmarks for its partner countries. In fact, many have sounded the alarm that these standards are generating a 'mass effect in support of the adoption of Chinese standards at the broader international level'.[52] China, however, claims that these technical standards are predicated upon 'local needs and based on local cultural resource',[53] making them flexible and also socially attuned.[54] Moreover, these are hailed as being intimately tied to development and represent a view that digital and cyber governance ought to serve the needs of specific country populations.

However, several concerns remain, particularly the fact that the diffusion of these technical standards allows China to exert significant influence over the choice of national strategy for BRI partners concerning information technology and surveillance practices.[55] In this sense, some authors have used the concept of 'the Beijing effect' to qualify this double move. On the one hand, China promotes the idea of cyber sovereignty and digital development for BRI-partnered countries. And yet, China expands its own influence through the digital infrastructures it builds and the international standards for digital communications that it diffuses worldwide at the expense of BRI-partnered countries' cyber sovereignty.[56] This

Security (September 2019) <www.un.org/disarmament/wp-content/uploads/2019/09/china-submissions-oewg-en.pdf> 2–3, under '(ii) State sovereignty in cyber space'.

[50] People's Republic of China, National Cyber Security Strategy, Non-Official Translation, 2016, <https://chinacopyrightandmedia.wordpress.com/2016/12/27/national-cyber-security-strategy/> under 'IV, strategic tasks', '(1) Resolutely defending sovereignty in cyberspace'.
[51] ibid, under 'III, Principles', '(1) Respecting and protecting sovereignty in cyberspace'.
[52] Alice Ekman (ed), 'China's Belt & Road and the World: Competing Forms of Globalization', Etudes de l'Institut français de recherches internationales (April 2019) <www.ifri.org/en/publications/etudes-de-lifri/chinas-belt-road-and-world-competing-forms-globalization>34–36; MERICS, 'Networking the 'Belt and Road'—The Future is Digital' (28 August 2019) <https://merics.org/en/analysis/networking-belt-and-road-future-digital>.
[53] Ministry of Foreign Affairs of the People's Republic of China, International Strategy Cooperation on Cyberspace (1 March 2017) <http://news.xinhuanet.com/english/china/2017-03/01/c_136094371_5.htm> under 'Chapter IV. Plan of action', '9. Exchange of Cyber Cultures'.
[54] ibid under '2. The Principle of Sovereignty'.
[55] Anna Gross and Madhumita Murgia, 'China Shows its Dominance in Surveillance Technology' Financial Times (London, 27 December 2019).
[56] Matthew S Erie and Thomas Streinz, 'The Beijing Effect: China's "Digital Silk Road" as Transnational Data Governance' (2021) 54 New York University Journal of International Law and Politics 1 <https://papers.ssrn.com/sol3/papers.cfm?abstract_id=3810256>.

has already stirred controversy and concern in countries such as Vietnam[57] and Pakistan.[58] Thus, in the technology and cyber field, BRI materially contributes towards creating and sustaining technological dependence on Chinese technology and infrastructure.

3. The Rhetoric of Multilateralism and the Role of Power

Many thought that with intergovernmental multilateralism no longer forming part of the mainstream American foreign policy, other powers, especially China, was likely to take up the mantle and provide the international system with renewed stability and direction. To a large extent, such predictions seemed rather plausible. In several forums, China continues to insist on a strengthened, multilateral, rules-based[59] international system that is able to infuse predictability and withstand power politics. The overall vision of the BRI seems to echo a similar sentiment, in that the BRI reinforces its commitment and continued engagement with existing multilateral institutions such as the UN and the World Trade Organization and puts much effort into creating and rejuvenating a plethora of multilateral forums across the board with Asia, Africa, and the Gulf, to mention just a few.[60] Normatively, too, China's message of building a 'global community of shared future' or a 'community of common human destiny' that would transpire by 'working together' and establishing a 'fairer and more equitable' international order projects, at its core, the indispensability of a multilateral process.

Yet, as the contours of the BRI unfold, it is becoming more certain that China's rhetoric on multilateralism is mediated by its preferences for bilateralism. Benvenisti even characterized the BRI as 'perfection of the bilateralism approach',[61] while Gregory Shaffer and Henry Gao show how the BRI, in essence, operates through 'packages of bilateral arrangements'.[62] These bilateral commitments are often concluded through extremely informal means including Memoranda of Understanding, standardization agreements, joint communiqués, press releases,

---

[57] Human Rights Watch, 'Vietnam: Withdraw Problematic Cyber Security Law: National Assembly to Vote on Repressive Bill Restricting Internet Freedom' (7 June 2018) <www.hrw.org/news/2018/06/07/vietnam-withdraw-problematic-cyber-security-law>.
[58] Digital Rights Foundation, *The Right to Privacy in Pakistan's Digital Spaces*, Human Rights Council Report (April 2018) 11–12, para 39.
[59] See eg, with respect to international security law, Permanent Mission of the PRC to the UN, Statement by Ambassador FU Cong at the General Debate of the First Committee of the 74th Session of the UNGA (11 October 2019) <www.un.org/disarmament/wp-content/uploads/2019/10/statement-by-china-e-gd-oct-11-19.pdf>.
[60] Vision and Actions Document 2015 (n 17).
[61] Eyal Benvenisti, 'International Law in the Age of Bilateralism', Draft Paper 2019 <www.law.nyu.edu/sites/default/files/InternationalLawintheAgeofBilateralism.pdf>.
[62] Gregory C Schaffer and Henry S Gao, 'A New Chinese Economic Law Order?', UC Irvine School of Law Research Paper No 2019-21, Singapore Management University School of Law Research Paper No 31 (11 April 2019) <https://ssrn.com/abstract=3370452>.

and other such formats that all fall somewhere between principle-led diplomatic formulations and concrete technical announcements. While these bilateral engagements are distinguishable through their different titles, the language employed, and the formats used, broadly they share similar traits: a lack of legal bindingness, a vague and open-ended commitment towards future engagement, and the absence of any institutional framework. Legally, the use of soft law is widespread as a means of governing relationships under the BRI that maintains a non-coercive and discretionary architecture for participating countries.[63]

Reflecting on this, Heng Wang regards the BRI as encompassing an approach that desires to 'maximize flexibility' through legal frameworks that are both 'fluid and malleable'.[64] Flexibility within the BRI is crucial for China as it not only tries to include vastly different countries with equally varied political and economic systems, but also because bilateralism and loose cooperation provide a relatively 'decentralized' and 'non-hierarchical' structure of engagement as opposed to the top-down rules-based framework of the Post-World War II US-led liberal international order. Given that a strict understanding of sovereignty and non-interference lies at the core of Chinese approaches to international law,[65] bilateral engagements under the BRI promise to leave substantial 'policy space' for partner countries. This is close to what Jiangyu Wang characterizes as 'a partnership based, relational approach' to global governance that is high on results but relatively flexible on rules and procedures.[66]

For China, this provides an opportunity to brandish a multi-perspective and plural approach to cooperation and coordination that welcomes 'a more variegated global order, with different regions guided by their own cultural, social, and political norms'.[67] More critically, this fragmented and dispersed international order, argues Tomer Broude, provides in some sense a refined form of power and centralization by forming 'complex intertwined networks' with China at the centre.[68] Thus, between the rhetoric of multilateralism and the practice of bilateralism lie spaces that are marked by shifting legalities, from 'soft' to 'hard' and 'informal' to 'formal' and provide enough scope for shaping and concretizing a distinctly

---

[63] Heng Wang, 'China's Approach to the Belt and Road Initiative: Scope, Character and Sustainability' (2019) 22 Journal of International Economic Law 29–55.
[64] ibid 43–45.
[65] The Ministry of Foreign Affairs of the Russian Federation, The Declaration of the Russian Federation and the People's Republic of China on the Promotion of International Law, 1202-25-06-2016 (25 June 2016) <www.mid.ru/en/foreign_policy/position_word_order/-/asset_publisher/6S4RuXfeYlKr/content/id/2331698>.
[66] Jiangyu Wang, 'China's Governance Approach to the Belt and Road Initiative (BRI): Relations, Partnership, and Law' (2019) 14(5) Global Trade and Customs Journal 222–28.
[67] Charles A Kupchan, 'Unpacking Hegemony: the Social Foundations of Hierarchical Order' in G John Ikenberry (ed), *Power, Order, and Change in World Politics* (CUP 2014).
[68] Tomer Broude, 'Belt, Road and (Legal) Suspenders: Entangled Legalities on the 'New Silk Road'', in Nico Krisch (ed) *Entangled Legalities Beyond the State* (CUP 2021) 107–29, 111. <https://papers.ssrn.com/sol3/papers.cfm?abstract_id=3489749&download=yes>.

Chinese narrative, that is still nestled within the current framework of international law.

This brings us to the question of power and dominance that permeates the structures and processes of the BRI, irrespective of whether they acquire a more formalized system or remain informal and decentralized. While the Chinese approach within the BRI speaks of 'mutual benefits', 'mutual dialogue', and 'consultation' as means to resolving disputes, it is clear that China indeed holds significant leverage over its weaker BRI partners.[69] Moreover, the BRI adopts a modus operandi that hardly provides any space for substantive engagement for other states, especially developing and least developed states, that arguably form the main addressees of the BRI. So even though the BRI may be explicit about 'jointly' undertaking and 'mutually' reinforcing its contours, it essentially translates into China substantially and materially laying out the normative and ideational framework for the same. It reflects what is classically known as the 'hub and spokes' model that puts China at the centre (hub) allowing it to maintain hegemony over its partners, who are themselves kept far apart. From this follows the crucial question of whether *peoples* in the 'Global South' are condemned to a double occultation?[70] The first time as a result of the imperial legacies of Western international law and now because of their own states being beholden to a 'Chinese dream' that seems to mirror similar patterns of exclusion. As Sornarajah reminds us, China has not always mounted attacks on the international legal system, especially in those areas which are likely to benefit its own elites and its national agenda.[71] In this regard, the BRI is riddled with tension between its assertion of a 'shared dream' of coexisting nationalisms and the fact that it allows very little room for different national perspectives to prosper given the dominance of China in the architecture of BRI. These tensions are what make the 'co-option' and 'contestation' lens important, but not fully comprehensive to explain the BRI, that remains fragmented, dispersed, and most importantly, constantly evolving.

Our attempt in this chapter has been to sketch out possible lines of enquiry as to what the BRI means for the universality of international law. If we take as our starting point the evolution of international law towards a 'pluralistic' system, there is a possibility for the BRI to complement rather than to principally disrupt or destroy the universalistic reach of international law. In this regard, the looming shadow of China's normative and ideational agenda predicated on the BRI remains hard to ignore. It is however important to highlight that the BRI defies a

---

[69] See eg nn 57 and 58.

[70] Mushakoji (n 2) 107, fn 1; Muthucumaraswamy Sornarajah and Jiangyu Wang, 'China, India, and International Law: A Justice Based Vision Between the Romantic and Realist Perceptions' [2019] Asian Journal of International Law 217–50, 331; Antony Anghie, 'Imperialism and International Legal Theory', in Anne Orford and Florian Hoffmann, The Oxford Handbook of the Theory of International Law (OUP, 2016), 156–172.

[71] Muthucumaraswamy Sornarajah, 'Asian International Law: Where Is It Now?' [2008] *Asian Yearbook of International Law* 265–72, 270.

purely statist analysis and does not fully correspond to traditional categories of international law. Legal scholarship cannot ignore how the BRI creates regulatory effects through creating infrastructures and through soft, legal, non-legal means,[72] which is accompanied by discourses that may shape international law in the twenty-first century. This becomes even more pronounced especially given that Chinese intervention is supported by material conditions, power, and persuasive ideals. In essence, it offers an opportunity for international lawyers to look beyond the operation of dichotomy and embrace our call for imagining new spaces that the BRI is so forcefully trying to generate on the global stage.

---

[72] Benedict Kingsbury, 'Infrastructure and InfraReg: On Rousing the International Law "Wizards of Is"' (2019) 8 Cambridge International Law Journal 171–86, 182–83 and 184–85.

VI

UNIVERSALITY AND THE LANGUAGES OF INTERNATIONAL LAW

14
The Power of Images
Questioning the Universality of International Human Rights Law

Elisabeth Roy-Trudel

Introduction

Images appeal to our emotions, and they are subjective and particularistic.[1] They can convey much more than text, or the written and spoken word, alone ever could. Images can tap into the heart, into the otherwise hidden soul of law and the pursuit of justice, in a way that is not amenable to conscious reflection.[2] As Costas Douzinas and Lynda Nead note, '[i]mages are sensual and fleshy; they address the labile elements of the self, they speak to the emotions, and they organize the unconscious. They have the power to short-circuit reason and enter the soul without the interpolation or intervention of language or interpretation.'[3]

The power of images is rarely recognized in the context of modern law, including international law, although the visual is omnipresent in the legal sphere. As this chapter demonstrates, modern law is heavily focused and relies on the sense of vision. It commonly uses images to translate and further develop abstract legal concepts, such as justice, human rights, and legal subjectivity. Images, however, are not neutral, and relying on vision is not a neutral endeavour either. Indeed, European modern thought and its emphasis on rationality, with vision considered the most rational and hence privileged sense, had significant consequences for the legal sphere: it arguably led to the imposition of the supremacy of vision—as opposed to other senses such as hearing or touch—and the visual in law, thus reifying the European mode of understanding the world and facilitating the claim to universality of Eurocentric international law.

Based on the premise that the universality of human rights should concern their applicability *and* their form and content, this chapter argues that more attention

---

[1] Richard K Sherwin, *Visualizing Law in the Age of the Digital Baroque—Arabesques and Entanglements* (Routledge 2011) 38.
[2] Peter Goodrich, 'Visiocracy: On the Futures of the Fingerpost' (2013) 39(3) Critical Inquiry 498; Sherwin (n 1) 38.
[3] Costas Douzinas and Lynda Nead, 'Introduction' in Costas Douzinas and Lynda Nead (eds), *Law and the Image: The Authority of Art and the Aesthetics of Law* (University of Chicago Press 1999) 7.

needs to be paid to the visual discourse in international law, although—or rather because—not everyone would naturally or primarily rely on this mode of expression. International human rights law, in particular, must be aware of its visual biases that create and entrench certain forms of domination and exclusion. This seems essential precisely because of its claim to universal authority and applicability, in a spatial and also in a moral sense. The visual discourse used in international human rights law may be conceived as a universal language that is part of a 'legal system that speaks to everyone'.[4] Yet this language can also be understood as a hegemonic one in the Gramscian sense.[5] Indeed, while the visual discourse, in other words the formation, expression, and transfer of ideas through the visual, is sometimes presented and perceived as natural, it has been developed and is often employed by dominant actors to sustain their influence and power.

Although the visual legal environment is full of meanings and values and exercises great power, the authority of visual governance and the rich relationship between law and the aesthetics are rarely discussed and even less questioned, either in theory or in practice.[6] However, as will be demonstrated in the first section of this chapter, exploring this relationship can shed light on how legal and visual discourses have influenced and constituted each other. Moreover, a critical visual discourse analysis of key moments in the history of human rights, pursued in the following section, reveals some of the ways in which images have shaped legal ideology, consciousness, and subjectivities. Challenging the supremacy of vision in law and considering alternative sensoria are consistent with Martti Koskenniemi's call, as echoed by the editors of this collection in their introduction, to have a real conversation about the right thing to do in international law. Drawing on sensuous scholarship, the chapter ends by suggesting that recognizing and accepting a sensorial plurality is hence also a crucial step towards the realization of international human rights law's promise of global justice.

1. The Visiocracy of Law

Considering vision as a higher sense has a long tradition in the Western world that predates the era of human rights. The importance given to vision emerged in the high Middle Ages for practical reasons, with Europeans embracing writing to preserve information and maintain traditions. The authority of the written word

---

[4] Işıl Aral and Jean d'Aspremont, 'Introduction: The Universalizing Narratives of International Law and their Binary Contestations' in Işıl Aral and Jean d'Aspremont (eds), *International Law and Universality* (OUP 2024) 1, 2.

[5] Antonio Gramsci, *Selections from the Prison Notebooks* (Quintin Hoare and Geoffrey Nowell-Smith tr and ed, Lawrence & Wishart 1971).

[6] Goodrich, 'Visiocracy' (n 2) 500–01; Bernard J Hibbitts, '"Coming to Our Senses": Communication and Legal Expression in Performance Cultures' (1992) 41(4) Emory Law Journal 873, 880.

became so strong that the sense of vision was privileged altogether, and other channels of communication were sidelined; institutions and groups that still relied on sound, touch, taste, and smell as main forms of expression were denigrated, and their significance declined markedly.[7] This supremacy of vision only grew with time. Indeed, with modernity,[8] vision and knowledge became inseparable. The reign of science and its alleged rationality was established, along with its method of relying almost exclusively on eye-centred techniques such as measuring and observing,[9] and they have not been successfully challenged up to this day.

Law is no exception: vision clearly dominates Western law, including international human rights law, and the visual is omnipresent. The metaphors used in the context of law are telling: law is a 'body', a 'text', a 'structure'. It is always something that can be looked at.[10] Visual evidence has long played a predominant role in the context of trials.[11] Fundamentally, it is through visual representations and through images that the whole Western legal tradition operates. It is important to recall that images are not merely generated by our perception but created thanks to collective knowledge.[12] Every image is part of a specific social context, although its meaning can resonate for a long time.[13] This is why centuries-old representations, such as that of Justice blindfolded and holding a balance, are still common and easily understood today.

1.1 Modernity's Grip on Law and Aesthetics

One of the priorities of Western modernity has been to establish the legitimacy of the rational, autonomous individual, and law was highly influenced by, but also contributed to, this goal. Rooted in Immanuel Kant's philosophy, law and justice have been presented as impartial and oblivious to feelings in the Western legal tradition. Law developed a specialized 'self-knowledge' and identified itself as a dispassionate science that could objectively manage society[14] and that could also be

---

[7] Hibbitts, 'Coming to our Senses' (n 6) 875.
[8] For a discussion on the term 'modernity' and its lack of clarity, see Jean Comaroff and John L Comaroff, 'Theory from the South: Or, how Euro-America is Evolving Toward Africa' (2012) 22(2) Anthropological Forum 113, 118–19.
[9] Leo Flynn, 'See What I Mean: The Authority of Law and Visions of Women' in Lionel Bently and Leo Flynn (eds), *Law and the Senses: Sensational Jurisprudence* (Pluto Press 1996) 146.
[10] Bernard J Hibbitts, 'Senses of Difference: A Sociology of Metaphors in American Legal Discourse' in Bently and Flynn (eds) (n 9) 97.
[11] Although aurality has admittedly a long tradition and important presence in law, with legal rhetoric playing a central role in a trial, it ranks only second in law's hierarchy of the senses. Sherwin (n 1) 39.
[12] Leif Dahlberg, 'Introduction: Visualising Law and Authority' in Leif Dahlberg (ed), *Visualizing Law and Authority. Essays on Legal Aesthetics* (Walter de Gruyter 2012) 4.
[13] Desmond Manderson, 'Introduction—Imaginal Law' in Desmond Manderson (ed), *Law and the Visual: Representations, Technologies, and Critique* (University of Toronto Press 2018) 3–4.
[14] Boaventura de Sousa Santos, 'Three Metaphors for a New Conception of Law: The Frontier, the Baroque, and the South' (1995) 29 Law & Society Review 569, 570.

studied systematically. Law's aesthetic dimensions were sidelined, and modern law evolved in isolation from art: 'Art is assigned to imagination, creativity, and playfulness, law to control, discipline and sobriety.'[15] A creator of art enjoys freedom and is imagined as a desiring and corporeal subject whose past and social context are recognized; the legal subject, in turn, is limited to having rights and obligations and has no desires, history, or gender.[16] Indeed, the Western legal tradition has always presumed a strong—even if implicit—relationship between legal subjectivity and rationality, with the focus lying on the rational mind and the thinking subject. The full meaning and potential of legal subjectivity was hence curtailed, and the legal discipline has made great efforts to preserve the illusion that law is a rational and comprehensive normative regime.[17]

Modern thought also sanitized the concept of aesthetics and rendered it vision-centred. While *aisthetikos*, the original Greek word, referred to an inclusive and unbiased perception by all the senses,[18] with premodern aesthetic experiences possibly appealing to more than one sense simultaneously,[19] modernity attempted to separate the senses from each other and developed an artificial hierarchy of the senses in which vision and hearing were placed at the top, whereas touch, smell, and taste were relegated to the bottom as lower senses not contributing to aesthetic experiences.[20] But, in reality, the aesthetic cannot be rationalized. It 'appeals not to our judgment of truth and logic, but to our senses. It finds expression not in a judgment of goodness or rightness, but rather in a feeling of attraction or repulsion.'[21] As such, the aesthetic has considerable power: it generates influential sensorial discourses that can even 'reify, overwhelm, and lay claim to a totalising authority.'[22] Appealing to the senses may hence have positive and negative effects, such as social inclusion or exclusion of specific groups or individuals.

Despite modernist attempts to keep things apart, law and the aesthetics are thoroughly related and interact with each other across the alleged rationality/non-rationality divide. It is, in fact, because of law's legitimate forms that justice becomes possible.[23] As Desmond Manderson contends by recalling the inseparability of form and content, '[l]aw is one of the ways in which form is developed in society, and law expresses itself through form and structure and style and ritual.'[24]

[15] Douzinas and Nead (n 3) 3.
[16] ibid.
[17] Martha-Marie Kleinhans and Roderick A Macdonald, 'What is a *Critical* Legal Pluralism?' (1997) 12 Canadian Journal of Law and Society 25, 28–29.
[18] Online Etymology Dictionary <www.etymonline.com>.
[19] David Howes, 'The Aesthetics of Mixing the Senses: Cross-Modal Aesthetics' <www.david-howes.com/senses/aestheticsofmixingthesenses.pdf> accessed 1 September 2018, 75.
[20] ibid.
[21] Desmond Manderson, 'Senses and Symbols: The Construction of 'Drugs' in Historic and Aesthetic Perspective' in Bently and Flynn (eds) (n 9) 200.
[22] ibid 201.
[23] Goodrich, 'Visiocracy' (n 2) 517.
[24] Desmond Manderson, *Songs without Music—Aesthetic Dimensions of Law and Justice* (University of California Press 2000) 191.

It has even been argued that if one were to destroy the aesthetics of law, law would lose its persuasiveness.[25] In other words, it is an illusion to imagine justice without aesthetics, with the latter containing strong and specific normative claims about justice. Both the form and the content of a legal system are revealing of the values of such a system and the kind of justice one can expect to obtain. Each legal tradition might have its own aesthetics, which manifests itself differently in different times, but the form of a legal system, or its aesthetic dimension, always matters.

1.2 The Power of Images in Law

Given their great powers, images have become one of the principal media through which political and legal discourses are constructed and maintained.[26] Images are powerful both as physical objects and as abstract entities. As material objects, whether in physical or digital form, they enter into direct, tangible contact with their surroundings; as abstract or conceptual representations, they are malleable carriers of messages, render visible what would otherwise remain hidden, and reveal meaning and ideology, including with respect to law and justice.[27] Images hence contribute to making and changing the world. Visual media, such as paintings, sculptures, and photographs, contribute to the discursive creation and interpretation of law and other social structures. Put differently, images not only illustrate and reflect but also—and perhaps most importantly—determine questions of law and authority.[28] Law uses the power of the visual to assert and maintain its authority, whether through emblems, architecture, clothing, graffiti, stamps, films, or other works of art.[29] For instance, the design of courts of justice has always followed careful considerations in order to establish the authority of the law.

Vision also fulfils an important function in translating the idea of justice, one of the main motivations of most legal systems but an abstract concept and very much 'a matter of faith'.[30] If the source of law is always abstract and even absent, the visual discourse used inside and outside the courtroom—not unlike props in a photographer's studio—plays the crucial role of continuously alluding to its existence and power. The idea of relying on the visual to establish power is very much alive in the twenty-first century, where digital images have largely replaced official painted portraits of sovereign rulers and state-sponsored parades and fireworks that were meant to impress.[31]

---

[25] Dahlberg (n 12) 4.
[26] Chiara Bottici, *Imaginal Politics—Images Beyond Imagination and the Imagery* (Columbia University Press 2014) ch 1.
[27] ibid 12.
[28] ibid 7.
[29] Manderson, 'Introduction' (n 13) 8.
[30] Goodrich, 'Visiocracy' (n 2) 516.
[31] Sherwin (n 1) 9.

Visual discourses influence the quest for justice because they determine the ways in which law exercises its power to define, in particular with respect to legal subjects, often with negative consequences. It is through a heavily vision-centred epistemology that law determines legal subjects and their position in society, with the rational—and seeing—white man who makes law and enjoys rights still being the privileged subject of Western law. As Leo Flynn argues, '[t]he sense of vision or, rather, particular versions of that sense, underlie the law's perception, the manner in which it obtains and structures knowledge about individuals, objectives and events'.[32] Photographs of subjects, because they express 'power or weakness, amity or aggressivity, attractiveness or repulsion',[33] are tools to define, categorize, and delineate legal subjectivity. Marginalized individuals and groups, such as women, visible minorities, and Indigenous peoples are defined and entrapped by law and its visual discourse in their construction and representation as 'others'.[34] These dynamics hence contribute to preventing many human beings, who are marginalized and not granted full legal subjectivity because of law's visual bias, from accessing the rights that are supposed to be universal.

Visual discourses are hence not only embedded within a particular context but are influenced by and sustain power relations and social difference.[35] As Gillian Rose writes, '[v]isual images do not exist in a vacuum, and looking at them for "what they are" neglects the ways in which they are produced and interpreted through particular social practices'.[36] Importantly, the effects that an image has are not only created by what is represented, and in which ways, but also by the way it is looked at.[37] The crucial role of the viewer in the (post)colonial context, notably the 'white gaze', was highlighted by Frantz Fanon;[38] more recently, feminist critiques have been crucial in further theorizing dominant 'practices of looking'.[39] Vision, as Donna Haraway writes, 'is *always* a question of the power to see—and perhaps of the violence implicit in our visualizing practices'.[40] The viewers matter and play an active role in the meaning-making of images and the production and reproduction of power relations through visual discourses. In other words, an image does not only consist of what can be seen, but the spectators contribute to what they see.

---

[32] Flynn, 'See What I Mean' (n 9) 139.
[33] David Howes and Constance Classen, *Ways of Sensing: Understanding the Senses in Society* (Routledge 2014) 1.
[34] Flynn, 'See What I Mean' (n 9) 140.
[35] See Gillian Rose, *Visual Methodologist: An Introduction to Researching with Visual Materials* (3rd edn, Sage 2012) 14–15.
[36] ibid 55.
[37] John Berger, *Ways of Seeing* (Penguin 1972).
[38] Frantz Fanon, *Peau noire, masques blancs* (Les Éditions du Seuil 1952).
[39] Marita Sturken and Lisa Cartwright, *Practices of Looking: An Introduction to Visual Culture* (2nd edn, OUP 2009).
[40] Donna Haraway, 'The Persistence of Vision' in Nicholas Mirzoeff (ed), *The Visual Culture Reader* (3rd edn, Routledge 2013) 359.

What is often constructed as an objective world to be apprehended is, in fact, 'permeated with bodily "subjectivity"'.[41]

The non-neutrality of visual discourses is particularly obvious when it comes to representational practices of difference and 'otherness', which are often prone to stereotyping. People who are not part of the majority population 'seem to be represented through sharply opposed, polarized, binary extremes—good/bad, civilized/primitive, ugly/excessively attractive, repelling-because-different/compelling-because-strange-and-exotic. And they are often required to be *both things at the same time!*'[42] Marginalized individuals and groups are defined and entrapped by law and its visual discourse in their construction and representation as 'Others'.[43] Reducing those represented to a few signifiers through stereotyping creates or reinforces inequalities and classifies 'people according to a norm that constructs the excluded as "other"'.[44] In a Foucauldian approach, such representational practices can be understood as practices of power/knowledge, which includes the power to represent.[45] In fact, there is a long history of racialized visual discourses that operate with sets of binaries, like black/white, savage/civilized, male/female, that express and reify the superiority and domination of one pole of the binary over the other, and that are rendered even more polarized through the image.[46]

The importance of visual discourses, for instance in the context of human rights, has arguably increased over the past few decades, as television became a privileged and widespread medium and digital technologies contributed to the proliferation of images, which, in turn, facilitated the reification of the dominant visual culture that lies beneath these developments.[47] New technologies have created further possibilities for representing violence and human rights violations for all actors involved, including victims, perpetrators, journalists, and defenders of human rights. Striking examples include the live visual coverage of the first Gulf War; photographs of horrific abuses at Guantanamo and Abu Ghraib; the wide coverage of migrants mainly from Africa and the Middle East desperately trying to reach Europe; and the staging of another development in what has been called a border crisis at the United States-Mexican border, with migrants and those 'facilitating' their journey being shown wearing surgical masks in the context of the Covid-19 pandemic.[48] In fact, while images have arguably always been used for ideological purposes, key events such as the wars in Iraq and 9/11 have led to an 'iconography

---

[41] Amelia Jones, 'The Body and/in Representation' in Mirzoeff (ed) (n 40) 369.
[42] Stuart Hall, 'The Spectacle of the "Other"' in Stuart Hall (ed), *Representation: Cultural Representations and Signifying Practices* (Sage 1997) 229.
[43] Flynn, 'See What I Mean' (n 9) 140.
[44] Hall (n 42) 259.
[45] ibid.
[46] ibid 243.
[47] Rose (n 35) 5–9.
[48] Nina Lakhani, 'Is There a Crisis at the Border?' *The Guardian* (19 March 2021) <www.theguardian.com/us-news/2021/mar/18/us-mexico-immigration-border-crisis> accessed 24 April 2021.

of threat' that serves various political purposes.[49] Yet, as it should be recalled, easier access to digital technologies and the possibility of rapidly distributing images has allowed victims of human rights violations to draw attention to their situation; the almost instant circulation of images via social media has even set off political movements, as demonstrated particularly well by the Arab Spring. At the same time, the proliferation of images and the amplification of visual discourses also mean that what is not represented can be rendered invisible, hidden, inexistent.[50]

2. A Visual Discourse Analysis of Key Moments in Human Rights

Law is constructed, transmitted, and rendered accessible in sophisticated detail by images;[51] yet relying on a particular visual discourse, as international human rights law does, always risks creating exclusions and is hence problematic. This section analyses a few emblematic images in the history of human rights as well as a couple of contemporary examples of images used in the field. The purpose of pursuing a critical visual discourse analysis does not only consist in understanding how law is expressed through images; it also entails exploring how images have shaped legal ideology, consciousness, and subjectivities.[52] Images that were produced at key moments in the history of human rights and that are still looked upon today represent the essence of important changes in legal thought. Some of these key moments that have been captured visually are the adoption of the 1789 *Déclaration des droits de l'homme et du citoyen* and the adoption of the Universal Declaration of Human Rights in 1948. While it should be remembered that the drafting of these declarations occurred, of course, within a complex context, carefully looking at the images produced at such decisive moments can nonetheless reveal much about, and give us a critical perspective on, the lengthy development of international human rights law and the crystallization of particular concepts and norms.[53] Inspired by iconography and iconology, which are methods commonly used in the social sciences and humanities to study different visual materials, the analysis is pursued at a formal and a contextual level: it considers visual elements, such as the colours, lines, space, and composition of the images. In addition to studying the composition of images, the analysis also draws on knowledge about the social and political context and considers the ways in which images are put to work by dominant actors.

---

[49] Allen Feldman, 'On the Actuarial Gaze: From 9/11 to Abu Ghraib' in Mirzoeff (ed) (n 40) 163.
[50] ibid 170.
[51] Goodrich, 'Visiocracy' (n 2) 508, 520.
[52] Manderson, 'Introduction' (n 13) 8.
[53] ibid 9.

One of the most famous images of the 1789 *Déclaration des droits de l'homme et du citoyen* (hereafter *Déclaration*) was painted, probably in 1789,[54] by Jean-Jacques-François Le Barbier, an artist who was heavily involved in politics and adhered to the ideas of the Revolution (see Figure 14.1).

This painting consists of two horizontal sections: two female figures occupy the top third while the rest of the image is filled with written text in the form of a detailed list. The figure in the upper left corner, dressed in blue, red and white—the colours of France—represents the French people. She has just broken the chains of the old regime and absolute monarchy. The figure on the right side, the one with wings, is an angel that embodies Liberty and possibly the new *Assemblée nationale*. With her left arm, she directs the viewer's gaze to the text below, ie the new *Déclaration*. With a power-symbolizing sceptre in her right arm, she points to an eye, which stands for reason and consciousness. The eye is the centre of a triangle that evokes the biblical trinity but arguably also symbolizes the French trinity, ie *liberté, égalité, fraternité*. In the lower and larger part of the painting, the rights and freedoms in the form of articles are listed on a support that evokes Moses' tables of law with the Ten Commandments. The pike—and not the sword of the king, previously a common symbol of power—between the two rows of rights and liberties represents the force of the law.

This painting hence makes use of well-known and common symbols at the time (the tables of law, an angel, a sceptre, and an eye) to give authority to a groundbreaking new concept, namely a declaration of rights and freedoms that belong to the people. The viewer understands or can be convinced by looking at this painting that rights need to be codified and, despite certain references to democratic ideas, that they are handed down, or at least supported by, a higher authority. Indeed, elements like the shining light in the sky and the angel make it clear that God—not the king, as was previously the case—gives the French people his benediction for declaring rights.

The influence of this painting can perhaps be detected in another prominent image associated with human rights, namely a 1949 photograph of Eleanor Roosevelt, a distinguished human rights activist, holding and immersed in a printed version of the United Nations Universal Declaration of Human Rights (UDHR). This picture (see Figure 14.2) is one of a few that illustrate the United Nations webpage on the UDHR;[55] it is also the image used by prominent non-governmental human rights organizations, such as Amnesty International, in their presentation of the UDHR.[56]

---

[54] Musée Carnavalet, 'Déclaration des droits de l'homme et du citoyen' <www.carnavalet.paris.fr/fr/collections/declaration-des-droits-de-l-homme-et-du-citoyen> accessed 1 September 2018.

[55] United Nations, 'Universal Declaration of Human Rights' <www.un.org/en/universal-declaration-human-rights/index.html> accessed 1 September 2018.

[56] Amnesty International UK, 'What is the Universal Declaration of Human Rights?' <www.amnesty.org.uk/universal-declaration-human-rights-UDHR> accessed 1 September 2018.

266 ELISABETH ROY-TRUDEL

Figure 14.1 Le Barbier's painting of the 1789 *Déclaration des droits de l'homme et du citoyen*.
Photo credit: <www.carnavalet.paris.fr/en/collections/declaration-des-droits-de-lhomme-et-du-cito yen> accessed 1 September 2018

In the tradition of European depictions of authority, and as was the case in Le Barbier's painting, a figure is used to bestow authority. This time it is not an allegorical figure, but a prominent member of the drafting committee of the UDHR, Eleanor Roosevelt. In this picture, the main lines consist of Roosevelt's two arms that link her body to the poster, and thus create a circle that suggests a coherent or consistent whole. With this embrace, the first chairperson of the UN body that

Figure 14.2 Eleanor Roosevelt holding a poster of the 1948 Universal Declaration of Human Rights.
Photo credit: <www.fdrlibrary.org/eleanor-roosevelt> accessed 1 September 2018

oversaw the coming together of the UDHR, who was also a former first lady of the United States, brings authority to the UDHR. This is underlined by the tight frame bringing the focus on Roosevelt and the poster; there is not much else in the picture that could divert the viewer's attention. At the same time, the main source of light comes from the poster itself, which, it can be argued, suggests that no higher or external authority is needed anymore: as the preamble of the UDHR stipulates, the authority comes from the 'inherent dignity' of all members of the big human family.[57] The most fundamental message to be conveyed by the photograph is precisely the importance and authority of this seminal text, and the tight composition and the soft shades create a sense of intimacy, which helps anyone looking at the photograph to feel a connection to the figure, the text, and the message.

In light of the traditional concept of the human, it is highly relevant that the UDHR is presented by a woman, namely the only female member of the drafting committee. The 1789 *Déclaration des droits de l'homme et du citoyen* had clearly been conceived in such a way as to restrict the concept of human to men, and hence

---

[57] United Nations, 'Universal Declaration of Human Rights' (n 55).

imagined men, as the only rights-bearers. This was highlighted by the rejection of Olympe de Gouges' 1791 attempt to broaden the meaning of the *Déclaration* by ironically renaming it *Déclaration des droits de la femme et de la citoyenne*.[58] Given this historical bias of human rights as men's rights, the choice of having Eleanor Roosevelt in the 1949 photograph can be interpreted as an appeal to women (at least of the Western world), so that they too recognize the authority of human rights and embrace the values underlying the UDHR, such as equality.

It is also interesting to remember that the international political context, at the time the picture was taken, started to be dominated by the Cold War. Notwithstanding Roosevelt's achievements as a human rights activist, it is worth noting that she was a wealthy woman, as her pearl necklace and sober yet elegant clothes remind the viewer; one could infer from this image that it is liberal democracy that brings about and guarantees human rights. She was, after all, a former first lady of the United States, the self-proclaimed champion of democracy and liberalism.

The same poster of the 1948 UDHR is used again by the United Nations, yet in a different context: taken in 1950, the photograph below (see Figure 14.3) celebrates the second anniversary of the adoption of the UDHR, and, at the time of writing, it illustrates the UN 'History of the Document' webpage and the entry on human rights of the UN Information Service.[59]

A first reading of this picture shows a group of children from a UN nursery standing or sitting outside in a half circle around the poster of the UDHR. A little girl on the right side points to the UDHR, with the gaze of the children—not all of whom are white—following her finger. With the swing in the background and some clothes lying on the grass, it looks as if the children have just stopped playing to gather around this poster. The UDHR—and its rights and freedoms—has been taken out of Geneva offices and animated and incorporated into everyday life.[60] Here again, the text itself is the main source of light, hinting at its self-referential authority. The rights and freedoms are no longer reserved for white people, but they are embraced by individuals from different ethnic backgrounds. The authority of the UDHR is now enhanced by being accessible to all and a promise for future generations.

On a closer look, one wonders: is the little girl pointing to an article, a fleck, or a blank spot? And what does the gaze of the other children really say—are these children seriously concentrating on the UDHR, are they doubtful, or maybe just bored? In fact, only literate persons can read the UDHR, which, ironically, is

---

[58] Bottici (n 26) 163–64; Rebecca Adami, *Women and the Universal Declaration of Human Rights* (Routledge 2019) 89.

[59] United Nations, 'History of the Document' <www.un.org/en/sections/universal-declaration/history-document/index.html> accessed 1 September 2018; UN Information Service, 'Human Rights' <https://unis.unvienna.org/unis/en/topics/human-rights.html> accessed 1 September 2018.

[60] This draws on Peter Goodrich, 'Faces and Frames of Government' in Manderson (ed) (n 13) 65.

THE POWER OF IMAGES   269

Figure 14.3 A 1950 photograph of a group of children looking at a poster of the *Universal Declaration of Human Rights*.
Photo credit: <https://unis.unvienna.org/unis/en/topics/human-rights.html> accessed 1 September 2018

probably not the case of most of these pre-school children, who are, moreover, 'reading' the text upside down. As for universality, one can notice that only a couple of children are clearly non-Caucasian; the great majority still represent the dominant part of society. Moreover, as their clothes and overall appearance show, these children seem healthy and to come from middle-class or wealthy families. In short, in spite of the obvious efforts made, the UDHR is still not reflective of and accessible to all. This illustrates the point that images, in all their meanings, are not only used by law; they are 'unruly' and reveal the 'excessive and subconscious meaning' of legal culture.[61]

---

[61] Manderson, 'Introduction' (n 13) 12.

In both photographs of the UDHR—the one of Roosevelt and the one of the children—there is a certain indeterminacy and ambiguity. The title of the poster can easily be read and attracts attention, but the body of the text—the rights and freedoms themselves—is not readable. This could be considered a weakness of the photograph, maybe resulting from a bad focus by the photographer. But, in fact, this ambiguity can be empowering by allowing human rights to be reinterpreted and appropriated in different contexts. In a way, blurring the text in such a way means that everyone can claim credit for and relate to the UDHR. This was particularly useful in the context of the fundamental ideological divide between political and civil rights, which were promoted by Western, liberal countries, and economic, social, and cultural rights, dear to the communist countries and also Latin American states. In this sense, images are always more complex than they appear, and what matters is often what is not represented.[62]

Considering contemporary visual discourses in human rights, an interesting shift from the earlier images analysed is noticeable. While the large number and great variety of photographs produced and circulated nowadays by governmental and non-governmental organizations in the field makes it difficult to draw definite conclusions based on the analysis of a few images, and while the historical distance that would allow the identification of certain images as iconic or as representing the essence of a key moment or change is lacking, it is nonetheless possible to identify what seems to be an emerging trend in international human rights. Two pictures used in recent years by influential UN bodies in important documents are revealing in this regard. The first one, reproduced below (in Figure 14.4), is the cover image of the 2013 Annual Report of the UN Office of the High Commissioner for Human Rights. The second telling picture illustrates the 2016–17 Global Appeal published by the UN High Commissioner for Refugees;[63] since this institution was not able to grant permission for the reproduction of this photograph, a more detailed description follows. These two documents have been chosen because they are major publications that are widely shared to explain, justify, and promote the work of these UN bodies, which are among the most prominent actors in international human rights.

The cover image of the 2016–17 Global Appeal published by the UN High Commissioner for Refugees shows a dozen people sitting on concrete. These people form a line that seems to start at the bottom right corner and to continue behind the last person shown in the top left corner. The focus is sharp in the bottom right corner, and the image becomes blurry in the top left corner. There are children, women, and men, wearing dark clothes, mostly with long sleeves. The men wear dark blue caps and the women scarves on their heads. They sit in front of a body of water, on which at least one blurry boat can be seen in the background. At least two people stand behind the people sitting, but only the lower part of their body is visible. Two children, wearing dark purple sweaters, look directly into the

---

[62] Goodrich, 'Faces and Frames of Government' (n 60) 71.
[63] Initially retrieved from <www.unhcr.org/ga16/index.xml> accessed 1 September 2018.

THE POWER OF IMAGES 271

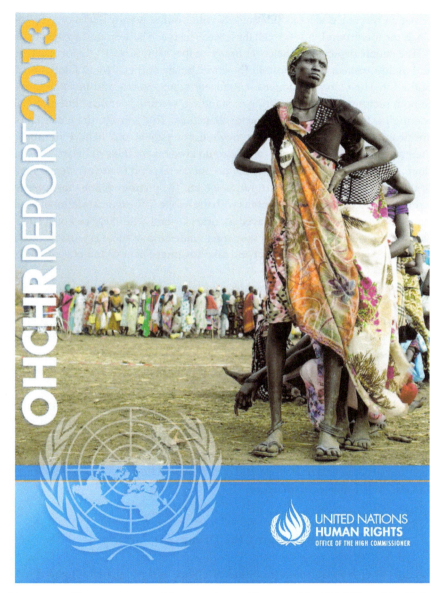

Figure 14.4 The cover image of the 2013 Annual Report of the UN Office of the High Commissioner for Human Rights.

Photo credit: <www2.ohchr.org/english/OHCHRReport2013/WEB_version/index.html> accessed 1 September 2018

camera; everyone else looks sideways. No one smiles. A baby sleeps on a woman's lap in the foreground. A few small dark travel bags can be seen next to the people.

The people depicted in the cover image of the 2013 OHCHR Report look poor and malnourished, while those in the cover image of the 2016-17 Global Appeal of the UN High Commissioner for Refugees seem anxious and in some distress. In both pictures, they form, sitting or standing, seemingly endless lines, probably waiting for further instructions or for their turn. This conveys the idea that they are awaiting help or relief, and that they must be patient and 'behave' in order for their rights claims to be heard—or one could even say for their rights to be given to them. The persons represented clearly do not correspond to the privileged subject of Western law, namely the white, rational man. The pictures define these people in a very restricted manner, one that fits with the image of the typical victim of human rights violations; they are portrayed as 'others'—and will likely be considered as such by the viewers constituting the target readership of these reports—who lack agency and who cannot construct and take advantage of any kind of genuine legal subjectivity.

It emerges that victims—and not legal instruments conveying a sense of hope—have become the focus of the visual discourse in human rights, which is arguably part of a larger shift that has occurred in international human rights in recent decades.[64] Children and women are overrepresented in the last two images, suggesting that human rights are first and foremost for members of certain vulnerable groups, and conveying an image of an ideal victim of human rights violations who 'deserves' the viewer's attention and reaction. In other words, recent visual discourses of UN bodies reflect and reinforce the idea that human rights reduce the possible agency of those in need of protection by assigning them the role of helpless recipients of humanitarian assistance.[65] As will be argued in the next section, it would be important for human rights scholars and advocates to be conscious of the imagery that they produce and reproduce, and of the fact that they are influenced by images and also utilize images to influence.

3. Challenging the Dominant Paradigm

Paying closer attention to law's visual discourse and acquiring a higher level of visual literacy can be important tools in challenging law's conscious or unconscious (mis)representations and associated hegemonic tendencies, including in international human rights law. It may also help us understand the ways in which

---

[64] For instance, on the recent emphasis on victims' rights, see Theo van Boven, 'Reparative Justice: Focus on Victims' (2007) 25(4) Netherlands Quarterly of Human Rights 723.

[65] Jacques Rancière, 'Who is the Subject of the Rights of Man?' (2004) 103(2) The South Atlantic Quarterly 297, 308.

images support law's reliance on dogmas and presumed truths,[66] and how images enhance the meaning of words and appeal to and evoke emotions. Some individuals and groups currently marginalized by law have therefore, in their quest for full legal recognition and for greater emancipation, chosen to engage with the predominance of vision in law and with problematic images. By way of example, some feminists claim that the deployment of law's authority, inter alia through its visual discourse, legitimizes patriarchal assumptions.[67] They have attempted to confront misrepresentations and to replace dominant visual discourses by alternative images that embrace their own understanding of the world,[68] which can certainly be empowering strategies.

While focusing on the visual arsenal utilized by law and understanding its implications—as the analysis above attempts to do with respect to international human rights—are important and revealing, such an approach arguably does not go to the heart of a deeply rooted structural problem. Images typically operate on a monosensorial level that does not transcend the double centrality of vision and rationality in Western thought. The way in which images are usually perceived and analysed in the West is also problematic, for instance because of the overreliance on binary pairs,[69] a common feature of Western modernity that tends to oversimplify and cannot capture other ways of thinking about and seeing the world.[70] This means that this line of critique can only be a first step, since it does not genuinely challenge or alter the dominant conception of law nor the alleged universal yet inherently biased visual language of human rights. In fact, without taking the critique further, it risks reinforcing, at least to some extent, modernity's rationalization of law, the alleged estrangement of legal subject and object, as well as the separation and hierarchization of the senses.

A much more radical shift, closely related to challenging law's rationality, would consist in overturning the supremacy of the visual in legal discourses, particularly in international law and human rights law given their claim to universal application. This does not imply abandoning the visual altogether, in a scopophobic move, since visual experiences obviously contribute to the creation of identities in important and not necessarily negative ways. It is the supremacy of the visual—in other words visiocracy—that must be questioned. This would also allow the embracing of the fact that law is embodied in various forms in different cultural and social contexts.

---

[66] Peter Goodrich, *Legal Emblems and the Art of Law: Obiter Depicta as the Vision of Governance* (CUP 2014) 248.
[67] Flynn, 'See What I Mean' (n 9) 139.
[68] ibid 142.
[69] Anne D'Alleva, *How to Write Art History* (Laurence King 2006) 34.
[70] Moreover, every analysis, including the present one, is tainted by the background—education, ethnicity, gender, etc—of the person pursuing it.

3.1. 'Go South': Alternative Epistemologies

Once the pervasive concept of Western rationality is transcended, alternative conceptions of law and of legal subjectivity, which comprise the unconscious, the non-rational, and the non-visual, can develop and thrive. The understanding of the world is not limited to Western worldviews, and so-called modernization and progress do not necessarily result from Westernization.[71] Although this has long been ignored by the West—or rather the North, as it is now often referred to in opposition to colonized non-European peoples in the Global South[72]—the South experiences the world differently, produces theory, and can offer explanations for historical events that have influenced the world, including modernity.[73] As Boaventura de Sousa Santos argues, the North can only provide limited and weak answers to crucial contemporary questions since it takes for granted the relevance and supremacy of the current paradigm.[74] Recall that Western law privileges what is perceptible to the eye, knowable, and measurable, and therefore 'ignores the unknowable, spiritual, and less tangible aspects of human experience'.[75] The importance of dreaming in Indigenous traditions, and its direct relevance for decision-making in everyday life, is a good example.[76] In addition to different kinds of knowledge, the South might also understand and *feel* the world differently, notably beyond rationality and cognition, and through different sensorial experiences. For instance, some Aboriginal peoples in Australia consider that animals, objects, and spirits are all—just like human beings—potential subjects that act with intention, and it is common practice to monitor one's environment to interpret messages.[77]

In order to possibly achieve justice at a global level, equity between different epistemologies must be attained.[78] However, as it stands, even liberal societies that claim to be committed to recognizing different traditions and worldviews, such as Indigenous customary laws, allocate to themselves the right to recognize this

---

[71] Boaventura de Sousa Santos, *Epistemologies of the South: Justice Against Epistemicide* (Paradigm Publisher 2014) viii; Comaroff and Comaroff (n 8) 119.

[72] The term Global South is also problematic, among other reasons because it does not capture the great diversity of perspectives in the South. Comaroff and Comaroff (n 8) 113, 117, 126–27. Moreover, the Global South is not limited to the geographical localization but can be considered 'a metaphor for the systematic suffering inflicted upon large bodies of population by Western-centric colonialism, capitalism, and patriarchy'; it is found both outside and inside Europe, North America, and other dominant societies. Boaventura de Sousa Santos, 'Epilogue: A New Vision of Europe: Learning from the South' in John Narayan and Gurminder Bhambra (eds), *European Cosmopolitanism: Colonial Histories and Postcolonial Societies* (Routledge 2017) 172, 175–76.

[73] Comaroff and Comaroff (n 8) 113.

[74] Santos, *Epistemologies of the South* (n 71) 20.

[75] Kristina Stern, 'Law and the Lack of Sense' in Bently and Flynn (eds) (n 9) 43.

[76] Elizabeth A Povinelli, 'Do Rocks Listen? The Cultural Politics of Apprehending Australian Aboriginal Labor' (1995) 97(3) American Anthropologist 505, 509.

[77] ibid 509–10.

[78] Santos, *Epistemologies of the South* (n 71) viii.

alterity, with genuine recognition always being extremely limited. Even in groundbreaking judgments, the courts of settler colonial societies clearly do not consider Indigenous law to be on an equal footing with Western law.[79] For international human rights law, which is deeply rooted in the Western tradition, epistemological equity would mean not only recognizing its visual biases but also considering other, non-hegemonic ways of knowing, being, and sensing as equally valid.

3.2 Toward a Fuller Sensorium in Law

The constitution and meaning of legal subjectivity are important and powerful since law, which is a system of symbols and meanings itself,[80] embodies and signals social values and aspirations, transforms desires into rights, and expresses anxiety about contentious social issues.[81] To give justice a chance, one might, therefore, have to go beyond abstract rules and try to pay attention to the particular, to the subjective specificity of each situation,[82] and the different ways in which legal subjects construct their identities, including through their senses.[83] International human rights law arguably plays a particular role in this context. In the face of various forms of violence—called human rights violations—it promises relief, hope, and justice. In the absence of other tangible forms of legal protection, it is human rights law that (somewhat ironically) constitutes the legal subject whose rights are violated.

All the senses contribute to the construction of individual and group identities, including legal subjectivity, and to the pursuit of global justice. Justice begins 'with an effort at comprehension',[84] and visual means alone cannot always enable this comprehension. If visual discourses tend to become hegemonic, they are not—and can arguably never be—truly universal; the multiple and plural identities in our worlds are, in fact, constructed in various ways and through a variety and different *mélanges* of senses.[85] The auditory, tactile, olfactory, and gustatory also play important communicative and educative roles. From socializing children into hygienic practices to transmitting conceptions of morality and acceptable postures, the senses are involved in the creation of perceptions of outsiders and serve to

---

[79] For Australia, see eg Elizabeth A Povinelli, 'The Cunning of Recognition: Real Being and Aboriginal Recognition in Settler Australia' (1998) 11(1) Australian Feminist Law Journal 3, 22.
[80] Sally Engle Merry, 'Legal Pluralism' (1988) 22 Law & Society Review 869, 886.
[81] Anna Grear, 'Human Rights—Human Bodies? Some Reflections on Corporate Human Rights Distortion, The Legal Subject, Embodiment and Human Rights Theory' (2006) 17(2) Law and Critique 171, 191; David Fagundes, 'What We Talk about When We Talk about Persons: The Language of Legal Fiction' (2001) 114(6) Harvard Law Review 1745, 1766.
[82] Manderson, *Songs Without Music* (n 24) 195.
[83] ibid 198.
[84] ibid 198.
[85] Howes (n 19).

differentiate and as markers of identities.[86] The senses also inform sentiments such as fear vis-à-vis others,[87] including in the supposedly more rational Western world. Different accents and allegedly bad smells have even been used explicitly as reasons for the exclusion of certain minority groups.[88]

However, human rights law, because of its focus on the allegedly higher senses of vision and hearing, can hardly capture these multisensorial dimensions, including different forms of discrimination based on the senses. If it can be said that '[s]ensory experience is socially made and mediated',[89] no society or culture is characterized by a unique and uniform sensorium. Although common elements within a society may be identified and compared to those present or absent in another society, sensory realities are often quite complex, and there can be important variation within a given culture. Sensory experiences, and cultures more generally, should hence not be essentialized.[90]

Allowing and enabling legal subjects to construct themselves along the full—and perhaps not yet fully recognized—sensorial spectrum would, therefore, constitute empowerment, enhance legal agency, and suggest novel avenues to achieve justice. Since the senses and the interplay between them are involved in the forging of personal perspectives as well as of social expectations, honouring all the senses can give a greater variety of actors the possibility to experience the world according to their values and preferred modes of expression and perception.

4. Conclusion

This chapter has argued that Western law's visiocracy—combined with modernity's conception of law as rational, positivist, and secular—has resulted in the limitation of legal subjectivity and has arguably afforded legal agency only to certain Western citizens. In light of the persistent and problematic hegemony of vision in the domain of international human rights law and its claim to universality, plurisensoriality should be embraced. This would contribute to rendering international human rights law and the concept of legal subjectivity more inclusive and dynamic, and therefore also more empowering and emancipatory. Indeed, different sensory practices—whether also primarily focused on vision or relying on other senses—are just as, or maybe even more, legitimate and effective ways of imagining law. Encouraging a diversity of metaphors in international law and legal

---

[86] Susanna Trnka, Christine Dureau, and Julie Park, 'Introduction: Senses and Citizenships' in Susanna Trnka, Christine Dureau, and Julie Park (eds), *Senses and Citizenships: Embodying Political Life* (Routledge 2013) 5.
[87] ibid 2–3.
[88] ibid 5.
[89] Elisabeth Hsu, 'The Senses and the Social: An Introduction' (2008) 73(4) Ethnos 433, 433.
[90] Koen Stroeken, 'Sensory Shifts and "Synaesthetics" in Sukuma Healing' (2008) 73(4) Ethnos 466, 473.

discourses would be one way to bring about greater comprehension and tolerance of difference.[91]

While such a shift in the relationship between law and the senses would certainly imply major challenges for orthodox law and legal theory as well as society as a whole, effectively pluralizing legal subjectivities and law itself might, in fact, bring us—that is all those working in or with international law—closer to achieving global justice. It would, at least, be a serious attempt to recognize and value difference and to enhance mutual understanding. Finally, the above-mentioned non-essentialist approach also implies a commitment to non-prescriptivism: if one is honest about valorizing different sensory experiences in the context of law, then there can be no legal solutions, and no law at all, outside and apart from legal and sensing actors.[92] International human rights law, in its quest for universality—if such an objective is attainable—should therefore appreciate the diversity of modes of understanding, sensing, and being in the world.

[91] Hibbitts, 'Senses of Difference' (n 10) 113.
[92] This draws on Kleinhans and Macdonald (n 17) 40–41; see also Mark Antaki, 'Le tournant sensoriel en droit: vers un droit sensible et sensé?' (2019) 34(2) Revue Canadienne Droit et Société 361, 366.

15
German 'Dogmatik'—An Untranslatable Concept if Ever There Was One?

Markus Beham

Hardly an academic debate among German(-speaking) scholars goes by without accusations of something being 'dogmatically' flawed or misguided. Judges and academics are valued based upon their 'dogmatic solutions' for having properly dealt with unprecedented factual situations. Stalemates within scholarly debate are lamented for having remained 'dogmatically unsatisfactory'. At the same time, academic adversaries can easily be accused of being 'too dogmatic', while an eminent professor may sometimes be humbled—as one might speak of an artist skilful enough to be painting in the style of the 'old masters'—as a 'proper dogmatic'.

'Dogmatik'[1] is one of those concepts that mean many different things to many different people.[2] The term has been described in the German literature as 'illustrious'

---

[1] For lack of a suitable translation, the German term 'Dogmatik' is used throughout this chapter. In discussions leading up to this contribution, 'legal doctrinalism' was suggested as an alternative. Similar to the term 'legal doctrine' and other possible variations, this translation conveys nuanced meanings that do not accurately reflect what is meant by the corresponding 'Dogmatik' or composite 'Rechtsdogmatik', seemingly elevating the role of academia within the process. In addition, for the international lawyer, it may invoke the notion of policy choices in international relations (such as in the 'Bush doctrine' or the 'Reagan doctrine') or for the US lawyer a certain stance in relation to constitutional interpretation. See, on the issue of translation, also Anthea Roberts, *Is International Law International?* (OUP 2017) 218, finding that the term 'translates somewhat awkwardly into English as "legal dogmatics"' (by way of disclosure, the present author was involved in the drafting of sections on German academia in the book). Another alternative, 'legal dogmatism', has a much more negative ring, implying some sort of narrow-mindedness. See on this, with regard to the German term 'Dogmatismus', also Matthias Jestaedt, 'Wissenschaftliches Recht—Rechtsdogmatik als gemeinsames Kommunikationsformat von Rechtswissenschaft und Rechtspraxis' in Gregor Kirchhof, Stefan Magen, and Karsten Schneider (eds), *Was weiß Dogmatik? Was leistet und wie steuert die Dogmatik des Öffentlichen Rechts?* (Mohr Siebeck 2012) 131–32; Bernd Rüthers, 'Rechtsdogmatik und Rechtspolitik unter dem Einfluß des Richterrechts' (1999) 15 Rechtspolitisches Forum/Legal Policy Forum 5–6 <www.ssoar.info/ssoar/handle/document/32172> accessed 12 January 2024; Ewald J Thul, 'Die Denkform der Rechtsdogmatik' (1960) 46 Archiv für Rechts- und Sozialphilosophie 241, 245.

[2] See, on this issue, already Walter Selb, 'Dogmen und Dogmatik, Dogmengeschichte und Dogmatikgeschichte in der Rechtswissenschaft' in Claus-Wilhelm Canaris and Uwe Diederichsen (eds), *Festschrift für Karl Larenz zum 80. Geburtstag am 23. April 1983* (CH Beck 1983). For a concise overview of different definitions and points of emphasis in its use, see Christian Waldhoff, 'Kritik und Lob der Dogmatik: Rechtsdogmatik im Spannungsfeld von Gesetzesbindung und Funktionsorientierung' in Gregor Kirchhof, Stefan Magen and Karsten Schneider (eds), *Was weiß Dogmatik? Was leistet und wie steuert die Dogmatik des Öffentlichen Rechts?* (Mohr Siebeck 2012) 22–26. For attempts at consolidation, see Jestaedt (n 1) 121; Rüthers (n 1) 5; Andreas Voßkuhle, 'Was leistet Rechtsdogmatik? Zusammenführung und Ausblick in 12 Thesen' in Gregor Kirchhof, Stefan Magen and Karsten

---

Markus Beham, *German 'Dogmatik'—An Untranslatable Concept if Ever There Was One?* In: *International Law and Universality*. Edited by: Işıl Aral and Jean d'Aspremont, Oxford University Press. © Markus Beham 2024.
DOI: 10.1093/oso/9780198889419.003.0016

and 'subject to different use',[3] some say 'vague'.[4] Others have called it anachronistic[5] or have already sounded its death knell,[6] a claim refuted by the ongoing discussion decades later.[7] 'Dogmatik' remains the hegemon of Germanophone legal scholarship.

This chapter traces the meaning of the concept within the Germanophone legal tradition and places it within the context of international legal scholarship to demonstrate its often implicit workings. Unbeknownst to many beyond the stereotype of the 'German professor', 'Dogmatik' has long infiltrated English language discourse through internationally minded representatives of the trade with their commentary tradition and encyclopaedic reference works.

While domestic legal education and scholarship in less accessible languages insert particularity into the understanding of the international legal system, they bring colour to its universal implementation. However, without a thorough understanding of these underlying processes at work, the true nature of the international legal system remains opaque. At the same time, the insufficient recognition of such phenomena accentuates the linguistic and intellectual challenges to the normative project of international law.

This makes the preoccupation with individual legal traditions a fundamental exercise in the study of universality and its many critiques.[8] How could the narrative of a *Ius Publicum Europaeum* or the accusation of Eurocentrism stand empirical scrutiny if even 'Western' scholars fail to communicate amongst themselves? If the 'European international law tradition "imagines itself as universal"',[9] it should first be aware of what that tradition is.

Attempting to fill one of the larger gaps in the legal vocabulary of English-speaking international lawyers and legal theorists,[10] this contribution highlights how a deeply particular approach to legal study and understanding has helped consolidate the body of international law.

Schneider (eds), *Was weiß Dogmatik? Was leistet und wie steuert die Dogmatik des Öffentlichen Rechts?* (Mohr Siebeck 2012).

[3] Markus H Müller, 'Neutralität und Parität als dogmatikleitende Rechtsprinzipien des Religionsverfassungsrechts—eine Intervention' in Julian Krüper, Heike Merten, and Martin Morlok (eds), *An den Grenzen der Rechtsdogmatik* (Mohr Siebeck 2010) 43.
[4] Martin Eifert, 'Zum Verhältnis von Dogmatik und pluralisierter Rechtswissenschaft' in Kirchhof, Magen, and Schneider (eds) (n 2) 80.
[5] See Frank Schorkopf, 'Dogmatik und Kohärenz' in Kirchhof, Magen, and Schneider (eds) (n 2) 139.
[6] See Ulrich Meyer-Cording, *Kann der Jurist heute noch Dogmatiker sein?* (Mohr Siebeck 1973) 32. See, on this issue, also Waldhoff (n 2) 21.
[7] See Oliver Lepsius, 'Kritik der Dogmatik' in Kirchhof, Magen, and Schneider (eds) (n 2) 46–49.
[8] Particularly arising from critical legal studies as indicated in the introductory chapter of this volume.
[9] See Martti Koskenniemi as quoted in the introductory chapter of this volume.
[10] Anthea Roberts has referred to this phenomenon as a 'tension between multiple languages'. See Roberts (n 1) 3.

While the relevance of transplanting[11] concepts and terminology of other legal traditions into the English language discourse may be up for debate, international lawyers should strive to appreciate the intellectual frameworks that guide parts of their faculty at the invisible college,[12] starting with what hides behind this most untranslatable term: 'Dogmatik'.

This chapter begins by mapping out the concept within the legal tradition of the German-speaking world in Section 1. It goes on, in Section 2, to discuss the particularities induced by it before highlighting, in Section 3, the impact it has had on the study and understanding of international law. Section 4 provides a brief conclusion.

1. What is 'Dogmatik'?

The *Concise Oxford English Dictionary* tells us that 'dogmatic' means 'inclined to assert principles or opinions as inconvertibly true' or 'a system of dogma, especially one laid down by the Roman Catholic Church'. Neither of these definitions comes close to the corresponding German word 'Dogmatik' in its legal sense.[13] The sometimes synonymously used 'Jurisprudenz'[14] goes far beyond the seemingly equivalent 'jurisprudence' that is more akin to legal theory.[15] Anglophone contributions on the question have been scarce.[16] Surprisingly, for a *terminus technicus* so pivotal to and dominant within the Germanophone legal tradition, most legal systems seem to get by happily without this 'favourite child'[17] of Austrian, German, and Swiss lawyers.

The difficulty of clearly defining 'Dogmatik' is apparent in the common approach of simply distinguishing it from a number of other 'disciplines':[18] legal philosophy, legal theory, legal sociology, legal history, and comparative law,[19]

---

[11] See Alan Watson, *Legal Transplants. An Approach to Comparative Law* (2nd edn, University of Georgia Press 1993).

[12] See Oscar Schachter, 'The Invisible College of International Lawyers' (1977) 72 Northwestern University Law Review 217.

[13] For explanation why this might be the case see Nils Jareborg, 'Legal Dogmatics and the Concept of Science' in René Bloy and others (eds), *Grundlagen und Dogmatik des gesamten Strafrechtssystems: Festschrift für Wolfgang Frisch zum 70. Geburtstag* (Duncker & Humblot 2013) 49.

[14] Eg Claus-Wilhelm Canaris and Karl Larenz, *Methodenlehre der Rechtswissenschaft* (3rd edn, Springer 1995) 11; Roland Dubischar, *Einführung in die Rechtstheorie* (Wissenschaftliche Buchgesellschaft 1983) 1.

[15] Its equivalents in French and Italian are closer to the German concept but this delineation cannot be part of the present contribution.

[16] See Jareborg (n 13); Neil MacCormick, 'Reconstruction after Deconstruction: A Response to CLS' (1990) 10 Oxford Journal of Legal Studies 539; Roberts (n 1) 218–19. However, none of these contributions seek to engage with the relevant literature, let alone the substantive German debate.

[17] Jestaedt (n 1) 117–18. See also Gregor Kirchhof and Stefan Magen, 'Dogmatik: Rechtliche Notwendigkeit und Grundlage fächerübergreifenden Dialogs—eine systematisierende Übersicht' in Kirchhof, Magen, and Schneider (eds) (n 2) 166.

[18] See also Waldhoff (n 2) 26.

[19] See eg Canaris and Larenz (n 14) 11; Waldhoff (n 2) 30–32.

others adding 'psychology of law, criminology, and so on'.[20] While all of these are depicted as 'essentially subspecies of other types of sciences',[21] '[l]egal dogmatics (Rechtsdogmatik) is the principal legal science'[22] and constitutes the 'centre piece' of legal scholarship.[23]

The German word 'Dogmatik' originates from the Greek 'δόγμα' [dogma], which in turn derives from 'δοκέω' [dokeo], meaning 'to think' or 'to suppose', which has its roots in 'δέκομαι' or 'δέχομαι' [dékomai/déchomai], translatable as 'to accept' in the sense of having received something or other. The grammatical structure of the German language—that demonstrates many similarities to Ancient Greek—has been considered formative for the concept of 'Dogmatik' and the precondition for formulating such ideas in the minds of generations of legal scholars.[24]

The term made its way through late antiquity into Christian theology to describe an axiom, a fundamental truth, a doctrine, or an opinion.[25] In the Catholic conception, it becomes an infallible postulation of faith.[26] As a legal term, it has been criticized for its bridge into the realm of theology, which supposedly gives it a somewhat transcendent, unquestionable appeal (some authors have indeed attested that only law and theology deal with the authoritative manifestation of intellect within the systematic context of a discipline).[27] Instead, the 'more modest' terms of 'legal systematics' and 'legal structure' have been suggested.[28]

Some find the concept of 'Dogmatik' already present in Pomponius' digests when he writes of 'quod sine scripto in sola prudentium interpretatione consistit'[29] and its features may be identified in other legal traditions such as common law.[30] Still, it is mostly thought of as a uniquely German phenomenon that can be traced back to the attempt to structure (civil private) law towards the end of the eighteenth

---

[20] Jareborg (n 13) 49.
[21] ibid.
[22] ibid.
[23] See Ralf Dreier, 'Zum Selbstverstandnis der Jurisprudenz als Wissenschaft' (1971) 2 Rechtstheorie 37, 41: 'Mit dem Terminus "Jurisprudenz" ist das Kernstück der Rechtswissenschaft, die juristische Dogmatik, gemeint.' See also Bernd Grzeszick, 'Steuert die Dogmatik? Inwiefern steuert die Dogmatik des Öffentlichen Rechts? Gibt es eine rechtliche Steuerungswissenschaft jenseits der Rechtsdogmatik?' in Kirchhof, Magen, and Schneider (eds) (n 2) 97; Kirchhof and Magen (n 17) 151; Michael Potacs, 'Rechtsdogmatik als empirische Wissenschaft' (1994) 25 Rechtstheorie 191, 191.
[24] See, on this relationship between language and the development of 'Dogmatik', Armin von Bogdandy, 'Internationalisierung der deutschen Rechtswissenschaft. Betrachtungen zu einem identitätswandelnden Prozess' in Eric Hilgendorf (ed), Selbstreflexion der Rechtswissenschaft (Mohr Siebeck 2015) 141.
[25] See also Rüthers (n 1) 9.
[26] See also ibid 12–13.
[27] See eg Kurt Ballerstedt, 'Dulckeit als Rechtsdogmatiker' in Wolfgang Kunkel, Karl Larenz, and Kurt Ballerstedt (eds), Gerhard Dulckeit als Rechtshistoriker, Rechtsphilosoph und Rechtsdogmatiker (Ferdinand Hirt 1955) 27.
[28] See Müller (n 3) 43: ' "Rechtssystematik" oder Rechtsstruktur'.
[29] See Rüthers (n 1) 12.
[30] See on this M Goldmann, 'Dogmatik als rationale Rekonstruktion: Versuch einer Metatheorie am Beispiel völkerrechtlicher Prinzipien' (2014) 53(3) Der Staat 373, 379.

century[31] and throughout the nineteenth century as the idea of inductive knowledge about the law.[32] A general tendency of German legal scholarship has been described as identifying an abstract 'general part' that controls the application of specific provisions in any area of law, even where this is not necessarily inherent in a statute.[33]

This preference for abstract and systemic reasoning[34] is reflected today in German legal education, with its almost exclusive emphasis on applying law to hypotheticals along a preconceived framework that strictly follows the structure known in legal writing terms as 'IRAC' ('issue', 'rule', 'analysis', and 'conclusion'):[35] the 'Gutachtenstil',[36] 'which is equally crucial to the thinking of every German lawyer'.[37]

'Dogmatik' has been described as a discipline that aims to permeate and sort the law, in order to guide legal work, and that seeks to provide answers to the questions brought up by legal practice.[38] Its efforts lie in exploring conceptions and understandings of the law and to secure them by forming terminology, introducing distinctions, elaborating arguments or principles, and compiling the *travaux*.[39]

But 'Dogmatik' also questions existing conceptions of, or decisions made in, practice; picks up new developments; and enquires into the resulting needs for change, tracing back and forth. It provides a reservoir of knowledge for practice, conveys an approach to practical legal work, and makes a contribution to the rationalization and, thereby, to the legitimization of the law.[40]

While academia seeks to comprehend and order the legal system, practice applies 'Dogmatik' to individual cases as standard procedures and arguments for regularly recurring problems.[41] This purpose also necessitates that any approach meet the requirements of effective application, providing both simplicity and

---

[31] See Nils Jansen, 'Rechtsdogmatik im Zivilrecht', *Enzyklopädie zur Rechtsphilosophie* (8 April 2011) <www.enzyklopaedie-rechtsphilosophie.net/inhaltsverzeichnis/19-beitraege/98-rechtsdogmatik-im-zivilrecht> accessed 29 June 2018. See also Lepsius (n 7) 49; Roberts (n 1) 218 fn 42; Waldhoff (n 2) 32–33 and 36.
[32] See Andreas Funke, *Allgemeine Rechtslehre als juristische Strukturtheorie* (Mohr Siebeck 2004) 102. On the historical development of the debate in this period and beyond, see recently and comprehensively also Christian Bumke, *Rechtsdogmatik* (Mohr Siebeck 2017) ch 1 and *passim*. See also Dubischar (n 14) 24–27.
[33] See Uwe Kischel, *Comparative Law* (OUP 2019) 386–87, para 61.
[34] ibid 421, para 128.
[35] Familiar to US law school students from the requirements for writing a case brief. See Linda H Edwards, *Legal Writing and Analysis* (5th edn, Wolters Kluwer 2019).
[36] See Kischel (n 33) 417–21, paras 120–28; Carl-Friedrich Stuckenberg, 'Der juristische Gutachtenstil als cartesische Methode' (2019) 4 Zeitschrift für Didaktik der Rechtswissenschaft 323. The term 'Gutachtenstil' is equally difficult to translate as 'Dogmatik' and literally means 'opinion style', sometimes translated as 'appraisal style', 'expert opinion style', or 'in the style of a legal opinion'.
[37] Kischel (n 33) 417, para 120.
[38] See Bumke (n 32) 1.
[39] ibid.
[40] ibid 1–2.
[41] ibid 11–12; Martin Morlok, *Was heißt und zu welchem Ende studiert man Verfassungstheorie?* (Duncker & Humblot 1988) 39–40.

pragmatism.[42] The resulting statements cannot be too concrete, so as to preserve their claim to universal applicability.[43]

In this constant cross-fertilization between academia and practice, 'Dogmatik' is normative, exploring the 'universal elements, mechanisms, and structures of legal practice',[44] elaborating the 'fundamental values, reasonings, and solutions' within positive law.[45] As a result, fixed sets of argumentation are offered to the legal practitioner,[46] inoculating application of the law against outside agendas.[47] In the absence of such clear aspirations, related concepts such as 'doctrine', 'interpretation', and 'legal theory' also known to the Anglophone legal scholar do not equate to this offspring of the continental law tradition.

Ultimately, one of the main reasons for moving within the confines of 'Dogmatik' is the constant urge towards quality assurance. The discipline seeks the use of certain principles and standards within the legal argument,[48] creating a comprehensive system that cannot be achieved through legislation alone.[49] Against the background of a multitude of argumentative paths, the approach strives towards fully integrated solutions and holistic answers to any given question.

2. 'Dogmatik' as a Catalyst for Particularity

While a number of German scholars[50] have previously publicized the specificities of German-speaking academia,[51] the assessment of its influence on international

[42] See Morlok (n 41) 40–41.
[43] See Stefan Baufeld, 'Rechtsanwendung und Rechtsdogmatik—Parallelwelten' (2006) 37 Rechtstheorie 171, 183–84.
[44] See Bumke (n 32) 12. cf Baufeld (n 43) 192.
[45] See Rüthers (n 1) 10. See also Anne Peters, 'Die Zukunft der Völkerrechtswissenschaft: Wider den epistemischen Nationalismus' (2007) 67 Zeitschrift für ausländisches öffentliches Recht und Völkerrecht 721, 738, refuting the argument often raised that there are no discoveries to be made in law.
[46] See Baufeld (n 43) 172; Dubischar (n 14) 1; Morlok (n 41) 39.
[47] See Uwe Diederichsen, 'Auf dem Weg zur Rechtsdogmatik' in Reinhard Zimmermann (ed), *Rechtsgeschichte und Privatrechtsdogmatik* (CF Müller 1999) 70. See also Baufeld (n 43) 178; Bumke (n 32) 45–46; Peters, 'Die Zukunft der Völkerrechtswissenschaft' (n 45) 771.
[48] See Jareborg (n 13) 55.
[49] See Baufeld (n 43) 171–72.
[50] von Bogdandy (n 24); Nico Krisch, 'The Many Fields of (German) International Law' in Anthea Roberts and others (eds), *Comparative International Law* (OUP 2018); Stefan Oeter, 'Die Zukunft der Völkerrechtswissenschaft in Deutschland' (2007) 67 Zeitschrift für ausländisches öffentliches Recht und Völkerrecht 675; Peters, 'Die Zukunft der Völkerrechtswissenschaft' (n 45); Andreas Zimmermann, 'Die Zukunft der Völkerrechtswissenschaft in Deutschland' (2007) 67 Zeitschrift für ausländisches öffentliches Recht und Völkerrecht 799.
[51] See Roberts (n 1). This form of sociological approach to international law is not entirely novel. For an ambitious compilation of activities of Austrian scholars, see Waldemar Hummer, 'Die österreichische Völkerrechtslehre und ihre Vertreter' in Waldemar Hummer (ed), *Paradigmenwechsel im Völkerrecht zur Jahrtausendwende. Ansichten österreichischer Völkerrechtler zu aktuellen Problemlagen* (Manz 2002) 354 and, on scholarship in Germany, the 2007 special edition of the *German Yearbook of International Law* on such questions. Such contributions could serve as further building blocks to help advance the project aspired to by Roberts.

legal scholarship has not been overly optimistic. Armin von Bogdandy finds that although Germans prefer visiting institutions in the UK and the US, rather than countries which base their laws on German role models, influence there is minimal.[52] He emphasizes the competitive disadvantage of a 'Dogmatik' mindset as opposed to the interdisciplinary aspirations of US legal scholars.[53] Some go as far as to say that this legal tradition has a self-exclusionary effect vis-à-vis the international scientific discourse.[54] Nico Krisch finds two indicators to substantiate the proposition of limited visibility of German scholarship in international law: presence at the Hague Academy of International Law and in international journals.[55]

Anthea Roberts sees the domestic orientation of scholars in Germany as a reason for their reduced presence in international publications.[56] The general academic profile of a German law scholar is that of a polymath, showing a holistic grasp of public, private, or criminal law.[57] This *homo universalis* is naturally burdened by the ideas and concepts of constitutional and administrative law. This domestic orientation comes at the cost of specialization in public international law, let alone any of its subfields.[58] Anne Peters see this as resulting in certain parts of German legal scholarship no longer being communicable transnationally.[59]

This phenomenon becomes visible when reviewing different textbooks on international law. A brief look at the table of contents shows diverging structural approaches to the treatment of concepts of international law. Whereas English textbooks take a broad approach and rely heavily on individual case law,[60] German textbooks tend to portray the individual concepts themselves and draw stricter lines, such as between the question of immunities of states as well as international organizations and those of their respective organs.[61]

---

[52] See von Bogdandy (n 24) 135.
[53] ibid 142. See on this also Oeter (n 50) 687; Roberts (n 1) 219; Zimmermann, 'Die Zukunft der Völkerrechtswissenschaft' (n 50) 805.
[54] See Lepsius (n 7) 46.
[55] See Krisch (n 50) 100. It would be interesting to contrast this with an analysis of the networks at play in selecting lecturers and conducting peer review.
[56] See Roberts (n 1) 106. cf, on the potentially negative effects of this, von Bogdandy (n 24) 143. Also arguing for the importance of publishing in both languages Oeter (n 50) 691; Zimmermann, 'Die Zukunft der Völkerrechtswissenschaft' (n 50) 820 and 823.
[57] Not so different from the profile in US law schools.
[58] See Zimmermann, 'Die Zukunft der Völkerrechtswissenschaft' (n 50) 806.
[59] See Peters, 'Die Zukunft der Völkerrechtswissenschaft' (n 45) 771. See also the argument made by Zimmermann, 'Die Zukunft der Völkerrechtswissenschaft' (n 50) 805. See also generally Waldhoff (n 2) 36–37.
[60] See, prominently and almost as a *pars pro toto*, Malcolm N Shaw, *International Law* (8th edn, CUP 2017) ch 12. See also Antonio Cassese, *International Law* (2nd edn, OUP 2005) ch 6, taking a somewhat hybrid approach of individual subchapters but with a strong emphasis on case law; James Crawford, *Brownlie's Principles of Public International Law* (8th edn, OUP 2012) ch 22, but with a separate treatment of diplomats and consuls in ch 17; Jan Klabbers, *International Law* (2nd edn, CUP 2017) ch 5. cf, however, Malcolm Evans (ed), *International Law* (5th edn, OUP 2018) chs 11 and 12.
[61] See eg Markus P Beham, Melanie Fink, and Ralph Janik, *Völkerrecht verstehen* (Facultas 2015) chs 8 and 9; Wolfgang Graf Vitzthum and Andreas Proelß (eds), *Völkerrecht* (7th edn, De Gruyter 2016) chs 2.IV.1 and 3.I.2; Matthias Herdegen, *Völkerrecht* (17th edn, CH Beck 2018) chs §37, §38, and §10; Stephan Hobe, *Einführung in das Völkerrecht* (10th edn, UTB 2014) chs 6.2.3.5 and 9; Knut Ipsen (ed),

Different issues arise at the micro-level. Looking again at immunities, Anglophone scholarship makes little to no terminological distinction when it comes to privileges and immunities. As Schermers and Blokker hold in their seminal treatise on international institutions, '[t]here is no sharp distinction between privileges and immunities'.[62] In contrast, the *Austrian Handbook on Public International Law* distinguishes between 'inviolability', 'immunity', 'privileges', and 'exemptions'.[63] August Reinisch, an Austrian scholar who is currently a member of the International Law Commission, seeks in his Habilitation thesis[64] to introduce the terminological differentiation into the international discourse:

> Normally, an international organization is immune only in respect of adjudicative enforcement jurisdiction, i.e., it remains liable to obey the law of the state where it is operating, and is merely exempt from judicial process to enforce that law. But there are some areas of national law which regularly do not apply to an international organization, e.g. customs, tax, immigration, financial (e.g., foreign exchange) controls, work permit regulations, etc. These areas should properly be referred to as privileges of international organisations.[65]

More in-depth enquiries into the literature and into other areas of law would, of course, be necessary to see if these illustrative examples can be reproduced elsewhere. But they do show a tendency—both at the macro- and micro-levels— towards more systematic and structured accounts of the law.

Völkerrecht (6th edn, CH Beck 2014) chs 2 §5 VII.4, 2 §6 I.7.b, and 5; Markus Krajeweski, *Völkerrecht* (Nomos 2017) ch §8 A.3 and F.2; Bruno Simma and Alfred Verdroß, *Universelles Völkerrecht. Theorie und Praxis* (3rd edn, Duncker & Humblot 1984) chs 6 and 8.3. cf, for a somewhat holistic approach, though with individual subchapters, Karl Doehring, *Völkerrecht. Ein Lehrbuch* (2nd edn, CF Müller 2004) ch § 12; Markus Kotzur, Torsten Stein, and Christian von Buttlar, *Völkerrecht* (14th edn, Franz Vahlen 2017) ch 13; Anne Peters, *Völkerrecht. Allgemeiner Teil* (2nd edn, Schulthess 2008) ch 5. cf also Hans-Georg Dederer and Michael Schweitzer, *Staatsrecht III. Staatsrecht. Europarecht* (11th edn, CF Müller 2016) ch §5 IV, looking only at the immunity of states and their central organs; Andreas von Arnauld, *Völkerrecht* (3rd edn, CF Müller 2016) chs §4 B.II and §8 C, discussing diplomatic and consular immunities separately but questions of the immunity of central state organs alongside state immunity. Interestingly, the *Austrian Handbook on Public International Law* makes a shift from the fourth edition to the fifth, the latter orienting itself towards the Anglophone approach. See the chapters by Ursula Kriebaum, 'Privilegien und Immunitäten im Völkerrecht' in A Reinisch (ed), *Österreichisches Handbuch des Völkerrechts* (5th edn, Manz 2013) 404 and, in the previous edition, by Ignaz Seidl-Hohenveldern and Waldemar Hummer, 'Die Staaten' in Waldemar Hummer, Hans-Peter Neuhold, and Christoph Schreuer (eds), *Österreichisches Handbuch des Völkerrechts* (4th edn, Manz 2004) 135, by Christoph Schreuer, 'Die Internationalen Organisationen' in ibid 173, as well as by Heribert F Köck, 'Die Organe des völkerrechtlichen Verkehrs' in ibid 324.

[62] Niels M Blokker and Henry G Schermers, *International Institutional Law* (5th edn, Martinus Nijhoff 2011) 257–58.
[63] See Kriebaum (n 61) 418–20 and also, in the previous edition, Schreuer (n 61) 181–83.
[64] Post-doctoral qualification for a full professorship.
[65] August Reinisch, *International Organisations Before National Courts* (CUP 2000) 14. See ibid 13–14 for further examples.

However, it may be exactly this German approach that anticipates the deficiencies identified in other academic cultures. At the ASIL 2012 Midyear Meeting in Athens, Georgia, Harold Hongju Koh criticized US law review articles as useless for the work at the Office of the Legal Adviser of the State Department.[66] 'Dogmatik', on the other hand, specifically seeks to provide answers to the questions brought up by legal practice.

3. 'Dogmatik' as a Catalyst for Universality

The above evaluations as to the relevance of German-speaking academia seem to somewhat undervalue the (implicit) impact of its international law tradition upon international discourse, both historically[67] and in recent times, particularly against the background of Harald Koh's critique of US scholarship.

> I guess you do have a point. I always have the impression after reading on something in an English textbook that one has been presented with the relevant cases there are to be known on a certain subject but one is none the wiser as to the application of the law. Maybe it does need the Germans to sort all the material and fashion it into a systematic framework.

So went the response by a colleague kind enough to conduct a preliminary review of this chapter.

Of course, this conversational comment on the idea that the German legal tradition provides a unique contribution to international legal scholarship is a broad generalization. Although coming from a representative of German academia, it does stretch the stereotype. Yet, it is not the first time that this Linnaean urge[68] has been identified as a positive feature of Germanophone scholarship. External perspectives have attested that 'German and German-speaking international law scholars evidence noteworthy strength in doctrinal analysis' and that '[a] traditional specialty of German legal analysis lies in *Rechtsdogmatik*'.[69] Internal perspectives have recognized this German exceptionalism[70] as 'its trademark, its

---

[66] Speech by Harold Hongu Koh at the ASIL 2012 Midyear Meeting in Athens, Georgia <https://youtu.be/COjHyHIpgwQ> accessed 12 January 2024.

[67] One need only think of the contributions of the many émigré scholars in the UK and the US following the events of the 1930s in Europe.

[68] Since the eighteenth-century Swedish botanist and zoologist Carl von Linné may stand here as a representative of formal categorizations with his championing of a binomial nomenclature to identify the species of the world. The present contribution concerns itself with the species *iurisprudentia germanica*.

[69] Roberts (n 1) 218.

[70] See Gregor Kirchhof, Stefan Magen, and Karsten Schneider, 'Vorwort' in Kirchhof, Magen, and Schneider (eds) (n 2) v; Kirchhof and Magen (n 17) 151; Lepsius (n 7) 47. See also Krisch (n 50) 96; Peters, 'Die Zukunft der Völkerrechtswissenschaft' (n 45) 748 and 771.

signature tune'[71] and it seems to be part of a (German) self-perception of getting things done right.[72]

How relevant is 'Dogmatik' to international legal scholarship? While German is not generally understood as one of the 'dominant' languages of international law, its speakers have taken their ideas above and beyond through their capacity as internationally minded professors or as judges and arbitrators at international courts or tribunals. 'Dogmatik' has found reflection in the global teaching and understanding of international law. Thereby, legal education 'made in' Austria, Germany, and Switzerland[73] has inevitably had a universal impact. The presence of German speakers in international fora is not equally bleak wherever one goes. The International Law Commission has seen a number of eminent German-speaking scholars over the past three decades.[74] German Karl-Heinz Böckstiegel is the thirteenth most appointed arbitrator in proceedings at the International Centre for Settlement of Investment Disputes.[75] Bruno Simma is surely not the only 'outlier', as has been held.[76] Further, Germanophone domestic jurisprudence on key issues of international law has been commonly picked up by the literature, thereby shaping the common understanding of key concepts of international law.[77]

As to the influence of German scholars upon the global discourse on international law, Roberts points out in her monograph *Is International Law International?* the project of constitutionalism as a consequence of German domestic orientation,[78] listing Andreas Paulus, Anne Peters, Bruno Simma, Christian Tomuschat, and Alfred Verdroß as primary representatives of this school of thought.[79]

---

[71] See Jestaedt (n 1) 118. See also Kirchhof and Magen (n 17) 152 and 171–72.
[72] See eg Kirchhof and Magen (n 17) 152 and 171–72.
[73] See also, on the impact of a common language on this, Roberts (n 1) 46.
[74] Christian Tomuschat (Germany, 1985–96); Bernhard Graefrath (Germany, 1987–91); Gerhard Hafner (Austria, 1997–2001); Bruno Simma (Germany, 1997–2002); Lucius Caflisch (Switzerland, 2007–16); Georg Nolte (Germany, 2007–present); and August Reinisch (Austria, 2017–present). In addition, Austrians Stephan Verosta and Alfred Verdroß were members 1977–81 and 1957–66, respectively. See International Law Commission, Present and Former Members of the International Law Commission (1949–present) <http://legal.un.org/ilc/guide/annex2.shtml> accessed 29 June 2018. Of course, among 229 members to date, the enumeration is probably more conclusive in qualitative than quantitative terms.
[75] UN Conference on Trade and Development, World Investment Report 2018 <http://unctad.org/en/PublicationsLibrary/wir2018_en.pdf> accessed 6 September 2018.
[76] Krisch (n 50) 107–08.
[77] Due to the fact that Vienna is home to a large number of international organizations and one of the headquarters of the United Nations, Austrian domestic courts have continuously had to deal with various issues concerning the immunities of international organizations. See eg the cases listed in the commentary of August Reinisch (ed), *The Conventions on the Privileges and Immunities of the United Nations and Its Specialized Agencies* (OUP 2016). Dissemination of such cases has increased through projects such as the Oxford Reports on International Law in Domestic Courts <http://opil.ouplaw.com/page/ILDC/oxford-reports-on-international-law-in-domestic-courts> accessed 29 June 2018.
[78] See on this also Krisch (n 50) 97–99.
[79] See Roberts (n 1) 106–07.

In the words of Andreas Zimmermann, Germans have taken the term 'public international law' seriously, emphasizing its binding, normative character.[80] In particular, by applying 'Dogmatik' to public international law, they have continuously attempted to provide reasoned and substantiated solutions to issues of public international law, avoiding the pitfalls of descriptively tracing state practice and developing a normative legal order based on overarching, universal principles.[81] Not only may its content be assessed but also aggregated, sorted, and structured.[82]

This draw towards systemization has found its expression in the Germanophone commentary tradition,[83] this 'most typical of dogmatic genres',[84] committing itself to international agreements, in particular through the Oxford Commentaries on International Law[85] but also works from other publishing houses. Contributions by German-speaking academics include commentaries on such essential documents as the Charter of the United Nations,[86] the Statute of the International Court of Justice,[87] the Vienna Convention on the Law of Treaties,[88] agreements surrounding the World Trade Organization,[89] the Conventions on the Privileges and Immunities of the United Nations and its Specialized Agencies,[90] and the Convention Relating to the Status of Refugees.[91]

The Charter commentary edited by Bruno Simma and others[92] is given additional 'authoritative gloss'[93] through its presence as a recommended reference work on the website of the Dag Hammarskjöld Library of the United Nations.[94]

---

[80] Emphasis in the translation as in the original, see Zimmermann, 'Die Zukunft der Völkerrechtswissenschaft' (n 50) 804.
[81] See Peters, 'Die Zukunft der Völkerrechtswissenschaft' (n 45) 747; Zimmermann, 'Die Zukunft der Völkerrechtswissenschaft' (n 50) 805.
[82] See Peters, 'Die Zukunft der Völkerrechtswissenschaft' (n 45) 747–48.
[83] See on this also ibid 771; Roberts (n 1) 218–21.
[84] See Lepsius (n 7) 45.
[85] Oxford Commentaries on International Law <https://global.oup.com/academic/content/series/o/oxford-commentaries-on-international-law-ocils/?cc=at&lang=en&> accessed 29 June 2018.
[86] Daniel-Erasmus Khan and others (eds), *The Charter of the United Nations. A Commentary* (3rd edn, OUP 2013).
[87] Christian J Tams and others (eds), *The Statute of the International Court of Justice* (3rd edn, OUP 2019).
[88] Oliver Dörr and Kirsten Schmalenbach (eds), *Vienna Convention on the Law of Treaties. A Commentary* (2nd edn, Springer 2018); Mark Villiger, *Commentary on the 1969 Vienna Convention on the Law of Treaties* (Brill 2019).
[89] See the *Max Planck Commentaries on World Trade Law* <https://brill.com/view/serial/MPCO> accessed 29 June 2018.
[90] Reinisch, *The Conventions* (n 77).
[91] Andreas Zimmermann (ed), *The 1951 Convention Relating to the Status of Refugees and Its 1967 Protocol. A Commentary* (OUP 2011).
[92] Khan and others (n 86).
[93] See, on this expression, Michael P Scharf, *Customary International Law in Times of Fundamental Change. Recognizing Grotian Moments* (CUP 2013) 218.
[94] See Dag Hammarskjöld Library, UN Documentation: Overview <https://research.un.org/en/docs/charter> accessed 29 June 2018.

Hans Kelsen already provided commentaries on the Covenant of the League of Nations[95] and the Charter of the United Nations.[96] At the time, Kelsen was criticized for his legalist assessment of such documents.[97] Today, this genre aimed at and connecting academia and practice has become an international professional standard. Elaborating individual treaty provisions, thereby providing a reservoir of knowledge for practice, the commentary tradition serves as an ambassador of 'Dogmatik' to the study of international law.

In addition, the systematization of international law finds its culmination in encyclopaedic projects ranging from smaller compendiums[98] to such colossal projects as the *Max Planck Encyclopedia of Public International Law*, now available online as a reference work for all issues related to public international law.[99] The latter project traces its origins to the three-volume *Dictionary of Public International Law and Diplomacy*[100] of the interwar years and the three-volume *Dictionary of Public International Law* of the early 1960s,[101] two German language publications, before these became the English language *Encyclopedia of Public International Law*,[102] the last precursor of the current database.[103] Considering the extent of participation by German-speaking scholars in this project,[104] it can hardly be deemed an 'outlier in terms of its internationalization'.[105] The streamlined presentation of various topics of international law introduces the aspiration of 'Dogmatik' to the English language discourse.

Equally, Germany has an active team reporting for the International Law in Domestic Courts database, and Austrian professor August Reinisch serves as one of its editors-in-chief.[106] This makes Austrian, German, and Swiss domestic jurisprudence on key issues of international law accessible to an international audience,

---

[95] Hans Kelsen, *Legal Technique in International Law. A Textual Critique of the League Covenant* (Geneva Research Centre 1939).

[96] Hans Kelsen, *The Law of the United Nations. A Critical Analysis of Its Fundamental Problems* (Stevens & Sons 1950) and the supplement *Recent Trends in the Law of the United Nations. A Supplement to 'The Law of the United Nations'* (Stevens & Sons 1951).

[97] See Bardo Fassbender, 'Hans Kelsen und die Vereinten Nationen' in Pierre-Marie Dupuy and others (eds), *Völkerrecht als Wertordnung. Common Values in International Law. Festschrift für/Essays in Honour of Christian Tomuschat* (NP Engel 2006) 775–76.

[98] See eg Burkhard Schöbener, *Völkerrecht. Lexikon zentraler Begriffe und Themen* (CF Müller 2014).

[99] *Max Planck Encyclopedia of Public International Law* <http://opil.ouplaw.com/home/epil> accessed 29 June 2018.

[100] Karl Strupp (ed), *Wörterbuch des Völkerrechts und der Diplomatie. Begonnen von Prof. Dr. Julius Hatschek* (De Gruyter 1924).

[101] Hans-Jürgen Schlochauer and Karl Strupp (eds), *Wörterbuch des Völkerrechts* (De Gruyter 1960) 4 vols.

[102] Rudolf Bernhardt (ed), *Encyclopedia of Public International Law* (North Holland 1993) 4 vols.

[103] See Rudolf Bernhardt and Karin Oellers-Frahm, *Das Max-Planck-Institut für Ausländisches Öffentliches Recht und Völkerrecht. Geschichte und Entwicklungen von 1949 bis 2013* (Springer 2018) 88–91. See on this also Roberts (n 1) 220.

[104] Figures on file with the author, data as evaluated by Roberts (n 1) 220: 31 per cent German, 4 per cent Austrian, and 4 per cent Swiss authors.

[105] ibid.

[106] See Oxford Reports on International Law in Domestic Courts <http://opil.ouplaw.com/page/ILDC/oxford-reports-on-international-law-in-domestic-courts> accessed 29 June 2018.

implicitly offering the legal education underlying these decisions to colour the understanding of different questions of international law.

4. Conclusion

Matthias Goldmann finds an interesting convergence between the idea of 'Dogmatik' and the Anglophone idea of 'doctrine' in Article 38(1)(d) of the Statute of the International Court of Justice: whereas 'judicial decisions and the teachings of the most highly qualified publicists of the various nations' are merely considered 'as subsidiary means for the determination of rules of law', scholarly work is placed upon an equal footing with legal practice, allowing academic preoccupation with the law to exert a level of influence upon its conceptualization.[107] Could 'Dogmatik' have been a universal idea all along?

This chapter has attempted to highlight how a particular legal tradition may support the universal aspirations of a normative project, as international law is, and thereby transcend the binary understanding of the universal.[108] 'Dogmatik' organizes and systematizes what did not previously come together together by inferring common principles from the interplay of individual norms. While the Germanophone legal tradition, through its emphasis on 'Dogmatik', runs the risk of over-conceptualizing beyond original intentions, it may also serve as a gatekeeper to bold assertions beyond positive law, thereby favouring universal denominators.

Among the multitude of legal techniques and instruments of international legal theory, the concept is surely among the more obscure, illustrated by its lack of a corresponding technical term in the working languages of international law. At the same time, it is a precondition for much systematization that has occurred in creating a 'universal language' of international law. Amidst the perceived chaos of international relations and the isolation of individual cases, its power lies in painting the picture of an overarching 'higher legal order', battling fragmentation and stabilizing the aspiration to universality.

If universality is achieved by creating unity, the project of international law as a rules-based order reflects the aspirations of 'Dogmatik'. If universality is achieved by reflecting such different traditions, this is certainly the case here, even if perhaps unconsciously so. A cursory look at the contributions of Austrian, German, and Swiss scholarship to international law suggests that its contribution has already been—if not express—substantial.

Having mapped out 'Dogmatik' as a distinct trait of the Germanophone academic tradition and appreciating its potential impact on the consolidation of a

---

[107] See Matthias Goldmann, 'Dogmatik als rationale Rekonstruktion: Versuch einer Metatheorie am Beispiel völkerrechtlicher Prinzipien' (2014) 53 Der Staat 373, 379.
[108] As suggested in the introductory chapter of this volume.

body of international law, parts of the linguistic and intellectual challenges of the field—now often the subject of what is called 'comparative international law'[109]—may be overcome, adding a piece in the puzzle to better comprehend the nature of the international legal system.

---

[109] See Roberts (n 1) 2 and 20, with further references, as well as Anthea Roberts and others, 'Comparative International Law: Framing the Field' (2015) 109 American Journal of International Law 467.

VII
CRITIQUE AND RESISTANCE TO UNIVERSALITY

16
The Retreat of the State in International Law?
The Paris Agreement as a Case Study

Maiko Meguro

Political and legal discourses on climate change have, from the start, been associated with the narrative of 'the global'. For instance, the United Nations Framework Convention on Climate Change (UNFCCC), in its preamble, states that 'the global nature of climate change calls for the widest possible cooperation by all countries and their participation in an effective and appropriate international response'. The UNFCCC aims to establish a regime to respond to the global nature of climate change in order to minimize the adverse effects of human activities on nature.

Concurrently, climate change has been associated with the narrative of 'the local', in particular in the context of policymaking. According to this narrative, the patterns of greenhouse gas (GHG) emission are shaped by a wide range of production and consumption patterns of people and businesses in societies with various social and economic conditions. The preamble of the UNFCCC, therefore, declares that states' response to climate change should be 'in accordance with their common but differentiated responsibilities and respective capabilities and their social and economic conditions'.

The narrative of the global that informs political and legal discourses on climate change seemingly boils down to the image of overcoming the symbolic Westphalian notion of modern states, and the rise of manoeuvring for the global governing authority in what was once the exclusive purview of each state now involves many institutions, interest-based consortiums, or 'civil society' beyond state borders. Yet, from the perspective of 'the local', tackling climate change requires drastic change in consumption and production patterns for the political economy of each state, switching to green, yet possibly more costly, economic and energy systems. This obviously affects the daily life of citizens and economic activities of enterprises and requires careful policy responses since the cost of such reforms differs considerably depending on the different social and economic conditions of states, which makes it hard to distribute internationally the efforts of tackling climate change in fair and equitable ways. This is why the issue came to be called the 'super wicked problem'[1] by policymakers engaged in the topic.

---

[1] The term was originally introduced by Kelly Levin, Benjamin Cashore, Steven Bernstein, and Graeme Auld in 2007. They have published analysis on the nature of climate change as 'super

Maiko Meguro, *The Retreat of the State in International Law?* In: *International Law and Universality*. Edited by: Işıl Aral and Jean d'Aspremont, Oxford University Press. © Maiko Meguro 2024. DOI: 10.1093/oso/9780198899419.003.0017

The foregoing explains why the history of international rulemaking under the UNFCCC, from the Kyoto Protocol to the Paris Agreement, has seen a constant oscillation between the global and the local. The negotiations that led to the Paris Agreement and the key political agreements adopted by the previous Conferences of the Parties (COPs) show the efforts to embrace this oscillation in order to find the right formula for maximizing the number of participants while securing satisfactory results for the climate. It can be argued that controversies related to international lawmaking on climate change have become a very illuminating case study for international law's capacity to tackle complex problems.

Despite this sophisticated balancing exercise, the regime established by the Paris Agreement was not wholeheartedly welcomed by international lawyers and environmental activists. The Paris Agreement has been criticized for providing more control and discretion to the member states in determining the content and extent of their respective contributions, disregarding what is scientifically necessary to keep the global temperature increase below 2 degrees Celsius.[2] Others suggest that the Paris Agreement cannot be considered a 'win' for the traditional international rule of law.[3]

It is against this backdrop that the chapter analyses the discourses on new forms of climate governance beyond state power, that is, beyond the traditional state-based modes of generating normativity. In doing so, this chapter engages with recent claims of a de-emphasizing of the state through the increasing number of transnational actors and activities, the growing role of universal institutions such as the UN, the universal ratification of multilateral treaties that protect international common interests, and the expanding jurisdiction of international courts and tribunals with quasi-compulsory jurisdiction.[4]

---

wicked problem' in 2012; see Kelly Levin and others, 'Overcoming the Tragedy of Super Wicked Problems: Constraining Our Future Selves to Ameliorate Global Climate Change' (2012) 45 Policy Sciences 123.

[2] See Section 4.

[3] Jutta Brunnée, 'The Rule of International (Environmental) Law and Complex Problem' in Heike Krieger, Georg Nolte, and Andreas Zimmermann (eds), *The International Rule of Law: Rise or Decline?* (CUP 2019) 24.

[4] eg Anna Peters, 'Compensatory Constitutionalism: The Function and Potential of Fundamental International Norms and Structures' (2006) 19 Leiden Journal of International Law 579; David Held, 'Law of States, Law of Peoples' (2002) 8 Legal Theory 1; Armin von Bogdandy, Philipp Dann, and Matthias Goldmann, 'Developing the Publicness of Public International Law: Towards a Legal Framework for Global Governance Activities' (2008) 9 German Law Journal 1; Mattias Kumm, 'The Cosmopolitan Turn in Constitutionalism: An Integrated Conception of Public Law' (2013) 20 Indiana Journal of Global Legal Studies 629; Larissa van den Herik 'The Individualization and Formalization of UN Sanctions' in Larissa van den Herik (eds), *Research Handbook on UN Sanctions and International Law* (Edward Elgar 2017); André Nollkaemper, 'Concurrence between Individual Responsibility and State Responsibility in International Law' (2003) 52 International Comparative Law Quarterly 615; Nico Krisch, 'The Decay of Consent: International Law in an Age of Global Public Goods'(2014) 108(1) American Journal of International Law 1; Jeffrey L Dunoff, 'Constitutional Conceits: The WTO's 'Constitution' and the Discipline of International Law' (2006) 17 European Journal of International Law 647.

This chapter is structured as follows. Section 1 first discusses current debates about authority beyond the state and the scholarly claims of a move away from the monopoly of states over global norm-making. Section 2 shows how similar scholarly debates were heard during the transition period from the Kyoto Protocol to the Paris Agreement. It also argues that the Paris Agreement offers a new understanding of climate governance in which the state is reconfigured as the coordinator of different governance levels and actors. Section 3 puts environmental law aside and draws some general lessons with respect to the question of the universality of international law. It ends with a few concluding remarks in Section 4.

1. Global Governance and Authority beyond the State

The idea of overcoming the fundamental premise of state centrism is most typically prevalent in discourses of international law and globalization. Globalization gave rise to a sense of urgency among international lawyers in coping with the 'new' global reality, such as the growing influence of networks of transnational actors, international institutions, the emerging space of global administrative law, and a myriad of informal and transnational rule-making processes.

International environmental cooperation is a good example of the foregoing. Coping with global environmental problems requires concerted actions by states with global coverage of substantial changes in domestic regulations and a serious commitment from both public and private actors. Most importantly, the response requires international institutions to manage *globally concerted actions* on a permanent basis. The increasing visibility of global problems requires a comprehensive and robust commitment from states and transnational actors while the decentralized structure of international law suffers from weak incentives for collective action.[5] While public goods cannot be completely spared from free riders as enforcement reciprocity does not work here, international organizations and institutions have been making efforts to enhance collective action by providing systems of monitoring and opportunities for capacity building.

In order to tackle global environmental problems, one may ask what type of agencies can be established beyond states.[6] 'Global governance' is a typical example of the new epistemic frameworks for constructing the responses to the challenges

---

[5] For climate change, the IPCC also repeatedly mentioned the issue of free riders in its assessment reports on mitigation (WG III). See eg the Third Assessment Report of the Intergovernmental Panel on Climate Change (IPCC) 'Climate Change 2001: Mitigation' (10.2.5 Partial Agreements); the Fourth Assessment Report of the Intergovernmental Panel on Climate Change (IPCC) 'Climate Change 2007: Mitigation' (1.2.3.6 Public good).

[6] It is in this sense that Paterson and others called governance one of 'the key themes in global environmental politics', see Matthew Paterson, David Humphreys, and Lloyd Pettiford, 'Conceptualizing Global Environmental Governance: From Interstate Regimes to Counter-Hegemonic Struggles' (2003) 3 Global Environmental Politics 1.

that concern these global problems. While the term 'global governance' 'means different things to different authors',[7] they agree that a type of cooperation required in fields such as global environmental law must be distinguished from traditional interstate cooperation. Since the 1970s, global politics on the topic has focused on the establishment of global governance structures to facilitate the process of enhancing collective engagement on a permanent basis.[8]

The concept of global governance is developed on the basis of recognition of a governance gap caused by a vacuum of sovereign authority beyond states and corresponding to a limited rule of law at the international level.[9] The notion of global governance has been sustained by the strong demand to keep international cooperation alive, despite the difficulty—stemming from its non-reciprocal nature—of cooperating on the maintenance of global public goods and free-riding incentives under the state-centric and consent-based construction of international relations and international law.

Young, for instance, aptly summarized the need for developing an alternative to the current anarchic regime of international governance: '[a]lthough the state is a positive force in managing natural resources and regulating pollution in domestic settings, the anarchic character of international society treated as a society of sovereign states constitutes a barrier to successful governance at the international level.'[10]

In order to enhance, manage, and anticipate global concerted action, international legal scholarship increasingly studies and delves into types of norm that are not fully captured by the interstate framework. Even after a series of doubts and concerns cast upon global governance during the 1990s and 2000s,[11] the basic

---

[7] Frank Biermann 'Global Governance and the Environment' in Michele M Betsill, Kathryn Hochstetler, and Dimitris Stevis (eds), *Palgrave Advances in International Environmental Politics* (Springer 2005) 239. Also see, in general, Paolo Contini and Peter H Sand, 'Methods to Expedite Environment Protection: International Ecostandards' (1972) 66 The American Journal of International Law 37.

[8] eg Frank Biermann, 'The Emerging Debate on the Need for a World Environment Organization: A Commentary' [2006] Global Environmental Politics 45; Steven Bernstein and Benjamin Cashore, 'Complex Global Governance and Domestic Policies: Four Pathways of Influence' (2012) 88 International Affairs 585; Rakhyun E Kim and Harro van Asselt, 'Global Governance: Problem Shifting in the Anthropocene and the Limits of International Law' in Elisa Morgera and Kati Kulovesi (eds), *Research Handbook on International Law and Natural Resources* (Edward Elgar 2016).

[9] eg Henrik Enroth 'The Concept of Authority Transnationalised' (2013) 4 Transnational Legal Theory 336, 345–46.

[10] Oran Young, 'Effectiveness of International Environmental Regimes: Existing Knowledge, Cutting-edge Themes, and Research Strategies' (2001) 108 Proceedings of the National Academy of Sciences of the United States of America 19853.

[11] Michael Zürn, 'Global Governance and Legitimacy Problems' (2004) 39 Government and Opposition 260; Amichai Cohen, 'Bureaucratic Internalization: Domestic Governmental Agencies and the Legitimization of International Law' (2005) 30 Georgetown Journal of International Law 1079; David Kennedy, 'The Mystery of Global Governance' (2008) 34 Ohio Northern University Law Review 827; Joseph HH Weiler, 'The Geology of International Law—Governance, Democracy and Legitimacy' (2004) 64 Zeitschrift für ausländisches öffentliches Recht und Völkerrecht 547; Daniel Bodansky, 'The Legitimacy of International Governance: A Coming Challenge for International Environmental Law?' (1999) 93 American Journal of International Law 596.

idea to uphold 'agency beyond states',[12] based on 'authority beyond states'[13] is still repeatedly asserted in various forms under the wider theoretical endeavour to construct global law in international environmental cooperation and other areas of cooperation in administering 'commons'.

The focus of multilateral environmental treaties since the late 1980s has increasingly been 'longer-term, irreversible, global threats'. Among these, climate change requires extensive changes in the socio-economic practices of each state, which demonstrate the qualitative difference of the international governance required, in comparison with international cooperation on other environmental topics, characterized by the efforts to harmonize domestic regulations on particular pollutants.[14]

In responding with a sense of urgency to develop such governance, multilateral treaty mechanisms, especially those with large memberships, are facing difficulty in developing timely solutions. In particular, the consent-based structure of international treaties is increasingly seen as a hurdle in securing the necessary concerted global acts. By the concept of law behind the mechanism of treaties, the state is almost the only lawmaking subject, and states are only obliged to abide by the rules to which they have consented.

Given the dissatisfaction with the state-centric structure, there are growing calls for 'a turn to authority' in explaining the concept of international law, given that its power is not tied to the exclusive realm of state sovereignty. The discourse is driven by a mixture of empirical claims, in which non-state actors—such as international institutional actors, and private and public actors—are more visible, and epistemological claims in which the scholars capture what is empirical. Some scholars deploy the concept of authority as the framework to discuss what seems to confer upon international institutions a certain decisional autonomy, which influences 'their freedom by unilaterally shaping the legal or factual situation' of 'subjects—individuals, private associations, enterprises, states, or other public institutions' for its accepted public purpose.[15]

In line with the discourse on the turn to authority, the idea of authority beyond the state has come to be used as an epistemological tool to make better sense of the issues in the basic framework of international law, in light of what is already recognized in the process of globalism. Through the concept of authority,[16] scholars argue that the empirically recognized changes associated with globalization and

---

[12] eg the concept of 'transnational environmental law'. See Veerle Heyvaert and Thijs Etty, 'Introducing Transnational Environmental Law' (2012) 1 Transnational Environmental Law 1.

[13] eg Birgit Peters and Johan Karlsson Schaffer, 'The Turn to Authority beyond States' [2013] Transnational Legal Theory 315; Bogdandy, Dann, and Goldmann (n 4); Michael Zürn, *A Theory of Global Governance: Authority, Legitimacy, and Contestation* (OUP 2018) pt 2.

[14] Daniel Bodansky, 'The History of the Global Climate Change Regime' in Urs Luterbacher and Detlef Spirinz (eds), *International Relations and Global Climate Change* (MIT Press 2001) 23.

[15] Bogdandy, Dann, and Goldmann (n 4) 5.

[16] The concept of 'authority' referred to in this chapter is chosen in the light of existing studies on global governance and international law.

notions of international public goods indicate that key normative decisions on the management of global problems are increasingly escaping from exclusive dominance by states and the traditional legal bindingness, which is exclusively conferred by the states.[17] In other words, these scholars started to see the need to reconstruct international law by shifting from its original character of 'interstate law' based on sovereignty to 'the law beyond states' that is based on the new, more inclusive, and possibly hierarchical authority, reflecting empirical observation on the emergence of new actors and places of norm creation.

In moving away from state centrism, this new view dismisses the binary concept of law as the issue of 'legally binding or not' that is strongly associated with consent by states, and aspires to grasp the concept of international law based on the new notion of the normativity of international law *qua* gradation of authority. The focus of the concept of law based on this authority-beyond-the-state thinking is seemingly more on the effect of norms in restricting the defining of actors' conduct than on the form of norms that is tied to state will. Based on this new intellectual framework of authority, international law scholars attempt to grasp a foundation of normativity of international law wide enough to capture the ongoing phenomenon of globalism that is beyond interstate frames.

Despite a significant escalation of the negative impacts of climate change and the sense of urgency to find effective solutions to the governance of global GHG emissions, traditional multilateral treaty mechanisms are rather slow and have fallen into a stalemate due to the large number of member states and conflicting stakes among them.[18] The sense of urgency based on such recognition has been a strong driver for scholars to argue for a theoretical trajectory where the sovereign-based paradigm is gradually ceding authority to a more liberal and cosmopolitan type of international legal order.[19] While the chapter does not evaluate whether this trajectory itself is good or bad, it is submitted here that such a trajectory, set by the context described in this chapter, could underlie the idea that enhanced normativity

---

[17] Bogdandy, Dann, and Goldmann (n 4); Zürn, *A Theory of Global Governance* (n 13); see also Kenneth W Abbott and Duncan Snidal, 'Strengthening International Regulation Through Transnational New Governance: Overcoming the Orchestration Deficit' (2009) 42 Vanderbilt Journal of Transnational Law 501; Michael Zürn, Martin Binder, and Matthias Ecker-Ehrhardt, 'International Authority and its Politicization' (2012) 4 International Theory 69; Joost Pauwelyn, Ramses A Wessel, and Jan Wouters, 'The Exercise of Public Authority through Informal International Lawmaking: An Accountability Issue?' (2016) Jean Monnet Working Paper 6/11.

[18] A 'stalemate' is generally seen as a pitfall of multilateral treaties with a large number of parties. Robert Falkner, Hannes Stephan, and John Vogler, 'International Climate Policy after Copenhagen: Towards a 'Building Blocks' Approach' (2010) 1 Global Policy 252, 260; Matthew J Hoffmann, *Climate Governance at the Crossroads* (OUP 2011) 8–9, 69–70; Maria Ivanova, 'Introduction—Politics Economics and Society' in Daniel Klein and others, *The Paris Agreement on Climate Change: Analysis and Commentary* (OUP 2017).

[19] Duncan B Hollis, 'Why State Consent Still Matters: Non-State Actors, Treaties, and the Changing Sources of International Law' (2005) 23 Berkeley Journal of International Law 1; Matthias Goldmann and Alexandra Kemmerer, 'Sources in the Meta-theory of International Law' in Jean d'Aspremont and Samantha Besson (eds), *The Oxford Handbook of the Sources of International Law* (OUP 2017).

is tied to the shift away from state centrism, which is commonly seen among criticisms of the Paris Agreement.

2. The Discourse of the State's Retreat and the UNFCCC

This section turns to the example of climate change and illustrates how the debate on the state's retreat from global governance described in the previous section has been playing out in the context of the UNFCCC. It argues that scholarly debates related to the UNFCCC are loaded with certain questionable normative presumptions[20] which do away with issues of diversity, limit strategic choices, and undermine the efficacy of solutions to the climate crisis.[21]

As was explained in the introduction, global problems such as climate change have been major case studies for examining questions on 'multilateral' or 'global' norm-making problems, which cannot typically be solved through traditional intergovernmentalism. Climate change is, among the many global environmental problems, a relatively well-researched issue. In fact, it has long been established that domestic and transnational actors must directly engage in the reduction of GHG emission.

Over more than two decades, the UN climate change negotiations have witnessed intense debates on how to achieve the universal cooperation necessary to fight climate change while simultaneously preserving space for particularity, complexity, and diversity among member states.[22] During this process, the move from the UNFCCC, adopted in 1992, to the Kyoto Protocol in 1997 was said to be informed by a so-called 'top-down approach' in order to create a highly centralized regime with mandatory emission reduction targets binding on Annex I parties, that is, the developed states among the UNFCCC members. As is well known, however, this approach has been replaced by the Paris Agreement in 2015 and is nowadays considered to mark a shift in international law on global climate change. In fact, the Paris Agreement is widely seen as reflecting a new 'bottom-up

---

[20] Peerenboom pointed out that the rule of law is biased towards liberal democratic values underlying Western versions of the rule of law. See Randall Peerenboom, 'Let One Hundred Flowers Bloom, One Hundred Schools Contend: Debating Rule of Law in China' (2002) 23 Michigan Journal of International Law 471, 473. For a general criticism of liberal assumptions, see Martti Koskenniemi, *The Gentle Civilizer of Nations: The Rise and Fall of International Law* (CUP 2010).

[21] eg Krygier emphasized that the rule of law is inherently *sociological* since it must be in 'sync with local ecologies'. See Martin Krygier, 'Four Puzzles about the Rule of Law: Why, What, Where? And Who Cares?' (2011) 50 Nomos: Getting to the Rule of Law 64, 86. See also Machiko Kanetake and André Nollkaemper (eds), *The Rule of Law at the National and International Levels: Contestations and Deference* (Hart Publishing 2016), in particular, the introductory chapter 'The International Rule of Law in the Cycle of Contestations and Deference'. For an empirical approach to the international rule of law, see Marc Hertogh, 'Your Rule of Law is not Mine: Rethinking Empirical Approaches to EU Rule of Law Promotion' (2016) 14 Asia Europe Journal 43.

[22] For a general overview of the climate negotiations, see eg Joyeeta Gupta, *The History of Global Climate Governance* (CUP 2014).

approach', characterized by pledges and a review mechanism. This new approach is based largely on voluntary state actions sustained by a series of procedural obligations at the international level while setting an ambitious temperature target to be achieved collectively.[23]

When the Kyoto Protocol was adopted under the UNFCCC at COP3 in 1997, it was considered a partial victory—but a victory nonetheless—for the international community. On the one hand, it succeeded in imposing an ambitious and legally binding ceiling on GHG emissions through a 'prescriptive, quantitative, time-bound, compliance backed' mechanism.[24] This feature is widely taken as a sign of centralization[25] or depoliticization[26] of international law on climate change. When the major framework conventions were established in the late 1980s and early 1990s, it was a common expectation that the Multilateral Environmental Agreements (MEAs) would gradually impose more substantial legal obligations on states.[27] The Kyoto Protocol was a milestone in this progressive trajectory of international environmental law. On the other hand, that victory is still partial because only the developed states listed in Annex I of the Protocol were required to reduce emissions during the first period of Kyoto commitments (2005–12).

Although the Kyoto Protocol succeeded in instigating a centralized system for the determination and implementation of the legal commitment, there was the obvious deficit of this binary structure between the developing and developed states, namely 'carbon leakage'. Carbon leakage is a type of free-rider problems that takes the form of an increase in GHG emissions from states *not* taking domestic action to cap emissions[28] that undermines the effectiveness of the global emission reduction scheme.[29] The top-down model of the Kyoto Protocol also failed to scale up.[30]

---

[23] Art 2(1)a of the Paris Agreement.
[24] Lavanya Rajamani, Jutta Brunnée, and Meinhard Doelle, 'Introduction: The Role of Compliance in an Evolving Climate Regime' in Jutta Brunnée, Meinhard Doelle, and Lavanya Rajamani (eds), *Promoting Compliance in an Evolving Climate Regime* (CUP 2012) 7.
[25] eg Joseph E Aldy and Robert N Stavins, 'Designing the Post Kyoto Climate Regime: Lessons from the Harvard Project on International Climate Agreements', An Interim Progress Report for the 14th Conference of the Parties, Framework Convention on Climate Change (24 November 2008) Harvard Project on International Climate Agreements; Steinar Andresen, 'International Climate Negotiations: Top-down, Bottom-up or a Combination?' (2015) 50 Italian Journal of International Affairs 15.
[26] Geir Ulfstein, 'Depoliticizing Compliance' in Brunnée, Doelle, and Rajamani (n 24).
[27] Robert Hahn and Kenneth Richards, 'The Internationalization of Environmental Regulation' (1989) 30 Harvard International Law Journal 421; Marc Pallemaerts, 'International Environmental Law from Stockholm to Rio: Back to the Future?' (1992) 1 Review of European Community & International Environmental Law 254.
[28] <IBT>Inter-governmental Panels on Climate Change (IPCC), Fourth Assessment Report Working Group III (2007) ch 11.7.2 (Carbon Leakage)</IBT>.
[29] ibid.
[30] eg Robert O Keohane and David G Victor, 'After the Failure of Top-down Mandates: The Role of Experimental Governance in Climate Change Policy' in Scott Barrett, Carlo Carraro, and Jaime de Melo (eds), *Towards a Workable and Effective Climate Regime* (Centre for Economic Policy Research 2015), especially 202; Alexandre Durand, 'Common Responsibility: The Failure of Kyoto' (2012) 34 Harvard International Law Review 1; Cinnamon P Carlarne, 'Rethinking A Failing Framework: Adaptation

Before the start of the second Kyoto commitment period, Canada and Japan announced that they would not participate in this period. This raises the question of international environmental law's effectiveness, which is not only about the stringency of commitments but also the wider participation of states.[31]

In the shift from the Kyoto Protocol to the Paris Agreement, two features of the Kyoto Protocol disappeared. The first was the assumption that there is a single best way forward to achieve the required reduction in global emissions. Carlarne aptly characterizes the nature of this shift, stating that 'the valiant efforts of the global community to negotiate a post-Kyoto treaty system have arrived at a crossroads and ... instead of focusing on finding the "right" pathway forward, there is a need to pursue multiple pathways'.[32] For instance, Article 4.2 of the Paris Agreement sets out the obligation of parties to register 'nationally determined commitments (NDCs)', which are self-proclaimed measures and goals to reduce GHG emissions. This does not include any obligation to actually fulfil said commitments, although it is recommended to increase the level of commitment over time to reflect the 'highest possible ambition' with regard to respective capabilities (Article 4.3). While the Paris Agreement sets the procedural obligation to register respective NDCs, in terms of substantial content states are solely bound by their own commitments made with regard to their respective national circumstances.

The second feature that vanished with the Paris Agreement was the black and white structure of the idea of 'differentiation'. In light of the principle of common but differentiated responsibility,[33] the Kyoto Protocol adopted a binary approach to determining the responsibility of developed states on the one hand and developing states on the other. In the post-Kyoto negotiations, this binary structure became more nuanced in order to reflect different national circumstances among all UNFCCC parties, rather than developed versus developing states. In 2009, the Copenhagen Accord proposed a framework which includes the bottom-up pledge and review system for both developed and developing states' mitigation commitments or actions.[34] This pledge and review mechanism was formally

and Institutional Rebirth for the Global Climate Change Regime' (2012) 25 Georgetown International Environmental Law Review 1–3.

[31] Daniel Bodansky, Jutta Brunnée, and Lavanya Rajamani, *International Climate Change Law* (OUP 2018) 6.
[32] Carlarne (n 30) 2–3.
[33] Art 3.1 of United Nations Framework Convention on Climate Change (1992): 'The Parties should protect the climate system for the benefit of present and future generations of humankind, on the basis of equity and in accordance with their common but differentiated responsibilities and respective capabilities. Accordingly, the developed country Parties should take the lead in combating climate change and the adverse effects thereof.'
[34] Under Decision 2/CP.15, both Annex I and non-Annex I parties were to define their own target levels and submit them in a defined format to the Secretariat. It must be noted that the Annex I party was to submit quantified economy-wide emissions targets while the non-Annex I party was to submit mitigation actions. See paras 4 and 5.

endorsed through the Cancun Agreement in 2010.[35] At COP17, in 2011, the UNFCCC Parties created the Ad Hoc Working Group on the Durban Platform for Enhanced Action (hereafter ADP), which adopted a mandate to develop this new instrument: a protocol, another legal instrument, or an agreed outcome with legal force under the Convention 'applicable to all Parties'[36] was to be adopted no later than 2015.

The Paris Agreement, through these substantial changes, establishes a common legal framework that includes both developed and developing states, in which every state determines its own commitment with a view to its respective national circumstances. While the Paris Agreement is undoubtfully a major diplomatic success that brings together the UNFCCC parties under a single legal framework, a number of authors underlined its 'informal and soft nature'[37] or a 'lack'[38] of obligation, since its form is not internationally enforceable. Other scholars also placed the Paris Agreement in a broader perspective, describing nationally determined contributions as a symbol of the primacy of domestic politics in international cooperation on climate change.[39] If not meant as a criticism, they generally viewed this re-acknowledgment of the primacy of state discretion as a pragmatic result of negotiation rather than a reflection of the normative core of international environmental law. While the responses vary, a common element is the perception that the Paris Agreement deviates from the previous trajectory. These scholars point out the blurring role of a treaty instrument and an international institution in the overall climate change regime, which was traditionally considered a mechanism of international regulation in delivering the necessary responses.[40]

---

[35] Decision 1/CP.16.

[36] Decision 1/CP.17, para 2.

[37] Jennifer Jacquet and Dale Jamieson, 'Soft but Significant Power in the Paris Agreement' (2016) 6 Nature Climate Change 43; Harro van Asselt, 'International Climate Change Law in a Bottom-up World' (2016) 26 Questions of International Law; Sebastian Oberthur and Ralph Bodle, 'Legal Form and Nature of the Paris Outcome Special Issue on Paris Agreement' (2016) 6 Climate Law 58.

[38] Anne-Marie Slaughter, 'The Paris Approach to Global Governance' (*Project-Syndicate*, 28 December 2015) <https://www.project-syndicate.org/commentary/paris-agreement-model-for-global-governance-by-anne-marie-slaughter-2015-12 >accessed 18 January 2024; also Richard Falk, 'Voluntary International Law and the Paris Agreement' (*richardfalk.org*, 16 January 2016) <https://richardfalk.wordpress.com/2016/01/16/voluntary-international-law-andthe-paris-agreement/> accessed 18 January 2024.

[39] eg Radoslav S Dimitrov, 'The Paris Agreement on Climate Change: Behind Closed Doors' (2016) 16 Global Environmental Politics 8–10; Carlo Carraro, 'A Bottom-Up, Non-Cooperative Approach to Climate Change Control: Assessment and Comparison of Nationally Determined Contributions (NDCs)' (January 2018) CEPR Discussion Paper No DP12627; Robert Falkner, 'The Paris Agreement and the New Logic of International Climate Politics' (2016) 92(5) International Affairs 1107, 1116–18; Anne van Aaken, 'Is International Law Conducive to Preventing Looming Disasters?' (2016) 7 Global Policy 81, especially 83.

[40] See eg Jutta Brunnée, 'COPing with Consent: Law-Making Under Multilateral Environmental Agreements' (2002) 15 Leiden Journal of International Law 1, 2. (Observing 'the requirement of consent is seen to undercut the dynamic forces, such as growing consensus among parties regarding the problem at hand and appropriate response actions, that may unfold within a regime and pull participants towards collective action. Thus, the increasing sense of urgency in combating global environmental problems has prompted calls for new approaches to international environmental law-making, including approaches that help overcome the constraints of the consent requirement.')

Yet, it must be acknowledged that the question whether the Paris Agreement is a 'change' of trajectory by reluctant state parties or an 'improvement' that makes the legal regime more effective is a value judgement. For those who think that keeping state supremacy at bay is the self-expressed purpose of international law, it appears that the trajectory of progress set out by the Kyoto Protocol was interrupted by reluctant state parties. For them, the Paris Agreement can be a successful political compromise[41] but not a reflection of the normative body of international law applied to the field of climate change. In contrast, some authors argue that the Paris Agreement already goes beyond 'business as usual'.[42] But many express concerns that the respective procedural obligations are not tied to the global legal target of keeping temperature rise below 2 degrees.[43]

From the perspective defended in this chapter, it is contended that the transition from the Kyoto Protocol to the Paris Agreement indicates how much domestic actors matter in making international agreements of this kind, reflecting the subjects that directly influence the daily life of these actors.

From this view, it is not clear whether this can be solved through a vertical and top-down approach when reluctance to commit by some states results from a lack of consensus among their domestic actors. From this perspective, while international law may have gone through fundamental changes over recent decades, this does not mean that what replaces the traditional understanding of state centrism is a universal, cooperative, pluralistic, and liberal-cosmopolitan system. The interstate frame simplifies thinking, in the sense that international law does not have to deal with the politics behind the veil of state. This is where states continue to have unique role as 'intermediators' in creating a state position that can be unitary enough to be expressed as consent.

In that sense, the structure of the Paris Agreement can be seen as an evolution towards the clear recognition and internalizing of the necessary process of coordination by the states parties between diverse domestic demands of their respective national circumstances, in deciding their level of ambition as a state, and between the global demand of necessary reduction and the level of ambition that it commits to.

---

[41] eg Benoit Mayer, 'Construing International Climate Change Law as a Compliance Regime' (2018) 7 Transnational Environmental Law 118.
[42] eg Daniel Bodansky 'The Paris Climate Change Agreement: A New Hope?' (2016) 110 American Journal of International Law 316.
[43] Annalisa Savaresi 'The Paris Agreement: A New Beginning?' (2015) 34 Journal of Energy & Natural Resources Law 25–26;; Charlotte Streck, Paul Keenlyside, and Moritz von Unger, 'The Paris Agreement: A New Beginning' (2016) 13 Journal for European Environmental and Planning Law 3; Richard Falkner, 'The Paris Agreement and the New Logic of International Climate Politics' (2016) 92 International Affairs 1107; Oran Young, 'The Paris Agreement: Destined to Succeed or Doomed to Fail?' (2016) 4 Politics and Governance 124; Robert O Keohane and David Victor, 'Cooperation and Discord in Global Climate Policy' (2016) 6 Nature Climate Change 570.

3. Where Does this Leave us? Redefining the Role of States beyond the Antagonism between Universality and Particularity

The previous section illustrated the transition from the Kyoto Protocol to the Paris Agreement that is characterized by an underlying dichotomy according to which the state is pitted against the top-down and centralized approach to enhancing international control over GHG emissions. While there are a number of areas where the contractual regime of international law is prevalent,[44] new challenges following the deepening of globalization accelerated the understanding that, for certain areas of international law, key political and legal decisions are moving beyond the purview of states. The previous sections showed that, on the one hand, all these perceived challenges of globalization strengthened discourses which claim that the paradigm of state centrism is becoming obsolete and, accordingly, a renewal in the framework of international law is necessary.[45] On the other hand, these concepts may structurally underestimate the remaining complexity currently mediated by states as intermediaries.

This brings us back to the theme of this volume and the antagonism between universality and particularity. In discussing global governance and international law, it must be recalled that the idea of 'law as system' inevitably requires, at least, the construction of a universal base of a logical nature, which creates a point of struggle for international law.[46] The struggle remains even for the case where one attempts to conceive of international law only in a functional sense.[47] A similar intention to construct a universal base exists for the discourse of authority beyond states, building upon the empirical observation of decades of continued efforts to keep international cooperation functioning.

In constructing universality, however, it is necessary to pay attention to critiques touching on the existence of regional and national diversities, as well as the uneven allocation of political power, that are easily cloaked under sound universalistic presumptions. This pattern of critique echoes the postmodern critique[48] which

---

[44] eg Catherine Brölmann, 'Law-Making Treaties: Form and Function in International Law' (2005) 74 Nordic Journal of International Law 383.

[45] Brunnée, 'COPing with Consent' (n 40); Krisch (n 4); Judith Goldstein and others, 'Introduction: Legalization and World Politics' in Judith Goldstein and others (eds), *Legalization and World Politics* (MIT Press 2001); Richard A Falk, 'Toward a New World Order' in Saul H Mendlovitz (ed), *On the Creation of Just World Order: Preferred Worlds for the 1990s* (FreePress 1975). See also other references in n 7.

[46] Austin is known for his statement that international law is not law 'properly so called'—John Austin, *The Province of Jurisprudence Determined* (1832). Hart also distinguished the system of international law from any system of municipal law. See Herbert Hart, *The Concept of Law* (Penelope A Bulloch and Joseph Raz eds, 2nd edn, Clarendon Press 1997) particularly ch 10.

[47] For a hidden universalism in 'the turn to function' for comparative legal studies, see Anne Peters and Heiner Schwenke, 'Comparative Law beyond Post-Modernism' (2000) 49 The International and Comparative Law Quarterly 800, 808–10.

[48] For the sake of this chapter, 'postmodern critique' refers to a series of reactions towards uncritical submission to the ideas of the Enlightenment, whereby God is substituted by equally uncontested

casts doubt on the postulation of readily recognizable and universally applicable principles.[49]

In short, antagonism between seeking and denying universality is part of the life cycle of healthy legal discourses.[50] For the sake of innovating international law in response to new challenges, the problem is rather the extreme oscillation between (over-)scepticism and (over-)affirmation of the universality of international law.[51]

The logical necessity of universality is rooted in the very pattern of legal reasoning. In this regard, international legal discourses necessarily pursue two seemingly contradictory goals—one is to *neutralize* conflict among the political powers by *overcoming* particularity to generate a universal basis, and the other is to *preserve* the plurality of conflicting political powers by *uplifting* particularity.[52] This dynamic is itself an indispensable part of how legal discourses reimagine how international law applies.

It can be stated that international law can only exist between universality and particularity. Law, by its very nature, depends on the existence of manageable discrepancy. Should it reach either end, law is equated either with the supreme authority that there is no discrepancy among legal subjects, or complete relativity where anything goes. From this perspective, the existence of law is dependent on the coexistence of universality and particularity. Complete universality will never be achieved through law: once such universality is achieved, law can only be equated with supreme, hence absolute, authority. This is why it is important to

---

grounds (eg reason, progress, justice, or being 'scientific'). Many of those postmodern reactions have fuelled the critical attitude of critical legal scholars.

[49] This is the basis of Carl Schmitt's criticism of Kelsen. See, in general, Sylvie Delacroix, 'Schmitt's Critique of Kelsenian Normativism' [2005] Ratio Juris 30; for similar views, Anne Orford, 'The Destiny of International Law' (2004) 17 Leiden Journal of International Law 441; David Kennedy, *International Legal Structures* (Nomos Verlagsgesellschaft mbH & Co 1987); Friedrich V Kratochwil, *Rules, Norms and Decisions: On the Conditions of Practical and Legal Reasoning in Internacional Relations and Domestic Affairs* (CUP 1989).

[50] See eg Maiko Meguro 'Appraisal of Diversity in International Law: A Note on Self-Serving Biases and Interdisciplinarity' in Pauline Westerman, Kostiantyn Gorobets, and Andreas Hadjigeorgiou (eds), *Philosophical (De)Constructions of International Law* (Edward Elgar 2022) Available at SSRN: <https://ssrn.com/abstract=3871186> accessed 18 January 2024.

[51] The image of oscillation, or antagonism, between universality and particularity is recurring in various streams of legal thought; eg Ernesto Laclau, *Emancipation(s)* (Verso 2007); Martti Koskenniemi, *The Gentle Civilizer of Nations: The Rise and Fall of International Law 1870–1960* (CUP 2004); Armin von Bogdandy and Sergio Dellavalle 'The Paradigms of Universalism and Particularism as Paradigms of International Law' (2008) IILJ Working Paper 2008/3; Orford (n 49); Philippe Allot, 'The Concept of International Law' (1999) 10 European Journal of International Law 31; Bruno Simma, 'Universality of International Law from the Perspective of a Practitioner' (2009) 20 European Journal of International Law 265; Joost Pauwelyn 'Europe, America and the Unity of International Law' (2006) Duke Law School Legal Studies Paper No 103; Dirk Pulkowski 'Narratives of Fragmentation: International Law between Unity and Multiplicity' (2005) ESIL Agora Paper.

[52] According to Carlo Galli, this antagonism is the core of Carl Schmitt's theoretical inquiry. Introduced by Thalin Zarmanian, 'Carl Schmitt and the Problem of Legal Order: From Domestic to International' (2006) 19 Leiden Journal of International Law 41, 48–49.

appreciate that, while law is always based on a move towards universality, one must always seek to reveal the power structure at work in law.

As was mentioned in the previous sections, the normative biases underlying existing thinking patterns or the 'trajectory' on globalism lead some international lawyers to make assumptions about the challenges which seemingly cause friction with the existing state-centred frameworks and concepts. While a state is rendered a problem rather than a solution in the realization of the communal ideal from these standpoints, they rarely explore the possible structural reasons for why, precisely, states are acting problematically. The reason why moving away from the consent-based model would effectively deal with the lack of consensus has not been addressed in international law.[53] The state can even be a defensive wall against interventionism under the name of 'interest beyond the borders', given the uneven political and normative powers in the world.

Even if one claims that, in the name of progressive universality, the old paradigm of state centrism must be changed in order to enhance the ongoing verticalization and individualization of global law, there must be an alternative solution to uplift and protect particularity. The argumentation is shaped without actually evaluating the degree of diversity across the different legal traditions of the world,[54] and without actually studying the functions that states serve in the contemporary landscape. Considering the importance of civil society in climate change discussions, it might be questioned whether states are blocking civil society's demands. In that sense, we must question whether people in different parts of the world and different social segments actually share the same values and political priorities with a view to the 'international common interests'. From a different perspective,[55] states can also be seen as the actors to fill the gap between the expectations of international and national communities. All these various arguments and perspectives are driven by different assumptions about the role of the state in international law and the maintenance of international order which this chapter has tried to unpack.

---

[53] For this point, see Maiko Meguro 'Tracing Influence in International Law: Beyond the Antagonism between Doctrine of Law and Social Science', forthcoming in Rossana Deplano and Nicholas Tsagourias (eds), *Research Methods in International Law: A Handbook* (Edward Elgar), available at SSRN: <https://ssrn.com/abstract=3597945> accessed 18 January 2024. From this perspective, there have been a few studies from 'insiders' of climate change negotiations. See Radoslav Dimitrov and others, 'Institutional and Environmental Effectiveness: Will the Paris Agreement Work?' (2019) 10 WIREs Climate Change.

[54] The alleged consensus for fundamental values and principles remains vague and general, and the substantial content can differ to a significant degree. See eg Maiko Meguro 'Backlash against International Law by the East?—How the Concept of Transplantation Helps Us to Better Understand Reception Processes of International Law' (*Völkerrechtsblog*, 11 January 2019) <https://voelkerrechtsblog.org/articles/backlash-against-international-law-by-the-east/> accessed 18 January 2024.

[55] There has been some debate on the fictious nature of unitary state. For example, Kelsen claimed that the concept of state is a purely normative one, stating that 'the state is not a visible or tangible body': Hans Kelsen, *General Theory of Law and the State* (tr Anders Wedberg, Harvard University Press 1949) 191.

4. Concluding Remarks

The previous sections have shown that the Paris Agreement can be construed as reflecting a new way to strike a balance between universality and particularity by re-emphasizing the role of states in light of the actors behind them. The pedigree of international environmental law has commonly been characterized by a centralized approach to setting a common standard to harmonize domestic regulations in a top-down way. However, the Kyoto Protocol, as the primary example, faced political constraints at the domestic level on the part of major emitters, including the United States. Article 4.2. of the Paris Agreement adopted the 'nationally determined commitment', which allows each state to define its own commitment towards the reduction of emissions in terms of the amount and means according to its respective national circumstances. From the viewpoint defended in this chapter, the Paris Agreement establishes a new normative account that reflects particularities without forsaking the framework of international law. The Agreement represents a new vision whereby the role of the state as the coordinator of different governance levels and actors is recognized. In this regard, allowing for discretion rather than policing it is not a sign of the weakness of the law on the matter.

It goes without saying that this chapter does not claim that states are the only effective unit for enhancing international common interests. The role of transnational movements and institutions is never discounted in mobilizing support and the necessary attention to what is happening at the domestic level. Together with adequate financing and technological cooperation, the role of various internet and social media tools in transnational and domestic arenas should also be recognized for encouraging various actors at the domestic level, and also states.

The chapter invited readers to envisage the possibility of an alternative path for international lawyers by looking beyond the traditional antagonism between universality and particularity. According to the depiction of the law's state of limbo between universality and particularity presented here, replacing state centrism with vague authorities stemming from an undisclosed normative orientation can be equally 'lawless'.

This ultimately means, as far as the particularities behind the veil of the state are concerned, that states play an important role in collecting and coordinating the various interests of domestic actors in the cycle of international lawmaking, interpretation, and application. In this regard, when international lawyers face the question of necessary but unattainable universality, the recalibration of states as the focal point of particularities can be proposed as a key feature. Advancing this alternative vision for redefining the role of states can only be done by empirically studying the actual function that states play. This is not an exercise in deconstructing what renders international law 'law', but it rather suspends the tragic perpetuation of the gap between the over-scepticism and over-affirmation of universality due to different assumptions.

For climate change, the cost and combination of options for adopting measures differ significantly according to different national circumstances as well as the natural conditions of each state. In this regard, even where speaking of universal norms in the abstract is accepted, accusations or harsh criticisms of a particular country whose contribution is 'not ambitious enough' can be reminiscent of calling a certain category of states and peoples 'barbaric' or 'non-civilized'. These labelling exercises have always characterized certain actors as obstacles to the application of international law. And the same goes for the current climate change issue, if the standard of criticism does not take into account the diversity of demands and necessities in responding to climate change. As was shown in this chapter, the Paris Agreement crystallized the approach according to which the absence of a universal standard for legally evaluating each state's contribution to tackling climate change does not sideline the centrality of states, be they developed, developing, or vulnerable states.

17
Oscillating Justice
Between Universal and Particular

Zinaida Miller

Universalism has been both the proud rallying cry of international criminal law—delivering justice on behalf of humanity—and its downfall—subject to accusations of neocolonialism, tone-deaf legalism, and imperial imposition. In defence against the latter, international criminal law advocates have emphasized the International Criminal Court's (ICC) doctrine of complementarity and the support offered by international tribunals to domestic rules of law. Transitional justice has alternately been congratulated and condemned for its contextual flexibility and its 'toolkit' approach to legal and political change. Together, these interwoven threads form a complex mesh of international justice. That tapestry has long been characterized not just by claims to universality or particularity but by distress over the tensions between them. Focusing on distress or tension alone, however, misses the significance of both for the project of international justice, its justifications, and its limits. This chapter argues that continuously moving *between* claims to disinterested global application and contextualized, plural practice bolsters the legitimacy of international justice while contributing to an ongoing failure to attend fully to racialized and colonial dynamics and histories.

In this chapter, I track the performance of universality and particularity in the discourse and practice of these forms of justice. Justice advocates suggest that, like their fellow travellers in human rights and humanitarian law, these practices function optimally if they apply in the same manner to everyone everywhere at all times. Yet international justice enterprises justify their universality by emphasizing not just the critical need for a uniform response but the ability of the doctrines and institutions to differentiate, particularize, and contextualize. They do so through a combination of disciplinary, institutional, doctrinal, and discursive techniques. In the vocabulary of international justice, universality signifies practices that apply equally to diverse actors and situations; it has both a spatial dimension (global reach) and a temporal one (continuous applicability).

This chapter argues that international justice attempts to legitimize itself precisely through its oscillation between universal and particular. The latter is less hidden in the former than touted as its balancing (and thus legitimating) characteristic.[1] Following Ilana Feldman and Miriam Ticktin, the goal here is not to 'debunk' universality itself by demonstrating how particular it really is but rather to 'explore the ... claim-making itself'.[2] Claims about both universal and particular often reinforce (and obscure) familiar racialized and colonial hierarchies.[3] They do so through continual movement between the poles of universality (expressed as equal treatment of diverse actors through disinterested legal institutions and doctrines) and particularity (understood as contextualized justice tailored to specific needs and histories).

The universality claimed in international justice discourses is, as Sundhya Pahuja argues of international law more broadly, both 'unavoidable' and 'unstable'.[4] The instability derives not just from the oscillation between universal and particular but from its outer parameters. Whether it is the possibility of broad amnesties or the choice by a society to collectively forget rather than publicly remember, not every particular or plural option is available.[5] Thus the unavoidable universality of international justice depends upon its apparent local flexibility while remaining unstable within its unspoken limits.

This chapter focuses on the ways in which international justice discourses and practices fluctuate between a commitment to the universal and to the particular. Section 1 explores the establishment of a disciplinary and institutional divide between international criminal law (led by lawyers, focused on punitive justice, and centralized through courts) and transitional justice (comprised of multiple disciplines, focused on truth, open to amnesties, and represented by truth commissions). Separating the two in this fashion allows international criminal law to appear as the avatar of universal justice while transitional justice produces particularistic mechanisms premised on local need. In reality, however, this is a technique to reinforce the oscillation on which the international justice enterprise as an inclusive whole relies. The legitimacy and legitimation effects of international justice rely upon invoking the practices as both universally applied and contextually differentiated.

Section 2 explores international criminal law's contribution to the rise of anti-impunity in human rights. Anti-impunity reflects a dual commitment to standardizing approaches to (certain forms of) violence while supporting differentiated

---

[1] This is not, of course, to suggest that international criminal law or transitional justice do not share with the broader international legal sphere the tendency to declare as universal that which is eminently particular and usually Eurocentric. See Chapter 1. To the contrary, the final section explores those tendencies.

[2] Ilana Feldman and Miriam Ticktin, *In the Name of Humanity: The Government of Threat and Care* (Duke University Press 2010) 3.

[3] This chapter is indebted to TWAIL analyses of international justice, particularly but not only in its criminal law form. See eg Asad Kiyani, John Reynolds, and Sujith Xavier, 'Foreword: Third World Approaches to International Criminal Law' (2016) 14(4) Journal of International Criminal Justice 915.

[4] Sundhya Pahuja, *Decolonising International Law: Development, Economic Growth and the Politics of Universality* (CUP 2011) 41.

[5] Zinaida Miller, 'Temporal Governance: The Times of Transitional Justice' (2021) 21(5) International Criminal Law Review 848.

approaches to justice through complementarity. In doing so, international criminal law simultaneously enforces a narrowed conception of violence and justice while utilizing victims' centrality as a defence against accusations of neocolonialism or hegemonic imposition. Section 3 turns to the promotion of truth-telling in transitional justice, which invokes contextual particularity as a strength but also justifies a universalized human rights goal (right to truth) and narrative (about progress born from atrocity). In the process, 'truth' narrows within the political and legal parameters of place, structure, and history, reinforcing hierarchies of suffering and harm.

Section 4 suggests that the balancing between universal and particular enacted by international justice discourses diverts attention away from certain forms of particularity and towards others. The racialized and colonial aspects of both the discourse and practices of international justice are less visible when the enterprise as a whole is legitimized through its claims to integrate universality and particularity. This section briefly sketches two sites in which the particularities of race and coloniality are marginalized: victimhood and temporality.

1. Universal Criminal Law, Particular Transitional Justice

The international justice enterprise described here—comprised of a variety of practices designed to combat international crimes, reckon with past atrocities, prevent the recurrence of violence, and punish perpetrators—includes both international criminal and transitional justice. Among the ways in which that overarching enterprise has managed the tension between the universal and particular has been the historical, disciplinary, and discursive treatment of international justice as comprised of two distinct fields. That distinction emphasizes the ways in which one set of practices can balance the other: if international criminal prosecutions represent imperial overreach, truth commissions can focus on local histories. If governments allow too many amnesties or not enough due process, international criminal law can ensure equal treatment among diverse countries. As this chapter reveals, however, each practice itself encompasses an oscillation between universal and particular.

In many versions, international criminal law and transitional justice have separate histories that eventually converge. Ruti Teitel begins her genealogy of transitional justice with Nuremberg, although she situates these post-World War II efforts as a reaction to the failures after World War I to achieve either justice or conflict prevention.[6] For Teitel, the 'period immediately following World War II

---

[6] On the narrative and genealogical significance of Nuremberg for international law, see David Koller, '... and New York and The Hague and Tokyo and Geneva and Nuremberg and ... : The Geographies of International Law' (2012) 23 European Journal of International Law 97.

was the heyday of international justice', characterized by 'an internationalist policy [that] was thought to guarantee rule of law'.[7] Thus, the trials at Nuremberg are incorporated into the transitional justice genealogy, along with the ad hoc tribunals during what Teitel calls the third phase of transitional justice. By contrast, Paige Arthur focuses on the invention of the term 'transitional justice' rather than the conception of justice in times of domestic political transition; as a result, she dates the development of the field to the 1980s.[8] The genealogies of both remain heavily contested.[9]

As academic and doctrinal fields, international criminal law and transitional justice remain separate in ways that enact a division between universality and particularity. Despite the heavy-handed influence of lawyers and legalism on transitional justice, the praxis field remains defined in part by its trans-disciplinary approach. Transitional justice developed on the basis of transnational and comparative exchanges, both academically and institutionally.[10] International criminal law, by contrast, produces itself as a doctrinal legal field comprised of aspects of both domestic criminal law and the public international fields of humanitarian and human rights law whose norms it seeks to enforce.[11] In this sense, while international criminal law is sometimes interpreted as part and parcel of transitional justice—specifically, when prosecutions take place in, or with regard to, governmental transition or recent conflict—the field as a whole operates by different protocols.

Signature institutions and practices further emphasize the difference between a universalizing field focused on courts and a particular one characterized by truth commissions.[12] The combined growth in institutional apparatus for prosecutions and development of an accepted anti-impunity norm in human rights bolstered universalist conceptions of retributive and punitive justice. Whether in the export of particular models of criminal justice abroad, the increased emphasis on criminalization in the trafficking and immigration arenas, or amplified attention to a duty to prosecute mass human rights violations, criminal law became a key component of international governance.[13] The establishment of the International Criminal

---

[7] Ruti Teitel, 'Human Rights in Transition: Transitional Justice Genealogy' (2003) 13 Harvard Human Rights Journal 69, 73.

[8] Paige Arthur, 'How 'Transitions' Shaped Human Rights: A Conceptual History of Transitional Justice' (2009) 31 Human Rights Quarterly 321.

[9] Marcos Zunino, *Justice Framed: A Genealogy of Transitional Justice* (CUP 2019); Kevin Jon Heller and Gerry Simpson (eds), *The Hidden Histories of War Crimes Trials* (OUP 2013).

[10] Neil Kritz, *How Emerging Democracies Reckon with Former Regimes* (USIP Press 1995).

[11] One of the leading casebooks on international criminal law begins with a discussion of transitional justice but almost entirely as a discussion of the purposes of criminal justice; shortly thereafter, the casebook moves away from any discussion of transitional justice or non-retributive mechanisms. Beth Van Schaak and Ronald C Slye, *International Criminal Law and Its Enforcement: Cases and Materials* (4th edn, West 2020).

[12] Jamie Rowen, *Searching for Truth in the Transitional Justice Movement* (CUP 2017).

[13] Allegra McLeod, 'Exporting US Criminal Justice' (2010) 29 Yale L & Pol'y Rev 83; Janet Halley and others (eds), *Governance Feminism: Notes from the Field* (University of Minnesota Press 2019); Diane

Tribunals for the Former Yugoslavia and Rwanda, followed by the passage of the Rome Statute in 1998, reflected and contributed to a transformation of the human rights movement towards anti-impunity and of anti-impunity as code for retributive justice.[14] Domestic trials conducted under universal jurisdiction and hybrid institutions such as the Special Court for Sierra Leone reflected parallel commitments to criminal prosecutions in response to conflict and atrocity.

In her influential book, Kathryn Sikkink argued that a 'justice cascade' characterized by increasing prosecutions and the diminishing impunity of leaders reflected a positive, powerful, and unexpected global development.[15] Despite early scepticism in the human rights movement about state power as well as broader criticisms of national criminal justice systems, a triumphalist narrative of war crimes trials developed and hardened after the Cold War.[16] In the international and human rights arenas, fighting impunity through the specific technique of criminal prosecution offered a standardized, doctrinal response to atrocity crimes defined primarily as crimes against humanity, war crimes, and genocide. When critiques of the ICC emerged, they often focused on the gap between the Court's promises and its delivery rather than on the accuracy or desirability of the universality claim itself. Thus, even as more scholars and advocates argued that the ICC's claims to equal treatment were betrayed by an overweening focus on African perpetrators, fewer suggested that the claim of universality itself was problematic in an ineluctably unequal world.[17]

Transitional justice by contrast constructed the category of 'local' justice in response to criticisms of cookie-cutter institutions, encouraging a perception of transitional justice as a patchwork quilt rather than monochromatic justice.[18] Yet these institutions were dogged either by accusations that they were 'too local' (and thus failed to meet the expectations of primarily Global North donors or advocates looking for due process or quasi-retributive mechanisms) or that they were 'not local enough' (and thus not able to solve the problem). For example, the *mato*

Orentlicher, "Settling Accounts' Revisited: Reconciling Global Norms with Local Agency' (2007) 1 International Journal of Transitional Justice 10.

[14] Karen Engle, Zinaida Miller, and Dennis Davis (eds), *Anti-Impunity and the Human Rights Agenda* (CUP 2016).
[15] Kathryn Sikkink, *The Justice Cascade: How Human Rights Prosecutions Are Changing World Politics* (WW Norton & Co 2011).
[16] Karen Engle, 'Anti-Impunity and the Turn to Criminal Law in Human Rights' (2014) 100 Cornell Law Review 1070; Gary Bass, *Stay the Hand of Vengeance: The Politics of War Crimes Tribunals* (Princeton University Press 2002).
[17] New work in the field has both highlighted this point and expanded into more radical critiques of the conceptualizations of international justice. See eg Grietje Baars, *The Corporation, Law and Capitalism: A Radical Perspective on the Role of Law in the Global Political Economy* (Brill 2019); Kamari M Clarke, *Affective Justice: The International Criminal Court and the Pan-Africanist Pushback* (Duke University Press 2019).
[18] Rosalind Shaw, Lars Waldorf, and Pierre Hazan (eds), *Localizing Transitional Justice: Interventions and Priorities After Mass Violence* (Stanford University Press 2010).

oput ceremonies in Northern Uganda were often cited as exemplars of attempts by local communities to follow their own post-conflict rituals—and of resistance from a global transitional justice community that objected to any perceived lack of accountability for perpetrators.[19] Dustin Sharp suggests that the persistent and increasingly mainstream calls for 'local ownership' allowed a 'potentially radical concept' to slip ever more towards becoming an 'empty signifier'.[20]

The institutional and discursive divide established between different areas of international justice sometimes allows one to stand for the transcendence of retributive justice while the other appears as the contextualist and particularist answer to hegemony. In certain cases, this division reinforces the classical law/politics divide, placing universalist legal neutrality on the side of criminal law and particularist political investments on the side of transitional justice. In fact, however, this is only one of several techniques by which the articulation and institutionalization of justice and truth depend upon a constant oscillation between an ostensible universal and its various Others.

2. Punishing Wrongs: Universalizing Retribution, Particularizing Prosecution

Much of the 'allure' of international criminal law, John Reynolds and Sujith Xavier point out, lies in 'the illusion of universality [and] promises of accountability and deterrence'.[21] Claims to that illusory and elusive universality manifest in the assertion of international criminal law as the institutional and doctrinal home of an equitable, disinterested, and positivistic rule of law.[22] If the viability or privileging of those declarations comes under duress, international criminal discourses turn instead to claims of strengthening domestic rule of law or serving specific communities. In service of the latter, international criminal law accommodates, constructs, and is constituted by its own particularistic oppositions. Specific legal rules

---

[19] This was particularly acute in Uganda after the ICC indicted several Lord's Resistance Army leaders for crimes committed in northern Uganda. See Erin Baines, 'The Haunting of Alice: Local Approaches to Justice and Reconciliation in Northern Uganda' (2007) 1 International Journal of Transitional Justice 91. Similarly, some of the contestation over the gacaca trials in Rwanda revealed a struggle between praise for a local mechanism that differed from classic retributive justice and discomfort with the lack of classic due process guarantees in its practice. See eg Human Rights Watch, *Justice Compromised: The Legacy of Rwanda's Community-Based Gacaca Courts* (2011); Phil Clark, *The Gacaca Courts, Post-Genocide Justice and Reconciliation in Rwanda: Justice Without Lawyers* (CUP 2010).

[20] Dustin Sharp, *Rethinking Transitional Justice for the Twenty-First Century: Beyond the End of History* (CUP 2018) 42.

[21] John Reynolds and Sujith Xavier, "'The Dark Corners of the World': TWAIL and International Criminal Justice' (2016) 14(4) Journal of International Criminal Justice 959, 960.

[22] '[T]he notion of impunity galvanized a movement intent on eradicating the differential and unequal application of justice. Activists insisted that no one is above the law ... This core value of anti-impunity that is enshrined in the Rome Statute dates back to the World War I era', Clarke, *Affective Justice* (n 17) 70.

are mobilized to accommodate difference while upholding claims to universal applicability and audience. The doctrine, practice, and narrative of international retributive justice derive legitimacy from this intricate assertion of both broad reach and specific application.

While claiming a universal struggle against atrocity, international criminal justice has consistently targeted only some harms, countries, and perpetrators. For example, Vasuki Nesiah has argued that the history of anti-impunity demonstrates the persistence of impunity, revealing the particularity of the supposedly universal or hegemonic embrace of prosecution.[23] Nesiah's historical analysis reveals the ways in which claims to a universal struggle against atrocity, inhumanity, and violence obscure the narrow, biased definitions of those terms. Grietje Baars calls the endemic exclusion of corporations from international criminal accountability 'planned impunity' to mark the ways in which international criminal law facilitates corporate power by 'spiriting away the relationships of oppression' that underpin it.[24] Nesiah, Baars, and other critical scholars reveal the ways in which universalism hides not just a technical limitation but a structural bias, one produced by inequalities of power and resources.

The seemingly technical limitations (such as the limited subject-matter jurisdiction of the ICC) were hardly inherent but rather the outcome of political choice: Kamari Clarke reveals that the initial draft code by the International Law Commission originally included crimes such as colonial domination and wilful and severe damage to the environment.[25] Over several years of committee meetings, the list narrowed to the current four Rome Statute crimes. To call these the 'most universal' of the crimes drastically underestimates the background power relations; nonetheless, their encoding in the Rome Statute has elevated them to the stance of 'most grave' crimes—acts against, literally, 'humanity'. In addition, the multi-level system of selectivity—from the choice of whom to prosecute, where to look for crimes, and which crimes matter—reinforces the partial nature of both punishment and conflict narratives.[26]

The 'anti-impunity transnational legal order', as Manuel Iturralde calls it, functions by 'concealing and ignoring the historically, politically, and socially situated dimensions of the categories it uses, and the interest they reflect'.[27] The struggle to 'fight impunity' erases some aspects of its own origin story while foregrounding others, in ways that highlight an 'impunity gap' but downplay the structural

---

[23] Vasuki Nesiah, 'Doing History with Impunity' in Engle, Miller, and Davis (eds) (n 14).
[24] Baars (n 17) 13, 281.
[25] Kamari M Clarke, 'Is the ICC Targeting Africa Inappropriately?' (*Human Rights & International Criminal Law*, March 2013) <iccforum.com/Africa> accessed 8 June 2020.
[26] Barrie Sander, *Doing Justice to History: Confronting the Past in International Criminal Courts* (OUP 2021).
[27] Manuel Iturralde, 'Colombian Transitional Justice and the Political Economy of the Anti-Impunity Transnational Legal Order' in Gregory Shaffer and Ely Aaronson (eds), *Transnational Legal Ordering of Criminal Justice* (CUP 2020) 254.

implausibility of universal justice. As a result, anti-impunity advocates bolster the power and legitimacy of the Court as a scrappy institution attempting to fulfil its ambitious goals and stymied primarily by logistical limitations.[28]

The ICC's complementarity regime embodies the attempt to enforce universal anti-impunity measures while allowing for differentiated responses to particular cases. The Court invokes a singular standard of 'unwilling or unable' as part of a complementarity analysis that applies to the same crimes regardless of place, while accepting that the ways in which a country might pursue perpetrators need not be precisely the same. Complementarity functions conceptually to construct a workable oscillation between a universal norm (fighting impunity) and a plural response (international or domestic prosecutions). The Rome Statute's Article 17 regime requires that the ICC not pursue prosecutions that could otherwise be undertaken at the domestic level.[29] The ICC's lack of primacy through complementarity is meant to quell not just sovereignty concerns but complaints that fighting impunity obstructs diverse responses to violence. Thus, formally, Article 17 creates a limiting rule for admissibility to the Court.

As Sarah Nouwen has argued, however, the treatment of complementarity not in its purely doctrinal form but rather as a conceptual 'big idea' produces the paradox that in the process of endorsing domestic prosecution, it simultaneously undermines state interest and capacity in those prosecutions. This happens both because it promotes the Court as the institution that will 'take over from states the responsibility to investigate and prosecute conflict-related crimes' and because the development of a 'pro-ICC ideology' emphasizes the superiority of international courts for prosecuting international crimes 'against humanity'.[30] Phil Clark links the hierarchical assumptions of complementarity to the distancing function of the Court, one which pits the international and thus disinterested arbiter and dispenser of justice against the distant, political, and particular site of violence.[31] In other words, the universalist aspiration of the Court—to prosecute on behalf of humanity while theoretically allowing space for others to do the same—reveals a deeper hierarchy that places the international above the national or local precisely on the basis of universality. The betrayal of facial neutrality by continuous selectivity is possible not in spite of Article 17 but, rather, *because* of its ready accommodation of the long-running hierarchies embedded in public international law.[32]

The figure of the victim further instantiates the discourse of anti-impunity. The paradigmatic victim often represents the humanity on whose behalf the Court is

---

[28] Samuel Moyn, 'Anti-Impunity as Deflection of Argument' in Engle, Miller, and Davis (eds) (n 14).
[29] Rome Statute of the International Criminal Court 1998, art 17.
[30] Sarah MH Nouwen, *Complementarity in the Line of Fire: The Catalysing Effect of the International Criminal Court in Uganda and Sudan* (CUP 2013) 13.
[31] Phil Clark, *Distant Justice: The Impact of the International Criminal Court on African Politics* (CUP 2018) 17.
[32] Antony Anghie, *Imperialism, Sovereignty and the Making of International Law* (CUP 2005).

meant to operate, even as victims are habitually associated with a particular time and place. The wish of 'victims' as a whole for perpetrators' punishment represents a justification for prosecution; anti-impunity arguments often invoke victim need, desire, and demand for law, particularly for prosecution and punishment.[33] Thus, victims come to represent an undifferentiated universal group that calls for retributive justice. At the same time, victims represent the specificity of particular contexts and conflicts, legitimizing the institutions and practices of international criminal justice. In the process, these discourses sometimes marginalize victims' divergent wishes and understandings about what justice means to them.[34]

The construction of complementarity as both doctrine and 'rhetorical concept' emphasizes the need for a universal response to atrocity through the language of domestic diversity.[35] In this sense, it is exemplary of the larger anti-impunity discourse, which moves seamlessly between defending a disinterested international law and a set of contextually specific responses. The universal and hegemonic reproduce and depend upon the particular and heterogeneous.

3. Telling the Truth: Universal Truths, Particularistic Memories

Transitional justice distinguished itself institutionally and legally from the beginning by its focus on two issues: the particular context of social and political transition to democracy and the need to address the human rights violations that occurred prior to that transition. The first oriented the field away from blanket prosecutions; the second promoted the necessity of truth-telling both on its own terms and as an alternative to the retributive justice that might be impossible to achieve under transitional conditions. Both were understood to contribute to societal reconciliation after a divided era. The most common technique was the truth commission; the dilemma embodied by these commissions were commonly referenced as the 'truth vs. justice' debates.[36] While truth appeared initially as a 'second best' to punishment, the field contributed to a broader zeitgeist that embraced the need for truth on its own terms. Truth became a proxy term for both history and memory, as well as its own form of accountability. As a result, truth—understood as recovery

---

[33] Kamari M Clarke, 'We Ask for Justice, You Give Us Law' in Sara Kendall, Christian DeVos, and Carsten Stahn (eds), *Contested Justice: The Politics and Practice of International Criminal Court Interventions* (CUP 2015).

[34] Rosalind Shaw, 'Memory Frictions: Localizing the Truth and Reconciliation Commission in Sierra Leone' (2007) 1 International Journal of Transitional Justice 183; Ann Nee and Peter Uvin, 'Silence and Dialogue: Burundians' Alternatives to Transitional Justice' in Rosalind Shaw, Lars Waldorf, and Pierre Hazan (eds), *Localizing Transitional Justice* (Stanford University Press 2010).

[35] Nouwen (n 30) 11.

[36] Robert I Rotberg and Dennis F Thompson (eds), *Truth v. Justice: The Morality of Truth Commissions* (Princeton University Press 2000).

of the past—became a universal value. Eventually it was raised to the status of a right, further entrenching its importance and centrality.

Transitional justice offered an emphasis on truth-telling and truth commissions as exemplary of the need for careful particularity in transitional and post-conflict contexts. Over time, as the enterprise expanded, however, its claims to legitimacy began to rest equally on its universal reach. That expansiveness meant both that transitional justice advertised itself as applicable to almost any context (liberal, illiberal, post conflict, settled democracy, etc) and established that every society and individual needed the truths that transitional justice mechanisms could uncover.[37] The particular did not disappear as the universal developed; rather, as the reliance on truth-telling suggests, the discourse increasingly mobilized claims to both universality and particularity.

As the enterprise developed and consolidated, the promotion of truth-telling about the past as a universal necessity allowed truth to become a fellow traveller rather than a competitor with retributive justice.[38] The developing 'right to truth' and the institutional hybridity of truth commissions and courts brought truth and justice into each other's previously separate spheres.[39] Courts themselves increasingly became a (debated) site for the exposure of the past—in spite of the long history of critiques of the capacity of criminal trials to achieve historical truth.[40] The notion that a right to truth might frequently entail an entitlement to prosecute perpetrators entangled discourses around truth with those of anti-impunity.[41] The universality of truth became a further justification for prosecution in certain cases.

Although the interweaving of justice and truth appeared to create a more harmonious vision of international justice, it also altered the relationship between claims to universality and particularity. A greater emphasis on truth as discovered through prosecution limited not just the more potentially expansive and particularistic role of truth commissions but their power to promote amnesties—particularly for grave human rights violations. In the process, amnesties as a whole became not so much dormant as quiet. Post-conflict and post-authoritarians states

---

[37] Thomas Obel Hansen, 'The Vertical and Horizontal Expansion of Transitional Justice: Explanations and Implications for a Divided Field' in Susanne Buckley-Zistel and others (eds), *Transitional Justice Theories* (Routledge 2014).

[38] Bronwyn Anne Leebaw, 'The Irreconcilable Goals of Transitional Justice' (2008) 30 Human Rights Quarterly 95.

[39] 'Once hostile towards each other, supporters of TRCs and courts have now entered a new anti-impunity era of cooperation dominated by the paradigm of complementarity, to the extent that the opposition between truth and justice is negated as a "debate of the past" or a "false dilemma".' Patricia Naftali, 'The Politics of Truth: On Legal Fetishism and the Rhetoric of Complementarity' [2015] *Revue québécoise de droit international* 101, 104 (citations omitted).

[40] Examples can be found in Sander (n 26); Aldo Zammit Borda, *Histories Written by International Criminal Courts and Tribunals: Developing a Responsible History Framework* (Asser 2021); Hannah Arendt, *Eichmann in Jerusalem: A Report on the Banality of Evil* (Penguin 2006).

[41] Office of the High Commissioner for Human Rights, *Promotion and Protection of Human Rights: Study on the Right to the Truth* (8 February 2006).

continue to deploy amnesties but were now forced to reckon in many cases with judgements as to the legality (and political consequences) of the choice.[42]

The universality of the need to uncover the past was implicitly balanced by the particularities of the pasts uncovered. The broad reach of the need for truth was premised on the claims to contextual understanding and unique histories on which transitional justice was founded. Truth commissions in particular promoted specificity of place. Truth was both an individual and collective need, promoted as catharsis and healing but also as record and preventative measure. South Africa's famous inquiry helped stabilize both sides of the oscillating nature of truth: the Truth and Reconciliation Commission (TRC) promoted the need for truth as a fundamental value of human rights and dignity as well a particular requirement for South Africa to move forward. At the same time, the particular truths sought had limits: the Commission focused on gross human rights violations committed by perpetrators of individual acts of violence, not the legal structure of racialized inequality, the system of apartheid, or its beneficiaries. Moreover, while participation was hardly mandatory, 'opting out' was difficult at best.[43] Institutional processes made it harder to examine either historical facts or memories about economic need, dispossession, or displacement while focusing on the truth of physical violation and violence.

4. Unbalanced: Hierarchies of Time and Victimhood

Among the consequences of this continuous oscillation between universal and particular is the displacement from view of historical and contemporary racialized and colonial hierarchies embedded within the enterprise and its practices. In their oscillation between universal and particular, anti-impunity and truth-telling discourses both rely fundamentally on (often assumed) constructions of humanity, victimhood, temporality, and progress. The particular acts as a defence against accusations of an overwhelming universalism, while universal reach fortifies justice against charges of relativism or inequity. As a result, it can be more difficult to specify and problematize the universals and particulars themselves. Oscillation, then, is not neutral; rather, it helps burnish the legitimacy of international justice efforts by strengthening the conceptual scaffolding on which it rests.

---

[42] The Inter-American Court of Human Rights has been particularly explicit about the unlawfulness of amnesties granted for gross human rights violations. *Barrios Altos v Peru* Inter-American Court of Human Rights Series C No 75 (2001). On the recent case of Colombia, see Alexandra Huneeus and René Urueña, 'Introduction to Symposium on the Colombian Peace Talks and International Law' (2016) 110 AJIL Unbound 16; Helena Alviar and Karen Engle, 'The Distributive Politics of Impunity and Anti-Impunity: Lessons from Four Decades of Colombian Peace Negotiations' in Engle, Miller, and Davis (eds) (n 14).

[43] Richard A Wilson, *The Politics of Truth and Reconciliation in South Africa* (CUP 2001).

The definition and treatment of victimhood and victims represent an area in which the ostensible neutrality of balancing gives way to specific racialized and colonial dynamics. As the preceding sections discussed, the invocation of the victim as both a universal figure who stands in for humanity and a particular community or individual who has suffered at the hands of specific perpetrators saturates international justice discourses. Victims sometimes serve as a synecdoche for the general humanity against whom crimes are committed. At other times, they are the specific group or individual harmed in a given context. Victims appear in the rhetoric of international prosecutors, in the text of truth commission reports, in advocacy for non-traditional alternatives to prosecution, and in the institutional machinery and discourse of the ICC. They are cited as a primary reason for 'fighting impunity'. Victims are central to the notion of international criminal law as a humanitarian enterprise that will protect the many who are victimized from the few who victimize them.

The victim may be both universal and particular, but in both guises, *some* aspects of the particular—for example, racialized difference or colonial descent—are left out. Richard Wilson examines the International Criminal Tribunal for Rwanda's case law and finds that, in reckoning with the crime of genocide, the Court exhibits deep discomfort with discussing claims based on race and ethnicity, since 'cosmopolitan jurists are committed to the idea of "humanity" rather than to notions of racial and ethnic groups ...'.[44] The clash between doctrine and background beliefs forces judges to confront questions of race—but only, as Vasuki Nesiah points out, to prosecute it. Those 'cosmopolitan jurists' look to what Nesiah describes as a 'universal, race transcendent "humanity"' as both the engine and beneficiary of ICL'.[45] The result is a deracinated victim because race is 'unsayable' even as it vividly informs representations of victims and perpetrators.[46]

The selective characterization of victims depends in part on making them central to international justice while defining them through a series of decisions and assumptions about the timeframe of violence, the nature of harm, and the origins of conflict. Madlingozi, along with McEvoy and McConnachie, reads the ways in which the victim is both foregrounded and obscured in transitional justice through Spivak's famous inquiry into whether the subaltern can speak.[47] Moreover, the

---

[44] Richard Wilson, 'When Humanity Sits in Judgment: Crimes Against Humanity and the Conundrum of Race and Ethnicity at the International Criminal Tribunal for Rwanda' in Feldman and Ticktin (eds) (n 2) 50.

[45] Vasuki Nesiah, 'Crimes Against Humanity: Racialized Subjects and Deracialized Histories' in Immi Tallgren and Thomas Skouteris (eds), *The New Histories of International Criminal Law: Retrials* (OUP 2019) 187.

[46] Clarke, *Affective Justice* (n 17) 26.

[47] Kieran McEvoy and Kirsten McConnachie, 'Victims and Transitional Justice: Voice, Agency, and Blame' (2013) 22 Social and Legal Studies 489, 498; Tshepo Madlingozi, 'On Transitional Justice Entrepreneurs and the Production of Victims' (2010) 2 Journal of Human Rights Practice 209.

radical individualization of violence and harm in criminal law in particular allows '[s]tructural victimhood caused by deep and persistent conditions of economic or political disenfranchisement [to] fade' from justice discourses.[48] The 'persistent conditions' Clarke describes are closely linked to long-term racial and colonial forms of hierarchy and subjugation.

The limits exercised on the meaning of victimhood and violence are thus intertwined with the mobilization of temporality in international justice practices.[49] The naturalized assumptions of time as linear, progressive, and comprised of discrete events promote a focus on catastrophic, recent, and spectacular violence—and on the victims produced by it. The harms for which international justice will be done—in whatever form justice takes—are rarely located in the distant past and are at best fleetingly exposed as a reproduction or continuation of what has gone before.[50] For both individual prosecutions and collective societal narratives, establishing an origin point in turn determines the weight and address of responsibility for violence. Without examining the consequences more closely, the vision of accountability promoted in this form remains impoverished in very specific ways: for example, courts are ill-equipped to understand the ways in which colonial structures and dynamics inform not only contemporary violence but also the reception of international justice practices.[51]

As with narratives around victimhood, temporal discourses of justice represent the partial nature of both universal and particular. In international justice discourses, one particular temporality becomes understood as universal even as the institutions claim in certain cases a more expansive mandate or investigation. Moreover, when confronted with questions about its particularity, the response generally rests on plausibility—either law, limited resources, or institutional constraints make broader accountability unavailable and unrealistic. These are not unreasonable explanations, but they are partial: it is within the accepted universe of the field as already structured that such temporal choices are made, thus reflecting the solidification and tilt of both transitional justice and international criminal law.

Temporal decision-making undergirds every form of international justice. Those decisions change the trajectory of prosecutions, limit the truths sought, and establish the parameters of transition and peace. The application of this temporality is endemically particular and political, even as its rhetoric is universalist. The time period of violence examined determines who the victims are, how and why violence took place, and who was involved in perpetrating atrocities. The assumed

---

[48] Clarke, *Affective Justice* (n 17) 54.
[49] See Miller (n 5).
[50] Kamari Clarke, 'Refiguring the Perpetrator: Culpability, History, and International Criminal Law's Impunity Gap' (2015) 19 International Journal of Human Rights 592, 597
[51] Clarke, *Affective Justice* (n 17) 17–18.

universality of temporality also bolsters the legitimacy of international justice practices by making it less simple to investigate continuing violence and colonial dynamics. The result is a set of stories about terrible conflicts driven by bad actors making poor decisions and about justice institutions emerging and evolving to assist the victims of those decisions.

5. Conclusion

To proclaim justice at the level of the international requires a certain confidence in the ability of the enterprise to apply similarly to all and yet specifically to some. Without the particulars of place, international justice has little meaning; yet without projects of transplantation and uniform applicability, it would have less persuasive power and fewer resources. In many ways, international justice discourses build on the 'paradoxical intersection between the universal and the specific' that Scott and Straus identify in human rights. Scott and Straus argue that human rights derive their power precisely from the combination of transcendent claims (which overcome history, particularity, and context) and locality ('what constitutes an abuse, how one understands that it transgresses what is morally permissible').[52] In international justice, a similar mobilization of two apparently contradictory impulses provides a foundational legitimacy to the project. International justice practices are simultaneously hegemonic and disaggregated, internally contradictory, and ambivalent. Yet while the oscillation between universal and particular can imply a balanced practice, neither formulation is unbounded, neutral, or disinterested. Instead, they manifest in techniques, doctrines, and norms which are limited in specific, repetitive ways—and which restrict the practice and meaning of justice.

Both international criminal law and transitional justice are committed to constituting different areas as commensurable and are reflexive about the need to embrace pluralism through diverse practices and complementarity.[53] On one side there are predominant arguments: on behalf of prosecution and punishment; on behalf of transplantable 'best practices' and codified crimes; on behalf of an international legal practice of anti-impunity that can escape local politics and distribution. On the other there are equally important claims: for sovereignty and local practice; for pluralism and diversity; for redress and contextual truth-telling. These duelling commitments emerge at times as opposition, as 'friction', as outright resistance, as subjugation, but they are inescapably linked—not least because their dual existence benefits the overall standing of the justice project.[54] At the same

---

[52] Steve Stern and Scott Straus, *The Human Rights Paradox: Universality and Its Discontents* (University of Wisconsin Press 2014) 4.

[53] I discuss commensurability in much more detail in 'Embedded Ambivalence: Un-Governing Global Justice' (2020) 11(3) Transnational Legal Theory 353.

[54] Anna Tsing, *Friction: An Ethnography of Global Connection* (Princeton University Press 2005).

time, they enact specific arrangements with significant consequences: defining justice by excluding amnesties, sanctifying victims by limiting their numbers and character, universalizing truth by marrying it to prosecution, embedding excavation of the past by curbing its duration. The result is a thumb on the scale of the universal—and further proof that the universal of international justice is, in the end, particular indeed.

18
Conceptual Universality vs Pragmatic Particularity in International Adjudication

Andreas Kulick

International adjudication, traditionally, is hardly associated with universality. It requires states' consent and is supposed to settle the specific dispute between the parties involved. Universal and compulsory jurisdiction is rather the exception than the rule. Nothing evinces this better than Article 36 of the ICJ Statute: it permits a state's opt-in to the World Court's compulsory jurisdiction, which some, albeit the minority of states have chosen, and usually with reservations.[1] The default rule, however, is individual consent, either ad hoc or by treaty, as stated by Article 36(1) of the ICJ Statute. The same applies to international arbitration[2] and most other international judicial dispute settlement mechanisms, with a few notable exceptions, such as the World Trade Organization (WTO) regime[3] and regional human rights systems such as the European Convention Human on Rights.[4] Article 33 of the UN Charter lists international adjudication as merely one among many means of pacific dispute settlement and also the Friendly Relations Declaration does not grant it any preference over the other means.[5] Further, although the 'fragmentation' debate,[6] referenced in the introductory chapter,[7] has somewhat lost momentum in recent years,[8] the proliferation or

---

[1] See 'Declarations Recognizing the Jurisdiction of the Court as Compulsory' <www.icj-cij.org/en/declarations> accessed 9 December 2019.
[2] See John G Merrills, *International Dispute Settlement* (6th edn, CUP 2017) 88–92; Yoshifumi Tanaka, *The Peaceful Settlement of International Disputes* (CUP 2018) 116–17. However, note the 'general consent' usually granted in International Investment Agreements with regard to investor-state dispute settlement; see CL Lim, Jean Ho, and Martins Paparinskis, *International Investment Law and Arbitration—Commentary, Awards and other Material* (CUP 2018) 94–97, and on the lack of 'privity' between the parties to the dispute, see Jan Paulsson, 'Arbitration without Privity' (1994) 10 ICSID Review 232ff.
[3] cf art 1 of the Understanding on Rules and Procedures Governing the Settlement of Disputes (DSU) and its Appendix 1.
[4] cf arts 32–34 of the Convention for the Protection of Human Rights and Fundamental Freedoms.
[5] UNGA Res 2625 (1970) GAOR 25th Session, Annex, second principle, second and third paragraphs.
[6] See, instead of many, ILC, 'Fragmentation of International Law: Difficulties Arising from The Diversification and Expansion of International Law', Report of the Study Group of the International Law Commission, Finalized by Martti Koskenniemi, 58th Session (1 May–9 June and 3 July–11 August 2006) UN Doc A/CN.4/L.682.
[7] See 11 in this volume.
[8] See eg the contributions in Mads Andenas and Eirik Bjørge (eds), *A Farewell to Fragmentation—Reassertion and Convergence in International Law* (CUP 2015). See also Laurence Boisson de

'multiplication'[9] of specialized international courts and tribunals is a reality of international dispute settlement so obvious to any observer or participant that speaking of 'universality' vis-à-vis international adjudication seems to be futile if not simply ill-informed.

However, despite this apparently non-universalist setting, for the past three decades at least, a different narrative[10] arguably has shaped the prevailing understanding of international adjudication, advanced primarily by Western European countries and the United States. I will call this narrative the 'conceptual universality' of international adjudication. Universality of international adjudication for present purposes shall denote the view that all settlement of international disputes should ideally occur via formalized procedures before an independent judicial body, ie in the form of arbitration or litigation, that decides on the basis of international law. Thus, such universality is conceptual in the sense that it postulates a normative ideal of what international dispute settlement is supposed to look like, which affects the construction of its reality. Such an ideal, let us call it the 'Lauterpachtian ideal',[11] is only slightly overstated by Martti Koskenniemi's famous description of 'Lauterpacht's utopia' as 'a world ruled by lawyers':[12] international disputes are governed by international law and, as they are in that sense legal disputes, they are best settled by recourse to judicial dispute settlement, ie international adjudication.[13]

The narrative of 'conceptual universality', so I contend, consists of three elements. First, that international adjudication, despite lack of universal jurisdiction and dependent on state consent, serves as an overall effective means to curb state

---

Chazournes' recent attempt to demonstrate the innocuous or rather even positive features of the 'plurality' of international courts and tribunals and to reconcile potential conflicts by way of a 'managerial approach': Laurence Boisson de Chazournes, 'Plurality in the Fabric of International Courts and Tribunals: The Threads of a Managerial Approach' (2017) 28 European Journal of International Law 13ff.

[9] Allain Pellet, 'Should We (Still) Worry about Fragmentation?' in Andreas Føllesdal and Geir Ulfstein (eds), *The Judicialization of International Law—A Mixed Blessing?* (OUP 2018) 228, adopting the term from Mohammed Bedjaoui, 'La multiplication des tribunaux internationaux ou la bonne fortune du droit des gens' in SFDI, *La jurisdictionnalisation du droit international* (Pedone 2002) 529ff.

[10] On narratives in international law, see Matthew Windsor, 'Narrative Kill or Capture: Unreliable Narration in International Law' 28 (2015) Leiden Journal of International Law 743; Andreas Kulick, 'Narrating Narratives of International Investment Law: History and Epistemic Forces' in Stephan W Schill, Christian J Tams, and Rainer Hofmann (eds), *International Investment Law and History* (Edward Elgar 2018) 41ff. On the concept of narratives, see generally Paul Ricoeur, 'La Fonction Narrative' (1979) 54 Études théologiques et religieuses 209ff.

[11] See, most prominently, Hersch Lauterpacht, *The Function of Law in the International Community* (reprint of the 1933 original, OUP 2011); Hersch Lauterpacht, *The Development of International Law by the International Court* (Stevens & Sons 1958).

[12] Martti Koskenniemi, *The Gentle Civilizer of Nations: The Rise and Fall of International Law 1870–1960* (CUP 2002) 404.

[13] See eg Lauterpacht (n 11) 431–46. On Lauterpacht's concept of the international judicial function, see also Ian GM Scobbie, 'The Theorist as Judge: Hersch Lauterpacht's Concept of the International Judicial Function' (1997) 2 European Journal of International Law 264, 270ff.

sovereignty and to further the development of an international community, based on a set of shared international legal rules and principles. Second, that, save negotiation, international adjudication is the preferable means of international dispute settlement, regardless of the 'political' nature of the dispute at hand. Third, the progress story that there is a welcome development of increasing judicialization of international affairs, including the increasing number of international courts and tribunals.[14] All three elements are underscored by a liberal, 'Lauterpachtian'[15] concept of international relations that is normatively committed—at least as an ideal, if not yet always in practice—to the international rule of law. This includes an increased focus on the individual and the pursuit of the international rule of law through legal and thus formalized processes of dispute settlement, of which international adjudication is the most advanced and thus the preferable one.

Admittedly, the narrative of conceptual universality of international adjudication often has not been reflected in reality. Just taking the United States as an example, the *Nicaragua* case in the 1980s[16] and the Iraq War in the 2000s constitute merely the most prominent instances of a myriad of US actions undermining peaceful, rule-based international dispute settlement, let alone international adjudication. However, these deviations in practice from the aforesaid narrative arguably pertained to specific instances while the overall narrative was still being upheld—and promoted vis-à-vis third states. Similar things may be said with regard to Western European countries' approaches when the European Union (EU) and the US dominated international relations and international discourse, particularly in the 1990s. More generally, from the peace movement starting in the late nineteenth century until the years following the fall of the Berlin Wall, there is a discernible increasing narrative that—as a reaction to phases of hot and cold war—the preferable means of settling international disputes is through formalized procedures before an independent body deciding the matters before it on the basis of pre-established rules and principles. The conceptual universality narrative took its present form, so I argue, only after 1990 with the veritable sprouting of international and regional courts and tribunals.[17] However, some of its aspects may be

---

[14] This reverberates particularly in eg Karen Alter, *The New Terrain of International Law—Courts, Politics, Rights* (Princeton University Press 2014) 112ff as well as in Boisson de Chazournes (n 8) 13ff. However, note her considerably more modulated tone in Laurence Boisson de Chazournes, 'Plurality in the Fabric of International Courts and Tribunals: The Threads of a Managerial Approach: A Rejoinder—Fears and Anxieties' (2018) 28 European Journal of International Law 1275ff.

[15] ie in the sense of the above 'Lauterpachtian ideal' that is not necessarily identical with Sir Hersch's writings.

[16] The US famously withdrew its consent under art 36 of the ICJ Statute and refused to participate in the proceedings. For an overview of the proceedings, see the ICJ website <www.icj-cij.org/en/case/70> accessed 9 December 2019.

[17] For an overview of the historical development, see Mary Ellen O'Connell and Leonore Vanderzee, 'The History of International Adjudication' in Cesare PR Romano, Karen J Alter, and Yuval Shany (eds), *The Oxford Handbook of International Adjudication* (OUP 2014) 40, 44ff and Karen J Alter, 'The Multiplication of International Courts and Tribunals after the End of the Cold War' in ibid 63ff.

traced back to earlier times, such as the many contemporaneous views underlying the establishment of the Permanent Court of Arbitration in 1899, of the World Court after World War I and again after World War II.

What reverberates with this assessment is, finally, the hegemonic potential of the 'conceptually universal' narrative of international adjudication. Because it assumes universality and because it is aspirational, it may very well serve as a 'hegemonic technique':[18] International adjudication and international courts thereby become a means of dominance. While this may be argued vis-à-vis international law in general, international adjudication formalizes dispute settlement and transforms international law from a mere means of shaping international discourse into normative pronouncements by (considerably) independent and impartial third parties (courts and tribunals) on what international law requires. 'Conceptual universality' of international adjudication thus may be employed, or at least may tend, towards shaping the world in the image of a Western view on law and dispute settlement by way of dressing it as universal—or at least as universally desirable.[19]

1. Three Trends: Sinicization, Re-etatization, De-judicialization

Such narrative of conceptual universality, with its various aspects as described above, is set to be challenged by what I will refer to as 'pragmatic particularity' in international adjudication. Such a competing narrative of pragmatic particularity is closely linked to the increasing importance of China as a world power and of Asia as the potential focal point of international affairs in the twenty-first century. Three trends in international relations in general and in international dispute settlement in particular arguably bring about such pragmatic particularity: the sinicization, re-etatization, and de-judicialization of international relations and thus of international law and international adjudication.

1.1 Falling Eagle, Rising Dragon

The first trend pertains to the rise of China[20] as the dominant power of the twenty-first century as well as the simultaneous decline of US influence on international affairs, what I will refer to as the 'sinicization' of international relations. The parallel

---

[18] cf 7 in this volume. See also Martti Koskenniemi, 'International Law and Hegemony: A Reconfiguration' (2004) 17 Cambridge Review of International Affairs 197ff.
[19] See also, for the hegemony–universality duality, 8-9 in this volume.
[20] Historically, such 'rise' is rather a return for the 'Middle Kingdom' to old dominance—a dominance which had been tarnished in the Opium Wars. See on this Maria Adele Carrai, *Sovereignty in China: A Genealogy of a Concept since 1840* (CUP 2019).

phenomena—rising dragon, falling eagle—are on the one hand evinced by China's growing assertion of influence over economic and geopolitical issues. Increasing activism in matters of international trade, including a rise in participation in trade disputes under the helm of the WTO, testify to this. Further evidence constitutes China's leading role in international investment protection, particularly in Asia and Africa, as demonstrated by its currently 120 bilateral investment treaties (BITs) in force, most of the recent ones containing a general consent to investor-state dispute settlement.[21] Moreover, the ambitious 'Belt and Road Initiative' (BRI), seeking to establish a Chinese economic sphere of influence by a connection of trade and investment partnership networks that stretches from East Asia into Eastern Europe, inter alia, must be mentioned in this regard.[22] Geopolitically, the most prominent example of China's more forceful assertion of a dominant role on the world stage undoubtedly is its claim over most of the South China Sea (SCS)—what has become (in)famous as the 'nine-dash line'—that not only challenges other states in the region but maybe even more so the United States' authority in the Pacific hemisphere in the long run.[23] In addition, Xi Jingping's leadership has overseen China's enhanced engagement in international law debates, with law reviews such as the *Chinese Journal of International Law* gaining prominence and with forceful attempts to shape international legal discourse, most prominently again with respect to the SCS dispute.[24]

On the other hand, waning US influence and—particularly under Trump's presidency—waning US interest in the multi- or plurilateral organization of international affairs feature two main results. First, a diminished devotion, in rhetoric as well as in action, to international agreements and rule-based containment of international disputes by the United States. Secondly, increased China–US antagonism, which crystallizes in the issue of international trade, evinced not only by the Trump administration's 'trade war' with China[25] and its deadlocking of the WTO Appellate Body,[26] but already by the Obama administration's attempt to contain China's economic grasp over Asia by concluding the Trans-Pacific Partnership

---

[21] See <https://investmentpolicy.unctad.org/international-investment-agreements/countries/42/china> accessed 9 December 2019. cf also Sarah Jaramillo, 'China's Approach in Drafting the Investor-State Arbitration Clause: A Review from the "Belt and Road" Regions' Perspective' (2017) 5 Chinese Journal of Comparative Law 79ff.

[22] See Michael D Swaine, 'Chinese Views and Commentary on the "One Belt, One Road" Initiative' (Summer 2018) 47 China Leadership Monitor 1ff.

[23] On the SCS dispute, see Erik Franckx and Marco Benatar, 'Non-Participation in Compulsory Procedures of Dispute Settlement: The People's Republic of China's Position Paper in the South China Sea Arbitration and Beyond' in Føllesdal and Ulfstein (eds) (n 9) 184ff.

[24] See eg the Special Issue 'The South China Sea Arbitration Awards: A Critical Study' (2018) 17 Chinese Journal of International Law 207–748; see also Stefan Talmon and Bing Bing Ja (eds), *The South China Sea Arbitration: A Chinese Perspective* (Hart Publishing 2014).

[25] 'DealBook Briefing: Welcome to the Trade War' *New York Times* (New York, 6 July 2018).

[26] See eg Geraldo Vidigal, 'Living Without the Appellate Body: Multilateral, Bilateral and Plurilateral Solutions to the WTO Dispute Settlement Crisis' (2019) 20 The Journal of World Investment & Trade 862ff.

(TPP) agreement, albeit immediately cancelled by President Trump when taking office.[27]

1.2 The Return of the State

At the same time, a second relevant trend with serious repercussions on international law and international adjudication shapes current international relations. States increasingly attempt to reassert (national) control over issues that have become a matter of international regulation of some sort and thus subject to international law as well as international judicial dispute settlement. This trend of 're-nationalization' marks a veritable 'return of the state'[28] in international relations. It is not limited to traditionally more authoritarian states but is becoming increasingly pervasive in the old West as well. Manifestations of this trend come in different iterations, such as a blatant disregard of established rules of international law, eg Russia's annexation of Crimea,[29] or the casting aside or abandonment of pluri- and multilateral international or regional frameworks regulating, with regard to specific issues or more comprehensively, aspects of import to the international community. In recent years, this latter feature of nation-state reassertion has particularly concerned treaties on trade and investment matters (eg the Transatlantic Trade and Investment Partnership [TTIP], TPP et al) as well as the environment (the Trump administration's decision to withdraw from the Paris Agreement, since reversed by the Biden administration)[30] but also the exit of international and regional organizations, such as the US withdrawal from UNESCO (not yet reserved by the Biden administration as of May 2021)[31] or, most prominently, the UK leaving the EU. Moreover, investment protection, in particular by way of investor-state dispute settlement, has been witnessing a considerable 'reassertion of control' by both low- and middle-income as well as high-income countries, evinced in cancellation of BITs, withdrawals from the International Centre for Settlement of Investment Disputes (ICSID) Convention, and backlashes in civil society, mostly

---

[27] See <https://ustr.gov/trade-agreements/free-trade-agreements/trans-pacific-partnership> accessed 9 December 2019. On the divergent Chinese (more multilateral, more open) and US (more bilateral, more protectionist) approaches to regional trade agreements, see also Wang Heng, 'Divergence, Convergence or Crossvergence of Chinese and U.S. Approaches to Regional Integration: Evolving Trajectories and their Implications' (2018) 10 Tsinghua China Law Review 150ff.

[28] See, for this expression, already José E Alvarez, 'The Return of the State' (2011) 20 Minnesota Journal of International Law 223.

[29] See, for an appraisal of the factual and legal issues involved, Christian Marxsen, 'The Crimea Crisis—An International Law Perspective' (2014) 74 Zeitschrift für ausländisches öffentliches Recht und Völkerrecht 367ff.

[30] Paris Agreement under the United Nations Framework Convention on Climate Change, signed 22 April 2016, entered into force 4 November 2016.

[31] With effect from 31 December 2018, see <www.state.gov/r/pa/prs/ps/2017/10/274748.htm> accessed 9 December 2019.

in wealthy Western countries, that has led to a reconsideration of their investment arbitration policies by several important players, including the EU.[32]

Backlash against international law and internationalism in general is nothing new. The rather novel aspect to it, at least since World War II and particularly in Europe and the US, is instead the change in narrative that fuels such scaling back of multilateral international regulation, expressly emphasizing, and legitimizing, national interest over international cooperation. Among several factors responsible in this regard, I will focus on one specific aspect that in my opinion cuts through both Western and non-Western manifestations of such a 'return of the (nation-) state' on the international arena. Arguably, the common thread of phenomena as diverse as the Trump presidency, the Brexit vote, the opposition to free trade agreements (TTIP, Canada-European Comprehensive Economic and Trade Agreement (CETA), etc) in the EU, or the undermining of an independent judiciary in Eastern Europe, most notably in Hungary and Poland,[33] are increasingly pervasive substantive concepts of democracy and their relation to the nation state. Substantive concepts of democracy[34] focus less on the process (input and throughput) and more on the result (output).[35] They are less concerned with how policies are created and how those deciding over these policies are chosen but instead whether what is decided represents the 'will of the people'.[36] The focus on such will—and the assumption that such a homogenous will actually exists—permits the casting aside of established rule-of-law achievements on the national level and demanding enforced pursuit and primacy of national interests at the international level. Moreover, the more one emphasizes the output, the more collective—national—interests step into the foreground and the less emphasis is placed on the protection of individual rights. Victor Orbán's characterization of his style of government as 'illiberal democracy'[37] is thus right on point: substantive concepts of democracy, at least if taken to the extreme,[38] antagonize liberalism as a political philosophy,[39] which champions the protection of individual rights, the adherence to the rule of

---

[32] See, on all this, the contributions in Andreas Kulick (ed), *Reassertion of Control over the Investment Treaty Regime* (CUP 2017).

[33] For the most recent developments in Poland, see 'Collision Course' *The Economist* (London, 7 July 2018).

[34] For a famous example, see Carl Schmitt, *Verfassungslehre* (4th edn, reprint of the 1st edn of 1928, Duncker & Humblot 1954) 75ff, 221ff.

[35] For a classical account of the various concepts of democratic legitimacy, see classically Fritz W Scharpf, *Demokratietheorie zwischen Utopie und Anpassung* (Konstanz Universitätsverlag 1970).

[36] See also Cas Mudde and Cristòbal Rovira Kaltwasser, *Populism—A Very Short Introduction* (OUP 2017) 11ff.

[37] Viktor Orbán's speech at the XXV. Bálványos Free Summer University and Youth Camp, 26 July 2014, Băile Tuşnad (Tusnádfürdő) <https://budapestbeacon.com/full-text-of-viktor-orbans-speech-at-baile-tusnad-tusnadfurdo-of-26-july-2014/> accessed 9 December 2019.

[38] Carl Schmitt's political philosophy (see, in particular, Schmitt (n 34) 75ff, 221ff) is a good lesson in this regard.

[39] For its most influential iteration in recent decades, see John Rawls, *A Theory of Justice* (Belknap Press 1971).

law, particularly in its procedural iteration, and thus also to judicial settlement of disputes arising between different stakeholders.

1.3 A Farewell to Courts?

It is therefore no surprise, with liberal democracy eroding in Europe and the US, with an authoritarian China grasping a central role in world leadership, and with Russia asserting considerable influence on international affairs, in Eastern Europe and the Middle East in particular, that judicialized international dispute settlement is being much less firmly embraced in recent years. Three examples of this trend of 'de-judicialization' will suffice here. First, the so-called 'trade war' introduced by former US President Donald Trump against China and threatened against the EU does not only appear to have sidelined established approaches to international trade policy but at the same time strikingly sidelined WTO dispute settlement, which, until recently, had usually been cast as a veritable success story of international adjudication.[40] Most notably, the Trump administration had been pursuing a policy of deadlocking appointments of members to the WTO Appellate Body, which undermines and cripples the WTO dispute settlement system as a whole.[41] Due to this policy, since 11 December 2019, the Appellate Body only consists of one member[42] and is thus not operational, as Article 17(1) Dispute Settlement Understanding (DSU) requires at least three Members to hear a dispute. The Biden administration has, as of yet (May 2021), not broken this deadlock of the Appellate Body.

Second, recent years have witnessed an increased tendency of states to shun international adjudication by refusing to participate in international litigation or arbitration on the basis that the court or tribunal lacks jurisdiction. The resistance of both China and Russia to Annex VII arbitration under the United Nations Convention on the Law of the Sea in the *South China Sea* and *Arctic Sunrise* disputes represent two recent examples of authoritarian states refusing to accept international judicial dispute settlement on politically charged matters, where issues of 'sovereignty' were advanced in order to justify non-participation.[43] In 2018, Venezuela notified the Registrar of the International Court of Justice of 'the sovereign decision of Venezuela of not taking part in the action that has been unilaterally

---

[40] See only Matthias Herdegen, *Principles of International Economic Law* (2nd edn, OUP 2016) ch 20.
[41] See Ana Swanson, 'Once the W.T.O.'s Biggest Supporter, U.S. Is Its Biggest Skeptic' *New York Times* (New York, 10 December 2017) <www.nytimes.com/2017/12/10/business/wto-united-states-trade.html> accessed 9 December 2019. See also Geraldo Vidigal, 'Living Without the Appellate Body: Multilateral, Bilateral and Plurilateral Solutions to the WTO Dispute Settlement Crisis' (2019) 20 The Journal of World Investment & Trade 862ff.
[42] See <www.wto.org/english/tratop_e/dispu_e/ab_members_descrp_e.htm> accessed 13 May 2021.
[43] See, on the *SCS* and *Artic Sunrise* disputes, Franckx and Benatar (n 23) 183ff.

filed by our neighbouring country without Venezuela's consent'[44] in the *Case Concerning the Arbitral Award of 3 October 1899 (Guyana v Venezuela)*.[45] What is striking in this regard is not the fact that jurisdiction was challenged in these disputes—a usual claim of respondents in international adjudication. Rather, such challenge to jurisdiction was entertained as a justification for refusing overall participation in the proceedings and thus obviously to attempt undermining the legitimacy of the proceedings or even the specific dispute settlement mechanism itself. While non-participation has occurred in the past, we are currently witnessing the sharpest increase in the past forty years.[46]

Third, and more generally, major powers, such as China, Russia, or the US (particularly, but not exclusively, under the Trump administration), test established patterns of international political thinking embracing formalized triadic judicial dispute settlement as the preferred way of settling international disputes. This has not only been evinced by the Trump administration's hostility towards dispute settlement in matters of trade, as mentioned above vis-à-vis the WTO,[47] but was displayed by China and Russia even before Donald Trump came into office. In their joint declaration of 25 June 2016, setting forth, inter alia, their position on the settlement of international disputes, the absence of international adjudication as a means of international dispute settlement is striking.[48]

2. The End of International Adjudication? Pragmatic Particularity

These three trends heavily contest the conceptual universality narrative and will transform, so I contend, international adjudication in the decades to come. Given the increasing influence of China economically, militarily, and policy-wise, and the possible decline of US power and rise of protectionism, nationalism, antiliberalism, and substantive concepts of democracy in Western countries, the narrative of formalized and rule-based dispute settlement as the means of choice is set to be abandoned. This will probably result in a diminished prominence of international adjudication, albeit not at all its overall abandonment. Rather, so I posit,

---

[44] Communiqué of the Bolivarian Republic of Venezuela of 18 June 2018 <http://mppre.gob.ve/wp-content/uploads/2018/06/CancilleriaVE-20180618-EN-ComuniqueLaHaya.pdf> accessed 9 December 2019.
[45] See the ICJ website, 'Arbitral Award of 3 October 1899 (Guyana v Venezuela), Latest Developments' <www.icj-cij.org/en/case/171> accessed 9 December 2019.
[46] See, on the historical development of and the recent increase in non-participation, Peter Tzeng, 'A Strategy of Non-Participation before International Courts and Tribunals' (2020) 19 The Law and Practice of International Courts and Tribunals 5ff.
[47] See Section 1.2.
[48] See 'The Declaration of the Russian Federation and the People's Republic of China on the Promotion of International Law' of 25 June 2016 <www.mid.ru/en/foreign_policy/news/-/asset_publisher/cKNonkJE02Bw/content/id/2331698> accessed 9 December 2019.

the dominant approach towards international adjudication is shifting from 'conceptual universality' to what is best described as 'pragmatic particularity'. Such pragmatic particularity arguably consists of three, albeit interlinked, elements. First, bilateral agreements will become even more prominent as the jurisdictional basis in international adjudication. Second, certain 'sovereignty conflicts' will be mostly excluded from judicial dispute settlement, whereas in areas of particular interest to dominant players on the world stage international adjudication, based however on mainly bilateral agreements, will flourish. Finally, despite possible increase with respect to certain specific issues, international adjudication will more transparently be pursued as just one of a variety of means to promote self-interest and less as a means to promote a universal interest.

As to the first element of 'pragmatic particularity', while bilateralism is already the predominant pattern of international adjudication to date, advances towards multilateral frameworks as the basis of international judicial dispute settlement in various fields such as international trade (WTO DSU) and regional and international human rights law (eg the Inter-American Court of Human Rights, European Court of Human Rights, Human Rights Committee individual complaints procedure) are likely to be scaled back. If the above assessment is accurate, that national interests are increasingly being asserted by states in a forceful manner ('return of the state'),[49] multilateral frameworks will be shunned, and bilateral arrangements will be preferred. In particular, bilateralism offers the opportunity for major powers to negotiate agreements with less powerful states that are more in line with their specific interests. China's BRI is the prime example of such arrangements. For example, BITs with states along the 'new Silk Road' are intended to be tailored precisely towards the specific needs of Chinese investors, ie emphasizing investment protection provisions and featuring—differently from Chinese BITs with Western countries—robust investor-state dispute settlement clauses not dissimilar to the old BITs concluded by Western European countries and the US with developing countries in the 1980s and 1990s.[50] However, overall, the Chinese approach towards the regulation of economic relations with other states under the BRI favours a soft-law and informal dispute settlement approach that relies on the individual bilateral relationship between China and the BRI partner states, particularly Central Asian countries.[51] In addition, America, particularly under the Trump administration, has recently displayed a distinct preference for bilateral over multilateral arrangements—a policy that, given the considerable protectionist sentiments at both ends of the American political spectrum, is probably not to be

---

[49] See Section 1.2.
[50] See Harriet Moynihan, 'China's Evolving Approach to International Dispute Settlement' (Chatham House, March 2017) 8. Recently concluded Chinese BITs with BRI states and beyond contain robust investor-state dispute settlement clauses, see eg art 12 of the China-Uzbekistan BIT of 2011 and art 13 of the China-Tanzania BIT of 2014.
[51] See Heng (n 27) 162ff.

fully reversed, at least not in substance, even though the Biden administration considerably changed its rhetoric.

The second element pertains to the increasing differential treatment of such disputes that states perceive as particularly sensitive to matters of vital national interests ('sovereignty conflicts') and disputes in areas where they have a particular interest in formalized judicial dispute settlement. The first group of disputes comprises issues of territorial sovereignty and jurisdiction, such as the aforementioned 'SCS' and 'Artic Sunrise' disputes,[52] as well as the use of force, the *jus in bello*, and increasingly also highly contentious human rights issues.[53] However, as the approach of the Trump administration towards international trade relations or the severe backlash in Europe against investor-state arbitration mechanisms in free trade agreements such as TTIP and CETA[54] have demonstrated, international economic law too is certainly not excluded from the group of issues that may be regarded as highly intrusive of vital national interests and 'sovereignty'. On the other hand, as China's BRI policy as well as at least its current approach to WTO dispute settlement show, where specific forms of adjudication suit the particular interests of major powers, they may even promote them.

Nonetheless, coming to the third and final element, the change of narrative is distinctive. International adjudication, under this approach of pragmatic particularity, is to be treated—and promoted—as but one instrument to be selected from the toolbox of international dispute settlement. The underlying rationale here is the national interest in the particular dispute at hand, not a general, universal preference for international adjudication as formalized independent decision-making based on pre-established rules and principles. This, of course, is taking Article 33 of the UN Charter at face value. However, it represents a considerable deviation from the narrative of 'conceptual universality' arguably dominant in (Western) international legal discourse over the past decades.

From the perspective of hegemony and regionalism,[55] one may regard these developments as an attempt to posit a counter-narrative and hence a counter-hegemony: replacing the Western hegemonic view of international adjudication as 'conceptually universal' with an alternative view that is more suitable to the policy interests of the new hegemon.

---

[52] See *The South China Sea Arbitration (Republic of Philippines v People's Republic of China)*, PCA Case No 2013-19, <https://pca-cpa.org/en/cases/7/>; *The Arctic Sunrise Arbitration (Netherlands v Russia)*, PCA Case No 2014-02, <https://pca-cpa.org/en/cases/21/> both accessed 9 December 2019. See also Section 1.3.

[53] Note, however, that the stand-off between the Russian Constitutional Court and the European Court of Human Rights (ECtHR) was mostly prompted over investment issues pertaining to the *Yukos* dispute and its iteration as individual application before the ECtHR; see Rachel M Fleig-Goldstein, 'The Russian Constitutional Court versus the European Court of Human Rights: How the Strasbourg Court Should Respond to Russia's Refusal to Execute ECtHR Judgments' (2017) 56 Columbia Journal of Transnational Law 172ff.

[54] See the contributions in Kulick (n 32).

[55] See Ch. 1, pp. 7–9, 11–12 of the draft.

3. Conclusions

For the aforementioned reasons, I submit that international adjudication, in the years to come, will be shaped by states openly measuring international judicial dispute settlement exclusively or at least primarily according to its potential to promote national interests—thus changing the narrative of international adjudication. Diplomacy or even various forms of technological, economic, or military intervention will be promoted openly as the preferable means of dispute settlement in certain areas of international relations. However, arguably, we will not witness international adjudication's complete thwarting by the great powers of the twenty-first century. Rather, we will observe a more case-by-case and overall pragmatist approach to it that will shun international adjudication in some areas of international law and welcome it in certain other areas: pragmatic particularity will supersede conceptual universality as the predominant narrative of international adjudication in the decades to come.

Index

For the benefit of digital users, indexed terms that span two pages (e.g., 52–53) may, on occasion, appear on only one of those pages.

Figures are indicated by *f* following the page number

Adorno, Theodor W., 59, 61, 67, 68–69, 174–75
African, 12, 154, 212–13, 215, 231, 232, 315
Al-Shaybānī, Muhammad, 219–20, 228
Alvarez, 108, 109–10, 112–13, 118
American, 12, 17, 78, 205, 225, 250, 336–37
American Society of International Law (ASIL), 96, 97
animal ethics, 172–73
anti-impunity, 20, 312–13, 314–15, 317–19, 320, 321, 324–25
arbitration, 20, 191, 328, 329–30, 332–33, 334–35, 337
Asia, 27, 97, 202, 206–8, 216–17, 250, 330–31, 336–37
Asian, 12, 34, 81–82, 95, 97, 98, 100, 199–200, 205, 209, 212–13, 215, 231, 243, 247–48
Asian Society of International Law, 96

bilateralism, 250–51
Butler, Judith, 6–7, 36

cartography, 28–29
China, 20, 100, 201–2, 203, 204–5, 206–8, 209, 213, 239–40, 241–44, 245–47, 248, 249–52, 330–32, 334–37
Christianity, 204, 215–16, 225–26
cities, 23–24, 25, 31, 37, 39–41
civic friendship, 128, 130–31
civilization, 18–19, 69, 97, 157–58, 187, 199–200, 201, 202, 205, 206–7, 208–10, 211–12, 213–15, 217, 218–19, 221, 224, 225, 227, 228, 231, 234–35, 237, 243
climate change, 20, 23, 295, 296, 299, 301–2, 304, 305, 308, 310
colonial, 9, 20, 115–16, 149, 153, 155, 162–63, 172, 175–76, 179, 188, 212–14, 239, 274–75, 311–12, 313, 317, 321, 322–24
colonialism, 150, 151–52, 162–63, 242
common good, 17, 122, 124, 125, 126, 127–29, 220, 228
confucianism, 201–4
critical legal geography, 26, 28–29, 32–33
critical legal studies, 7–8

cultural relativism, 14–15, 138–39, 158–59, 203–4

de-judicialization, 20, 334
dialectics, 5–6, 29, 61
dichotomy, 14–15, 156–57, 252–53, 306
disagreement, 14–15, 60, 121–22, 131–32
discourse, 1–6, 10, 15, 19, 20, 24, 25–26, 34, 35, 36, 39, 40, 47–49, 50, 57, 60–62, 64, 66–68, 69, 71–73, 83, 85, 86, 124, 125, 127–28, 131–33, 182–83, 195, 200, 210, 225, 228, 229, 236, 243, 246, 252–53, 257–58, 261, 262–64, 270, 272–73, 275–77, 280, 281, 284–85, 286, 287, 288, 290, 295, 297, 299, 306–7, 311, 312, 313, 316–17, 318–19, 320, 322–23, 324, 329–31, 337
Divine Kingdom, 202, 205

epistomologies, 156–57, 158, 274–75
Eurocentrism, 98, 187–88, 200, 209–10, 215–16, 227, 280
Europe, 2–4, 15–16, 27–28, 97, 105, 112–13, 115, 117, 186, 187–88, 200, 205, 208, 215–16, 231, 263–64, 330–31, 333–34, 337
European, 8–12, 17, 18–19, 32, 73–74, 78, 81–82, 91, 95–96, 97, 98–99, 100, 103, 104, 105–6, 107, 108–11, 112, 116, 118, 140–41, 142–43, 144, 149, 151–52, 154, 155, 158, 159, 161–63, 172, 176–77, 182–83, 187–88, 191–92, 193–94, 199–200, 204, 205, 206–8, 209–10, 211–15, 218–19, 224, 225, 226, 230–31, 233–34, 236, 237, 257, 258–59, 266–67, 280, 328, 329–30, 336–37
European Convention on Human Rights, 327–28
European Court of Human Rights, 17, 336–37
European Society of International Law (ESIL), 1, 95
European Union, 24, 187–88, 329–30

false necessity, 91
feminist, 2–4, 10, 51–54, 58, 59, 60–61, 69–70, 152, 262–63, 272–73
fluid space, 25, 27–28, 37–38, 40

formalism, 57–58, 59, 78
fragmentation, 11–13, 74, 131–32, 139–40, 291, 327–28

Germany, 19, 166–67, 179–80, 285, 288, 290–91
global animal law, 18, 150, 162–63, 185–86, 187, 188–89, 191, 195
global governance, 39–40, 75–76, 242–43, 248–49, 251, 297–99, 301
Global North, 211, 212–13, 215–16, 233, 237, 315–16
Global South, 19, 211, 212–14, 240–41, 252, 274

Hanseatic League, 27–28, 37
Hegelian mystification, 81, 88
Hegelianism, 88–90
hegemonic, 4–5, 6–7, 8–9, 41, 61, 199–200, 201–9, 210, 212–14, 257–58, 272–73, 274–76, 312–13, 317, 319, 324, 330, 337
hegemony, 2–4, 8–9, 18–19, 20, 37–39, 44, 51–54, 75, 195, 200, 209–10, 212–13, 233, 239, 243, 252, 276–77, 316, 337
heterogeneity, 1, 13
homogenous space, 27, 29, 30, 32, 33
human domination, 159
humanitarian law, 311

iconography, 263–64
imperialism, 9, 14–15, 77–78, 80, 81–82, 87–88, 91–92, 154–56, 161–62, 185–86, 187, 188, 195, 199–200, 204, 207, 208–10, 212–13, 242, 305
indigenous peoples, 262, 263
inequality, 139, 242
international criminal law, 66–67, 211, 311, 312–13, 314, 316–17, 322, 323, 324–25
interspecies justice, 195

Jameson, Fredric, 16, 63

Kokugaku, 202, 203–4
kokutai, 204, 209
Korea, 201–2, 206–7
Koskenniemi, Martti, 1, 6–7, 60, 61–62, 65, 66, 69–70

Laclau, Ernesto, 4–5, 40, 65
Latin American, 12, 270
legal
  geography, 72, 74–75
  imaginary, 16
Le Guin, Ursula, 16, 58–59, 61–62, 69–70

liberalism, 18, 150–51, 175–77, 179–80, 182–83, 268, 333–34, 335–36

MacIntyre, Alasdair, 101–2, 123–24, 127–28, 129–30
margin of appreciation, 136, 138–39, 142–43, 144
Maritain, Jacques, 121–22, 132–33
Meiji Restoration, 205, 209
Middle Kingdom, 201, 202, 203–4, 205
misericordia, 128–29, 130–31
moral pluralism, 17, 122, 211, 213–14
multilateralism, 75, 76, 78–79, 235, 236, 250–53

natural law, 17, 122, 125, 126, 131–33, 151–52, 174–75
neocolonialism, 20, 311, 312–13
networked space, 25, 36–38, 39–40
nineteenth century, 18–19, 30, 73–74, 199, 200, 204, 209–10, 216–17, 227
non-human, 150–51, 161, 163–66, 173–74, 175, 182–83

Paris Peace Conference, 207–8
peace, 31, 48–49, 95–96, 98, 174–75, 208–9, 221–23, 234–35, 240, 242, 323–24, 329–30
politics of space, 24, 28–29, 32–33, 35, 36, 40, 41

rationality, 29–30, 39, 123, 124–25, 128–29, 132–33, 135, 136, 138, 139–40, 141–43, 145, 150–51, 159, 175, 177–78, 202–3, 248, 257, 258–61, 273–74
re-etatization, 20, 330
regional order, 199–200, 201–10
reason, the cunning of, 89–90
rhetoric, 19, 71, 165–66, 172, 205, 240–41, 244, 246–47, 248, 250–53, 322, 323–24, 331–32, 336–37
Russia, 17, 136, 207–8, 334–35
Russo-Japanese War, 207–8

Seals dispute, 18, 185–86, 191–92, 195
self-defence, 209, 233
senses, 239–40, 260, 273, 275–76, 277
sensorium, 275–76
Singer, Isaac Bashevis, 150–51, 177, 182–83
Sinocentric, 201–2, 204
Sino-Japanese War, 207
spaces of modernity, 27, 29–30, 34, 36, 39, 41
spatial imaginaries, 24–25, 32–33, 35, 36–37
spatiality, 25–26, 27, 29, 30, 31, 36–38, 41

INDEX   341

speciesism, 150–51, 172–75
standard of civilization, 18–19, 199–200, 205–6, 209, 210, 225, 228
subjectivity, 161–62, 257, 259–60, 262–63, 272, 274, 275–77
subsidiarity, 133, 136, 144
symptomatic reading, 72

Teitel, Ruti, 65, 66–67, 69–70, 313–14
Tokugawa, 202, 204
transitional justice, 311, 312–16, 319–20, 321, 322–23, 324–25
truth commissions, 312, 313, 320, 321
TWAIL, 2–4, 8–9

unequal treaties, 205, 209, 243
United Nations, 12, 20, 23, 81–82, 212, 214–15, 230, 265, 268, 289, 290, 295, 334–35
unity, 2, 11, 13–15, 204, 221–22, 291
Universal Declaration of Human Rights (UDHR), 121–22, 136, 266–69, 267f, 269f

universality
  as culture, 16, 77–81
  as equality for, 87
  as equality of, 87
  as reach, 16, 72–74
  as representation, 16, 74–77

validity, 12, 26, 43–44, 74, 217, 221, 232, 245, 306–7
virtues, 122, 123, 125, 126, 128–29, 130–31, 140–41
visual discourse, 19, 257–58, 261–64, 272–73

Western
  law, 234, 259, 262, 272, 274, 276–77
  legal tradition, 14–15, 259–60
  world, 18–19, 80, 98–99, 157, 234, 258–59, 267–68, 275–76
World Organisation for Animal Health, 18, 185–86
WTO, 18, 167–68, 185–86, 191–95, 327–28, 330–32, 334–35, 336–37